DISCERNING THE SPIRITS

How did Paul determine ethical and theological truth? Were all believers expected to be able to 'discern the spirits' (1 Cor. 12.10)? In contrast to previous studies, this conceptual investigation examines all the significant terms referring to discernment, leading to the insight that for Paul ethical and theological knowledge are inherently related. Understanding the will of God requires noetic and existential transformation, in short, the 'renewal of the mind' (Rom. 12.2). Munzinger argues that Paul implies a process of inspiration in which the Spirit sharpens the discerning functions of the mind because the believer is liberated from a value system dominated by status and performance. The love of God enables all believers to learn to interpret reality in a transformed manner and to develop creative solutions to questions facing their communities. Authentic discernment – as this study demonstrates – effectuates a comprehensive new sense of meaning.

DR ANDRÉ MUNZINGER teaches at the Institute for Protestant Theology, University of Köln, and is Academic Assistant to the Director, Professor Dr Konrad Stock.

SOCIETY FOR NEW TESTAMENT STUDIES

MONOGRAPH SERIES

General editor: John Court

140

DISCERNING THE SPIRITS

SOCIETY FOR NEW TESTAMENT STUDIES:

MONOGRAPH SERIES

Recent titles in the series

Discerning the Spirits

Theological and Ethical Hermeneutics in Paul

ANDRÉ MUNZINGER

CAMBRIDGE
UNIVERSITY PRESS

CAMBRIDGE UNIVERSITY PRESS
Cambridge, New York, Melbourne, Madrid, Cape Town, Singapore, São Paulo

Cambridge University Press
The Edinburgh Building, Cambridge CB2 8RU, UK

Published in the United States of America by Cambridge University Press, New York

www.cambridge.org
Information on this title: www.cambridge.org/9780521875943

First published 2007

Printed in the United Kingdom at the University Press, Cambridge

A catalogue record for this publication is available from the British Library

Library of Congress Cataloguing in Publication data
Munzinger, André, 1972–
Discerning the spirits : theological and ethical hermeneutics in Paul / by André Munzinger.
    p.   cm. – (Society for New Testament studies monograph series ; 140)
Includes bibliographical references and index.
ISBN-13: 978-0-521-87594-3 (hardback)
ISBN-10: 0-521-87594-3 (hardback)
1. Discernment of spirits – Biblical teaching.   2. Paul, the Apostle, Saint – Theology.
3. Paul, the Apostle, Saint – Ethics.   4. Bible. N.T. Epistles of Paul – Criticism,
interpretation, etc.   I. Title   II. Series.

BV5083.M86   2007
227′.06 – dc22
2007001749

ISBN 978-0-521-87594-3 hardback

For
Maria-Theresia Pinger
and
Hermann Eyl

CONTENTS

PREFACE

This is a revised and updated version of my thesis, which was accepted by Brunel University and London School of Theology in June 2004.

Discernment had long been a topic of interest to me. Various interpretations of 'Spirit guidance', 'promptings' and 'words of the Lord' had accompanied me throughout my schooling, church life and theological activities. I was consequently intrigued when Professor Max Turner mentioned that there was scope for research in this area and quite surprised by the extent to which Paul challenged the concepts I had previously encountered. The spiritual discernment that I found in Paul was dependent on a liberated perception of reality and mature self-understanding. This research reflects the attempt to elucidate this new perception.

It is a privilege to be allowed to name a number of people and organisations which have contributed to the completion of this work.

First of all I am greatly indebted to Professor Max Turner for his supervision of this work. His patience, his probing and his trust allowed me to develop freely and experience the conditions for the type of discernment described below.

I would like to thank the Laing Trust, which granted a generous scholarship over a number of years, hence making this work possible.

Similarly, I would like to express my deep gratitude to the Hilverkus family and Heidrun Helmer for their support. Very special thanks go to my sister and brother-in-law for sharing their home with me.

Annette Glaw, Desta Heliso, Cor Bennema and Volker Rabens enriched my studies in countless stimulating discussions, whereas Beate Killguss and Jenny Heimerdinger proved of enormous help in various details of the work.

I would like to express my appreciation to Dr John M. Court, the Society for New Testament Studies and Cambridge University Press for their willingness to accept this study and for their beneficial advice and kind assistance throughout the production procedure.

The work is dedicated to Hermann Eyl and Maria-Theresia Pinger for their enlightening guidance, which helped me learn what 'renewed thinking' can mean.

André Munzinger
Köln, February 2006

ABBREVIATIONS

Unless listed below, abbreviations are taken from S. Schwertner, *Theologische Realenzyklopädie. Abkürzungsverzeichnis* (Berlin: W. de Gruyter, 1994²) and R. M. Ritter, *The Oxford Dictionary for Writers and Editors* (Oxford: Oxford University Press, 2001²).

AB	Anchor Bible
CNT	Commentaire du Nouveau Testament
DPL	G. F. Hawthorne and R. P. Martin (eds.), *Dictionary of Paul and his Letters* (Leicester: InterVarsity Press, 1993)
EDNT	H. Balz and G. Schneider (eds.), *Exegetical Dictionary of the New Testament* I–III (Grand Rapids, MI: Eerdmans, 1993)
HTR	*Harvard Theological Review*
ITP	Intertestamental Period
Int.	*Interpretation*
JEThS	*Journal of the Evangelical Theological Society*
JPT	*Journal of Pentecostal Theology*
L-S	A. A. Long and D. N. Sedley (eds.), *The Hellenistic Philosophers* I. *Translations of the Principal Sources with Philosophical Commentary*; II. *Greek and Latin Texts with Notes and Bibliography* (Cambridge: Cambridge University Press, 1987; cited by volume and page number)
NICNT	New International Commentary on the New Testament
NIDNTT	Brown, C. (ed.), *New International Dictionary of New Testament Theology* I–IV (Exeter: Paternoster Press, 1975, 1976, 1978, 1976)
PNTC	The Pillar New Testament Commentary
SNTW	Studies of the New Testament and its World
ThBLNT	Theologisches Begriffslexikon zum Neuen Testament
Unpubl.	Unpublished
WBC	Word Biblical Commentary
ZNT	*Zeitschrift für Neues Testament*

PART I

Introduction

1

THE CONCEPTUAL APPROACH

A.   Why Discernment?

Modernity has struggled into the twenty-first century, sharply aware that its previously self-confident profile cannot be taken for granted anymore. Complex questions require immediate and attentive scrutiny: how can the looming worries of a 'clash of civilisations' be avoided? Wherein does the dignity of human life lie with respect to its beginning, its end and its relationship to other creatures? How can we evaluate such diverse phenomena as the changing expressions of sexuality, innovations in biotechnology or complex procedures of globalised interdependence? These pressing questions with their universal implications are accompanied by concerns of more personal and spiritual significance for believers of the Christian faith: does the Lord lead individuals in every detail of their lives? Is the will of God clearly defined? Is it easily accessible? How does the Spirit guide each believer personally?

These questions illustrate the interest in and need for discernment in a time far removed from Paul's. So can and should scholarship answer these questions with the aid of Paul? Is he a reliable guide for issues he had not foreseen? If we agree that Paul should be consulted, how concrete or abstract will that help be? Paul has intrigued scholars and believers for centuries with the gift he introduces in 1 Cor. 12.10, the ability to discern the spirits. What did he mean? Is it a secondary issue or a central part of his theology? Is it a gift for all believers or for a few gifted members of the church?

E. Käsemann, P. Stuhlmacher and J. C. Beker offer a basis for dealing with this gift in a comprehensive manner. All three situate discernment at the heart of Paul's theology, yet without clearly substantiating their claim. For Käsemann, 'rechte Theologie' is neither scholastic repetition of tradition nor is it defined by religious or enthusiastic experience. Rather, he claims, it occurs in the discernment of spirits

(1 Cor. 12.10).[1] Likewise, Stuhlmacher describes true Christian thought between the cross and the parousia in precisely the same terms: διάκρισις πνευμάτων.[2] And J. C. Beker has given the discernment of spirits a crucial role in his incisive presentation of Pauline theology: 'the locus of the interaction between coherence and contingency [the details of which we shall return to] is the Holy Spirit, which has the function of the διακρίσεις πνευμάτων (1 Cor 12:10)'.[3]

If the assessment of these scholars is correct, then this gift needs to be embedded in a broader discussion about the nature of Paul's theologising generally and the structure of epistemology in his letters more specifically.[4] Recent work has highlighted the need for this broad perspective. J. G. Lewis proposes that Paul 'theologizes by practising spiritual discernment, engaging in theo-ethical reasoning'.[5] 'Theo-ethical reasoning', according to Lewis, implies that Paul engages in 'reasoned ethical reflection'.[6] But what does this mean epistemologically for discernment? It is remarkable that, while Käsemann and Stuhlmacher appear to imply a process of human thought, Beker assumes that the Holy Spirit is the subject of discernment.[7] Do these assumptions contradict or complement

---

[1] E. Käsemann, '1 Korinther 2, 6–16', in *Exegetische Versuche und Besinnungen* I (Göttingen: Vandenhoek & Ruprecht, 1965[4]) 274.

[2] P. Stuhlmacher, 'Glauben und Verstehen bei Paulus', *Evangelische Theologie* 26 (1966) 337.

[3] J. C. Beker, 'Recasting Pauline Theology: The Coherence-Contingency Scheme as Interpretive Model', in J. M. Bassler (ed.), *Pauline Theology* I. *Thessalonians, Philippians, Galatians, Philemon* (Minneapolis: Fortress Press, 1991) 18–19.

[4] The primary interest of my research will lie in the seven undisputed Pauline letters. However, I will, at points, also include Ephesians and Colossians. While I do not intend to defend Pauline authorship for either one, it is possible to speak of the 'Pauline nature' of the theology presented there (L. Cerfaux, *The Christian in the Theology of Paul* [London: Geoffrey Chapman, 1967] 472). In the matter of wisdom, E. E. Ellis believes that Colossians and Ephesians (e.g. Col. 2.3 and Eph. 1.8f.; 3.9f.) 'only restate exegetical conclusions that are found in their more original commentary forms in 1 Corinthians 1–4 and Romans 11' ('"Wisdom" and "Knowledge" in I Corinthians', in *Prophecy and Hermeneutic in Early Christianity* [WUNT 18; Tübingen: Mohr/Siebeck, 1978] 60). Cf. J. D. G. Dunn, who uses both Ephesians and Colossians in *The Theology of Paul the Apostle* (Edinburgh: T&T Clark, 1998) 732, but does not claim Pauline authorship for them.

[5] J. G. Lewis, *Looking for Life: The Role of 'Theo-Ethical Reasoning' in Paul's Religion* (JSNT.S 291; London: T&T Clark, 2005) 222.

[6] Lewis, *Life*, 36–82, here 205.

[7] In a thesis in Greek, J. Jillions claims that Paul's aim is to contrast God's guidance with the 'first century world' which 'was characterised by allegiance to human guides of all kinds' ('Decision-Making and Divine Guidance: Greco-Roman, Jewish and Pauline Views' [Seminar Paper, SBL Conference, July 2003] 10). Although he does not wish to contrast this with 'rational thought', he does not explain how God's guidance and rational thought work together. This is a significant problem in scholarship generally, which I mean to rectify

one another? I. W. Scott has presented research on Paul's theological knowledge, which highlights both the rational and spiritual aspects of Paul's epistemology.[8] According to Scott, Paul's reasoning is structured as a story: Paul expects his audience to be 'emplotted' in the 'theological narrative' of Christ, which transforms believers and 'does not allow for the . . . gulf between religious dogma and lived experience'.[9] But this raises further questions: if theology and ethics are interdependent, what implications can we assume for the structure of Paul's hermeneutics?[10] If spiritual discernment is the 'center of his religion', can we establish a theory of how Paul believed it functioned?[11] How do mind and Spirit work together?

It is my aim in this book to attend to these questions. In order to establish an accurate understanding, I propose to broaden the scope of the study. I will include other terms which imply discernment (evaluation, interpretation and judgement) and other passages which highlight the epistemological, psychological and theological background of the process of verification and understanding, thereby offering an investigation into the *concept* of discernment in the Pauline literature. Such a conceptual approach stands in contrast to an exegetical thesis or a concentration on a word study, since it broadens research in a linguistically justifiable manner to include features (words, passages, discourses) which elucidate, but are not semantically tied to, discernment.[12]

The following introduction will delineate the scope of this book. While this will include an overview of the state of research, my primary aim is to substantiate the focus of my argument and the nature of my conceptual approach. In the course of the study, I will present more details of the

('Decision-Making', is taken from '"Let thy Good Spirit Guide me", Divine Guidance in Corinth: Greco-Roman, Jewish and Pauline Views' [Unpubl. PhD dissertation, University of Thessalonica, 2002]).

[8] I. W. Scott, *Implicit Epistemology in the Letters of Paul: Story, Experience and the Spirit* (WUNT 2,205; Tübingen, Mohr/Siebeck, 2006).

[9] Scott, *Epistemology*, 284.

[10] For Lewis, *Life*, 205ff., the connection of theology and ethics is also an important result of his work.

[11] Lewis, *Life*, 222.

[12] The legitimacy of traditional word studies as the basis for establishing theology has been rightly criticised, specifically by J. Barr, *The Semantics of Biblical Language* (Oxford: Oxford University Press, 1961). The alternative, more cautious approach of grouping words according to semantic domains, and hence basing theological observations on the shoulders of the broader discourse concepts, has given biblical interpretation firmer ground to stand on (cf. P. Cotterell and M. Turner, *Linguistics and Biblical Interpretation* [Downers Grove, IL InterVarsity Press: 1989] 106–23).

history of research into the relevant aspects of Pauline theology and when we encounter them.

B.   Delineating the Conceptual Approach

In the three points that follow I aim to outline the concept of discernment. First, I shall propose a semantic definition, secondly an elucidation of the epistemological focus on the sources of discernment and, finally, a structural and theological classification.

1.   Semantic Overview and Definition

The three terms which have been at the centre of attention with respect to Pauline discernment are διακρίνω/διάκρισις and δοκιμάζω. The debate about διάκρισις πνευμάτων[13] (1 Cor. 12.10, and διακρίνω in 1 Cor. 14.29) has focussed on its role as a regulative force within the charismatic community. Should it be understood exclusively as the interpretation of prophecy or also more generally as an evaluation of spiritual manifestations?[14] While this discussion continues to require our detailed attention, it is notable that it has not, in any significant manner, been related to the broader depictions of Pauline theology noted at the beginning.[15] A similar deficit applies to the detailed studies on δοκιμάζω.[16]

---

[13] Both plural and singular of διάκρισις have good textual evidence: the singular with Sinaiticus, C, D*, F, G, P, 0201, 33, 1175 (*pauci*), latt, sy^p, sa, Clemens Alexandrinus; the plural with P^46, A, B, D², Ψ, 1739, 1881, Maj, sy^h, bo. However, as G. Dautzenberg (*Urchristliche Prophetie: Ihre Erforschung, ihre Voraussetzungen im Judentum und ihre Struktur im ersten Korintherbrief* [BWANT 104; Stuttgart: Kohlhammer, 1975] 124) points out, the *lectio difficilior* is probably the plural, since it is plausible that the early church moved to the slightly easier understanding of the singular (cf. similarly English Bible translations). It is possible that the plural expresses the fact that the gift was used frequently. Nevertheless, I do not deduce any further meaning from the plural and hence interchange between plural (which I use when citing 1 Cor. 12.10) and the singular (which I generally use) without implying a difference in meaning or intention.

[14] The two positions are presented by G. Dautzenberg ('Zum religionsgeschichtlichen Hintergrund der διακρίσεις πνευμάτων [1 Kor 12:10]', *BZ* 15 [1971] 93–104) and W. Grudem ('A Response to Gerhard Dautzenberg on 1 Cor. 12.10', *BZ* 22 [1978] 253–70). While Dautzenberg has provoked debate with his innovative understanding of διάκρισις πνευμάτων as an interpretation of prophecy, Grudem insists on the traditional reading.

[15] This also applies to Jillions ('Decision-Making', 1) who has a conceptual approach and studies various terms in 1 Corinthians, but does not tie this in with broader questions of truth formation and theological verification.

[16] L. Asciutto, 'Decisione e liberta in Cristo. Δοκιμάζειν in alcuni passi di S. Paolo', *Rivista di Teologia Morale* 3 (1971) 229–45; G. Therrien, *Le discernement dans les écrits pauliniens* (Paris: Librairie Lecoffre, 1973).

Since O. Cullmann designated this verb as 'the key to all New Testament ethics', its significance has been noted primarily with respect to the ethical dimension of Pauline thought and, more problematically, has been tied to the word and its cognates.[17] G. Therrien's study is misleading as his focus on δοκιμάζω and cognates does not do justice to his conceptual title (*Discernement*) and therefore offers partially incorrect theological conclusions.[18]

Excursus: The Conceptual Inaccuracy of G. Therrien's Study

Gérard Therrien has presented a detailed study of δοκιμάζω and its cognates δοκιμή, δόκιμος and ἀδόκιμος (the latter three provide twenty of a total of thirty-seven occurrences he investigates). He takes this approach because he follows the traditional method of a word study.[19] This is inaccurate because, while the title and intent of his study presupposes a conceptual study, he offers an investigation of lexically related words.[20] On the basis of an *etymological* argument, he identifies the basic/proper meaning of δοκιμάζω as 'accepter ou être accepté après épreuve'.[21] However, such an approach does not do justice to the synchronic use of the terms and can be rejected as linguistically inaccurate.[22] While δοκιμάζω is linguistically linked to δόκιμος[23] and both may belong to the same semantic

---

[17] O. Cullmann (*Christ and Time: The Primitive Christian Conception of Time and History* [trans. F. V. Filson; London: SCM Press, 1962[2]] 228). He goes on to say that 'the working of the Holy Spirit shows itself chiefly in the testing (δοκιμάζειν), that is in the capacity of forming the correct Christian ethical judgement at each given moment...' While Therrien (*Discernement*) places ethical discernment in a broader eschatological context, the conceptual title is misleading, as his focus lies only on δοκιμάζω and its cognates.

[18] We shall return to Therrien's conclusions in chapter 2.

[19] Therrien, *Discernement*, 4f.

[20] Therrien, *Discernement*, 5. For the rationale behind concentrating only on δοκιμάζω and related words, he refers to Spicq ('Le langage humain est comme le sacrement de la pensée révélée... chaque terme doit faire l'objet d'une étude sémantique si l'on veut retrouver sa puissance et sa vérité d'évocation) and Congar ('la philologie a parfois renouvelé heureusement certains paragraphes de la théologie').

[21] Therrien, *Discernement*, 10 (following Prellwitz he refers back to δέχομαι and even back to Sanskrit for clarification); cf. W. Grundmann, 'δόκιμος κτλ.', *TDNT* II, 255: the 'Stammwort' is δοκή.

[22] Cotterell and Turner, *Linguistics*, 25, distinguish diachronic and synchronic linguistics as follows. A diachronic study takes a historical 'cross-section' whereas a synchronic study is the 'examination of a single cross-section'. 'The history of a word (a *diachronic* study of its use) may explain *how* a word came to be used with some particular sense at a specified time ... The state of a language, and of its lexical stock, can be understood entirely by direct observation of usage at the time in question (synchronous study)' (132, cf. 113).

[23] Δοκιμάζω 'ist Denominativ von δόκιμος' (G. Schunack, 'δοκιμάζω', *EDNT* I, 341). Cf. J. H. Moulton, W. F. Howard and N. Turner, *A Grammar of New Testament Greek* II (Edinburgh: T&T Clark, 1923) 405.

8   *Introduction*

domains ('to learn', 'to think'),[24] not all references relate to discernment. What terms are not relevant then for this discussion?

Except for the word play with δοκιμάζω, δόκιμος and ἀδόκιμος in 2 Cor. 13.4ff.,[25] the related terms (δόκιμος, δοκιμή, ἀδόκιμος) can all be eliminated from this study. They do not refer to my concept of discernment.[26] It is not justifiable to relate the 'worthiness' of the believers' or apostle's work to their discernment.[27] This criticism also calls into question the inclusion of those instances of the verb δοκιμάζω where God tests his people (1 Cor. 3.13; 1 Thess. 2.4).[28] Linking this aspect with the discernment that believers undertake is only supported on the basis of the same word-form being used in both contexts. For one, there is no contextual evidence that these two aspects are to be correlated.[29] Further, it is unthinkable to apply a similar logic to other verbs, such as πειράζω. For instance, Therrien would surely not explain Paul's exhortation to the Corinthians to *test* themselves (cf. 2 Cor 13.5 where πειράζω is used synonymously with δοκιμάζω) in the same way as Satan *tempts* (cf. πειράζω in 1 Cor. 7.5). It is also hard to conceive that he would see a parallel with those that tested God and were destroyed by serpents (cf. πειράζω in 1 Cor. 10.9).[30]

But what references of δοκιμάζω are applicable to my concept of discernment? It is helpful to organise these according to the objects of δοκιμάζω. The believers are to:

---

[24] J. P. Louw and E. A. Nida, *Greek–English Lexicon of the New Testament* II (New York: United Bible Societies, 1988) 364.

[25] The thrust of this passage (2 Cor. 12.19–13.10) is partially ironic and no doubt Paul is playing with different aspects of 'passing a test', cf. R. P. Martin, *2 Corinthians* (WBC 40; Waco, Tx: Word Books, 1986) 481f. 'Paul is concerned that the test imposed in 13:5 and 13:6, respectively, be passed. But he will be more than happy, if he does *not* pass the test of 13:7. If he fails this one that means he will not have to discipline the church, for its members will have repented' (*2 Corinthians*, 482). The 'common denominator for all uses' is 'that the presence and power of Christ be demonstrated in each instance'.

[26] Most of the occurrences can be translated by 'proven worthiness' or its negation (or by the more precise German term *Bewährung*; δοκιμή: Rom. 5.4; 2 Cor. 2.9; 8.2; 9.13; Phil. 2.22; δόκιμος: Rom. 16.10; 1 Cor. 11.19; 2 Cor. 10.18; 13.7; ἀδόκιμος: 1 Cor. 9.27). The rest can be understood as 'evidence/proof' (δοκιμή: 2 Cor. 13.3), 'human approval' (δόκιμος: Rom. 14.18), 'debased' (Rom. 1.28).

[27] If Therrien wanted to do that, he would have to also study synonymous words which signify the value of works such as δίκαιος.

[28] It is generally pointed out that this aspect has its origin in the OT: cf. Therrien (*Discernement*, 305ff.) and Grundmann ('δόκιμος', 257). Schunack ('δοκιμάζω', 341) shows that in the LXX the verb is used for the Hebrew *bahan* where it is found particularly in poetic texts and has Yahweh as subject twenty-two out of twenty-eight times, e.g. Pss. 16.3; 25.2; 138.1, 23.

[29] Neither in 1 Cor. 3.13 nor in 1 Thess. 2.4 is God's testing linked with human discernment.

[30] Finally, I exclude three occurrences of δοκιμάζω from my study because they refer to an approval by Paul (2 Cor. 8.8, 22) or by the Corinthians (1 Cor. 16.3) and are not linked in any particular manner to a process of discernment, but to other types of testing; so, correctly, Asciutto ('Decisione', 230), who excludes these.

- test themselves and their 'work' (Rom. 14.22; 1 Cor. 11.28; 2 Cor. 13.5; Gal. 6.4);
- test 'everything' (1 Thess. 5.21);
- discover 'the things that are important or pleasing to God' (Rom. 2.18; 12.2; Phil. 1.10; cf. Eph. 5.10).
- The Gentiles did not see fit to acknowledge God (Rom. 1.28).[31]

These objects call into question a further point of Therrien's study: his focus solely on ethical discernment.[32] My argument in this book will give evidence that such a focus does not do justice to Paul's thinking. At this point it must suffice to note that Therrien misses that δοκιμάζω is partially synonymous with other verbs denoting discernment.[33] In 1 Cor. 11.31 διακρίνω is used as an equivalent term to δοκιμάζω.[34] And, in 1 Thess. 5.21 it could be interchanged with ἀνακρίνω, which is used in a similar manner in 1 Cor. 2.15, where Paul also claims that all things can be evaluated. Nevertheless, not all occurrences of δοκιμάζω should be used identically. Some of the occurrences emphasise the *process* of examination (1 Cor 11.28; 2 Cor. 13.5; Gal. 6.4; 1 Thess. 5.21), others stress the *result* of the examination (Rom. 1.28; 14.22) and others combine both aspects (Rom. 2.18; 12.2; Phil. 1.10).[35]

[31] For the significance of the 'deliberate decision' of the Gentiles, cf. J. D. G. Dunn, *Romans 1–8* (WBC 38A; Dallas: Word Books, 1988) 66. H. Schlier (*Der Römerbrief* [HThK 6; Freiburg: Herder, 1977] 63) points out that the 'Verweigerung' of God is not a 'Fatum' but a decision, a 'Prüfung und ein Entschluß'. Rom. 1.28 also shows that both δοκιμάζω and ἀδόκιμος can be used in the same verse without any relationship to one another. There is no reason why Paul could not have used πονηρός or κοινός instead of ἀδόκιμος and hence there is no need to extrapolate meaning from them appearing together (contra Therrien, *Discernement*, 135).

[32] Therrien deals with and explains all the passages mostly within his 'moral' framework, even those clearly denoting a broader object (such as Rom. 1.28; 1 Thess. 5.21; *Discernement*, 78f., 302).

[33] Although, in his introduction, Therrien promises to touch on the other terms, the treatment is not only 'en proportion moindre', as he promises, it is essentially insubstantial (*Discernement*, 4). Διάκρισις/διακρίνω is referred to only in passing. 1 Cor. 12.10 and 14.29 are offered as parallels to 1 Thess. 5.19–21 (*Discernement*, 72–9) and he mentions these passages when he deals with 1 Cor. 11.28 (89f.). The links to σοφία, φρόνησις, σύνεσις and, for that matter, to 1 Cor. 2.6–16 appear as references in the concluding section of his work, where he synthesises the foundations and principles of δοκιμάζω, but they are not dealt with on their own terms (*Discernement*, 273f). Therrien's claim that Romans treats the concept of discernment in greatest detail is incorrect in view of the centrality of the issue in 1 Corinthians (*Discernement*, 264).

[34] Cf. W. Schrage, *Der erste Brief an die Korinther (1 Kor 11,17–14,40)* (EKK 7/III; Neukirchen-Vluyn: Neukirchener Verlag, 1999) 54, who shows διακρίνω and δοκιμάζω are interchangeable there. The same process is implied.

[35] Against G. D. Fee (*Paul's Letter to the Philippians* [NICNT; Grand Rapids, MI: Eerdmans, 1995] 101) who comments that δοκιμάζω 'always carries the connotation of "proving", thus "approving" something by putting it to the test'. This can be misleading as it is too categorical and does not allow the different nuances to stand out. See particularly Schunack ('δοκιμάζειν', 341), who warns that the meanings are not to be harmonised. There is a possible distinction to be made between 'put to the test, examine' and the result of the

Gérard Therrien's approach is too narrow and too broad at the same time. It is too narrow because, as my thesis will demonstrate, it misses the breadth of Paul's view by neglecting all the other terms denoting the concept of discernment. It is too broad because the information he does offer has in part no thematic link to discernment but only a lexical connection to δοκιμάζω.

Having clarified the inadequacy of a focus on certain words, what does my *conceptual* approach entail? While for analytical purposes I will study the evaluation and interpretation of ethical and spiritual (πνευματικά, 1 Cor. 2.13, and πνεύματα, 1 Cor. 12.10)[36] matters separately, my argument will be concerned to give a coherent depiction by interrelating the terms in a more extensive theological manner.[37]

This kind of extensive picture emerges when we position 'discernment' within the general semantic domain of intellectual ability, which includes the more specific domains 'know', 'learn', 'think', 'understand'.[38] The acquisition ('to learn')[39] and possession of information ('to know') or understanding ('to understand')[40] form the essential backdrop to my

---

examination, 'regard as worthwhile'. But the latter definition implies a certain amount of reflection preceding the approval, as in Louw and Nida (*Lexicon* I, 364).

[36] For a clarification of how and why I use 'spiritual' in contrast to 'theological' see n. 58 (chapter 1).

[37] Sometimes an explicit differentiation is given on the basis of a difference between διακρίνω and δοκιμάζω (J. Martucci, 'Diakriseis Pneumaton [1 Co 12,10]', *Église et Théologie* 9 [1978], 467), while at other times no clear reasoning is given. J. D. G. Dunn (*Jesus and the Spirit* [London: SCM Press, 1975] 223ff.) differentiates implicitly in concentrating on δοκιμάζω 'which refers to ethical decision making' and, on the other hand, the evaluation of inspired utterances (διάκρισις πνευμάτων; 233ff.). However, in *Theology of Paul* (648 n. 110) Dunn mentions that δοκιμάζω and διακρίνω should be seen in connection with one another, but he does not elaborate on this.

[38] Louw and Nida, *Lexicon* II, 380. These domains are 'fuzzy sets', as Louw and Nida call them, implying that 'considerable overlapping and indeterminate borders' are to be expected between them. Generally though, Louw and Nida differentiate these domains further: the domain 'Know' 'involves the possession of information' while 'Learn' 'involves the acquisition of information' and 'Understanding' is to comprehend (cf. *Lexicon*, 325, 349). 'Think' 'involves essentially the processing and manipulation of information, often leading to decision and choice' (349).

[39] For my purposes this may include general perceptive apprehension such as γινώσκω (e.g. 1 Cor. 13.12), ὁράω (Rom. 11.22; Gal. 2.4; 1 Thess. 5.15) but also specific terms of watchfulness/soberness such as πειράζω (2 Cor. 13.5), βλέπω (1 Cor. 1.26; 3.10; 8.9; 10.12; 2 Cor. 10.7), νήφω, ἐκνήφω (1 Cor. 15.34; 1 Thess. 5.6,8), προνοέω (Rom. 12.17), γρηγορέω (1 Cor. 16.13; 1 Thess. 5.6,10), cf. νουθετέω (Rom. 15.14; 1 Thess. 5.12,14).

[40] This includes the possession of γνῶσις (cf. particularly 1 Cor. 8.1), σύνεσις (1 Cor. 1.19), σοφία (throughout 1 Cor. 1–3) which Paul criticises, as well as ἐπίγνωσις, αἴσθησις, γνῶσις (e.g. 2 Cor. 1.13f.; Phil. 1.9; Philm. 6) which are a feature of the believers' lives (or a dialectic phenomenon, cf. 1 Cor. 8.3, 7–11; Gal. 4.9; Rom. 1.18–32. Here the misuse of noetic knowledge is emphasised). It is, of course, remarkable that the positive valuation becomes so much more frequent in the contested Pauline literature (cf. Eph. 1.17; 3.4, 19; 4.13; 5.15; Col. 1.9, 10, 28; 2.2; 3.10, 16; 4.5). However, an example of how much Paul generally expects his readers to consciously follow his argument can be shown by his

discussion. However, it is the manipulation and processing of thought to achieve certain ends ('to think') which more narrowly defines the term discernment.[41] Hence, I offer the following working definition of discernment: the process of reflective thought leading to decision and choice on the 'correctness, meaning, truth, or value of something or someone'.[42]

Excursus: Does Paul Use Δοκιμάζω in an Original Sense?

Two linguistic issues require clarification for our understanding of δοκιμάζω.

First of all, C. F. Evans assumes that δοκιμάζω when not followed by a direct object but by an indirect question appears for the first time in Greek literature in Rom. 12.2 and Eph. 5.10. This leads him to state that this 'would require a distinct shift in meaning from "testing" or "proving" by the application of known criteria to something like "ascertaining (by exploration) what still has to be discovered"'.[43] With that shift in meaning he claims to see Paul's 'emphatic affirmation of, and massive confidence in, the ability of the believer's renewed intellectual and moral judgement to discover and discern the divine will in its completeness'. First of all, we may note that δοκιμάζω *is* used with indirect questions in Greek literature and not in any novel sense.[44] Moreover, there is no need to overload the

---

appeal to the thinking of the Thessalonian church (καθὼς οἴδατε; 1 Thess. 1.5; 2.1, 5, 11; 3.3, 4; 4.2; 5.2, 12).

[41] Four interrelated aspects are important:

1. To think and to reason: λογίζομαι (Rom. 3.28; 1 Cor. 13.11; Phil. 3.13; 4.8), δοκέω (1 Cor. 7.40);
2. To think expressing intention: βουλεύομαι (2 Cor. 1.17), προνοέω (2 Cor. 8.21), cf. γνώμη (1 Cor. 1.10);
3. To think as the basis of valuation: φρονέω (Rom. 8.5; 12.3, 16; 14.6; 15.5; 1 Cor. 13.11; 2 Cor. 13.11; Phil. 1.7; 2.2, 5; 3.15, 19; 4.2; cf. Col. 3.2), οἶδα (Rom. 14.4), cf. πείθω (Rom. 8.38; Phil. 1.6), σωφρονέω (Rom. 12.3; 2 Cor. 5.13), φρόνησις (Eph. 1.8);
4. To decide: προαιρέω (2 Cor. 9.7), ἀνακρίνω (1 Cor. 2.14, 15; 14.24; cf. the judicial use in 4.3, 4; 9.3; 10.25, 27), συγκρίνω (1 Cor. 2.13; 2 Cor. 10.12), κρίνω (Rom. 14.5; 1 Cor. 7.37; 10.15; 11.13; 31; 2 Cor. 5.14), διακρίνω and δοκιμάζω (passages described in more detail in chapter 3).

[42] Louw and Nida, *Lexicon* I, 363. It could be argued that this definition is essentially that which Louw and Nida call the subdomain '*To Distinguish, To Evaluate, To Judge*', since they go on to argue that this 'normally implies careful thinking about various alternatives and then deciding what is to be regarded as more justified' (*Lexicon*, 363). Yet they also define this subdomain as the 'final result of the process of thinking', which narrows the scope too much as I will also incorporate reflective thought.

[43] C. F. Evans, 'Romans 12.1–2: The True Worship', in L. De Lorenzi (ed.), *Dimensions de la vie chrétienne (Rm 12–13)* (Rome: Abbaye de S. Paul h.l.m., 1979) 29.

[44] Used with an indirect question: Demosthenes, *Orationes* 60:17: ἔστι γὰρ ἔστιν ἁπάσης ἀρετῆς ἀρχὴ μὲν σύνεσις, πέρας δ᾽ ἀνδρεία. καὶ τῇ μὲν δοκιμάζεται τί πρακτέον ἐστί, τῇ δὲ ᾡζεται ('For of all virtue, I say, and I repeat it, the beginning is understanding and the

verb with a meaning that becomes apparent in a conceptual study of Paul. As I shall argue, Paul does have extensive confidence in the believer's discernment, but that need not be established on the basis of presuming a new meaning of δοκιμάζω.

The other point is that both Therrien and Grundmann claim (with slightly different emphases) that Paul is original in using δοκιμάζω in the religious sense of people discerning between right and wrong themselves.[45] A sample search (with a synchronic emphasis) of the use of δοκιμάζω and δοκιμασία in both Hellenistic and Jewish literature shows that the term was used in the technical sense of 'testing' or 'approving' a broad range of different objects.[46] There are numerous parallels to Paul's supposed originality. Particularly striking is that it is used in a moral sense,[47] but also in the context of assessing good and evil in a more general[48] and even religious sense[49]. Hence δοκιμάζω was used as a moral term with

fulfilment is courage; by the one it is judged [δοκιμάζω] what ought to be done and by the other this is carried to success').

[45] Therrien (*Discernement*, 15, 60; 263f.) sees this as a particularly important issue. Grundmann ('δόκιμος', 256) also claims 'this whole word group first acquires religious significance in the NT, the ideas of which are shaped by the OT'.

[46] E.g., wives are tested by their husbands (Josephus, *Bell.* 2.161); the points of swords on corpses (Josephus, *Bell.* 5.516); finding out and approving good qualities of writers (Dionysius of Halicarnassus, *Thucydides* 1.11).

[47] Philo, *Deus* 128: 'voluntary sins . . . are convicted by the judge within the soul and thus are proved [δοκιμάζω] to be unholy and foul and impure.'

[48] Philo, *Prob.* 23: 'though the evil lies in themselves and in their judgement, which makes them test [δοκιμάζω] the slave by the tasks he performs'. The issue is the fear of death and the desire to live and that these enslave the mind; cf. Demosthenes, *Orationes* 60, 17 (quoted earlier); Epictetus, *Dissertationes* 1.20.7f.: 'Therefore, the first and greatest task of the philosopher is to test [δοκιμάζω] the impressions and discriminate [διακρίνω] between them and to apply none that has not been tested. . . When therefore, you wish to realize how careless you are about the good and the evil, and how zealous you are about that which is indifferent, observe how you feel about physical blindness on the one hand, and mental delusion on the other, and you will find out that you are far from feeling as you ought about things good and things evil'; *Dissertationes* 2.12.20: the soul 'utilizes these other things [essentially all other abilities of man], and puts each of them to the test [δοκιμάζω], and exercises deliberation'; 2.23.5f.: Zeus 'has given you something better than all these things – the faculty which can make use of them [sight and hearing, life itself and what is conducive to it such as fruit, wine, oil], pass judgement upon them [δοκιμάζω], estimate the value of each'. He explains that this is the faculty of moral purpose (προαιρετική). Josephus, *Ant.* 7.321: 'Then God sent the prophet Gad to offer him a choice of three things from which to choose that which seemed best to him . . . [ἣν ἂν δοκιμάσῃ]'. The choices were famine, or face his enemies or pestilence and disease.

[49] Josephus, *Ant.* 1.15: 'I entreat those who will read these volumes to fix their thoughts on God, and to test [δοκιμάζω] whether our lawgiver has had a worthy conception of his nature and has always assigned to Him such actions as befit His power, keeping his words concerning Him pure of that unseemly mythology current among others'; *Ant.* 1.233: '[N]o, He [God] wished but to test [δοκιμάζω] [Abraham's] his soul and see whether even such orders would find him obedient'; *Ant.* 4.295: '[A]nd may ye continue to observe laws which God has approved [δοκιμάζω] as good and now delivers to you!' Cf. also the example Grundmann himself cites ('δόκιμος', 256) from an inscription (*Ditt. Syll.*): ἀνὴρ δεδοκιμασμένος τοῖς θείοις . . .

religious connotations and we cannot affirm that Paul coined a different sense or used the verb in a novel context.

Both of these examples show that care needs to be taken before making theological assumptions or attaching theological significance to words without providing sufficient linguistic evidence. While Paul may in part have an original concept of discernment, this assumption cannot be made on the basis of the word-form he uses.

2.   Epistemological Focus: What are the Sources
of Genuine Knowledge?

With respect to the above semantic definition, which highlights terms of cognitions, one could, naturally, argue that it misses the crucial point concerning Pauline discernment: is not true knowledge a gift of the Spirit? Are the intellectual faculties reliable and significant sources of discernment in Paul?[50] Is authentic knowledge not the result of revelation or immediate Spirit guidance? Hence, should we not focus on what some scholars have called *pneumatic* epistemology?[51] Three passages offer a preliminary clarification of these questions, which are crucial for the direction of this study.

In Rom. 12.2 Paul calls for a renewal of the reader's mind (ἡ ἀνακαίνωσις τοῦ νοός) as the basis of true discernment (εἰς τὸ δοκιμάζειν ὑμᾶς τί τὸ θέλημα τοῦ θεοῦ). While this emphasises the noetic dimension (and leaves out the Spirit), does Paul not presuppose his programmatic description of the Christ-like life in Rom. 8.6? If so, that passage implies a juncture of mind and Spirit (φρόνημα τοῦ πνεύματος), a Christological mindset. This in turn brings to mind 1 Cor. 2.16. There Paul ends his epistemological discussion by claiming that 'we have the mind of Christ' (ἡμεῖς δὲ νοῦν Χριστοῦ ἔχομεν). Of course, these passages require further examination, but for the moment we may posit that we must take a look at both the natural and revelatory epistemological processes and, more specifically, their interrelationship. In other words, we must investigate

---

[50] The tension in Paul is expressed well as follows: 'Reason is both indispensable to the task of explication and a source of embarrassment' (J. D. Moores, *Wrestling with Rationality in Paul: Romans 1–8 in a new Perspective* [MSSNTS 82; Cambridge: Cambridge University Press, 1995] 159).

[51] Cf. G. Sellin, 'Das "Geheimnis" der Weisheit und das Rätsel der "Christuspartei" (zu 1Kor 1–4)', *ZNW* 73 (1982) 86; S. W. Yu, 'Paul's Pneumatic Epistemology: Its Significance in his Letters' (Unpubl. PhD dissertation, Duke University, 1998) 206; P. Stuhlmacher, 'Zur hermeneutischen Bedeutung von 1Kor 2,6–16', in *Biblische Theologie und Evangelium* (WUNT 146; Tübingen: Mohr/Siebeck, 2002) 157ff., where he speaks of a '*geistliche Erkenntnistheorie*' and of an '*Erkenntnistheorie des Glaubens*' (159).

passages which describe the impact of the Spirit on the believer[52] and identify the role of the natural faculties.[53] However, my main interest will be in the juncture of mind and Spirit and the way in which it allows for correct and astute cognitive functioning.[54] In so doing we must attempt to understand what the nature of inspiration is. Is it of a spontaneous and charismatic or rather long-term and possibly ethical nature?[55]

In sum, however, this emphasis on the psychological and epistemological background of discernment will require justification and clarification. *Justification* is needed because it stands in stark contrast to the correlation of wisdom and law or, more precisely, discernment and external norms. Hence, while my argument stresses the role of the new creation (particularly the renewed mind) in Paul as the basis for authentic understanding, this differs from other approaches which focus on formal criteria.[56] In

---

[52] This will include Spirit 'leading' (πνεύματι ἄγονται; Rom. 8.14; Gal. 5.18), λόγος σοφίας and λόγος γνωσέως (1 Cor. 12.8), θεοδίδακτος (1 Thess. 4.9), ἀποκαλύπτω (particularly 1 Cor. 2.10; Phil. 3.15; Gal. 1.16). Clearly, revelation and inspiration are substantial concepts in Paul with which I can deal only insofar as they have a bearing on my subject.

[53] Particularly, νοῦς (Rom. 1.28; 7.23, 25; 11.34; 12.2; 14.5; 1 Cor. 1.10; 2.16; 14.14, 15, 19; Phil. 4.7; cf. Eph. 4.17, 23; Col. 2.18), συνείδησις (particularly Rom. 2.15; 9.1; 13.5; 1 Cor. 8.7, 10, 12; 10.25, 27, 28; 2 Cor. 1.12), καρδία (cf. particularly passages where mind and heart are partially synonymous, Rom. 1.21, 24; 2.5, 15, 29; 16.18; 1 Cor. 7.37; 2 Cor. 3.15; 4.6; 9.7; Phil. 4.7; cf. Eph. 1.18; 4.18; Col. 2.2. Other significant passages for our purposes: Rom. 5.5; 8.27; 1 Cor. 2.9; 4.5; 14.25; 2 Cor. 1.22; 2 Cor. 3.3), cf. φρόνημα (Rom. 8.5f.).

[54] We need to adjudicate whether or not Therrien (*Discernement*, 294) is correct when he claims that discernment is an 'acte *humano-divin*' in which one cannot isolate human and divine activity (*Discernement*, 269). Of particular benefit for our reflection on the impact of the Spirit on rationality will be the works by G. Theissen (*Psychological Aspects of Pauline Theology* [Philadelphia: Fortress Press, 1987]); W. Schrage ('Zum Verhältnis von Ethik und Vernunft', in H. Merklein [ed.], *Neues Testament und Ethik* [Freiburg: Herder, 1989] 482–507); F. Voss (*Das Wort vom Kreuz und die menschliche Vernunft: Eine Untersuchung zur Soteriologie des 1. Korintherbriefes* [FRLANT 199; Göttingen: Vandenhoeck & Ruprecht, 2002]). M. Healy ('"What the Heart of Man Has not Conceived". A Theological Approach to 1.Cor 2:6–16' [Unpubl. PhD dissertation, Pontifical Gregorian University, 2000] 14f.) also offers helpful insights into the epistemology expounded in 1 Cor. 2.6–16, but her portrayal of contemporary scholarship as 'reductive', in contrast to her innovative 'theological' approach, is not convincing.

[55] For purposes of introduction it is possible to identify two significant views. The first sees Spirit-activity as a spontaneous, '*charismatic recognition of God's will*', an '*inward compulsion of love*' (Dunn, *Jesus*, 225). The second emphasises the '*trained, habituated disposition, shaped and nourished by Holy Spirit . . .*' (A. C. Thiselton, *The First Epistle to the Corinthians* [NIGTC; Grand Rapids, MI: Eerdmans, 2000] 943).

[56] J. D. G. Dunn must be credited for his in-depth work on the criteria for the correct evaluation of spiritual manifestations (1 Cor. 12–14). He has given these criteria (love, tradition and edification) the most detailed attention ('Discernment of Spirits – A Neglected Gift', in W. Harrington [ed.], *Witness to the Spirit* [Dublin: Irish Biblical Association, 1979] 79–96; *Jesus*, 223ff., 233–6; 'Responsible Congregation [1 Cor. 14.26–40]', in L. de Lorenzi [ed.], *Charisma and Agape [1 Kor. 12–14]* [Rome: Abtei von St Paul vor den

other words, I shall place true knowledge and wisdom in direct dependence on the renewal of the believer.[57] The *clarification* of my argument
will come from an investigation into the manner in which Paul's Jewish
and Hellenistic contemporaries understood authentic epistemology. Of
particular interest will be the breadth of traditions, which help us to elucidate Paul's line of thought. These will range from apocalyptic theology
to Philo of Alexandria and extend to the philosophical interpretations in
the Stoics.

3.   Discernment as a Theological Concern

The third point illustrating my conceptual approach looks at discernment
within Paul's thought as a whole. As I mentioned earlier, initially we must
follow the lead presented by scholarship, which distinguishes between the
discernment of ethical and spiritual matters (based on the different terminology of δοκιμάζω and διακρίνω/διάκρισις, respectively). However,

---

Mauern, 1983] 201–36; *Theology*, 594–8). Some refer back to his work (cf. C. Claußen,
'Die Frage nach der "Unterscheidung der Geister"', *ZNT* 8 [2001] 31; Schrage, *Korinther*
III, 157). However, F. Hahn ('Charisma und Amt', *ZThK* 76 [1979] 418–49) does not refer
to Dunn but presents the same three criteria.

With respect to the correlation of wisdom and law, two important protagonists are E. J.
Schnabel (*Law and Wisdom from Ben Sira to Paul* [WUNT 2,16; Tübingen: Mohr/Siebeck,
1985]), who argues for a continued correlation concerning Pauline ethics, and C. M.
Pate (*The Reverse of the Curse: Paul, Wisdom and the Law* [WUNT 2,114; Tübingen:
Mohr/Siebeck, 2000]), who maintains a complete disassociation.

[57] Naturally, this leads to a focus on 1 Corinthians where true knowledge and wisdom are
key problems. I will not deal in detail with the Gnostic hypothesis (of the background to the
Corinthian problem) which has been criticised, as problems of the dating of 'gnosticism' as
an incipient system have been noted (R. M. Wilson, 'How Gnostic were the Corinthians?',
NTS 19 [1972–3] 65–73), and alternative explanations, such as sapiential Judaism, have
been more pressing. For the Gnostic hypothesis, cf. *inter alios* U. Wilckens, *Weisheit und
Torheit: Eine exegetisch-religionsgeschichtliche Untersuchung zu 1 Kor 1 und 2* (Tübingen:
Mohr/Siebeck, 1959); W. Schmithals, *Die Gnosis in Korinth* (Göttingen: Vandenhoeck &
Ruprecht, 1969³) 277–85. M. Winter, *Pneumatiker und Psychiker in Korinth* (Marburg:
N. G. Elwert Verlag, 1975), calls into question any Gnostic influence on Paul's own theology,
and U. Wilckens had a change of mind later and did not want to see any direct Gnostic
influence on Paul and the Corinthians ('Zu 1Kor 2,1–16', in C. Andresen and G. Klein
[eds.], *Theologia Crucis – Signum Crucis: Festschrift für Erich Dinkler zum 70. Geburtstag*
[Tübingen: Mohr/Siebeck, 1979] 501–37.

For work on sapiential Judaism, cf. particularly J. A. Davis, *Wisdom and Spirit: An
Investigation of 1 Corinthians 1.18–3.20 against the Background of Jewish Sapiential
Traditions in the Greco-Roman Period* (Lanham, MD: University Press of America, 1984),
which relies on the studies of B. A. Pearson, *The Pneumatikos-Psychikos Terminology
in 1 Corinthians* (Missoula: Scholars Press, 1973); R. A. Horsley, 'Pneumatikos versus
Psychikos: Distinctions of Status among the Corinthians', *HTR* 69 (1976) 269–88. But for
sapiential Judaism cf. also G. E. Sterling, '"Wisdom among the Perfect": Creation Traditions
in Alexandrian Judaism and Corinthian Christianity', *NT* 37 (1995) 355–84.

we will discover that this is an artificial separation that does not reflect
the interdependence of these levels of thought in a singular hermeneutical and theological movement.[58] That is to say, spiritual manifestations must be assessed in the light of their ethical outworking and ethical
life must be viewed in the light of spiritual realities. Macro- and micro-
cosmos interrelate. Spiritual realities have ethical implications, while at
the same time ethical transformation manifests the truth claim of a correct
knowledge of God. Given that I posit a certain amount of interrelationship between the apocalyptic Christ-event and existential reality (between
cosmology and anthropology), what does this imply for Paul's method of
truth verification? What are the *foundations* of true knowledge? Do his
various truth claims *cohere* with one another? How clearly are objective
and subjective reality distinguishable?[59] I shall argue that the interdependence of various forms of discernment reflects a holistic and comprehensive (not systematic or necessarily coherent) grasp of reality as perceived
through the Christ-event. (When I speak of 'Christ-event' I mean a broad
understanding of the life, death and resurrection of Jesus).[60]

---

[58] An important clarification must be made: I differentiate between 'theological' and
'spiritual' because the latter is used to translate a spiritual manifestation, πνευματικόν, as
used in 1 Cor. 2.13, are 'spiritual realities' (Lewis, *Life*, 68) and hence far broader than the
charisms (contra Dunn, *Theology of Paul*, 554f.). A 'Spiritual reality' is, for instance, for
Paul 'God's secret wisdom' that the 'rulers of this age' have not understood (1 Cor. 2.6f.).
However, as noted earlier 'spiritual' is an elusive term and should not be differentiated
rigidly from theological phenomena because all spiritual manifestations have theological
consequences. It is the goal of this book to show the *interdependence* of spiritual, theological and ethical levels of Pauline thought, which becomes reasonably evident in the use
of the term 'spirituality' in M. J. Gorman, *Apostle of the Crucified Lord: A Theological
Introduction to Paul and his Letters* (Grand Rapids, MI: Eerdmans, 2004) ch. 5.
[59] Two differing positions may be named here: O. Hofius ('"Die Wahrheit des Evangeliums". Exegetische und theologische Erwägungen zum Wahrheitsanspruch der paulinischen
Verkündigung', in *Paulusstudien* II [WUNT 143; Tübingen: Mohr/Siebeck, 2002] 17–37)
has a propositional understanding of truth whereas V. P. Furnish stresses its existential character ('Where is "The Truth" in Paul's Gospel?', in E. E. Johnson and D. M. Hay [eds.],
Pauline Theology IV. *Looking back, Pressing on* [Atlanta: Scholars Press, 1997] 161–78).
[60] Although broad in scope, it can be expressed simply: '"Christ died (for us) and was
raised (from the dead)"', which was the 'shared confession and bond which held together
the first Christian Churches' (Dunn, *Theology of Paul*, 177). Indeed, at points in this book
we shall be looking at only the first half of the confession, concentrating on the salvific
meaning of the incarnation and cross (particularly in chapter 4, where I argue for the contingent aspect of the interpretation of the gospel). However, other aspects, such as the life of
Jesus or the apocalyptic meaning associated with the event, are for Paul implicitly present
in the confession (cf. J. C. Beker, *Paul the Apostle: The Triumph of God in Life and
Truth* [Philadelphia: Fortress Press, 1984] 16–18; D. Flemming, 'Essence and Adaptation:
Contextualisation and the Heart of Paul's Gospel' I-II [Unpubl. PhD dissertation Univer-
sity of Aberdeen, 1987] 533ff.; L. Goppelt, *Theologie des Neuen Testaments* [Göttingen:
Vandenhoeck & Ruprecht, 1991³] 368).

This comprehensive understanding means that discernment is not only the result of the believer's transformation, but gives it a key role in the translation of theology into ethics and vice versa.[61] Hence, I understand discernment as having an *interpretative* role, through which meaning is established, and a *corrective* role, by which knowledge is qualified. The interpretative role plays a significant part in Paul's and the believers' development of an authentic interpretation of the Christ-event and the ensuing ethos.[62] Formerly hidden knowledge is brought to the light and hence can be appropriated. The corrective role reflects the constant need to evaluate experiences and claims to inspiration in the Pauline churches.[63] This means that discernment describes one of the principle features of Pauline epistemology. It dynamically balances the tension between provisional knowledge – which acknowledges the ambiguity of all existence – and the assured conviction that reality is ultimately exposed in the Christ-event.

C.   Focal Theory and Organisation of the Study

In sum my work will present a novel approach to discernment by elucidating the following elements. Firstly, in contrast to previous studies, which concentrated on specific words or passages denoting discernment, I intend to provide a comprehensive study, which not only includes all the terms referring to discernment but also those conceptually linked to it. Secondly, the need for such a conceptual approach will become apparent when clarifying the substantive interdependence of ethical and spiritual discernment. This in turn will be confirmed by, thirdly, understanding Paul's approach to truth formation and how an authentic interpretation of

---

[61] T. Engberg-Pedersen (*Paul and the Stoics* [Edinburgh: T&T Clark, 2000]) will be a helpful guide in the matter of understanding Paul's comprehensive grasp of reality (of theology and ethics) and how the Stoics offer a point of comparison. For the interrelationship of epistemology and ethics I will interact *inter alios* with A. R. Brown (*The Cross and Human Transformation: Paul's Apocalyptic Word in 1 Corinthians* [Minneapolis: Fortress Press, 1995]).

[62] As points of reference for understanding Paul's thought as a whole, we may name Beker (*Paul*) and D. Patte (*Paul's Faith and the Power of the Gospel: A Structural Introduction to the Pauline Letters* [Philadelphia: Fortress Press, 1983]). Cf. also C. A. Davis, *The Structure of Paul's Theology: 'The Truth which is the Gospel'* (Lewiston, NJ: Mellen Biblical Press, 1995).

[63] G. D. Fee (*The First Epistle to the Corinthians* [Grand Rapids, MI: Eerdmans, 1987] 118) points out that there is an obvious problem of 'discernment' at Corinth, hence the frequency of evaluative terminology in 1 Corinthians: (ἀνακρίνω [8×]; διακρίνω [5×]; κρίνω [15×]; συγκρίνω [1×]; δοκιμάζω [3×]) and Paul's concern that they 'make appropriate "judgments" about what God is doing in the world' (117).

the Christ-event interrelates with renewed identity and community formation. Fourthly, I will present an in-depth explanation of how human mediation and divine revelation (mind and Spirit) interact and affect rationality, consciousness and valuation and hence how authentic knowledge and authentic spirituality necessarily qualify one another leading to a renewed perception of self, others and the world. And, finally, I will substantiate and differentiate this portrayal of Pauline epistemology by presenting relevant contextual Hellenistic and Jewish material. Hence, my argument will present discernment as the nerve centre of Pauline thinking. It is existential theologising meaning an interpretation and translation of the Christ-event into the particulars of everyday life.

I aim to organise the material by concentrating on two major questions, namely: (1) What requires discernment and (2) how should and can authentic discernment function? I will deal with these two points in two separate sections that follow this introduction (Part I). The first of these (Part II) will include three chapters (2, 3, 4). In chapter 2 I will concentrate on the scope of ethical evaluation and the relationship between discernment and the law. In chapter 3 I will examine the extent of spiritual discernment. And in chapter 4 I will demonstrate how the previous two aspects of discernment (ethical and spiritual) belong together as I highlight how they have to be understood from Paul's more comprehensive grasp of reality and truth-formation. How this comprehensive grasp is to be understood will be further elucidated in part III (chapters 5 and 6). In chapter 5 I investigate Paul's religious and philosophical context – that is both Judaism and Hellenism – with the emphasis on the specific question as to how authentic discernment was believed to function. I will use this material to validate my portrayal of Pauline epistemology in chapter 6. Finally, in my concluding chapter (chapter 7) I will summarise the results of my investigation and draw attention to the significance of the concept of discernment for future Pauline research.

PART II

What requires Discernment? The Objects of Evaluation

2

THE DISCERNMENT OF ETHICAL QUESTIONS

A. **Introduction**

> I appeal to you therefore, brothers and sisters, by the mercies of God, to present your bodies as a living sacrifice, holy and acceptable to God, which is your spiritual worship. Do not be conformed to this world, but be transformed by the renewing of your minds, so that you may discern [δοκιμάζω] what is the will of God – what is good and acceptable and perfect.

Paul's admonition in Rom. 12.1–2, which is full of hope, is remarkable: after questioning the possibility of understanding God's paths and judgements in Rom. 11.33f., he now presents an approach to the knowledge of the will of God.[1] The prospect of attaining this knowledge was not only a 'determining factor in Paul's own life and plans'[2] but to 'live in tune with the divine, however conceptualized, was also a fundamental objective for *all* religious and quasi-religious systems of the age'.[3] Now, Paul posits, believers can fulfil this hope. The ethical implications of this vision inspired O. Cullmann to a keen statement of his own:

---

[1] With that I do not mean to suggest that the will of God is a synonymous expression for the inscrutable ways of the Lord in Rom. 11.33f. It does seem fair to say that Paul is offering a partial answer in 12.2 to his earlier questions. This answer has much potential for in-depth inquiry.

Essentially 'the will of God' needs to be studied conceptually, including terms like πρόθεσις (Rom. 8.28; Eph 1.11), but cf. V. P. Furnish (*Theology and Ethics in Paul* [Nashville: Abingdon Press, 1968] 188–91), who offers an overview of θέλημα and θέλειν in Paul; also G. Schrenk ('θέλημα κτλ.', *TDNT* III, 52–62 [particularly 57f.]); further, θέλημα τοῦ θεοῦ (Col. 1.9f.; Eph. 5.17), τί ἐστίν εὐάρωστον τῷ κυρίῳ (Eph. 5.10) and τὰ διαφέροντα (Phil. 1.9f.; cf. Rom. 2.18).

[2] Dunn, *Theology of Paul*, 40.

[3] (Italics mine) J. D. G. Dunn, *Romans 9–16* (WBC 8B; Dallas: Word Books, 1988) 717. Thus all people of 'spiritual and moral sensibility' (Dunn, *Romans 9–16*, 715) would have approved the goal of discernment expressed in philosophical principles in Rom. 12.2 (τὸ ἀγαθὸν καί εὐάρεστον καί τέλειον). Cf., for a similar reading, C. E. B. Cranfield, *The Epistle to the Romans* II (ICC; Edinburgh: T&T Clark, 1983³) 610.

This 'testing' (δοκιμάζειν) is the key to all New Testament ethics . . . Certainty of moral judgement in the concrete sense is in the last analysis the one great fruit that the Holy Spirit, this factor in redemptive history, produces in the individual man.[4]

Is this a correct interpretation of Paul's thought? If so, it means I need to offer an in-depth study of this 'testing'. Cullmann does not offer much evidence to support this assertion and does not elucidate what the implications are for Pauline theology. But G. Therrien has attempted to fill this gap in his monograph on discernment.[5]

Δοκιμάζω, Therrien argues, is a flexible and resourceful form of ethical deliberation as it enables the Christian to answer questions not addressed by Paul.[6] By applying the fundamentals of faith to everyday life, the believer avoids both legalism, 'la lettre', and situation ethics, 'l'amoralisme'.[7] While normative authority is still present,[8] the believer is now inwardly inclined to fulfil the will of God because he or she is renewed in knowledge and guided by the Spirit, the '*conscience prudente*',[9] and a 'clairvoyant' love.[10] This inward inclination requires of

[4] Cullmann, *Christ*, 228.

[5] Therrien, *Discernement*, 303. Therrien claims that Paul's vision of ethical discernment is original, but as I showed earlier this claim is linked to inaccurate evidence about δοκιμάζω.

[6] Therrien, *Discernement*, 306. Therrien concludes that Paul did not give ready-made solutions to every problem, but encouraged believers to seek the will of God by using the resources of faith, human reflection and experience in ever-changing historical contexts. He states that δοκιμάζω allows Christians to answer current questions not addressed by scripture (*Discernement*, 305).

[7] Therrien, *Discernement*, 264, 303f. Baptised into Christ, inspired by the Spirit and enlightened by faith, the believer (in contrast to Gentiles and Jews). While the Gentiles have been handed over by God to a ἀδόκιμος νοῦς, since they were not prepared to acknowledge God (Rom. 1.18–32), the discernment of the Jews, though defined by the law, shows a lack of coherence with their behaviour (Rom. 2.17–24; Therrien, *Discernement*, 264).

[8] Therrien, *Discernement*, 284ff. The norms are the 'laws' of the Spirit, love and Christ. His position on the Mosaic law is ambiguous. While in its enslaving function it is abrogated, when it is considered as a spiritual expression of the will of God it still has a normative function.

In part this authority is ecclesiastically defined. Therrien (*Discernement*, 286) is keen on the norm brought about by the teaching of the church. However, at points this foundation of discernment seems to originate rather neatly from his particular ecclesiastical background. Hence it is a discernment based on 'les fondements ontologico-sacramentels' and in 'l'être nouveau du baptisé' (*Discernement*, 304).

[9] Therrien, *Discernement*, 305. With regard to the Spirit he puts it like this: It is the same Spirit which resurrected Christ, spoke through the prophets, 'inscribes' on the hearts the requirements of the law, animates the church and keeps a safeguard over the apostolic authority (*Discernement*, 304).

[10] Therrien, *Discernement*, 264. There he also speaks of the necessity of 'charité fraternelle' (Rom. 14.22–23).

the believer to edify the church and apply the big picture of salvation history to every given situation.[11] Salvation history implies that every moral decision has an eschatological dimension.[12]

As explained earlier (pages 7ff.), Therrien's methodology of a word study does reflect the breadth of the concept of discernment in Paul. Therrien misses the obvious point that other, synonymous, terms expound in a significant manner Paul's thought and the connection of ethical and theological discrimination.[13] Nevertheless, a number of Therrien's conclusions elaborate crucial issues for my study.

First of all, Therrien's assertion that decision making is based on a synergy of mind and Spirit, an 'acte *humano-divin*', would appear to offer an answer to the epistemological questions raised in the first chapter. But how does this synergy affect valuation, consciousness and reason?[14] How should we conceptualise the inward inclination, which Therrien believes is guaranteed by the renewed mind? Secondly, Therrien's argument that the renewed mind is the resolution of the tension between legalism and autonomy in Paul is significant.[15] W. Schrage has taken this thought even further by claiming that Paul's vision of discernment makes it possible for the believer to evaluate all previous norms and traditions.[16] But is this a fair treatment of the complex issue of normativity and the role

[11] Therrien, *Discernement*, 290ff. His point is that situation ethics just looks at the immediate and individual criteria for decision making, whereas he believes that both the Christological and eschatological dimensions of each situation are significant and give each decision their full meaning (*Discernement*, 245f., 303f.).

[12] His procedure is as follows: In the first section he traces the meaning of the above words in the Greek and Jewish world and the non-Pauline NT texts (*Discernement*, 9–62). Then, after an exegetical analysis of the Pauline literature (including the Pastorals; *Discernement*, 63–238), Therrien offers a systematic overview of the religious value and moral dimension of δοκιμάζω and cognates (*Discernement*, 239–302).

[13] For instance, because Therrien does not address ἀνακρίνω and συγκρίνω, he misses 1 Cor. 1–2 and the epistemolgical and hermeneutical expositions found there.

[14] Therrien, *Discernement*, 294.

[15] We must find out where the locus of normativity lies without falling into the hermeneutical trap (perceivable in Therrien's work) of reading contemporary ecclesiology into Paul. As noted earlier, at places Therrien interprets Paul using language reminiscent of his ecclesiastical background. Hence, the will of God like the plan of salvation and the 'impératif moral' is realised in the church, in the '*prédication apostolique*' and in the '*célébration liturgique*' (*Discernement*, 289).

[16] W. Schrage, *Die konkreten Einzelgebote in der paulinischen Paränese: Ein Beitrag zur neutestamentlichen Ethik* (Gütersloh: Gerd Mohn, 1961) 170: 'Der Christ hat gerade durch kritisches Fragen, Sichten und Prüfen herauszufinden, was unter dem "bisher undurchsichtigen Angebot" von Willenskundgebungen aller Art" und der "bunten Fülle unterschiedener Vorschriften" (AT, Tradition, Lebenserfahrung u.ä.) dem Willen Gottes entspricht, denn das ist ihm auf Grund seiner erneuerten Urteilsfähigkeit möglich' (citing Schlier and Lohmeyer respectively).

of the Torah in Paul?[17] Thirdly, while the eschatological dimension is significant, should *every* decision be linked to the final judgement, and is eschatology the unifying concept behind discernment?[18]

I will deal with the eschatological question first and follow on with the relationship of normativity and discernment. The first, epistemological, question is given some attention here but will be dealt with more comprehensively in chapters 5 and 6.

B.   Is Ethical Discernment Defined by Eschatology?

In answering this question, we need to consider two aspects, which Therrien believes serve as the background of eschatological discernment.[19] On the one hand, God tests every believer and the value of his or her work (the '*dokimasie* eschatologique').[20] Believers need to be 'proven worthy', not only in the face of the final judgement, but also in the daily confrontation with a hostile world.[21] In particular, the apostles are subject to tests and, in turn, are required to test others.[22] On the other hand, each decision must be viewed as playing a part in salvation history.[23] The Christian is to reaffirm the two eschatological reference points, namely, the Christ-event ('*kairos central*') and the eschatological judgement ('*kairos final*') in every act of discernment.[24] These reference points give each decision eternal value.[25] But does this reflect Pauline ethics?

Therrien is in part right to stress this aspect of discernment. As J. L. Martyn suggests, Pauline epistemology must generally be seen against the background of 'the juncture of the ages'.[26] The believer's discernment

---

[17] The epistemological question at the heart of discernment (how can one know the truth?) intrinsically includes the issue of which norms and traditions are the basis for evaluation. I use the term 'normativity' to define this issue.

[18] 'La dimension eschatologique permet d'unifier tout le thème' (Therrien, *Discernement*, 3).

[19] According to Therrien, Paul is not original in highlighting the eschatological aspect of discernment, as this is also perceivable in other Jewish and NT texts (*Discernement*, 17–60).

[20] Therrien, *Discernement*, 246. He assigns this whole aspect of '*dokimasie* eschatologique' to the category of the religious value of δοκιμάζω, which he contrasts with the moral dimension (*Discernement*, 243).

[21] Therrien, *Discernement*, 245–54. He differentiates between the 'auteur' of the '*dokimasie*', which is God, and the 'sujets', who are the believers.

[22] Cf. Therrien (*Discernement*, 100–16) for 1 Cor. 3.12f.; 9.27; 2 Cor. 2.9; 10.18.

[23] Therrien, *Discernement*, 263f., 297–9.

[24] Therrien, *Discernement*, 295.   [25] Therrien, *Discernement*, 264.

[26] J. L. Martyn, 'Epistemology at the Turn of the Ages: 2 Corinthians 5:16', in W. R. Farmer, C. F. D. Moule and R. R. Niebuhr (eds.), *Christian History and Interpretation: Studies Presented to John Knox* (Cambridge: Cambridge University Press, 1967) 284.

is connected with eschatological judgement. Hence, Paul prays that the Philippians 'may determine [δοκιμάζω] what is best so that in the day of Christ you may be pure and blameless' (Phil. 1.10; cf. 1 Cor. 11.27–34). Nevertheless, two important caveats must be issued.

First, the eschatological dimension should not be stressed to the detriment of understanding that Paul's ethics are founded in 'the present reality – of God, the created world and people in particular'.[27] Future judgement alone does not determine discernment. Rather believers are to expound the meaning of salvation for every given moment (2 Cor. 6.2).[28] Even in 1 Cor. 11, where discernment is embedded within a 'whole chain of forensic language' and is accorded eschatological significance, the problem at the heart of the issue is a sociological one.[29] The rich have not been paying appropriate attention to the poor and, consequently, they have done an injustice not only to members of the church but also to Christ.[30] For Paul, the relational dimension cannot be divorced from the theological issue.[31] Judgement begins in the manner in which members of the community treat one another. Sole concentration on eschatological judgement would neglect the need to examine the present context implying a need for self-examination, whether or not a 'genuine appropriation of grace anchored in identification with the crucified Christ' has taken place (1 Cor. 11.31f.).[32]

[27] J. F. Kilner, 'A Pauline Approach to Ethical Decision-Making', *Int.* 44 (1989) 371.

[28] Cf. F. Lang, *Die Briefe an die Korinther* (NTD 7; Göttingen: Vandenhoeck & Ruprecht, 1986) 303f.

[29] Fee, *Corinthians*, 561. Cf. the forensic language: ἀναξίως, ἔνοχος (v. 27); δοκιμάζω (v. 28); διακρίνω, (vv. 29,31); κρίμα (vv. 29,34); κρίνω (vv. 31, 32).

[30] Fee, *Corinthians*, 533. Cultic meals as part of worship were a known phenomenon, and it is probable that the Lord's Supper was eaten in connection with such a meal. The rich (those with enough food and drink and their own houses), who may have been hosting the meals, were starting them (the breaking of bread was at the beginning of the meal) before the poorer members arrived and possibly even giving them food of poorer quality; cf. G. Theissen, 'Social Integration and Sacramental Activity: An Analysis of 1 Cor. 11:17–34', in *The Social Setting of Pauline Christianity* (Edinburgh: T&T Clark, 1982) 145–69; Dunn, *Theology of Paul*, 609–13.

[31] There is some discussion of how to understand 'not discerning the body' in v. 29. Some see 'body' as a direct reference to the church (G. Bornkamm, 'Lord's Supper and Church in Paul', in *Early Christian Experience* [trans. P. L. Hammer; London: SCM Press, 1969] 148f.; Fee, *Corinthians*, 563f.). Others see the reference to the church as secondary to a reference to Christ and his uniqueness (Thiselton, *Corinthians*, 891–4; Schrage, *Korinther* III, 51f.). In either case, to my mind, both the health of church life and the correct understanding of Christ are inextricably tied together. The disregard for members of the church is clearly as dangerous as a disregard for Christ, contra A. Robertson and A. Plummer (*First Epistle of St. Paul to the Corinthians* [Edinburgh: T&T Clark, 1955²] 252), who do not think τὸ σῶμα (1 Cor. 11.29) denotes 'the body of Christians'.

[32] Thiselton, *Corinthians*, 898. He also warns against understanding the examination as a 'pietist psychologism' (similarly Schrage, *Korinther* III, 57f).

Secondly, the reason why eschatological significance is accentuated so much by Therrien is because he has confused conceptual research with a word study (cf. Excursus a in chapter 1). If we restrict ourselves to examining those senses of δοκιμάζω which are conceptually linked to discernment, eschatology cannot be seen as the unifying concept behind discernment. As argued earlier, it is confusing to relate God's testing of his people with human evaluation,[33] apart from which the linguistically related terms (δόκιμος, δοκιμή, ἀδόκιμος) are not relevant (except 2 Cor. 13.5): it is not justifiable to correlate the 'worthiness' of the believers' or apostle's work with their discernment. On the contrary, I claim that discernment is linked to a self-understanding liberated from such estimation.

In the final analysis, this means that the emphasis Therrien places on the eschatological dimension needs to be curtailed. While the Christ-event is crucial for epistemology, it is not necessary to place *every* decision in the context of the final judgement.

C.   Discernment and Normativity

In this section we must deal with distinctly differing opinions regarding the issue of normativity in Paul. On the one hand, we have O. Cullmann's assertion and G. Therrien's endorsement that the key to ethics in Paul is a process of testing, which is based on the renewed mind. And we noted that W. Schrage believes that this testing will make it possible for the believer to assess all previous norms and traditions. E. J. Schnabel, on the other hand, sees this entirely differently. He has claimed that the will of God has sufficiently been revealed 'in the law, in the words of Jesus Christ, in the pronouncements of the apostles, and in the orders of creation'.[34] Discernment here is only a secondary process of application.

Obviously then, Paul's hopeful admonition in Rom. 12.1–2, quoted at the beginning of this chapter, raises some crucial questions for the concept of discernment. Does Paul have a fixed concept of what constitutes the will of God? Where does the locus of normativity lie? To what extent do external norms and traditions play a role? Do the norms themselves require discernment?[35]

---

[33] For instance, this calls into question the inclusion of those instances of the verb δοκιμάζω where God tests his people (1 Cor. 3.13; 1 Thess. 2.4).

[34] Schnabel, *Wisdom*, 342.

[35] These questions lead us into a broader discussion regarding the structure and foundation of Pauline ethics. While on the one side some scholars have investigated the more extensive horizon of Paul's moral thinking, others have focussed on the particulars of his

1.   The Selective Use of Traditions

In order to understand what the locus of normativity is in Paul's ethics, we must take the various possibilities one by one. We will look first at the significance of Jesus' teaching, then at the apostolic commands, followed by Hellenistic and wisdom morality and, finally in some depth, the role of the law (Torah). This discussion will then serve as a backdrop for my own proposal in which I will elucidate how the renewed mind is the basis of discernment.

Jesus, Paul and Hellenism

Given the Christological focus of Paul's theology, one would expect that the believer could find ethical orientation in the teachings of Jesus. Paul does on occasion appeal to the authority of Jesus' sayings, and the Christ-event in general terms (as I shall further elucidate) serves as the focal point of the new ethos.[36] However, 'the scarcity' of any direct appeal is 'itself enough to show that Jesus' teachings by no means become a "Christian law" analogous to the Jewish'.[37] Rather, it seems that Paul expects the

---

ethical teaching. The former group acknowledges the fluidity of Pauline ethics, while the latter stresses the finality and efficacy of binding norms. These two sides can also be correlated with the dialectic that we find in Paul in which a stark emphasis on the freedom that the gospel brings (the indicative) is present alongside a resolute demand for obedience to particular apostolic commands (the imperative). I cannot resolve the tension, but in this book we will return to this issue at various points and I will attempt to highlight how discernment offers a key aspect for its clarification.

For an overview, cf. W. L. Willis, 'Bibliography: Pauline Ethics, 1964–1994', in E. H. Lovering, Jr and J. L. Sumney (eds.), *Theology and Ethics in Paul and his Interpreters: Essays in Honor of Victor Paul Furnish* (Nashville: Abingdon Press, 1996) 306–19. W. A. Meeks (*The Moral World of the First Christians* [Philadelphia: Westminster Press, 1986] 14ff., 162) stresses that only by understanding the symbolised universe of the early Christians can one understand the particulars. P. Richardson (*Paul's Ethic of Freedom* [Philadelphia: Westminster Press, 1979] 164) emphasises Paul's unique and strong emphasis on the '*theology* of freedom'. For the difficulty of the imperative-indicative classification, cf. M. Wolter, 'Die ethische Identität christlicher Gemeinden in neutestamentlicher Zeit', in W. Härle and R. Preul (eds.), *Woran orientiert sich Ethik?* (Marburg: Elwert Verlag, 2001) 61–90.

[36] As argued by R. Penna ('The Problem of the Law in Paul's Letters', in *Paul the Apostle* II. *Wisdom and Folly of the Cross* [trans. P. Wahl; Collegeville, MN: Liturgical Press, 1996] 132). Further: 'only Christ . . . represents the real alternative to νόμος . . . and ἀνομία (i.e., sin) alike. . . [T]he only norm of reference is Christ himself' ('Problem', 134).

[37] Furnish, *Ethics*, 228, cf. 49ff. and 218ff.; H. D. Betz, 'Das Problem der Grundlagen der paulinischen Ethik (Röm 12,1–2)', in *Paulinische Studien: Gesammelte Aufsätze* III (Tübingen: Mohr/Siebeck, 1994) 187f.; R. Penna, 'Problems of Pauline Morality: The Present State of the Question', in *Paul*, 166–7. It is probable but largely an argument from silence to argue that, despite the 'paucity of explicit evidence', the believer 'seeking to live in accord with the law of Christ could refer to the Jesus tradition known widely among the

believers to attain a maturity which reflects the 'mind of Christ' (1 Cor. 2.16).[38]

The apostolic directives are the other obvious place to look for ethical guidance. W. Schrage has stressed the material significance of these for a true understanding of Pauline ethics.[39] However, Paul also calls believers to assess these directives (1 Cor. 10.15; 11.13). At least at certain points Paul does not wish for 'unquestioning obedience' but rather for 'responsible decision', 'to have them decide for themselves upon their own gift and call' (1 Cor. 7).[40] That means, to a great extent it is left up to the believer to know when the apostolic maxims conclude an argument and when they are the beginning of reflection.[41]

A further possibility that has been stressed is that apart from the Christ-event there is no new substance in Paul's ethics, nothing that the estimation of unbelievers would not also acknowledge as good.[42] Indeed, it is remarkable how much of Paul's ethics converge with Hellenistic ethics.[43] Parallels can be found in the details of his parenesis and in the broader texture of his thought (the latter of which we shall return to in chapter 5).[44] However, it is not possible to find a complete identification of Pauline and Hellenistic morality. There are foundational elements

churches' (Dunn, *Theology of Paul*, 658). Indeed, even where Paul is sure that his instructions are a 'command of the Lord', 'they must be *recognised* as the Lord's command' and then obeyed on that basis (italics mine; Dunn, 'Discernment', 94).

[38] Even Schnabel (*Wisdom*, 316) must agree: 'It is nevertheless obvious that Paul has hardly drawn upon the historical life and work of Jesus for the concrete orientation of Christian conduct.'

[39] W. Schrage's position has developed somewhat. While in *Einzelgebote*, 9–12, his main point was to highlight the significance of Paul's commands, in 'Verhältnis', 505, he states: 'Ebensowenig wird einfach auf apostolische Autorität oder ein festes Normensystem reklamiert oder gar rationale Uneinsehbarkeit der Gebote als radikaler Gehorsamstest hingestellt.'

[40] W. Gooch (*Partial Knowledge: Philosophical Studies in Paul* [Notre Dame: University of Notre Dame Press, 1987] 99–100) concerning 1 Cor.7. Otherwise in 1 Corinthians he sees Paul taking a more authoritative approach.

[41] J. P. Sampley, *Walking between the Times: Paul's Moral Reasoning* (Minneapolis: Fortress Press, 1991) 95.

[42] So, R. Bultmann, 'Das Problem der Ethik bei Paulus', *ZNW* 23 (1924) 123–40, here 138. Similarly, H. Conzelmann, *Grundriß der Theologie des Neuen Testaments* (Tübingen: Mohr/Siebeck, 1976) 310.

[43] M. Bockmuehl (*Jewish Law in Gentile Churches: Halakhah and the Beginning of Christian Public Ethics* [Edinburgh: T&T Clark, 2000] xiv) shows 'the remarkable extent to which early Christianity adopted Jewish tradition of a "public" or "international" morality' (cf. also 127–43). Cf. H. Merklein, 'Die Weisheit Gottes und die Weisheit der Welt (1 Kor 1,21)', in *Studien zu Jesus und Paulus* (WUNT 43; Tübingen: Mohr/Siebeck, 1987) 384; Penna, 'Morality', 164f.; Betz, 'Problem', 186f.

[44] As with Stoic discernment, Paul expects that the believers can discern 'what counts' (τὰ διαφέροντα, Phil. 1.10). 'The identification of ἀδιάφορα [matters, neutral in and of themselves, which neither benefit nor harm] was an important part of the moralists'

that do not cohere with Paul's ethics (cf. Rom. 1.18–2.5).[45] Hence, the believer may look to the outside world for input for his conduct, but the key is his ability to select.

> With all Paul's incorporation of contemporary ethics, there is a concurrent process of selection and sifting applied . . . All acceptance was therefore selective and critical, not absolute.[46]

Thus, instead of offering a basis for discernment, Hellenistic morality itself *requires* discernment.

It could be suggested then that Paul's discriminating use of Hellenistic ethical thought is no different from that found in the wisdom tradition. There, too, we find a dialectic of an acceptance of certain ethical traditions, on the one hand, and condemnation of Gentile morality, on the other.[47] Moreover, Paul does clothe some of his material in wisdom terminology.[48] And he 'dramatically' vivifies 'the importance of wisdom by locating it in the person of Christ'.[49] However, in the uncontested letters we find a hesitance with regard to wisdom and partial critique of it (1 Cor. 1–2).[50]

---

pedagogy' in order to weather 'the vicissitudes of fortune'. 'Such evaluation served to warn listeners against mistaken placement of values and, via negation, to highlight what really mattered' (J. L. Jaquette, *Discerning what Counts: The Function of the Adiaphora Topos in Paul's Letters* [SBL.DS 147; Atlanta: Scholars Press, 1995] 197). Jaquette goes on to show that in his letters Paul often uses the same argumentative strategy to show that certain items and issues are ἀδιάφορα, such as the shiftings and variations of life (Phil. 4.10ff), circumcision (Galatians) or elitism (*Adiaphora*, 199–207). However, Paul's objectives are different from the moralists' (*Adiaphora*, 225).

Moreover, Paul draws on a broad range of philosophical material in his ethics and can approve existing orders of creation (marriage, family, work etc.). Cf. the Stoic/Hellenistic vocabulary: τὸ ἀγαθόν (1 Thess. 5.15; Rom. 12.9; 13.3; 14.16; 15.2; 16.19); τὰ καθήκοντα (Rom. 1.28); ἀληθής, σεμνός, δίκαιος, προσφιλής, εὔφημος, ἀρετή (Phil. 4.8).

[45] Cf. Betz, 'Grundlagen', 187, and my argument in chapter 5.

[46] W. Schrage, *The Ethics of the New Testament* (trans. D. E. Green; Edinburgh: T&T Clark, 1988) 201. This is also argued well, although from a broader perspective than Paul's theology, by T. Herr, (*Naturrecht aus der kritischen Sicht des Neuen Testaments* [Munich: Ferdinand Schöningh, 1976] 277 [and throughout]). He points out that first-century Christians 'die antike Ethik ihrer Zeit an dem Maßstab der Christusbotschaft gemessen und kritisch geprüft und, wo erforderlich, korrigiert haben'.

[47] Dunn, *Theology of Paul*, 661–7.

[48] Cf. E. J. Schnabel ('Wisdom', *DPL*, 967–73) who has correctly argued that 'the notion of wisdom is not restricted to the occurrence of the term *wisdom*' and offers a helpful overview of the semantic field ('Wisdom', 967). Examples of wisdom concepts are the vice lists (Rom. 1.29–31; 13.13; 1 Cor. 5.10f.; 6.9f.) and Paul's hope that the believers will discover the good (cf. Rom. 15.14; 16.19) and avoid evil amongst themselves (1 Thess. 5.15, 21).

[49] J. S. Lamp, *First Corinthians 1–4 in Light of Jewish Wisdom Traditions* (Studies in the Bible and Early Christianity 42; Lampeter: Edwin Mellen Press, 2000) 193.

[50] Explicit wisdom language increases in Ephesians and Colossians. For instance, the believers were taught ἐν σοφί (Col. 1.28) and receive understanding of God's will ἐν πάσῃ

R. Penna has suggested that this differentiated stance towards the wisdom tradition is due to the identification of wisdom and law.[51] But did Paul want to avoid such an identification? There are two antithetical answers, which we must deal with separately.

The Relevance of the Law[52]

Although a consensus has partially emerged that Paul does not follow the equation of wisdom and law with regard to salvation,[53] for a number of scholars the law remains applicable for ethical deliberation. These scholars rely on two ideas: first, to varying degrees they follow E. P. Sanders' portrayal of 'covenantal nomism'.[54] Hence, for Paul Christ has replaced the law as the outer boundary marker but it remains authoritative for the ordering of daily life. Indeed, because of the liberation in Christ and the guidance of the Spirit, there is a renewed freedom for the law.[55]

Secondly, those advocating a continued relevance of the law have pointed to the factual evidence that some dependence on the Torah is still present in Paul's writings and have shown that the Hellenistic churches patterned their lives to some extent according to the law.[56]

σοφία καὶ συνέσει (Col. 1.9f; cf. Eph 1.17), and they are expected to teach and admonish each other in wisdom (Col. 4.5).

[51] 'Paul did not do a real exploitation of the wisdom theme precisely because of the strict linkage at his time between Hokmah [wisdom] and Torah, so that one reality carried the other with it; he wanted to avoid the danger of bringing about a restoration of the Law along with wisdom' (R. Penna, 'Dissolution and Restoration of the Relationship of Law and Wisdom in Paul', in *Paul*, 147). For a different angle on Paul's attitude to wisdom as Law, cf. M. D. Goulder, 'ΣΟΦΙΑ in 1 Corinthians', *NTS* 37 (1991) 516–34.

[52] For a differentiated discussion of what νόμος denotes, cf. M. Winger, *By what Law? The Meaning of* Νόμος *in the Letters of Paul* (SBL.DS 128; Atlanta: Scholars Press 1990) 197f.

[53] Cf. M. Hengel, *Der Sohn Gottes: Die Entstehung der Christologie und die jüdisch-hellenistische Religionsgeschichte* (Tübingen: Mohr/Siebeck, 1975) and M. Wolter, 'Verborgene Weisheit und Heil für die Heiden. Zur Traditionsgeschichte und Intention des "Revelationsschemas"', *ZThK* 84 (1987) 297–319 and Pate, *Curse*, 11, cf. 2, n. 2.

[54] E. P. Sanders, *Paul and Palestinian Judaism* (Philadelphia: Fortress Press, 1977) 517: '"Good deeds" are a condition for remaining "in", but they do not earn salvation.'

[55] Cf. Dunn, *Theology of Paul*, 721: 'As long as the weakness of the flesh and the power of sin endure, the law will continue to be a force for death. But under the power of the Spirit (as spiritual) it remains God's holy and good guide and yardstick'. H. Hübner (*Das Gesetz bei Paulus* [Göttingen: Vandenhoeck & Ruprecht, 1980 ²] 128f.) believes 'Existenz im Geiste Gottes' makes it possible to abide by the law (although he differentiates between Galatians and Romans). Similarly N. T. Wright (*The Climax of the Covenant* [Edinburgh: T&T Clark, 1991] 191f.), insists that the Torah *is* reaffirmed (*Climax*, 266). S. J. Hafemann (*Paul, Moses, and the History of Israel* [WUNT 81; Tübingen: Mohr/Siebeck, 1995] 405) speaks of a 'freedom "for the Law"' (cf. 429–36; 438–58; Donaldson, *Paul*, 167, 230f.).

[56] Cf. particularly K. Finsterbusch (*Die Thora als Lebensweisung für Heidenchristen: Studien zur Bedeutung der Thora für die paulinische Ethik* [Göttingen: Vandenhoeck &

Hence, E. J. Schnabel has taken these arguments to maintain that 'the Christian ethic . . . is based on, or rather derived from, specific and binding norms' in which the law still 'has a constitutive significance for the Christian ethos'.[57]

Others have adamantly taken the opposing view. For one, covenantal nomism as such has been the object of continued debate, with a far more variegated result being developed than depicted by E. P. Sanders et al.[58] Moreover, some scholars have argued that it is not possible for Paul to reject the law as *conditio salutis* and retain it as an ethical guideline.[59] C. M. Pate holds that the approach of covenantal nomism dilutes Paul's

Ruprecht, 1996] 186–7) who offers evidence that the Torah should 'als Maßstab ethischen Handelns . . . Gültigkeit haben'. Indeed she believes that Paul would have understood his ethical deliberation as an exposition of the Torah. P. J. Thomson (*Paul and the Jewish Law: Halakha in the Letters of the Apostle to the Gentiles* [Compendia Rerum Iudaicarum ad Novum Testamentum; Minneapolis: Fortress Press, 1990] 264) writes that 'halakha was pervasive in Paul' and even sees 'every reason to call him a Hellenistic Pharisee'. B. S. Rosner (*Paul, Scripture and Ethics* [AGJU 22; Leiden: Brill, 1994] 177) finds the OT to be a 'crucial and formative source' for Paul's ethics. For a continued significance of OT tradition, cf. further Schrage, *Einzelgebote*, 173 and M. Bockmuehl, *Revelation and Mystery* (WUNT 2,36; Tübingen: Mohr/Siebeck, 1990) 228.

[57] Schnabel, *Wisdom*, 321; idem, 'How Paul Developed his Ethics', in B. Rosner (ed.), *Understanding Paul's Ethics: Twentieth-Century Approaches* (Grand Rapids, MI: Eerdmans, 1995) 273. He suggests that, on the Christological level, Paul 'abandoned the functional identity of Torah and wisdom' (*Wisdom*, 299), but on the ethical level there is still a 'correlation', even an 'identification' of law and wisdom (*Wisdom*, 344f.).

[58] D. A. Carson ('Summaries and Conclusions', in D. A. Carson, P. T. O'Brien and M. A. Seifrid [eds.], *Justification and Variegated Nomism* I. *The Complexities of Second Temple Judaism* [WUNT 2,140; Tübingen: Mohr/Siebeck, 2001] 543) claims: 'There is strong agreement [amongst the authors of this volume] that covenantal nomism is at best a reductionistic category'. Further see, M. A. Elliott, *The Survivors of Israel: A Reconsideration of the Theology of Pre-Christian Judaism* (Grand Rapids, MI: Eerdmans, 2000). S. Kim (*Paul and the New Perspective: Second Thoughts on the Origin of Paul's Gospel* [WUNT 140; Tübingen: Mohr/Siebeck, 2002] 293–95) calls into question the 'dogma' of the new perspective, both with respect to Judaism and Paul. S. J. Gathercole (*Where is Boasting? Early Jewish Soteriology and Paul's Response in Romans 1–5* [Grand Rapids, MI: Eerdmans, 2002] 266) argues for a more differentiated approach to Second Temple Judaism than with 'vague catchall terms like "legalism" and "works-righteousness"', and that Paul's dialogue partners in Romans 'did indeed hold to a theology of final salvation for the righteous on the basis of works'. While P. Stuhlmacher (and D. A. Hagner, *Revisiting Paul's Doctrine of Justification: A Challenge to the New Perspective* [Downers Grove, IL: InterVarsity Press, 2001] offers a strong critique of the new perspective, S. Westerholm (*Perspectives Old and New on Paul: The "Lutheran" Paul and his Critics* [Grand Rapids, MI: Eerdmans, 2004] 445) argues for a more helpful balance between old and new.

[59] Cf. H. Räisänen, *Paul and the Law* (WUNT 29; Tübingen: Mohr/Siebeck, 1983) 200ff.; S. Westerholm, *Israel's Law and the Church's Faith* (Grand Rapids, MI: Eerdmans, 1988) 198–222; Pate, *Reverse*, 408–28. Furnish (*Ethics*, 33f.) says that '[t]here is no evidence which indicates that the apostle regarded [the law] as in any sense a source book for detailed moral instruction or even a manual of ethical norms . . . Paul himself never seeks to assemble, codify, or interpret in a legalistic way the statutes or wisdom of the Old Testament'. S. K. Davis (*The Antithesis of the Ages: Paul's Reconfiguration of Torah*

'scandalous messages of a crucified messiah, whose death terminated the whole law'.[60] Accordingly, the Christ-event would lose its full significance if it were merely the replacement of a boundary marker. Moreover, Pate believes that the Torah is 'an indivisible unity; either all or none of the Torah remains in the light of Christ's death'.[61]

While my own argument cannot solve these issues conclusively, I propose that both sides of the argument require qualification. That means, first of all, that we must question the bifurcation of salvation and ethics. This applies particularly to the treatment of the relevance of the Torah. And, secondly, we must counter those positions that wish to see a complete abrogation of the Torah because of the factual but selective use of the law. I deal with these one by one.

First, although this book cannot offer a substantial critique of covenantal nomism, I do agree that it is artificial to argue for a division of the Christological impact on salvation and ethics. As chapter 4 will show, ethics is not an addendum to salvation but an inherent part of what the Christ-event means. There I will argue that Christology necessitates, and is the paradigm for, a new existence.[62] This new existence implies the beginning of a new identity, which requires objectification in an ethos.[63] Hence, the Christ-event not only generates the boundary markers, but also

[CBQ.MS 33; Washington, DC: Catholic Biblical Association, 2002] 215f.) believes that for Paul, 'Torah was God's time-bound revelation' only for Jews, and that he reconfigured it so that Christ filled the same theological space reserved for the Torah; cf. A. Lindemann, 'Die biblischen Toragebote und die paulinische Ethik', in *Paulus, Apostel und Lehrer der Kirche* (Tübingen: Mohr/Siebeck, 1999) 113: the Torah 'ist ihm nicht mehr Quelle der Weisungen Gottes für das Verhalten der Menschen, soweit sie Christen sind'; Betz, 'Grundlagen', 205. H. Sonntag (ΝΟΜΟΣ ΣωΤΗΡ: *Zur politischen Theologie des Gesetzes bei Paulus und im antiken Kontext* [TANZ 34; Tübingen: Francke, 2000] 300) claims that the law is not able to aid in a constructive 'Zusammenleben' between God and humanity, and that the νόμος-free norm is Christ, since it makes a life possible not available under νόμος. Further compare F. Thielmann (*Paul and the Law: A Contextual Approach* [Downers Grove, IL: InterVarsity Press, 1994] 243) who claims that the 'Mosaic Law is absorbed by the gospel' in contrast to his *From Plight to Solution* (NT.S 61; Leiden: Brill, 1989), where he sees more continuity with the law. Winger (*Meaning*, 199) states that 'the gospel is free of Jewish νόμος'.

[60] Pate, *Reverse*, 411.   [61] Pate, *Reverse*, 425, concerning Gal. 5.3.

[62] W. Marxsen, *'Christliche' und christliche Ethik im Neuen Testament* (Gütersloh: Gütersloher Verlagshaus, 1989) 15: ethics is not an addendum or only a 'Konsequenz' of theology but rather an 'integrierender Bestandteil' of theology; 'ohne Ethik ist Theologie nicht mehr Theologie'. Similarly T. Söding (*Das Liebesgebot bei Paulus* [Münster: Aschendorff, 1995] 276) writes that, while not every directive is directly related to the gospel, the 'Grundausrichtung' of Pauline ethics must be according to the gospel (*Liebesgebot*, 273).

[63] How Christology is the defining point for the identity of the community and that the new existence combines both soteriology and ethics is shown by M. Wolter, 'Ethos und Identität in paulinischen Gemeinden', *NTS* 43 (1997) 440f.; D. G. Horrell, '"No Longer Jew or Greek." Paul's Corporate Christology and the Construction of Christian Community', in D. G. Horrell and C. M. Tuckett (eds.), *Christology, Controversy and Community: New Testament Essays in Honour of D. R. Catchpole* (NT. S. 99; Leiden: Brill, 2000) 279–302. Cf.

inspires its everyday practice.[64] It (the Christ-event) serves as the basis for a completely new *Lebensraum*, a new being.[65] Therefore, any bifurcation of salvation and ethics will not do justice to Paul. The ethos of the believer is governed to the same extent by Christology, as is soteriology. This in turn implies that the law loses its dominating role for both. But does it imply that it is completely abrogated? This leads us to my next point.

Secondly, Pate's argument requires critique. The Torah is only indivisible to a certain extent. It is indivisible in the sense that there is something comprehensive and internalised about the fulfilment of its demand. Again, we will return to this for a more comprehensive treatment later.[66] However, the Torah *is* divisible in the sense that certain elements can be reappropriated and certain elements rejected. This acknowledges the factual evidence that Paul can make some use of the law but that it is always a selective use. All those positions, which retain a significance for the Torah, must do this in a discriminating manner.[67] *Hence, the Torah*

G. Theissen (*Die Religion der ersten Christen: Eine Theorie des Urchristentums* [Gütersloh: Kaiser Verlag, 2000] 120), who rightly writes that 'Ethos' and 'Mythos' 'verstärken einander'. But the ethos is a constitutive element of the 'Mythos', it is the meaning of the myth in the language 'des Verhaltens' (*Religion*, 101).

[64] Cf. U. Schnelle (*Paulus: Leben und Denken* [Berlin: W. de Gruyter, 2003] 635), who suggests that the starting point and foundation of ethics in Paul is the '*Lebens- und Handlungseinheit* des neuen Seins' as a participation in the 'Christusgeschehen'. M. D. Hooker ('Interchange in Christ and Ethics', *JSNT* 25 [1985] 14) claims: 'That is why conformity to the gospel affects his whole lifestyle'. Similarly, cf. H. D. Betz, 'Humanisierung des Menschen: Delphi, Plato, Paulus', in *Hellenismus und Urchristentum: Gesammelte Aufsätze* I (Tübingen: Mohr/Siebeck, 1990) 120–34.

[65] Cf. K. Backhaus ('Evangelium als Lebensraum. Christologie und Ethik bei Paulus', in U. Schnelle and T. Söding [eds.], *Paulinische Christologie: Exegetische Beiträge. Hans Hübner zum 70. Geburtstag* [Göttingen: Vandenhoeck & Ruprecht, 2000] 9–31) who believes that the Pauline ethos is the 'raum-gemäß' unfolding of the gospel 'mit Sinn, Hand und Fuß'. Ethics fills the space given by the gospel and 'gestaltet' it (31). M. Pfeiffer (*Einweisung in das neue Sein: Neutestamentliche Erwägungen zur Grundlegung der Ethik* [Gütersloh: Gütersloher Verlagshaus, 2001] 318f.) eloquently describes how Christian ethics means allowing oneself to be guided into the new being: 'Da ereignet sich neue Schöpfung, die Auferweckung aus dem Tode im Jetzt, und bricht sich das eigentliche Wunder Bahn: die Menschwerdung des Menschen.'

[66] There I will show that, while the 'claim of the law' (Rom. 8.4) still offers an element of 'continuity', 'Christians do not "observe" the law, they "fulfil" it' (J. Barclay, *Obeying the Truth* [SNTW; Edinburgh: T&T Clark, 1988] 142). Moreover, for Paul it is significant that this satisfying of the 'real' intention of the law is a result (of life in the Spirit) rather than an imperative and hence cannot be seen in any form as a new bondage.

[67] This point is particularly evident behind the comments by Finsterbusch (*Thora*, 185), who claims that the Gentile Christians do not need to follow the law to the same extent as the Jews but, she insists, they have to 'sie *auf ihre Weise* halten'. 'Mit der Aufhebung der Sündenherrschaft durch Christus sind nicht *alle* Funktionen der Thora abgetan.' Another example is Schnabel ('Ethics', 273), who is similarly selective and essentially inconsistent

requires discernment. While scripture serves as a backdrop for ethical (and theological) reflection,[68] for concrete decisions its applicability may be confirmed as well as rejected.[69] As Bultmann claims, this manner of criticism is implied within the δοκιμάζειν τί τὸ θέλημα τοῦ θεοῦ (Rom. 12.2).[70]

In sum, we have seen that the various traditions are used in a selective manner. They require a discerned appropriation. Rather than providing

when he states: 'Consequently large parts of the Torah, particularly of the cultic Torah, have no further factual validity as normative will of God. But the Torah remains the revelation of God's will in its new relation to Jesus Christ.' Cf. L. Thurén, *Derhetorizing Paul: A Dynamic Perspective on Pauline Theology and the Law* (WUNT 124; Tübingen: Mohr/Siebeck, 2000) 181–5, who argues that, although the 'law is no longer valid', it 'is still holy and of divine origin' and hence he needs to persuade his readers of this tension that 'the requirement of the law is still valid, but it is fulfilled by other means, viz. by the Spirit' (181).

The discriminating understanding also applies to those scholars who have attempted to differentiate the roles of discernment and law and to establish an ellipse with two foci: the 'mind of Christ' and the 'law of Christ' (cf. R. N. Longenecker, *Paul, Apostle of Liberty* [Grand Rapids, MI: Baker Book, 1977] 181–208; Dunn, *Jesus*, 224f.; *Theology of Paul*, 647–649). Schnabel (*Wisdom*, 299–342) has also rigidly divided Paul's ethics, differentiating between the law, which is equivalent to 'binding norms', and wisdom, equivalent to 'guiding criteria'. For a critique of this position, cf. R. Bauckham ('Book Review of E. J. Schnabel, Law and Wisdom', *Expository Times* 98 [1986–87] 54) and Barclay (*Truth*, 230) and his criticism that 'Schnabel's approach . . . is vitiated by his unsupported assumption that law is equivalent to "binding norms" and wisdom equivalent to "guiding criteria"'.

[68] 'Working out the specific behaviour associated with this vision [the message of reconciliation, the righteousness of God, their identity as God's covenant people] requires Spirit-led discernment and the transformation of the community's life. But Paul was convinced that the Spirit would lead his churches to become more *discerning readers of scripture*, to hear themselves addressed directly by scripture, and to shape their lives accordingly' (R. B. Hays, 'The Role of Scripture in Paul's Ethics', in Lovering and Sumney [eds.], *Theology*, 47; italics mine). K. Ehrensperger ('Scriptural Reasoning – the Dynamic that Informed Paul's Theologizing' [Seminar Paper, British New Testament Conference, September 2003] 1–12) contextualises Paul 'in the symbolic universe of the Scriptures and of contemporary Jewish exegesis' which means perceiving him 'as living, thinking and acting from within this "cultural-linguistic" system with its own specific forms of reasoning. These forms are perceived as comparable to "Scriptural Reasoning", a practice of dialogic thinking around a text which is not opposed but distinguished from Western philosophical logic' ('Reasoning', 10).

[69] Lindemann ('Toragebote', 113) writes that in concrete ethical conflicts Paul can decide against the Torah, and he does not even necessarily use it as an authority when he agrees with it. 'Ethik ist für Paulus also keinesfalls die Praktizierung der Tora; ethische Entscheidungen trifft der Apostel vielmehr vom Bekenntnis her' (114; cf. also O. Merk, *Handeln aus Glauben: Die Motivierungen der paulinischen Ethik* [Marburg: Elwert, 1968] 247f.).

[70] R. Bultmann, *Theologie des Neuen Testaments* (Tübingen: Mohr/Siebeck, 1968[6]) 342. His argument is that the freedom from the law is realised in the freedom 'innerhalb des überlieferten Gesetzes zu unterscheiden zwischen dem seinem Inhalt nach Gültigen und Ungültigen. Pls [Paulus] hat dieses Problem nicht entwickelt; aber die Verpflichtung zu solcher Kritik ist in dem Vermögen des δοκιμάζειν τί τὸ θέλημα τοῦ θεοῦ, τὸ ἀγαθὸν καὶ εὐάρεστον καὶ τέλειον (Rm 12,2), bzw. des δοκιμάζειν τὰ διαφέροντα (Phl 1,10) enthalten.'

'ready made formula[e]' the various norms need to be evaluated.[71] 'Believers must determine God's will as they meet the everyday challenges of their lives.'[72] But does this not leave the believer with a high ethical risk potential?[73] What is the ultimate touchstone? What is the reference point for decision making? My argument proposes that the *locus of normativity is in the renewed mind* (Rom. 8.6; 12.2; 1 Cor. 2.16). By renewed mind I mean the cognitive and reflective aspect of the new creation, defined by the Christ-event and empowered by the Spirit. That is to say that Christ and the Spirit are the warrants, whereas the renewed mind is the point at which normativity is established and processed.[74] How I can assert this requires further elaboration.

2.   The Renewed Mind as the Locus of Normativity

Four different but interrelated aspects of Paul's ethics clarify how the renewed mind is the locus of normativity. In various manners Paul expresses his trust in the ability of the new creation to discern the will of God.

a. First of all, each individual is called upon to make full use of their reflective potential. This potential has a broad span. It includes the macro-level of basic knowledge of the Creator (Rom. 1.20)[75] and the micro-level

---

[71] S. Westerholm, 'Letter and Spirit: The Foundation of Pauline *Ethics*', *NTS* 30 (1984) 247. Cf. E. Käsemann (*An die Römer* [HNT 8a; Tübingen: Mohr/Siebeck, 1980[4]] 319) who suggests that the demand of God's will is not set once and for all because it can be found and done only in the concrete decision for a given situation. As noted earlier in the introduction to this chapter, Schrage (*Einzelgebote*, 170) supports this need for discernment. Cf. Furnish (*Ethics*, 105): 'Paul refuses to define the law and God's will as coextensive entities or to think that his will has been once and for all revealed.' Indeed any reference to the law is missing in Rom. 12.1–2.

[72] Sampley, *Reasoning*, 54.

[73] G. Strecker ('Ziele einer neutestamentlichen Ethik', *NTS* 25 [1978] 14) shows that 'sich dem Risiko der ethischen Entscheidung auszusetzen' is not only a side effect but an objective of Paul's ethics.

[74] For the differentiation of warrants and norms (although with a different emphasis), cf. R. Scroggs, 'New Being: Renewed Mind: New Perception. Paul's View of the Source of Ethical Insight', in *The Text and the Times* (Minneapolis: Fortress Press, 1993) 171f. The warrant is the 'authoritative source', whereas the 'norm is the description of what sort of action is correct, whether that description be of a very specific act or a set of general principles'. However, W. Schrage (*Ethik des Neuen Testaments* [NTD 4; Göttingen: Vandenhoeck & Ruprecht, 1982] 189) issues an important caveat: 'Schon angesichts der Bedeutung dieses vom Geist geleiteten Unterscheidens, das alles prüft und das Gute behält (1 Thess. 5,19f.), spricht man besser auch bei Paulus nicht von Normen – zumal diese leicht das gesetzliche Mißverständnis einer "deontologischen" Ethik provozieren und von den Folgen des Tuns und damit "teleologischer" Argumentation dispensieren könnten.'

[75] This does *not* imply full 'natural theology'. Paul is not particularly original or contentious in stating this (Dunn, *Theology of Paul*, 74) and consequently we should not stress

of an assessment of matters of personal significance such as marriage
(1 Cor. 7.36f.) or the amount given in offerings (2 Cor. 9.7). The latter
type of individual reflection will imply that in some 'cherished but con-
troverted traditions governing social behaviour' various different opinions and lifestyles must exist next to one another (Rom. 14.5,22; 1 Cor.
8–10).[76] 'Conscience'[77] and 'conviction' are key boundary markers of
individuality, although never to the detriment of the community.[78] That
means that while discernment is ultimately a communal process, it begins
in the deliberation by each individual believer. And this is linked to my
next point.

b. An important (and often neglected) aspect of Paul's ethics is the
call for believers to examine themselves in order for them to retrieve the
focal point of their faith and hence reconfigure their ethical conduct (1
Cor. 10.12; 11.27–32; 14.37f.; 2 Cor. 13.5; Gal. 6.4).[79] Acquiring a true
self-understanding as the prerequisite for authentic knowledge is a well-
known teaching of Hellenism.[80] To be sure, Paul is not concerned with
that aspect of the tradition in which introspection uncovers a person's
divine potential.[81] However, he does believe that self-examination will
lead to a correct perception of one's limitations.[82] And, more significantly,

the point too much (cf. K. Haacker, *Der Brief des Paulus an die Römer* [ThHK 6; Leipzig: Evangelische Verlagsanstalt, 1999] 48–9).

[76] Dunn (*Theology of Paul*, 687) claims that Paul challenges the Roman church 'to recognize that *God accepted people whose views and practices they regarded as unacceptable*.' He points out that the 'issue [what can be eaten] was one of considerable importance for all parties, and one whose resolution was integral to Paul's own understanding of the Gospel and its corporate outworking' (*Theology of Paul*, 681).

[77] Cf. my discussion in the final chapter.

[78] J. A. Fitzmyer (*Romans* [AB 33; New York: Doubleday, 1993] 687) says that in Rom. 14 Paul means 'conscience' but says 'conviction' (Rom. 14.22).

[79] Barclay (*Truth*, 159ff.) claims that 'such self-scrutiny is a favourite theme in Paul's challenge to his churches' (*Truth*, 160): Paul realises that on the one hand it is dangerously easy to overestimate one's importance and so delude oneself (*Truth*, 160) and on the other hand that it is right to boast in certain limits (*Truth*, 161). In 2 Cor. 13.5 Paul exhorts (note the imperatives,πειράζετε, δοκιμάζετε) the church twice to critically examine themselves (Martin, *Corinthians*, 478f.). I argue for the importance of self-knowledge against P. Ciholas ('Knowledge and Faith: Pauline Platonisms and the Spiritualization of Reality', *Perspectives in Religious Studies* 3 [1976] 200): 'The Socratic γνῶθι σαυτόν [sic] is totally invalidated in Paul to be replaced by the γνῶθι κύριον.'

[80] C. Göbel, *Griechische Selbsterkenntnis: Platon-Parmenides-Stoa-Aristipp* (Stuttgart: Kohlhammer, 2002) 68ff., 165ff., 234ff.

[81] H. D. Betz, *Der Apostel Paulus und die sokratische Tradition* (Tübingen: Mohr/Siebeck, 1972) 118ff., 132ff.; idem, 'The Delphic Maxim ΓΝΩΘΙ ΣΑΥΤΟΝ in Hermetic Interpretation', in *Hellenismus*, 92–111; *Galatians* (Philadelphia: Fortress Press, 1979) 302.

[82] 'Paul shares with antiquity the view that man is incessantly trying to show himself to be "somebody"' (Betz, *Galatians*, 303). In Gal. 6.3 and Rom. 12.3 Paul explains that the objective of such testing and introspection is an authentic self-understanding and a correct

only by means of a correct self-understanding can the contours of gifting and identity be perceived (Rom. 12.3–8).[83] Self-examination is then the beginning of an ethos shaped in the light of the Christ-event.[84] Remembering where believers started and came from helps them to verify their perspective of themselves and their relation to God (Rom. 11.18; cf. 2 Cor. 10.7).[85] What this precisely implies requires further elaboration in the latter half of the book. Important for now is that critical, reflective ethical deliberation begins with each believer finding his or her correct self-understanding.[86]

c. Of course, Paul does not remain at the individual level. A stronger emphasis lies on his expectation that believing communities are to sort

estimation of how one stands in relation to others (1 Cor. 1.26; 3.18; 8.2). This enables legitimate 'boasting' which Paul gives examples of in Rom. 4.2 and 1 Cor. 15.10. Such 'boasting' is based on grace rather than reason (in contrast to Hellenistic philosophy; Betz, *Galatians*, 303).

[83] N. Baumert ('Zur "Unterscheidung der Geister"', *ZKTh* 111 [1989] 183–95) offers a different interpretation of Rom. 12.3–8 by positing that the passage deals with discernment and correct self-evaluation. Everyone can find the measure for correct self-evaluation in the fruits of their actions or rather in their personally granted gift, which, according to the grace granted them, will be of various kinds (N. Baumert, 'Charisma und Amt bei Paulus', in A. Vanhoye [ed.], *L'apôtre Paul: personalité, style et conception du ministère* [Leuven: Leuven University Press, 1986] 216). This interpretation hinges on understanding the μέτρον πίστεως in 12.3b not as the measure of faith, but as the measure of authenticity ('Unterscheidung', 184. For the lexical reasoning behind the translation of πίστις, see 'Charisma', 217). Each gift is a 'Gütezeichen Gottes', forming the basis for correct discernment and self-evaluation, which Paul demanded in v. 3 ('Unterscheidung', 193f.). Baumert's work deserves further attention, but his insistence is questionable that discernment, because it is a gift given by the Spirit, cannot be studied or learnt ('Unterscheidung', 194).

[84] In 2 Cor. 13.5 Paul urges the Corinthians to examine themselves if they are ἐν τῇ πίστει. Here, faith has been understood as 'obedience' (V. P. Furnish, *II Corinthians* [AB 32A; New York: Doubleday, 1984] 576f.) or 'profession' (L. L. Belleville, *2 Corinthians* [Leicester: InterVarsity Press, 1996] 331), or in a broader sense, incorporating these dimensions, as 'a correct appreciation of the Pauline Gospel versus the rival kerygma (11:4) . . . For Paul, "faith is the reality of the presence of Christ" . . . What Paul is doing is expressing the hope that the Corinthians will examine themselves to deal with the issue of whether or not they are walking in the way of Christ by following his apostle (1 Cor. 11:1)' (Martin, *Corinthians*, 478, quoting H. D. Wendland).

[85] In 1 Cor. 1.26 Paul says: 'Consider [βλέπετε] your own call, brothers and sisters: not many of you were wise by human standards, not many were powerful, not many were of noble birth.' In other words, the believers are to remember that they 'did not stumble onto a great thing in hearing the good news as it was preached by Paul, rather "God chose" the likes of them' (Fee, *Corinthians*, 82).

[86] Cf. H. Schürmann, 'Die Gemeinde des Neuen Bundes als der Quellort des sittlichen Erkennens nach Paulus', in T. Söding (ed.), *Studien zur neutestamentlichen Ethik* (Stuttgart: Katholisches Bibelwerk, 1990) 24–6.

Furthermore, note the cognitive emphasis in 2 Cor. 13.5ff.: ἐπιγινώσκετε and γνώσεσθε, cf. R. Bultmann (*Der zweite Brief an die Korinther* [KEK 6; Göttingen: Vandenhoeck & Ruprecht, 1976] 248), who believes that knowing Christ 'in us' means understanding oneself, and Christ as a 'kritische Macht'.

out many issues for themselves. On the one hand, this means finding a common mind on issues which require unity (cf. Rom. 15.5; 2 Cor. 13.11; Phil. 2.2, 5; 4.2). On the other hand, this will imply being able to discern in what areas difference is tolerable and to arbitrate between personal liberty and communal duty (cf. particularly 1 Cor. 8; 10.25ff.). Individual rights are to be brought into consonance with a respect for the strengths and weaknesses of others.[87]

Particularly important is that Paul requires of the believers to participate in the ethical deliberation of which his letters also form a part (Rom. 15.14; 1 Cor. 10.15; 11.13; 14.37; Phil. 3.15). That means that, although Paul does not shun giving advice to his churches, the underlying expectation seems to be that they should 'be capable of settling the disputes in its [their] midst'.[88] This applies to issues of pastoral concern as well as conflicts which the Corinthians, for example, are taking before the courts (1 Cor. 6.1–6).[89] Moreover, while Paul expects the strong to follow his and Christ's example in giving up their rights, he anticipates that they will come to this decision on the basis of their free choice (1 Cor. 8.8; 10.23).[90] Truth cannot be applied without the consent of each individual.[91] J. C. Beker correctly states that Paul envisages the whole church taking part in this process of reflective deliberation:

> Within the unity of the Spirit, the members of the body in their diversity, multiformity, and mutuality plot the necessary strategies for their contingent situation in accordance with the coherent truth of the gospel. Indeed, the body of Christ constitutes a

---

[87] Kilner, 'Approach', 375; cf. Hooker, 'Interchange', 14.

[88] M. Rissi, 'κρίνω', *EDNT* II, 320. Cf. H. D. Wendland (*Die Briefe an die Korinther* [NTD 7; Göttingen: Vandenhoeck & Ruprecht, 1964[10]] 43) who comments: 'Er [Paulus] fordert, daß die Gemeinde stark genug sein muß, solchen Streit in sich selber auszutragen und zu beseitigen.'

[89] Concerning 1 Cor. 6.1–6, and how judgement within the community and the 'discouragement of lawsuits between brothers of the faith were common themes of contemporary Judaism', cf. C. J. Roetzel, *Judgement in the Community: A Study of the Relationship between Eschatology and Ecclesiology in Paul* (Leiden: Brill, 1972) 130. The underlying criticism of Paul is that 'it reveals how lacking in truly Christian wisdom the Corinthians are, and therefore how poorly they understand their true place in Christ' (Fee, *Corinthians*, 231).
See also the comments on how pastoral discipline can be seen in connection with the difficult pericope of 1 Cor. 5, in G. W. H. Lampe, 'Church Discipline and the Epistles to the Corinthians', in Farmer et al. (eds.), *History*, 337–61.

[90] Cf. A. J. Malherbe, 'Determinism and Free Will in Paul: The Argument of 1 Corinthians 8 and 9', in T. Engberg-Pedersen (ed.), *Paul in his Hellenistic Context* (Edinburgh: T&T Clark, 1994) 231–55.

[91] Sampley, *Reasoning*, 54: 'One inquires whether the action or matter is good in terms of its impact on oneself; is it appropriate to the individual?'

pneumatic democracy where – under the guidance of the apostle and his coworkers – the members of the body 'find out,' 'test,' and 'approve' (δοκιμάζειν) 'what is the will of God . . .' [This is not] an abstract or individualistic [hermeneutic] of the apostle, nor an activity of learned rabbis in a rabbinic school, but a pragmatic consensus-building activity in the body of Christ, where relevant and authentic 'gospel' strategies are devised for particular problems.[92]

This is an incisive depiction of Paul's vision of discernment, but it needs to be enhanced: the 'intensely communal dimension' of deliberation is only possible if and because love is the foundation.[93] That means that the circle of reference can be within the community because it is based on an egalitarian reciprocity.[94] The respect for the other believers makes a fair evaluation of their life/conduct possible.[95]

d. My final point reminds us of the beginning of this chapter: in both Rom. 11.34–12.2 and 1 Cor. 2.16 Paul answers an otherwise rhetorical question in a remarkable manner. The question is a citation from Isa. 40.13: 'For who has known the mind of the Lord (τίς γὰρ ἔγνω νοῦν κυρίου)?' Normally the expected answer is 'no-one' (cf. *Wis.Sol.* 9.13f.; *syrBar* 14.8f.; *4 Ezra* 4.11). And indeed in both Rom. 11 and 1 Cor. 1–2 Paul has been intent on showing the transcendence of true knowledge and its subversion of human constructions. The surprise is then that in both

---

[92] Beker, 'Theology', 211. Cf. Schürmann, 'Gemeinde', 26ff.: '[D]er eigentliche "Quellort" sittlicher Erkenntnis, der alle "Quellen" in sich versammelt, – ist für die praktische sittliche Unterweisung und Mahnung des Paulus die Kirche als die "Gemeinde des Neuen Bundes"'; D. Fredrickson, 'Pauline Ethics: Congregations as Communities of Moral Deliberation', in K. L. Bloomquist and J. R. Stumme (eds.), *The Promise of Lutheran Ethics* (Minneapolis: Fortress Press, 1998) 120: 'Paul is not asserting that the moral life is an imitation of universal order; nor is it conformity to a particular historical tradition. Neither is it obedience to divine command. Instead persons in community pursue consensus through testing.'

[93] F. J. Matera, *New Testament Ethics: The Legacies of Jesus and Paul* (Louisville, KY: Westminster/John Knox Press, 1996) 251: 'The church is the post-resurrection community of disciples; it is the place in which the moral life is learned and lived' (cf. Furnish, *Ethics*, 235; Schrage, *Ethics*, 211–17).

[94] For a differentiated discussion of how the various reference groups interact, cf. W. A. Meeks, 'The Circle of Reference in Pauline Morality', in D. L. Balch, E. F. Ferguson and W. A. Meeks (eds.), *Greeks, Romans, Christians* (Minneapolis: Fortress Press, 1990) 305–17; for egalitarian reciprocity, see Wolter, 'Identität', 84ff.

[95] Cf. Söding, *Liebesgebot*, 270, who eloquently describes the significance of love in Paul's ethics: 'Liebe ist die rückhaltlose, von Herzen kommende Bejahung eines anderen Menschen, von daher die ganzheitliche Hinwendung zu ihm . . . damit ist sie zugleich Antriebsfeder eines Handelns, das dem anderen um seinetwillen in allem dienen will . . .' 'Aber es gehört doch zu ihrem Wesen, nach Mitteln und Wegen zu suchen, um den Nächsten zu unterstützen und seine Sache zu fördern.'

cases there is an affirmative answer. In a bold manner Paul optimistically asserts that knowledge is possible.[96] In 1 Cor. 2.16 the answer is: 'We have the mind of Christ.' In Rom. 12.2 Paul writes that the believers can discern the will of God.[97] Although commentators have acknowledged the parallel reference for the *question*, they have missed the parallel *answer*.[98] This is partially due to the artificially added chapter breaks, which can create the impression of a substantial pause in the argument. But the οὖν, 'therefore', in Rom. 12.1 'must be given its full weight'.[99] It 'is a vital logical link in Paul's argument'.[100] Paul is expounding 'what has gone before'.[101] G. Fee reminds us to note 'what the first readers of this letter could hardly have missed, namely that these words [the affirmative in Rom. 12.2 concerning attaining insight into the will of God] follow hard on the heels of the doxology of 11:33–36'.[102] This implies that the renewed mind in Rom. 12.2 is at least a partial answer to the inscrutable ways of God in 11.33–36.[103] Consequently, in both 1 Cor. 2.16 and Rom.

---

[96] The affirmative answer is recognised for 1 Cor. 2.16 by Voss (*Wort*, 188), who argues that, although essentially the question should be answered with 'no', Paul answers with 'einer überaus kühnen, "wir haben den Sinn Gottes und können ihn verstehen"'. See A. Lindemann, *Der erste Korintherbrief* (HNT 9,1; Tübingen: Mohr/Siebeck, 2001) 73: 'Vielmehr ist die Aussage in V.16b uneingeschränkt als positive Aussage zu verstehen.'

[97] The scope of the knowledge is limited by some in differentiating between not knowing 'Gottes Heilsgedanken' but only 'pneumatischer Urteilsfähigkeit' (Schrage, *Korinther* III, 267); similarly, compare, G. D. Fee, *God's Empowering Presence* (Peabody, MA: Hendrickson, 1994) 603. Bultmann (*Theologie*, 481) differentiates between a γνῶσις or σοφία which concerns God's will ('also die Urteilskraft des sittlichen Wollens') and which all believers are to have and a special γνῶσις which regards God's '*Heilsplan*'. The latter is a mystery, requires interpretation and the question: 'welche theologischen und christologischen, kosmologischen und anthropologischen Konsequenzen sind notwendig, welche sind legitim?' This special knowledge is not a matter for all believers! But as I shall argue in chapter 4, such a differentiation is not Pauline.

[98] This applies to all commentators of 1 Corinthians and Romans I questioned, evident in my bibliography. All miss the parallel question and answer in Rom. 12.2 and 1 Cor. 2.16. Fitzmyer (*Romans*, 634) even claims that the answer in Rom. 11.34 is 'of course, "No one!"' but misses the (possibly ironic) point that Paul makes in Rom. 12.2. Käsemann, *Römer*, 309f., believes an affirmative answer is possible but does not note that this is given in Rom. 12.2.

It is particularly surprising that neither Fee, *Corinthians*, 119, nor Thiselton, *Corinthians*, 274, see Paul's irony here as they are keen on Paul's 'double intent' with the quotation of Isa. 40.13 in 1 Cor. 2.16.

[99] D. J. Moo, *The Epistle to the Romans* (NICNT; Grand Rapids, MI: Eerdmans, 1996) 748.

[100] Hooker, 'Interchange', 3–4.

[101] Dunn, *Romans 9–16*, 708; cf. Wilckens, *Römer* III, 2; Cranfield, *Romans* II, 595.

[102] Fee, *Presence*, 603.

[103] Moreover, they probably would have also deduced that there is a reversal of the ἀδόκιμος νοῦς in Rom. 1.28 to a 'verstehenden Urteilsfähigkeit' in 12.2 (Lohse, *Römer*, 337).

12.2 Paul's argument is the same: it is possible to discern God's will.[104] And, significantly, this knowledge is not found in scripture or in apostolic authority or even transcendent wisdom.[105] It can be found in the renewed νοῦς (or in its equivalent, the 'mind of Christ' (1 Cor. 2.16)). Discernment becomes anthropologically centred.[106] True wisdom is now accessible for all (in Christ).[107] However, and this is key, the affirmation in both passages is linked to the transformation of those involved.

True knowledge is tied to an inherently different type of existence.[108] As I shall elucidate later, this existence must be defined by the Christ-event and empowered by the Spirit. Important here is that this new creation is a far more comprehensive fulfilment of God's demand than the adherence to individual demands of a moral standard.[109] Rather than a new cult

[104] In different words and a different context, Marxsen (*Ethik*, 199) expresses the same thrust: 'Für den erneuerten Menschen wird das Unmögliche dennoch zu einer Möglichkeit, aber eben zu einer Möglichkeit von etwas, was ihm unmöglich bleibt.'

[105] Against B. Witherington III (*Conflict and Community in Corinth: A Socio-Rhetorical Commentary on 1 and 2 Corinthians* [Grand Rapids, MI: Eerdmans, 1995] 129), Paul does not allow '*the Word* to have the last word' but uses scripture in a question which he answers in a completely unexpected manner.

[106] K. Haldimann ('Kreuz – Wort vom Kreuz – Kreuzetheologie. Zu einer Begriffsdifferenzierung in der Paulusinterpretation', in A. Dettwiler and J. Zumstein [eds.], *Kreuzestheologie im Neuen Testament* [WUNT 151; Tübingen: Mohr/Siebeck, 2002] 21) argues for the '*Subjektzentriertheit*' of the theology of the cross. 'Kreuzestheologie zielt in einer Weise auf das Subjektsein des Menschen, die dessen Verflüchtungen in Selbstkonstruktionen und Selbstaufhebungen a limine unterläuft.' Marxsen (*Ethik*, 198) shows how important it is to acknowledge the 'Täter' in Christian ethics, because without doing that one misses the point of the whole endeavour. For the centrality of the new creation in Pauline ethics, cf. R. B. Hays, *The Moral Vision of the New Testament: A Contemporary Introduction to New Testament Ethics* (Edinburgh: T&T Clark, 1997) 46; M. V. Hubbard, *New Creation in Paul's Letters and Thought* (MSSNTS 119; Cambridge: Cambridge University Press, 2002) 235.

[107] Theissen (*Religion*, 152, 372) correctly states that in early Christianity there is a downward transfer of true wisdom. Wisdom becomes accessible not only for an upper-class elite, but also for those who were traditionally excluded from it, such as the foolish and the weak (1 Cor. 1.26f.). That Paul believes all should be able to discern will be developed in the following chapter.

[108] R. Schnackenburg (*Die sittliche Botschaft des Neuen Testaments* II. *Die urchristlichen Verkündiger* [HThK.S 2; Freiburg: Herder, 1988] 30) writes that this is more than a religious motivation of ethics, it is a new orientation, a new existence in Christ; cf. Evans, 'Romans', 27f. See C. B. Armstrong, 'St. Paul's Theory of Knowledge', *Church Quarterly Review* 154 (1953) 441: 'ἐπίγνωσις springs from the whole personality'.

[109] As Furnish (*Ethics*, 104) lucidly points out, the claim on the Christian in Rom. 12.1–2 is much more radical than 'any prescribed code of requirements'; cf. Therrien, *Discernement*, 142–3; E. T. Charry, 'The Grace of God and the Law of Christ', *Int.* 57 (2003) 34–44: 'Far from abolishing the torah of God, Paul's life "in [under] the torah of Christ"(*ennomos Christou*, 1 Cor 9:21) is stricter and more difficult to fulfil than the torah of God according to the rabbis . . . It demands intentionality of self . . .' With respect to 1 Cor. 7.19 ('obeying the commandments of God is everything'), cf. C. K. Barrett (*A Commentary on the First Epistle to the Corinthians* [London: A. & C. Black, 1971²], 169), who says

or ritual as the locus of worship, Paul calls believers to 'present your bodies as a living sacrifice' (Rom. 12.1).[110] It is a holistic relocation from one sphere of influence to another.[111] In a similar manner, the appeal to discern everything in 1 Thess. 5.21 is based upon Paul's prayer in v. 23 that God 'sanctify you entirely'.[112] The whole person is in view, 'the totality of sanctification, extending throughout the person'.[113] This corresponds with S. Pedersen's assertion that the foundational matrix of Pauline thought is the Christological fulfilment of the 'original creation commandment', the 'fundamental norm for the relationship between the

that the 'commandments' mean 'an obedience to the will of God as disclosed in his Son far more radical than the observance of any code'.
Similarly, see the innovative but contested reading that Rom. 2.14–15 and 25–9 shames the Jewish interlocutor 'by showing that God is fulfilling his new covenant promises in Gentiles' in a '*comprehensive* doing of the law' (by virtue of Paul's reference to Jer. 31 in Rom. 2.15; S. J. Gathercole, 'A Law unto Themselves: The Gentiles in Romans 2.14–15 Revisited', *JSNT* 85 [2002] 27). This comprehensive and internal fulfilment is of a different quality from individual regulations and is no partial fulfilment of the Torah ('Law', 46). Against this reading, cf. M. D. Mathewson, 'Moral Intuitionism and the Law Inscribed on our Hearts', *JEThS* 42 (1999) 629–43, who reads Rom. 2.14f. as referring to a 'moderately foundationalist' 'innate intuitive faculty that allows us to apprehend and know God's basic moral demands' ('Intuitionism', 643).

[110] M. Thompson, *Clothed with Christ: The Example and Teaching of Jesus in Romans 12.1–15.13* (JSNT.S 59; Sheffield: Sheffield Academic Press, 1991) 85: '[U]nderpinning Rom. 12.1–2 is Jesus' foundational and exemplary sacrifice. For Paul, Christ's image is the goal of the transforming process, and his Spirit enables the renewal of the mind.' 'Thus, imitating his obedience of self-offering, Christians may hope to discern and perform God's perfect will.'

[111] 'To have the mind of Christ, therefore, is to complete by way of the cross the apocalyptic transfer to the new creation. It is to be relocated, to find oneself no longer under the powers of the world but liberated for a life of obedience to God . . .' (A. R. Brown, 'The Cross and Moral Discernment-2', *Doctrine and Life* 47, 4 [1997] 284). Hubbard (*Creation*, 233) suggests correctly that the new-creation metaphor denotes the 'transition from one state to another' within a broader 'soteriological matrix'. He maintains that '"resurrection," "new birth," and "new creation" are merely alternative formulations of the "life" side of the death-life equation.' Betz ('Grundlagen', 199) maintains that the 'Nonkoformismus' in Rom. 12.1–2 is possible due to the 'fortgesetzte Verwandlung' that characterises the ethical life of the Christian.

[112] I follow T. Holtz (*Der erste Brief an die Thessalonicher* [EKK 13; Neukirchen-Vluyn: Neukirchener Verlag, 1986] 266) who claims that 1 Thess. 5.12–24 is a unit. Moreover, he points out that the sanctification of the believer is 'ganz vollständig' (*Thessalonicher*, 264f.). Cf. C. A. Wanamaker, *The Epistles to the Thessalonians* (NIGTC; Grand Rapids, MI: Eerdmans, 1990) 204, who believes that the imperative to discern everything would have been understood by readers to have a more comprehensive applicability than just the spiritual manifestations. 'The need to test everything . . . had general relevance to every aspect of Christian thought and behaviour' (*Thessalonians*, 206).

[113] A. J. Malherbe, *The Letters to the Thessalonians* (AB 32B; New York: Doubleday, 2000) 338, in the matter of 5.23.

Creator and created man (Gen. 2:15–17)'.[114] That means not the Torah but the existential relationship to the Creator is the focal point of ethics.[115]

3.   Summary and Questions

Paul expects believers to become able to discern. The traditions and norms we have investigated do not offer a final compass for decision making. Rather, each requires selective appropriation. In contrast, my argument has shown that the renewed mind (or its equivalent, the 'mind of Christ') is placed at the centre of ethical deliberation. Paul counts on the fact that the believers not only sort out matters of individual choice themselves but also that they will be able to order their affairs independently. This deliberation begins with each believer finding the starting point of their faith and understanding their own gifting. It continues within the 'pneumatic democracy',[116] in which conduct is assessed and interpreted. In sum, the locus of normativity lies in the renewed mind.

D.   Conclusion

In concluding this chapter we may return to O. Cullmann's interpretation of Rom. 12.1–2 quoted in the introduction. Can we confirm that δοκιμάζω is the key to Pauline ethics? If and when we recognise that δοκιμάζω needs to be studied in parallel with other terms denoting discernment, its significance within Paul's thought becomes unmistakable. Discernment is crucial for understanding Paul's ethical thinking in particular and offers hope for those readers of Romans who were dismayed by Paul's earlier remark that God's inscrutable ways cannot be known (Rom. 11.33ff.).

---

[114] S. Pedersen ('Paul's Understanding of the Biblical Law', *NT* 44 [2002] 1–34) claims the centrality of the creation commandment, 'to rule over the created', because the hermeneutical emphasis is '*transferred from the depiction of Israel's deliverance and subsequent lawgiving to the account of the creation and fall at the beginning*' (11). Cf. S. Vollenweider, *Freiheit als neue Schöpfung: Eine Untersuchung zur Eleutheria bei Paulus und in seiner Umwelt* (Göttingen: Vandenhoeck & Ruprecht, 1989) 405: In 'diesem Schöpfungsbezug' is 'die theologische Mitte der paulinischen Freiheitsbotschaft'. With respect to creation theology, Schrage (*Ethik*, 192f.) is right to argue that Paul does not have a creation ethic or natural law but rather a creation Christology. However, he emphasises, the world is and remains God's creation (Rom. 1.20, 25; 1 Cor. 8.6; 10.26).

[115] 'To believe in Christ therefore means to let oneself be existentially incorporated into the reality of the new creation which has broken into man's world in Christ's historical submission . . . (cf. Gal. 2:19–20)' (Pedersen, 'Understanding', 31). It is not 'a predetermined rule or set of rules for conduct' but a new being (Hays, *Vision*, 43; cf. Schrage, *Einzelgebote*, 165).

[116] Beker, 'Theology', 211.

My argument has shown that this new ethical insight offers a new perception on normativity. The norms and traditions, which were part of Paul's plausibility structure, now require discernment. Against those positions, which, for instance, regarded the law as a sufficient and binding standard, I argued that discernment is essential in the process of selecting, validating and applying the norms and commandments. Moreover, I proposed that in Paul's emphasis on the renewed mind (or its equivalent, the 'mind of Christ' in 1 Cor. 2.16) as the locus of normativity, discernment becomes anthropologically centred. Wisdom becomes accessible for the whole church. However, some questions remain open.

First, at various points we observed that a limitation to ethical discernment will not do justice to Paul since he does not divide salvation and ethics.[117] Nevertheless, the relationship of ethics and theology requires further study. We shall return to this issue in chapter 4. Secondly, the renewed mind requires further investigation. The significance I have attached to it makes the questions of how it is attained and what it implies of all the more consequence.

---

[117] Such a distiniction between ethics and existence is remarkably stark in K. Stendahl, *Final Account: Paul's Letter to the Romans* (Minneapolis: Fortress Press, 1995) ch. 5.

3

THE DISCERNMENT OF SPIRITS

A.   Introduction

The 'discernment of spirits' in 1 Cor. 12.10 has caught the attention of scholarship throughout the centuries of Bible reading. In this chapter I need to deal in a detailed manner with this gift. Of particular interest is that some scholars have attempted to call into question Paul's request for discernment. Accordingly, it has been argued that a critical evaluation cannot be meant, since Paul does not believe that spiritual manifestations are ambivalent.[1] Hence, G. Dautzenberg particularly has confined the gift to a process of interpretation of prophetic utterances. On the other hand, others have highlighted the need for critical investigation and evaluation of all manifestations.[2] Consequently, a number of questions arise: does Paul or does he not call for an appraisal which will challenge and examine the subject and content of spiritual utterances? Would such an investigation endanger the community? How can positive impulses be differentiated from negative ones? My research must address these questions. Furthermore, I will keep in mind what we noted in the introductory chapter. There we saw that Stuhlmacher, Käsemann and Beker saw the gift of discernment in the broad sense of theologising, but they did not offer evidence for their case. Can the gift be interpreted as broadly as they do?

In order to answer these questions, three different aspects require investigation. First, does the gift refer to a process of interpretation or one of

---

[1] M. Frenschkowski (*Offenbarung und Epiphanie* I. *Grundlagen des spätantiken und frühchristlichen Offenbarungsglaubens* [WUNT 2,79; Tübingen: Mohr/Siebeck, 1995] 411) claims in his conclusion that the NT '*die Ambivalenz der pneumatischen Äußerungen schlechterdings nicht kennt*, jedenfalls nicht in Bezug auf die Doppeldeutigkeit des in der Inspiration redenden Numens'. Similarly, H.-C. Meier rejects the meaning '*Diakrisis als "Beurteilung"*' and favours '*Diakrisis als "Unterscheidung"*' on the basis that neither the Holy Spirit, nor the pneumatic, nor the apostle are to be evaluated or criticised (*Mystik bei Paulus: Zur Phänomenologie religiöser Erfahrung im Neuen Testament* [TANZ 26; Tübingen: Francke, 1998] 215–21).

[2] So Schrage, *Korinther* III, 156.

evaluation? Do these necessarily contradict each other? Secondly, what are the objects of διακρίνω? Are they merely prophetic utterances or also other spiritual manifestations or even spirits? Of what significance are these manifestations? What does their spiritual nature imply about their evaluation? Thirdly, whom does Paul envisage as the subject of this discernment? Finally, I will be able to offer an initial assessment of the relationship of the gift of διάκρισις πνευμάτων to the discernment mentioned in the previous chapter.

B.   Διάκρισις/διακρίνω:[3] **Interpretative Evaluation**

> I Cor can be read as a primer on decision-making and divine guidance, with 1:1–4:21 as an exposition of first principles and the remainder of the letter as a demonstration of how this works in practice.[4]

By the time Corinthian readers would have reached the gift of διάκρισις πνευμάτων in 1 Cor. 12.10 they would have realised that Paul is subverting the Corinthian understanding of spirituality and is keen on introducing an alternative of his own. In this context he is playing (in part quite polemically) with κρίν- words.[5] But then without clear elaboration he presents a gift in 12.10 which he only mentions here, and yet which sounds as if it would have relevance for all of the Corinthian problems.

---

[3] It is important to note that the word-forms in question here have numerous senses not necessarily related to one another, and that 'it is impossible to find a consistent rendering' of them in the Pauline letters (Barrett, *Corinthians*, 274). (I interchange 'sense' and 'meaning' freely while acknowledging that linguistically this can be difficult [cf. Cotterell and Turner, *Linguistics*, 178–81]). For the various meanings, cf. διάκρισις: a. ability to decide; b. dispute; διακρίνω: a. evaluate carefully; b. prefer; c. make a distinction (Louw and Nida, *Lexicon* II, 59). Liddell and Scott add 'interpretation'/ 'interpret' respectively (H. G. Liddell and R. Scott, *A Greek–English Lexicon* [Oxford: Clarendon Press, 1958[9]] 399).
    The list of the occurrences of both διακρίνω and διάκρισις in Paul shows that the meanings vary. Διακρίνω: Rom. 4.20, with the sense 'to waver' or 'to doubt'; Rom. 14.23, with the sense 'doubts'; 1 Cor. 4.7, with the meaning 'to prefer, to judge as superior, to regard as more valuable' in our case then, 'who judges that you surpass others?'(Louw and Nida, *Lexicon* I, 362); 1 Cor. 6.5, with the meaning 'to decide' or 'to evaluate carefully'; 1 Cor. 11.29, with the meaning 'to evaluate, judge carefully'; 1 Cor. 11.31, 'to evaluate, judge carefully'; 1 Cor. 14.29, meaning contested. Διάκρισις: Rom. 14.1, with the sense 'to argue, dispute'; 1 Cor. 12.10, meaning contested.
[4] Jillions, 'Decision-Making', 11. In his paper Jillions offers an outline of 1 Corinthians in which he shows how divine guidance 'can be seen as threads linking the various concerns Paul addresses', but he does not elaborate this assertion ('Decision-Making', 11).
[5] For instance, κρίνω: 1 Cor. 2.2; 4.5; 5.3, 12, 13; 6.1, 2, 3, 6; 7.37; 10.15, 29; 11.13, 31, 32; διακρίνω: 1 Cor. 4.7; 6.5; 11.29, 31; 14.29; ἀνακρίνω: 1 Cor. 2.14, 15; 4.3, 4; 9.3; 10.25, 27; 14.24.

The question is what exactly Paul has in mind when he introduces the gift of διάκρισις πνευμάτων?

I shall introduce the positions of G. Dautzenberg and W. Grudem who hold opposing views on the gift. In order to obtain an overview of the issues at hand I shall present their work separately. Following that I will assess and arbitrate between their positions and propose my own under-standing of these verses.

1.   The Conflicting Readings

Dautzenberg's Challenge

Gerhard Dautzenberg was the first to challenge the traditional reading of διάκρισις πνευμάτων (1 Cor. 12.10).[6] This tradition has understood the gift as discerning whether or not it is a godly, human or demonic spirit speaking out of an ecstatic person.[7] In contrast, he endeavours to show that the phrase should be understood as an inspired understanding and interpretation of prophecy.[8]

Dautzenberg's line of argument can be summed up as follows: first, he postulates that there is a direct connection between prophecy and διάκρι-σις πνευμάτων in 1 Cor. 12.10 just as there is in 14.29. This connection is parallel to the other gifts in 12.8–10, which, he postulates, are also grouped together (word of knowledge/word of wisdom; tongues/interpretation and faith/healings/miracles).[9] Then he claims that διάκρισις and διακρίνω mean 'interpretation' and 'interpret' in these verses. This assertion is based on a lexical and historical study demonstrating that διάκρισις and

---

[6] Dautzenberg, 'Hintergrund', 93–104; *Prophetie*, 120–48; 'Prophetie bei Paulus', in *Prophetie und Charisma, Jahrbuch für biblische Theologie* 14 (1999) 55–70. (Here he adds the meaning 'prüfen' to 'deuten' but this does not change the thrust of his argument ['Prophetie', 66]). It is Dautzenberg's main aim in *Prophetie* to question any apparent and often supported contrast between prophecy as depicted in 1 Cor. 12–14, in Revelation and the Jewish apocalyptic tradition of the time. Rather he sets them all in one tradition and shows that they are connected by numerous phenomena which they all have in common. The interpretative process discussed here is part of this common tradition. Dautzenberg does refer to A. Schweitzer as having questioned the traditional reading, and to Fascher and Kleinknecht who recognised that κρίνω is a technical term of Greek oracle interpretation. But none of the above has offered a new interpretation of διάκρισις πνευμάτων (Dautzenberg, 'Hintergrund', 93f.).

[7] Dautzenberg ('Hintergrund', 93) refers to a number of commentaries here, the more significant of which will be dealt with in the course of this chapter.

[8] Dautzenberg, *Prophetie*, 147.

[9] Dautzenberg, *Prophetie*, 123. Dautzenberg basically only describes the groups and offers no real evidence for his point. Yet his juxtaposition of prophecy and διάκρισις here is important for the rest of his argument.

διακρίνω belong to Greek interpretation terminology[10] and that they are variants for translating פשׁר and פתר in the biblical domain.[11]

Furthermore, Dautzenberg challenges the traditional reading by arguing that it does not make semantic sense. If one wanted to retain the meaning of 'distinguishing between' one would need *two* classes of things that are to be distinguished.[12] He also suggests that it does not fit into the context. For the meanings 'to judge' or 'to test' (in dependence on 1 Thess. 5.19; 1 Jn 4.16; *Didache* 11) one would need to find a problem with false prophecy in 1 Corinthians.[13] This, according to Dautzenberg, is not the case.[14] On the contrary, he shows that the context of 1 Cor. 12–14 attempts to enhance the significance of prophecy rather than view it as a threat. Hence, there is no room or need for testing.[15]

An additional important part of Dautzenberg's proposal is his interpretation of the πνεύματα. He objects that the traditional understanding of 1 Cor. 12.10, 'discerning between good and evil spirits', does not correspond to the Pauline understanding of πνεῦμα.[16] He argues that Paul does not use this term for demons or angels, and he points to 1 Cor. 2.13, 14.12, 32 and 2 Thess. 2.2 as offering substantiation for reading πνεύματα more broadly as the manifestations of the Spirit rather than the

---

[10] For an overview of where this is the case, see my summary of Grudem's critique below. Dautzenberg admits that the direct evidence for this is sparse, but he still insists on the point by asserting that κρίνω and διακρίνω can be exchanged ('sachlich kein Unterschied') and that κρίνω was part of the Greek interpretation terminology ('Hintergrund', 95f.). He also points out that προφητης and Greek interpretation terminology were closely associated ('Hintergrund', 97).

[11] Furthermore, he sees an expansion of the interpretation process from dreams to all areas of revelation (including prophetic texts) in post-biblical Judaism. Dautzenberg sees reason to understand διάκρισις πνευμάτων, parallel to the mentioned interpretation processes, as the interpretative panel of the revelations shown to prophets (*Prophetie*, 125).

[12] Dautzenberg, *Prophetie*, 128: the differentiation between good and bad spirits would need to be expressed as in Heb. 5.14, διάκρισιν καλοῦ τε καὶ κακοῦ.

[13] The other translation used, 'to judge', has a judicial connotation and, along with the translation 'to test', does not fit into the context of how prophecy is treated in 1 Cor. 12–14 (Dautzenberg, *Prophetie*, 129). As so often in Dautzenberg's logic (see also 132, 134), this of course presupposes that πνεύματά in 1 Cor. 12.10 is referring to prophecy.

[14] He questions the often-quoted parallels to 1 Cor. 12.10: in 1 Thess. 5.21, he argues, there is no direct link between δοκιμάζω and prophecy and the passage should, therefore, not serve as a parallel to 1 Cor. 12–14. In a similar manner, Dautzenberg excludes 1 Thess. 5.19; 1 Jn 4.16; *Didache* 11. His desire to shield prophecy from criticism does not cohere with 1 Cor. 12–14.

[15] Dautzenberg, *Prophetie*, 143–6. Moreover, he questions any link to 1 Cor. 12.1–3, which is often quoted with reference to 1 Cor. 12.10. He claims that there are no exegetical grounds to perceive 1 Cor. 12.1–3 as a rule for the discernment of spirits. He understands it more generally as a theological foundation for the whole discussion in the passage but not as a test for pneumatic phenomena.

[16] Dautzenberg, *Prophetie*, 135–42.

spirits themselves. However (and this is a central point), he then limits the manifestations to prophecies. Although it is a central presupposition of his whole theory, he does not explain why he makes this limitation.[17]

Dautzenberg's novel reading of διάκρισις πνευμάτων as the interpretation of prophecy has provoked others to rethink this passage.[18] While he has backed up his position with detailed semantic, historical and contextual material, a number of serious problems remain. Wayne Grudem has offered a thorough critique of Dautzenberg's results.[19]

Grudem's Reply

Grudem's review can be summarised as follows: first of all, he objects to Dautzenberg's connection between prophecy and διάκρισις πνευμάτων in 1 Cor. 12.10. He sees no convincing grammatical or logical reason to assume that Paul portrayed the gifts in 12.8–10 as belonging to four connected groups (except for tongues and interpretation). In 14.29 he questions any direct link of the verb διακρίνω to the gift in 12.10, on the grounds that the object and the subject of discernment are different.[20] He points out that Dautzenberg's reasoning is circular: by assuming the correctness of his results regarding 12.10 (διάκρισις is linked only to prophecy) he concludes that the same gift is discussed in 14.29.[21]

Further, Grudem has reviewed the linguistic material which Dautzenberg uses as evidence for his interpretation of διακρίνω and διάκρισις.[22] He concedes that there are instances where these terms are used for the interpretation of dreams,[23] for solving riddles,[24] for the interpretation of signs[25] and one instance where διάκρισις means to explain or interpret

---

[17] The intricate link, mentioned earlier, which he sees between prophecy and διάκρισις is essentially the only reasoning behind this assertion.

[18] E.g. Dunn, *Jesus*, 232f.; Wolff, *Korinther*, 104f.

[19] W. Grudem, *The Gift of Prophecy in 1 Corinthians* (Washington, DC: University Press of America, 1982) 263–88; first printed in: 'Response', 253–70.

[20] The objects of discernment are prophecies in 14.29, not generally spirits as in 12.10, and the subject is the entire congregation in 14.29, not just the carriers of the gift as in 12.10.

[21] Grudem, *Gift*, 265–71.   [22] Grudem, *Gift*, 270–3.

[23] Grudem (*Gift*, 271) identifies twenty instances, particularly: Philo: *Jos.* 90, 93, 98, 104, 110, 116, 125, 143, 248, 269; *Som.* 2.4, 7, 110; Pausanias, *Description of Greece* 1.34.5: (about Amphiaraos who has turned into a god) δοκῶ δὲ Ἀμφιάραον ὀνειράτων διακρίσει μάλιστα προσκεῖσθαι; Symmachus' translation of Gen. 40.8.

[24] Twice in Josephus (quoted in my proposal below).

[25] Once in Diodorus Siculus 17.10.15. But both Grudem and Dautzenberg miss the example in Aristophanes (*Birds* 719f.), translated into verse by B. B. Rogers (LCL): 'For whatever you do, if a trade you pursue, or goods in the market are buying, Or the wedding attend of a neighbour and friend, first you look to the Birds and their flying (ὄρνιν τε νομίζετε πάνθ᾽ ὅσαπερ περὶ μαντείας διακρίνει) . . .'

spoken oracles.[26] Yet Grudem does not agree that Dautzenberg has offered enough material to be able to translate these terms as 'interpret' or 'interpretation' on the following grounds. In the first place, contrary to Dautzenberg's contention, διακρίνω and διάκρισις are only used twice to translate פָּשַׁר and פְּתַר, while συγκρίνω (σύγκρισις) is used fifty-two times.[27] Related to this, secondly, it is not possible to generally interchange διάκρισις and διακρίνω with other κρίν- words in interpretation contexts. Thus Dautzenberg cannot assume that there is no substantial difference between κρίνω and διακρίνω. Grudem argues for such a difference.[28] Thirdly, there are no specific parallels in Jewish or Christian literature where διάκρισις and διακρίνω are used for the interpretation of prophecy. Fourthly, Grudem shows fifty-eight examples where Jewish or early Christian authors prefer to use other words when speaking about the interpretation of difficult or obscure utterances. Finally, Grudem shows that, contrary to Dautzenberg's objection, the translation 'distinguishing between spirits' (where only one class of things to be distinguished between is named) has stylistic parallels.[29] Grudem concludes that these objections call into question the legitimacy of Dautzenberg's interpretation.

Moreover, Grudem points out that it is an unwarranted assumption on Dautzenberg's part to limit πνεύματα to prophetic manifestations. While there is no other reference in early Christianity to an interpretation of prophecies, the evaluation of spirits fits into co-[30] and

---

[26] Grudem, *Gift*, 272. This one instance is in Stobaeus (*Eklogai* 4.50.95; fifth century AD), where he is quoting Juncus, a philosopher, assumed to be from the second century AD. Grudem questions its validity as a parallel due to its late date and the uncertainty of how similar the oracle was to early Christian prophecy.

[27] Grudem, *Gift*, 273ff. Moreover, I. Broer has pointed out that the Danielic interpretation process that Dautzenberg cites in his favour is not associated with prophecy but dreams ('Fundamentalistische Exegese oder kritische Bibelwissenschaft? Anmerkungen zum Fundamentalismusproblem anhand des paulinischen Offenbarungsverständnisses', in J. Werbick [ed.], *Offenbarungsanspruch und fundamentalistische Versuchung* [Freiburg: Herder, 1991] 59–88). Further, the *angelus interpres* in the apocalyptic literature that Dautzenberg relies on is always part of the revelation itself and is a heavenly being, of which Vos finds no examples in the New Testament (J. S. Vos, 'Het probleem van de onderscheiding der geesten bij Paulus', *Nederlands Theologisch Tijdschrift* 52 [1998] 196).

[28] Grudem, *Gift*, 275f.   [29] Grudem, *Gift*, 280f.

[30] Grudem counters Dautzenberg's argument concerning 1 Cor. 12.3. He finds that the differences between 12.3 and 12.10 do not prevent both speaking of a type of discernment. While 12.3 is a more general criterion and possibly more objective test, 12.10 should be seen in contrast as a special or highly developed ability and as a more subjective kind of evaluation (Grudem, *Gift*, 285f.).

Moreover, according to Grudem, οἱ ἄλλοι in 14.29 'implies evaluation not interpretation' (*Gift*, 287). Grudem bases this claim on the hypothetical thought that the prophet will not

context.[31] Indeed, Paul's highlighting the intelligible nature of prophecy in 1 Cor. 14 makes interpretation seem superfluous.[32]

Grudem also shows how he understands the discernment of prophecy in 1 Cor. 14.29, which is important for this research.[33] First, οἳ ἄλλοι refers to the entire congregation. But as this is a contested issue, I need to deal with this in some detail below. Secondly, it is the prophet's speech which is evaluated, and the prophet himself is not judged as true or false. Each prophecy may have both true and false elements in it. Hence, discernment is a differentiated process and one need not imagine an either/or decision when discernment took place. He follows on from this with the suggestion that the prophets at Corinth did not then speak with a 'divine authority of actual words, but rather with just a divine authority of general content, which made the prophecies subject to evaluation and questioning at every point'.[34]

Grudem's critique is extensive and touches on most of Dautzenberg's points, and his proposals are helpful and we must return to them. In the following critique, however, I will attempt to arbitrate between the categorical positions of Dautzenberg and Grudem. A far more likely solution lies in the middle ground.

be impartial enough to carry out an evaluation himself in contrast to an interpretation. (He assumes the interpretation of tongues can be done by the tongues-speaker him/herself.)

[31] Regarding Dautzenberg's history of religions argument, Grudem expresses the criticism that he has made an unwarranted assumption by only comparing 1 Cor. 12.10 with texts that mention prophecy, since this presupposes the result that πνεύματα are prophetic manifestations. Grudem sees no legitimate reason to restrict the gift in such a manner. On the one hand, he states that Paul would have used the much less ambiguous προφητεία, had he wanted to express such a limitation. On the other hand, he shows how the interpretation of distinguishing between a demonic spirit and the Holy Spirit fits into the context of the New Testament (*Gift*, 284).

The *Rezeptionsgeschichte* is not a helpful guide because it is not uniform. Vos offers early church and Patristic evidence that those who read Paul did not follow Dautzenberg's interpretation (Vos, 'Probleem', 195f.). Cf. also *Didache* 11, 12, particularly 12.1; Hermas, *Mand.* 11.1ff. In both the latter two cases the emphasis is on testing rather than on explanation or interpretation of the prophecies. Yet Vos has dismissed three instances, two of which seem quite clear in that διακρίνω is understood as διασαφέω (196 n. 14, and his dismissal there of Origen and Theodore of Mopsuestia).

[32] Grudem does not accept Dautzenberg's argument that prophecies in contrast to tongues are intelligible (no need for translation) but not understandable (just their meaning is obscure; Grudem, *Gift*, 288).

[33] Grudem, *Gift*, 62–67.

[34] Grudem, *Gift*, 67. He believes that the meaning of διακρίνω is 'making distinctions or carefully evaluating' (64) and the word-form is used instead of κρίνω because that has the sense of judging with only two possibilities for the outcome. Paul, by using these two different terms, distinguishes between judgement outside of the church (κρίνω) and more careful evaluation inside the church (διακρίνω).

2.   An Alternative Reading

I will first deal with the interrelationship of 1 Cor. 12.10 and 14.29 and then discuss the legitimacy of an interpretative element in διάκρισις/διακρίνω.

The Relationship of 1 Corinthians 12.10 and 14.29

Grudem must be agreed with when he objects to Dautzenberg's claim that prophecy and διάκρισις are directly connected in 1 Cor. 12.10. There is, indeed, no evidence that Paul would have wanted his readers to divide the gifts in 12.8–10 into four groups. Further, Dautzenberg does not clarify why he narrows down πνεύματα in 12.10 to prophecy. He is inconsistent in that on numerous occasions he states that the term is to be understood as 'Geistesoffenbarungen' and yet implies that these are only prophetic manifestations.[35] Since so much of his argument is built on this hypothesis, the reasoning is weakened considerably. In a similar manner, other scholars insist that discernment 'forms a pair with prophecy', but they likewise do not offer substantiation for their assertion.[36]

---

[35] Dautzenberg, *Prophetie*, 135, 146.

[36] D. Hill (*New Testament Prophecy* [London: Marshall, Morgan & Scott, 1979] 133f.) writes that, on the one hand, the gift of discernment (12.10) forms a pair with prophecy and *cannot* be seen as 'independent of that gift'. On the other hand, he sees the evaluation including 'people claiming to be inspired . . . miracle-workers, glossolalists, teachers, etc.' These two statements are not easily reconcilable. Similarly, see E. Fascher, *Prophētēs: Eine sprach- und religionsgeschichtliche Untersuchung* (Gießen: Töpelmann, 1927) 184f.; D. E. Aune, *Prophecy in Early Christianity and the Ancient Mediterranean World* (Grand Rapids, MI: Eerdmans, 1983), 220; Wolff, *Korinther*, 104f.

Dunn also asserts that the gift '*forms a pair with prophecy*', points to a number of commentaries that have apparently made a mistake in presuming the opposite but offers no evidence for this claim, except for a reference to 14.29 (Dunn, *Jesus*, 233). Moreover, while he mentions that there are only two options for translating πνεύματα (as spirits or as πνευματικά) he does not explain why he pairs it only with prophecy.

Gordon Fee explains his identifying πνεύματα with prophecy in a slightly more detailed manner (Fee, *Presence*, 171). He refers to 1 Cor. 14.29 and the parallel juxtaposition of tongues and interpretation in 12.10 in a similar way to Dautzenberg. He also points to 1 Thess. 5.20f. as another example of the appeal to test prophecy. However, Grudem has refuted the first point and the exclusive link to prophecy in 1 Thess. 5.21 is contested.

What can be affirmed from all these scholars is that some link to prophecy and 14.29 is evident. However, it is the exclusive link which I question. There seems little awareness of the possibility that πνεύματα is in fact referring to prophecy *and* other manifestations. J. S. Ukpong ('Pluralism and the Problem of the Discernment of Spirits', *Ecumenical Review* 41 [1989] 417f.) denies any exclusive connection between *diakrisis pneumaton* and prophecy. Other commentators who see the gift referring to more than just prophecy are: F. W. Grosheide, *Commentary on the First Epistle to the Corinthians* (London: Marshall Morgan & Scott 1954²) 287f.; R. C. H. Lenski, *St. Paul's First and Second Epistles to the Corinthians* (Minneapolis: Augsburg Publishing House, 1963) 503f. and A. Bittlinger, *Gifts and Graces* (London: Hodder & Stoughton, 1967) 46.

However, Grudem has taken the opposite extreme and denies any identification of the discernment in 14.29 with the gift in 12.10.[37] This is similarly not convincing. It is not necessary, as Grudem presumes, to have
precisely the same object and subject in both verses in order for them to be
describing the same process of discernment. As to the object, 14.29 can
be understood as describing a partial aspect or an example of the broad
gift in 12.10. Similarly, regarding the subject, the difference Grudem has
noted between the two verses also does not mean the two verses denote
two different processes. As I shall argue below, the existence of a gift
does not mean that the whole congregation cannot to some degree take
part in the gift. Therefore, the separation by Grudem of the activity in
14.29 from that in 12.10 is, at best, 'beyond what seems warranted – or
necessary'.[38]

It can be concluded at this point that neither an exclusive juxtaposition of prophecy with διάκρισις nor Grudem's sharp separation need
to be accepted as convincing. I propose that on the basis of a broader
understanding of πνεύματα (as spirits and their manifestations as argued
below), the gift in 12.10 depicts a broad range of discernment,[39] which
is exemplified in 14.29.[40]

An Interpretative Element in Διάκρισις/διακρίνω

With respect to the material Dautzenberg offers in support of his interpretation of διάκρισις and διακρίνω, Grudem's critique has been convincing insofar as the evidence is not sufficient to enable clear-cut support

---

[37] For many who take the traditional position of a 'discernment of spirits', it is not
particularly clear how close they see the relationship to prophecy, and sometimes 14.29
is not mentioned (cf. Lietzmann, *Korinther*, 63; J. Calvin, *The First Epistle of Paul the
Apostle to the Corinthians* [trans. J. W. Fraser; Edinburgh: Saint Andrew Press, 1960] 263,
302; T. M. Crone, *Early Christian Prophecy* [Baltimore, MD: St Mary's Press, 1973] 222).
Crone says that it is not clear what the discernment of spirits refers to, but presumes it
is prophecy, since this is the only example offered. H. Conzelmann (*Der erste Brief an
die Korinther* [KEK 5; Göttingen: Vandenhoeck & Ruprecht, 1981[2]] 255) just says that
'διακρίσεις πνευμάτων' 'wird erklärt' in 14.24f. But this passage describes the effect of
prophecy (on unbelievers) and not the discernment of prophecy.

[38] Fee, *Presence*, 252. It is especially noteworthy that Grudem's description of the gift
in 12.10 includes the possibility of an evaluation of prophecy (*Gift*, 58). Similarly, the only
actual difference I can detect between his definition of the discernment in 14.29 and that of
12.10 is that he believes Paul is only addressing the discernment of true prophets in 14.29.
This distinction to my mind is hypothetical.

[39] Cf. Barrett (*Corinthians*, 328): 'The whole section proceeds on the assumption that
all spiritual manifestations must be tested.'

[40] Cf. Wendland, *Korinther*, 94f., 115, who takes the traditional view of the discernment of spirits in 12.10 yet refers back to it when explaining 14.29. Similarly Grosheide
(*Corinthians*, 337) says 14.29 'reminds of 12.10'.

for Dautzenberg's theory. On the other hand, Grudem has completely dismissed Dautzenberg's theory and reconfirmed the traditional interpretation of 1 Cor. 12.10. This does not entirely do justice to the material presented by Dautzenberg. Particularly when we consider a *via media*, the acceptance of a broader definition of διάκρισις, which would do justice to both 12.10 and 14.29, Dautzenberg's argument becomes partially relevant again.

While I acknowledge that there is no consistent reading of διάκρισις in Paul and that some of the meanings are not connected, it does not mean that *all* the different lexical senses need be seen as opposing one another. In other words, a more flexible approach may show that the process of διάκρισις incorporates both an evaluative and an interpretative element and these need not be seen as alternative options.[41] I will attempt to offer such evidence by (a) looking at the linguistic plausibility and (b) reviewing the conceptual background of an interpretative element in the process of discernment.

The Linguistic Argument

It is important to clarify a number of points. As a general rule, 'in any one context, a word will only carry one of its possible senses'[42] unless the author intends a deliberate double-entendre. However, there is no clear marker to indicate this intention. Moreover, I recognise that essentially 'interpretation' and 'evaluation' belong to two different semantic domains, the former to 'communication' and the latter to 'thinking' or rather to 'the last stage of thought'. Nevertheless, in both cases Louw and Nida point out that these domains are not to be seen too rigidly and

---

[41] Other scholars have also pointed in a similar direction, but there has been little or no substantiation of such an argument. Dunn (*Jesus*, 233f.) has made a particularly helpful start: 'In fact there may be little ground for dispute between these two sets of alternatives [interpretation or discernment]. Paul's meaning may be less precise than either and so be able to embrace the different nuances of each . . . In this context *diakrisis pneumaton* is best understood as an *evaluation, an investigating, a testing, a weighing of the prophetic utterance* by the rest (of the assembly or of the prophets) to determine both its source as to inspiration and its significance for the assembly (source and significance being two sides of the one coin, so that the evaluation includes both interpretation of spirits = spiritual utterances, and distinguishing of spirits = sources of inspiration).' This is an incisive definition in both its breadth and specification of what Paul meant by πνεύματα and διάκρισις. But from a linguistic and theological point of view it is regrettable that he does not explain how he reaches this conclusion.

Similarly, see Broer, 'Exegese', 67 and Aune, *Prophecy*, 221, who follows Dunn: 'since this term combines the notions of discrimination, interpretation, and examination in a suitably ambiguous way'.

[42] Cotterell and Turner, *Linguistics*, 179.

overlap is to be accepted.[43] This becomes particularly evident when the definition of Louw and Nida for the subdomain 'to distinguish, to evaluate, to judge' is considered: it 'involves essentially the process of deciding the correctness, *meaning*, truth, or value of something or someone'.[44] In deciding the meaning of something, an interpretative element is an essential and integral part. It is in this respect that I argue for 'interpretation' as a 'connotative meaning'[45] or feature of the sense 'to evaluate carefully'. I support this with synchronic evidence that διάκρισις and διακρίνω were used in that manner.[46]

A number of examples in Philo are particularly worth looking at. These depict διακρίνω/διάκρισις being used with both an interpretative and an evaluative sense:

> [T]he shrewdness coupled with the resoluteness which enabled him to recognize the products of empty fancies which many accounted to be good, and to distinguish [διακρίνει καὶ διαστέλλει] them as mere dreams from those which are really so; and to confess that the true and certain interpretations [συγκρίσεις] of things are given under God's guidance.[47]

While there is no identification of interpretation and discernment here, διακρίνω and συγκρίνω are parallel to one another.

> On the former dream an interpretative judgement [διάκρισις] is pronounced . . .[48]

The διάκρισις of Joseph's dream here by his brothers and father is both interpretation and judgement/evaluation.

> The statesman is most certainly an interpreter [ὀνειροκριτικός] of dreams . . . [not like those who] use their art of interpreting [διακρίνω] the visions given . . . for making money; but one who is accustomed to judge with exactness [ἀκριβόω] that great general universal dream . . .[49]

The interpretation of dreams for money and exact judgement are actually contrasted. Yet the whole section deals with interpreting the dream of the 'life of man' correctly. The goal is an exhortation to let 'every man search into his own heart and he will test the truth' that this dream is 'fancy'. Hence, the interpreter is judging the validity and truth of the life-dream.

---

[43] Louw and Nida, *Lexicon* I, 380, 404.
[44] (My italics); Louw and Nida, *Lexicon* I, 363.
[45] Cotterell and Turner, *Linguistics*, 45ff.   [46] Cf. chapter 1, n. 25.
[47] Philo, *Mig.* 19.   [48] Philo, *Som.* 2.7.   [49] Philo, *Jos.* 125.

[The statesman must] interpret [διακρίνειν] the day-time visions and phantoms of those who think themselves awake, and with suggestions commended by reason and probability shew them the truth about each of these visions: that this is beautiful, that ugly, this just, that unjust, and so with all the rest; what is prudent, courageous, pious, religious, beneficial, profitable . . .[50]

The interpretation of the daytime visions is, in fact, describing discernment according to my earlier definition, in which the validity or truth of something is evaluated on the basis of reflective thought.

These examples show that interpretation and discernment can be closely linked when διάκρισις and διακρίνω are used.[51] While the emphasis remains on the possibility of translating διακρίνω as 'to interpret',[52] my point in this section has been that it is linguistically justifiable to assume that the communicative element, 'to interpret', can be an integral part of evaluation and discernment.

Excursus: Interpretation and Evaluation at Delphi

It is also noteworthy that Plato saw a need for interpretative discernment of ecstatic phenomena such as the dreams and oracular utterances at Delphi. Much attention in the past has been drawn to Plato, *Timaeus* 71e–72b:

[50] Philo, *Jos.* 143.

[51] Further examples can be mentioned where the sense of διακρίνω has a broader scope than just discernment: Mt. 16.3 'You know how to interpret (διακρίνω) the appearance of the sky, but you cannot interpret the signs of the times'; Josephus, *Ant.* 8.148: τὸν δὲ μὴ δυνηθέντα διακρῖναι τῷ λύσαντι χρήματα ἀποτίνειν (Solomon sent riddles 'proposing that he who was unable to interpret them should pay a fine to the one who did solve them'); cf. Plato, *Protagoras* 315.

[52] A random search of classical and contemporary (to Paul) authors reveals that this broader use is not frequent. (While it is awkward that Loeb Classical Library translates διακρίνω in part with nouns, I have followed their translation to remain consistent and the point is made in either case):
Pausanias, who has been quoted above for using διάκρισις once as interpretation, never does so otherwise in his work on the *Description of Greece*: 9.36.6, here used with the sense 'distinguishing'. And for διακρίνω: 1.42.5, 'sorting' (herbs); 3.9.11, 'grievance'; 4.6.1, 'decision'; 4.8.8, in the passive as 'being hurt'; 6.22.9, 'distinguish'; 7.14.3, 'separate'; 8.26.1f., 'separate'; 9.13.7, 'decision'; 10.33.7, 'decision'.
Demosthenes, *Exordia* 34.3, 'decide'; *Orationes* 12.17, 'dispute'; 32.28, 'determine'; 57.6, 'decide'.
Xenophon, a classical writer, only uses the 'normal' translations: διακρίνω: *Cyropaedia* 7.5.39, 'discriminate'; *Hellenica* 5.2.10, 'dispute'; *Anabasis* 6.1.22, 'decide'; *Memorabilia* 1.1.9, 'decide'; *Scripta Minora, Agesilaus* 1.33, 'decision'; *Oeconimicus* 9.6, 'separating'; *Symposium* 4.20, 'discriminatory contest'; διάκρισις: *Cyropaedia* 8.2.27, twice as 'adjudication'; *Scripta Minora, On Hunting* 4.1, 'division'.

But it belongs to a man when in his right mind to recollect and ponder both the things spoken in dream or waking vision by the divining and inspired nature, and all the visionary forms that were seen, and by means of reasoning to discern [συννοέω] about them all wherein they are significant and for whom they portend evil or good in the future, the past, or the present. But it is not the task of him who has been in a state of frenzy, and still continues therein, to judge the apparitions and voices seen or uttered by himself; for it was well said of old that to do and to know one's own and oneself belongs only to him who is sound of mind. Wherefore also it is customary to set the tribe of prophets to pass judgement [κρίνειν] upon these inspired divinations; and they, indeed, themselves are named 'diviners' by certain who are wholly ignorant of the truth that they are not diviners but interpreters [ὑποκριταί] of the mysterious voice and apparition, for whom the most fitting name would be 'prophets of things divined'.

Scholarship has rightly been warned against identifying the role of the μάντις/προφήτης at the Delphic Oracle with tongues (and their interpretation) or prophecy,[53] since there are obvious semantic[54] and conceptual differences.[55] However, for this study, it is significant that the ambiguity of inspired utterances was recognised and hence it was deemed helpful for another person to judge and discern.[56] It is particularly of interest that the manifestations required a blend of both evaluation and interpretation. In this regard, M. Turner rightly points out that although the utterances may have been intelligible, this 'does not preclude that prophetic oracles were regularly cryptic, laden with metaphor, vague and ambiguous'.[57]

The Conceptual Argument

Now that I have established the possibility of a broader understanding of διάκρισις and διακρίνω, how probable is it? Or rather, does it fit with Paul's conceptual framework?

[53] C. Forbes, *Prophecy and Inspired Speech in Early Christianity and its Hellenistic Environment* (WUNT 2,75; Tübingen: Mohr/Siebeck, 1995) 103ff.

[54] Even those scholars who see a parallel here acknowledge this (cf. Dunn, *Jesus*, 228; H. Kleinknecht, 'πνεῦμα κτλ.', *TDNT* VI, 348f.).

[55] Paul would probably not have followed Plato's differentiation of ecstatic and rational. As Aune (*Prophecy*, 39) points out, 'Plato appears to use this oracular practice as a precedent for advocating the subordination of those with a less rational basis for knowledge to those with a more fully rational grasp of knowledge, i.e. philosophers and rulers.' Further, Forbes (*Prophecy*, 318f.) points out that the conceptual and sociological differences between the Pauline churches (and other early Christian groups) and the Delphic oracle make them difficult to compare with one another.

[56] See also Kleinknecht, 'πνεῦμα', 348, who shows how Plato comments that, in the case of the famous Delphic oracle imparted to Socrates, Socrates himself became its critic and thus made it 'true'.

[57] M. Turner, *The Holy Spirit and Spiritual Gifts* (Carlisle: Paternoster Press, 1996) 189.

First of all, we should remind ourselves that the objections to Dautzenberg's theory are based on his linking interpretation and prophecy. Yet, by not confining πνεύματα in 1 Cor. 12.10 to prophecies but opening it to 'spirits/spiritual manifestations' (as I propose), the concept of interpretation becomes increasingly applicable. For one thing, the use of διακρίνω/διάκρισις in an interpretative manner with such manifestations has been established. But the conceptual level is also important here. Dautzenberg's legitimate point was that the process of interpretation was not only known and practised in Hellenism and Judaism in connection with pneumatic and mantic phenomena, but that there was an increase of such interpretation processes in all areas which could disclose the will of God.[58] Grudem, in his list of terms denoting interpretation, comes up with fifty-eight instances where 'Jewish or early Christian authors had occasion to speak about the interpretation or explanation of difficult or obscure words or sayings'.[59] While Grudem offers this evidence in order to deny a link between interpretation and prophecy, my point is that spiritual manifestations and divination (of various natures) were commonly interpreted so that their significance or relevance could be explained. Hence, these processes belonged to Paul's conceptual framework and in that manner confirm the plausibility of an interpretation of spiritual manifestations.

Yet, while this is clearly applicable to cryptic messages, does not the difficulty remain that Paul's point is that prophecies were intelligible (1 Cor. 14) and hence not in need of interpretation?[60] In response it should be noted that my proposal of διάκρισις as a broad term is quite flexible. By incorporating both elements, it would allow for more evaluation

---

[58] Dautzenberg, *Prophetie*, 43–121, 125; 'Hintergrund', 94ff. He supports his case specifically from post-biblical evidence.

[59] Grudem, *Gift*, 278ff. (quote from p. 280). It is astonishing that Grudem himself did not come up with the solution that I am attempting to portray. In his nuanced understanding of how the evaluation took place, noted earlier, an interpretative element is not difficult to perceive (*Gift*, 60–7).

Further, see 1QpHabVII 1ff. for the rationale for interpreting prophecies: God tells Habakkuk, the prophet, to write down that something is going to happen, but he does not understand when it will come about. 'When it says, "so that with ease someone can read it," this refers to the Teacher of Righteousness to whom God made known all the mysterious revelations of his servants the prophets . . . for God's revelations are truly mysterious' (M. Wise, M. Abegg and E. Cook, *The Dead Sea Scrolls* [London: Harper, 1996] 119). See also Dan. 2.45, where Daniel, in his interpretation, validates the truth of the dream.

For the fact that prophecies were not categorically differentiated from other forms of divination, cf. 'The prophet and the dreamer of dreams are both considered as receiving divine communications.' (H. A. Wolfson, *Philo* II [Cambridge, MA: Harvard University Press, 1982[5]] 56f.). For the fluid boundaries, see also Turner, *Spirit*, 190–6 or Philo, *Jos.* 96, for an example of the interpreter of dreams being a prophet of the 'divine will'.

[60] This argument is often used (e.g. Wolff, *Korinther*, 105).

or interpretation depending on the nature of the prophecy.[61] Such an understanding leaves the possibility open that some prophecies did not require any interpretation.[62] Other prophecies, on the other hand, would have required further clarification as well as interpretation.[63] '[E]ven if a prophetic utterance is correct . . . the congregation has the duty to "discern" what must be done with such an utterance.'[64] Indeed, it is surprising that even Grudem admits that prophecies 'are often difficult to understand'.[65] Therefore, however one understands prophecy (cf. the discussion below), it is plausible that the utterance was intelligible but not yet understandable.

3.   Conclusion

In sum, then, it has been my aim to avoid an either/or position whereby διάκρισις/διακρίνω is understood as interpretation or evaluation, and to advance a case that does not limit the sense unnecessarily. Supported by both linguistic and conceptual material, I have presented an open-minded, flexible and pastorally sensitive process,[66] which not only identifies the source of spiritual manifestations but also offers some explanation of their meaning and significance so that the community can be edified appropriately.[67] This is significant for the development of my thesis. Discernment has both an evaluative and an interpretative function. Hence, the contours of *a hermeneutical and theological act* become visible, the details of which will require more in-depth treatment in the next chapter. For now I must attend to the objects of discernment in 1 Cor. 12.10 and 14.29: prophecy and spirits. What precisely does Paul have in mind when calling for their interpretative evaluation?

---

[61] Similarly Broer, 'Offenbarungsanspruch', 67.

[62] Some prophecies seem to have been both intelligible and understandable, as Grudem (*Gift*, 288) points out.

[63] A. C. Wire (*The Corinthian Women Prophets* [Minneapolis: Fortress Press, 1990] 148) suggests that Paul wanted 'to clarify meanings, narrow down options, and get a common mind'. Wire thinks examples of this may be the evaluation Paul expected from the Corinthians when he wanted them to confirm his assessment of the 'man living with his father's wife (5:3–5)', or the acceptance he required in 14.37f.

[64] Grosheide, *Corinthians*, 337f.   [65] Grudem, *Prophecy*, 149.

[66] This is a debatable aspect. Yet an interpretative element eases the difficulty of giving an absolute evaluation of the validity of a spiritual phenomenon. It is possible to imagine that a spiritual manifestation may be theoretically true but still confusing or counter-productive. Here, interpretative discernment could explain or refocus the utterance.

[67] The link between interpretation and evaluation, or communication and discernment is evident in 1 Cor. 2.6–16. I shall deal with this in chapter 4, D, so I have refrained from using that as evidence here since my argument would become circular.

C.   The Interpretative Evaluation of Prophecies and Spirits

Having established the plausibility of an interpretative element in discernment in 1 Cor. 12.10 and 14.29, we need to gain some insight into what Paul means when he insists on the interpretation and evaluation[68] of prophecies and πνεύματα.[69] While the two objects are interrelated and should not be categorically divided, we may deal with them separately, as both refer to significant aspects of Paul's ecclesiology.

1.   Prophecies

Paul singles out prophecy as requiring discernment (1 Cor. 14.29) despite his encouragement of prophetic activity (1 Thess. 5.20) and his stress on its significance (1 Cor. 14.1).[70] Although over the past few decades the phenomenon of prophecy in the New Testament has increasingly come to the attention of scholarship, its discernment has not received the same attention.[71] However, understanding discernment also helps clarify the role of prophecy in the community. I propose that by emphasising

[68] It may be noted from the start that I interchange 'to evaluate carefully' and 'to discern' without presupposing any difference in meaning. While I recognise the differentiation that has been made by Dautzenberg (*Prophetie*, 126ff.) and Meier (*Mystik*, 216f., who argues against 'Beurteilung' and for 'Unterscheidung'), this should not be held too rigidly. Both these senses ('to evaluate carefully' and 'to distinguish') are found in one subdomain, for which Louw and Nida make a point of elucidating that it 'normally implies careful thinking about various alternatives and then deciding what is to be regarded as more justified' (Louw and Nida, *Lexicon* I, 363).

[69] Dautzenberg's objection against the evaluation of prophecy on the basis that the context of 1 Corinthians does not hint at any negative or judgemental attitude towards prophecy can be dealt with in a straightforward manner. 1 Cor. 14 definitely refers to various 'constraints and restraints with respect to inspired utterance' (Dunn, 'Congregation', 216). However, the following section will establish the legitimacy of the evaluative element in more detail.

[70] Dautzenberg's criticism of the traditional understanding of διάκρισις has been that if prophecy is to be evaluated, then the gift of discernment is the more significant one, and he questions why Paul has not set this gift over the gift of prophecy. However, I. Broer perceptively shows that this also applies to Dautzenberg's understanding of διάκρισις, since if prophecy is dependent on an interpretation process, this also sets the latter over the prior ('Exegese', 67).

[71] See *inter alios*: Fascher, *Prophētēs*; U. B. Müller, *Prophetie und Predigt im Neuen Testament* (StNT 10; Gütersloh: Gütersloher Verlagshaus, 1975); E. Cothonet, 'Les prophètes chrétiens comme exégètes charismatiques de l'écriture', in J. Panagopoulos (ed.), *Prophetic Vocation in the New Testament and Today* (NT.S 45; Leiden: Brill, 1977) 77–107; Aune, *Prophecy*; M. E. Boring, *Sayings of the Risen Jesus: Christian Prophecy in the Synoptic Tradition* (MSSNTS 46; Cambridge: Cambridge University Press, 1982); Crone, *Prophecy*; E. E. Ellis, 'Prophecy in the New Testament Church – and Today', in Panagopoulos (ed.), *Vocation*, 46–57; Forbes, *Prophecy*; G. Friedrich, 'προφήτης κτλ.', *TDNT* VI, 781–861; T. W. Gillespie, *The First Theologians: A Study in Early Christian Prophecy* (Grand Rapids, MI: Eerdmans, 1994); Hill, *Prophecy*; J. Panagopoulos, 'Die urchristliche Prophetie', in idem (ed.), *Vocation*, 1–32; Thiselton, *Corinthians*, 956–65, 1087–94; Turner, *Spirit*, 185–

the need for the discernment of prophecy, Paul is presenting a vision against triumphalism and for a self-regulating community.[72] Three aspects are important.

First of all, the process of discernment grounds prophecies in the reality of community life. What do I mean by this? While its nature is still contested, it seems fair to say that prophecy is perceived to be of a spiritual origin.[73] (This differentiated it to some degree from exegesis or teaching).[74] This *perception* enhances rather than reduces the danger of spiritual elitism (specifically at Corinth).[75] But this elitism in turn is one

---

220; Wire, *Prophets*. In the matter of discernment, it is noteworthy that the important works by Forbes and Aune do not particularly elaborate on the subject. The *Wirkungsgeschichte* of 1 Cor. 14.29, as presented by Schrage (*Korinther* III, 466–9), shows that the main controversy has been regarding the subject of discernment. Schrage's comments on the different conceptions of office (particularly in the post-reformation period) and on who has authority within the church are revealing. But this debate is too broad to be based on this passage alone.

[72] H. Schürmann, 'Die geistlichen Gnadengaben in den paulinischen Gemeinden', in *Ursprung und Gestalt* (Düsseldorf: Patmos, 1970) 261.

[73] From a number of significant studies on the subject a consensus has emerged that it is 'a specific form of divination that consists of intelligible verbal messages believed to originate with God and communicated through inspired human intermediaries' (Aune, *Prophecy*, 339; cf. Forbes, *Prophecy*, 219; Turner, *Spirit*, 187; Dunn, *Jesus*, 228; Grudem, *Gift*, 118, 143). Turner (*Spirit*, 189) states that 'the content of a message was often short and usually specific'. Aune suggests that the 'distinctive feature' of prophetic speech was 'not so much *content* or *form*, but its *supernatural origin*' (*Prophecy*, 338. That definition does not prevent Aune from offering an extensive discussion and identification of basic and complex forms [*Prophecy*, 320–7] and style [*Prophecy*, 327–37] of prophetic speech). Thiselton warns against seeing prophecy as a 'spontaneous' phenomenon because this restricts '"revelation" to a kind of *Deus ex machina* worldview' (*Corinthians*, 1093), against M. Turner ('Spiritual Gifts Then and Now', *Vox Evangelica* 15 [1985] 10; Dunn, *Jesus*, 228). I shall discuss these epistemological questions in more detail in chapter 6. However, against Thiselton, the fact that prophecy requires discernment speaks for prophecy being a less rather than more rational process.

[74] It 'need not be doubted that prophecies had didactic and prescriptive elements' and that Paul saw some similarity between prophecy and other forms of inspired speech. However, 'the burden of proof rests with those who wish to claim charismatic preaching and exegesis were normal aspects of *prophecy* rather than of *teaching*' (Turner, *Spirit*, 205–12 [quotations taken from pp. 206 and 212 respectively]; cf. also Grudem, *Gift*, 139–44). For such an identification, see, e.g., Ellis, *Prophecy*, 147–254; Gillespie, *Theologians*; in a nuanced fashion, D. Hill, 'Christian Prophets as Teachers or Instructors in the Church', in Panagopoulos (ed.), *Vocation*, 108–30; Cothonet, 'Prophètes', 77–107.

[75] 'While the speaker believes that such utterances or discourses come from the Holy Spirit, mistakes can be made, and since believers, including ministers or prophets, remain humanly fallible, claims to prophecy must be weighed and tested' (Thiselton, *Corinthians*, 965). Cf. Forbes (*Prophecy*, 321) for the problem of spiritual elitism at Corinth. Forbes thinks that those who believed themselves to be mature began to 'restrict the practice of prophecy to their own number' who in turn were also the only ones who were allowed to evaluate prophecy (*Prophecy*, 321). Paul counters this spiritual elitism in 1 Cor. 12–14 and attempts to call upon the entire congregation to evaluate prophecies (*Prophecy*, 265–9).

of the major problems Paul is attempting to address.[76] In the discernment of prophecies, as Aune has helpfully suggested, the content rather than the origin is the most important criterion for the evaluation.[77] Not the prophets, nor a speculation about spiritual origins, but the manifestations themselves are to be discerned.[78] This implies that the discernment of prophecies has an *unambiguous* starting point: in the concrete effect upon church life. In that sense prophecies are grounded, and triumphalism and consequently elitism are reduced.

Secondly, by requiring the church to discern prophecies, Paul is making it possible to encourage their use without threatening the unity of the church. How is this so? Paul is clearly keen on both unity and prophecy. The discernment of prophecy gives the whole community (as I shall later argue) a part in establishing its influence. Hence, Paul introduces a safeguard against too much significance being attached only to those prophesying. This safeguard is not in the form of an authoritative leadership but lies in the interdependence of all church members, in listening to and learning from one another.[79] Hans von Campenhausen has described this community not as 'just another constitutional organisation with grades and classes, but a unitary, living cosmos of free, spiritual gifts, which serve and complement one another'.[80]

---

[76] The issue of elitism at Corinth is often tied to the use of tongues. However, Forbes (as presented in the previous footnote) seems correct in his insistence that we also consider prophecies in this regard, as the problems of triumphalism in 1 Cor. 1–2 appear to be of a very broad nature, including wisdom (1.18) and spiritual manifestations (2.12). The problem of undisciplined exercise of prophecy (14.29) is then secondary to the larger issue of elitism.

[77] Aune, *Prophecy*, 219f. Even for Grudem the starting point of any evaluation lies in the manifestation: 'the congregation would simply evaluate the prophecy and form opinions about it' (Grudem, *Gift*, 67).

[78] However, this should not lead to an unnecessary bifurcation of source and manifestation. Aune further remarks (*Prophecy*, 222) that 'the purpose of evaluation does not appear to be negative in orientation, i.e. for the sole purpose of unmasking oracles which were inspired by demonic powers'. However, it is not a 'negative' process by which to unmask false manifestations and retain the authentic, but a cautious and constructive (rather than triumphalistic) approach.

[79] 'Die Vorsteherschaft innerhalb der Gemeinde begründet kein einseitiges Verhältnis des Befehlens, dem ein ebenso einseitiges Gehorchen entspräche, sondern setzt im willigen Befolgen und Anerkennen eine gegenseitige Übereinstimmung, ein Hörenwollen und Hörenkönnen in freier Wechselseitigkeit voraus . . .' (H. von Campenhausen, 'Zur Auslegung von Röm 13: Die dämonistische Deutung des ἐξουσία-Begriffes', in W. Baumgartner, O. Eissfeldt, K. Elliger and L. Rost [eds.], *Festschrift Alfred Bertholet zum 80. Geburtstag* [Tübingen: Mohr/Siebeck, 1950] 111). Cf. also Dunn, *Jesus*, 291; K. Wengst, 'Das Zusammenkommen der Gemeinde und ihr "Gottesdienst" nach Paulus', *EvTh* 33 (1973) 554.

[80] H. von Campenhausen, *Ecclesiastical Authority and Spiritual Power* (trans. J. A. Baker; London: A. & C. Black, 1969) 63f. For the discussion concerning the pneumatic community in the Pauline churches, cf. Dunn, *Theology of Paul*, 562–4, 566–71. What is

Thirdly, the discernment of prophecy solves a problem which a number of scholars have addressed. They attempt to differentiate between different types of prophecy so as to identify a qualitative difference in category between Paul's own prophetic call and the prophecies of church members.[81] This argument rests on the a priori belief that the more authoritative type of prophecy would not require discernment. However, this line of thought is not convincing. It neglects the fact that discernment not only has a critical function but should also be seen as a *constructive element* in theological and ethical deliberation. Rather than an a priori categorisation, all prophecies are, in the first instance, to be treated equally. Discernment, then, establishes a spectrum of authority in which all prophecies find their correct place. The burden lies on the shoulders of the whole congregation to decide how authoritative prophecies are. [82] Congregational

important is that the use of the gift ensures 'the cohesion and consistency of the witness of fallible believers to the work of the Holy Spirit as a witnessing community faithful to the gospel' (Thiselton, *Corinthians*, 969). Unity is a key objective of the gift of discernment.

[81] Here I refer to Grudem, Sandnes, Bockmuehl and Penney: Wayne Grudem has differentiated between the various types of prophecy and classified them as an authoritative (basically a form of word-for-word inspiration) and a weaker type (the congregational prophecy with lesser authority; *Gift*, 43–73). One of the many arguments he uses to substantiate his claim is that the demand to evaluate prophecy shows that there is a weaker type of prophecy which should not be equated with the more authoritative type. However, Turner has rightly pointed out that this debate has been somewhat motivated by an anachronistic canonical approach, which 'confuses the issues' (*Spirit*, 215). Cessationists explicitly state that all NT prophecy had to be inerrant in order to sustain the inerrancy and infallibility of scripture (cf. F. D. Farnell, 'The Gift of Prophecy in the Old and New Testament', *Bibliotheca Sacra* 149 [1992] 410).

Karl Olav Sandnes has approached the subject from a different angle. He has studied Paul's self-understanding and has concluded that he really did understand his apostolate and his commission in prophetic terms (*Paul – One of the Prophets?* [WUNT 2,43; Tübingen: Mohr/Siebeck, 1991] 240–5). Yet the nature of Paul's commissioning ἀποκάλυψις (Gal. 1.16) differed from the revelations of the early Christian prophets in that Paul's was a 'once-for-all call' of Christ whereas the prophets were in need of ever-new revelation. Paul's gospel (his 'mystery') was therefore, in contrast to the prophetic utterances, not open for testing (*Paul*, 245).

Similarly, Markus Bockmuehl in his research into the concepts of revelation and mystery in Paul and Judaism believes there are different qualities of revelation (*Revelation*, 226f). He points out that even Paul discloses 'doctrinal' mysteries (e.g. Rom. 11.25 and 1 Cor. 15.51) with 'considerable caution' and embeds them into a context of 'traditional language and careful Scriptural proof' (*Revelation*, 227).

In the same manner, J. Penney ('The Testing of New Testament Prophecy', *JPT* 10 [1997] 35–84) distinguishes between different types of prophecy (canonical and lesser revelation). The secondary type of prophecy (lesser revelation) was in need of testing by the gathered community and their various gifts ('Testing', 81).

[82] The concept of a spectrum makes rigid categorisation unnecessary; cf. Turner, *Spirit*, 216: 'In the final analysis Paul does not say that all New Testament prophets see through a glass darkly while apostles see clearly: the apostles' prophecy, too is *ek merous* and *en ainigmati* (1 Cor. 13:9,12).' For a discussion of the relationship of prophecy to the gospel

64   *What requires discernment?*

discernment, then, is the means by which authority is granted or rejected. But this in turn places all prophecies under the scrutiny of the community as it verifies and validates the significance of each prophecy.[83] Finally, this means that authentic prophecy is strengthened and enhanced.

In sum, Paul was keen on the use of the gift of prophecy. But he needed to find a way in which prophetic activity could take place without spiritual elitism (and hence factionalism) being enhanced, which in turn would have nullified any positive impulses. I have proposed that it is for this reason that Paul called for the discernment of prophecy. In a constructive manner, Paul grounds every prophecy in the discernment of the community as a part of its self-regulation. Discernment can reject some utterances, reinterpret others and finally endorse those which authentically speak to the life of the community.

2.   The Spirits?

The object of διάκρισις in 1 Cor. 12.10, πνεύματα, has received varied interpretations. The position of Dautzenberg, who understands it solely as prophecy, has been rightly dismissed. But what then are the 'spirits'? Does Paul really mean to denote the Spirit of God and evil spirits in the same word?[84] Is the term to be understood in the light of Jewish apocalyptic demonology and angelology,[85] as 'different phenomena of Christian life',[86] or as the dispositions of the human heart?[87] Or are these various

---

or *kerygma*, see G. Dautzenberg, 'Botschaft und Bedeutung der urchristlichen Prophetie', in Panagopoulos (ed.), *Vocation*, 131–61; Turner, *Spirit*, 213–20. See also H. Merklein ('Der Theologe als Prophet. Zur Funktion prophetischen Redens im theologischen Diskurs des Paulus', *NTS* 38 [1992] 402–29) who claims that prophecy has the purpose of '[um] Leerstellen zu füllen, die im Rahmen eines argumentativen Diskurses des Kerygmas nicht zu schließen sind'.

[83] Dunn has also brought the testing of New Testament prophecy to bear against the claims of Käsemann and Bultmann that the gospel tradition was augmented by prophecies ascribed to the risen Lord (J. D. G. Dunn, 'Prophetic "I"-Sayings and the Jesus Tradition: The Importance of Testing Prophetic Utterances within Early Christianity', *NTS* 24 [1977–78] 175–98). Dunn suggests that if this were the case (which he questions), evaluation and discernment would have minimised any development of such post-resurrection prophetic traditions. (Cf. similarly D. Hill, 'On the Evidence for the Creative Role of Christian Prophets', *NTS* 20 [1974] 262–74; Turner, *Spirit*, 220 n.102).

[84] The precise terminology is not much help. Paul does not otherwise speak of πνεύματα in the plural to speak of evil spirits *together with* the Holy Spirit, although the singular is used to denote an/the evil spirit (2 Cor. 11.4; cf. Eph. 2.2; 2 Thess. 2.2). Grudem (*Gift*, 284) in his reply to Dautzenberg on the issue also points to the rest of the NT: 1 Jn 4.1 (δοκιμάζετε τὰ πνεύματα); Mt. 8.16; 12.45; Acts 19.12; 23.8, 9; 1 Tim. 4.1; Rev. 16.14.

[85] Cf. the discussion in Meier, *Mystik*, 220f.   [86] Grundmann, 'δόκιμος', 260.

[87] Cf. Lazure and Schnackenburg in Therrien, *Discernement*, 56f., although some of the references Therrien offers concern 1 Jn 4.1.

interpretations related? I propose that discerning the spirits means understanding the macro-microcosmic link of reality *and* evaluating that link.
That implies placing everyday existence into relationship with cosmology
and spirituality, and, on the other hand, evaluating spiritual manifestations
according to their ethical results. What do I mean by this and how can I
assert this? I propose to consider three aspects.

Acknowledging a Dualistic Framework

First, it is important to acknowledge how pervasive Paul's dualistic framework is. There is a cosmological battle of good and evil, which has an
effect on all areas of life.[88] Within this battle Paul recognises the existence of various personal spiritual beings[89] who possess authority in the
spiritual realm.[90] While there is discussion about the background of these

---

[88] Cf. J. B. Russell, *The Devil: Perceptions of Evil from Antiquity to Primitive Christianity* (Ithaca, NY: Cornell University Press, 1977) 229, 237; H. Gunkel, *The Influence
of the Holy Spirit* (Philadelphia: Fortress Press, 1979) 37; A. Schlatter, *Paulus der Bote
Jesu* (Stuttgart: Calwer Verlag, 1985[5]) 342; Bittlinger, *Gifts*, 45f. Even a helpful attempt,
such as the one by W. Wink (*Naming the Powers: The Language of Power in the New
Testament* [The Powers 1; Philadelphia: Fortress Press, 1984] 5), which demythologises
the 'powers' into categories of 'modern sociology, depth psychology, and general systems
theory', concedes that the 'principalities and powers' (in the NT) are 'the inner and outer
aspects of any given manifestation of power' with 'something that would not reduce to
physical structures – something invisible, immaterial, spiritual, and very, very real'. Yet see
also the attempt to show how 'small an extent the notion of demonic and hostile powers
generally featured in the thought of the earliest Christians . . . [and that t]here is nothing
in the Pauline writings that refers to a battle between Christ and hostile forces' in W. Carr,
Angels and Principalities (MSSNTS 42; Cambridge: Cambridge University Press, 1981)
176. Whether or not there was neutral ground is not entirely clear. However, Bittlinger (*Gifts*,
45) pleads for 'the ability to distinguish between divine, *human* and demonic powers' (italics
mine).

[89] These need to be studied in a conceptual (although not necessarily systematic) manner. Russell (*Devil*, 237) writes that the evil powers are equivalent to the 'larger symbols of
Satan'.
  For instance, E. E. Ellis has seen a close affinity between angels and spirits in Paul,
although the identification of the two is not attested ('"Spiritual" Gifts in the Pauline Community', *NTS* 20 [1973] 138). Note the presence of angels requires the veiling of women
(1 Cor. 11.4–10), the tongues of angels (1 Cor. 13.1), the co-activity of angels with his
opponents (2 Cor. 11.3f.), the worship of angels (Col. 2.18) and the angel of Satan (2 Cor.
12.7; cf. Gal.1.8).
  But there are also other 'personal, evil, spiritual beings whose purposes are opposed to
God, his people and his cosmos' (D. G. Reid, 'Satan, Devil', *DPL*, 862); cf. 2 Cor. 2.11;
δαιμόνιοι (1 Cor. 10.14–21); στοιχεῖα (Gal. 4.3, 8; Col. 2.8, 20). For the cosmological
significance of the ἄρχόντες, cf. O. Cullmann, *Der Staat im Neuen Testament* (Tübingen:
Mohr/Siebeck, 1961[2]) 75ff.; G. Theissen, *Psychologische Aspekte paulinischer Theologie*
(FRLANT 131; Göttingen: Vandenhoeck & Ruprecht, 1983) 365ff.

[90] Cf. P. T. O'Brien, 'Principalities and Powers: Opponents of the Church', in D. A.
Carson (ed.), *Biblical Interpretation and the Church: Text and Context* (Exeter: Paternoster

realities, it is clear that they have a direct effect on everyday life.[91] 'Human agents, historical entities, and natural phenomena are dominated and pervaded by transcendent spiritual forces.'[92] These forces can blind (2 Cor. 4.4), deceive (Rom. 7.10) and tempt (1 Thess. 3.5; 2.18). Discernment requires of the believers to acknowledge and identify the presence of these realities.[93] However, does that make their identification merely a speculative affair? This takes us to my next aspect.

Observing the Ethical Results

We should note that the term πνεῦμα is in itself slightly ambiguous in Paul.[94] In other words, Paul's language may be intentionally

Press, 1984) 110–50; C. E. Arnold, *Ephesians: Power and Magic. The Concept of Power in Ephesians in Light of its Historical Setting* (MSSNTS 63; Cambridge: Cambridge University Press, 1989); idem, *Powers of Darkness* (Leicester: InterVarsity Press, 1992) 87–161.

[91] While Beker (*Paul*, 181) is keen to point out that apocalyptic is both the 'material content' and the 'linguistic medium' of Paul's framework, C. Forbes has shown that Paul is combining creatively the angelology and demonology of Judaism, and the Graeco-Roman world-view ('Paul's Principalities and Powers. Demythologising Apocalyptic?', *JSNT* 82 [2001] 61–88; 'Pauline Demonology and/or Cosmology? Principalities, Powers and the Elements of the World in their Hellenistic Context', *JSNT* 85 [2002] 51–73). But see also the lucid attempt by E. Schweizer to identify the 'elementary spirits' with Pythagorean ideas (and the elements fire, earth, water, air), which informed the situations at Colossae and in Galatia. Yet Schweizer admits that 'it is difficult to draw a clear line between these views and a belief in personal demonic beings' ('Slaves of the Elements and Worshipers of Angels: Gal 4:3, 9 and Col 2:8, 18, 20', *JBL* 107 [1988] 468). Another plausible interpretation is that of 'local presiding deities' or 'national gods', put forward by N. T. Wright (*The Epistles of Paul to the Colossians and to Philemon* [Leicester, InterVarsity Press, 1986] 101f.). Cf. for further elaboration, G. B. Caird, *Principalities and Powers: A Study in Pauline Theology* (Oxford: Clarendon Press, 1956) 1–30.

[92] Beker, *Paul*, 188.

[93] Cf. Dunn, *Theology of Paul*, 432–4, who points out that, although spiritual experience is a frequent phenomenon in Paul, he was farsighted enough to realise that it could lead to 'esoteric and elitist factionalism' (*Theology*, 433) and become 'uncritical', and correspondingly began to 'hedge' these experiences in with certain tests (*Theology*, 434). Furthermore, discernment will acknowledge these experiences without bringing about fear of demons, because in Christ there is victory over their influence (O. Böcher, *Das Neue Testament und die dämonischen Mächte* [Stuttgart: Katholisches Bibelwerk, 1972] 73f.). As I argued earlier (C1), with regard to the discernment of prophecy, Paul is aware of the speculative and ambiguous dangers of attempting to clarify the origins of manifestations directly.

[94] While the majority of references denote the Spirit of God (over 100 of the 146 references, cf. Dunn, *Theology of Paul*, 76 n. 117), Paul uses the same word to refer to the human spirit (Rom. 1.9; 8.16; 1 Cor. 2.11; 5.3–5; 7.34; 14.14; 16.18; 2 Cor. 2.13; 7.1, 13; Gal. 6.18; Eph. 4.23; Phil. 4.23; Col. 2.5; 1 Thess. 5.23; Philm. 25). In a number of cases it is so elusive that it is not clear what he is referring to (cf. 1 Cor. 4.21; 14.15, 32; 2 Cor. 4.13; Gal. 6.1; Eph. 1.17; Phil. 1.27). Indeed, to some extent, 'the human spirit is but a manifestation of the divine Spirit' (Dunn, *Theology of Paul*, 77; R. Jewett, *Paul's Anthropological Terms: A Study of their Use in Conflict Settings* [AGJU 10; Leiden: Brill, 1971] 451ff.; Fee,

fluid.[95] It is to be presumed that Paul also has the anthropological spirit in view.[96] Paul was realistic about people: he knew about intentional deceit through some apostles and workers and he knew of the twisted motives (Gal. 1.7ff.) and haughty thinking (Rom. 12.3) which were difficult to detect and required discernment. It is important that believers recognise that such phenomena are related to the macrocosm.[97] In 2 Cor. 11.13–15 Paul warns that 'appearances are deceptive' and that the church should not be fooled 'by the superficial attractiveness of teachers who claim to be heaven-sent messengers'.[98] Discernment will unveil the teachers as false and the fact that they are mere διάκονοι, 'agents' of Satan.[99] That means there is an interpretative move in which the link between ethical results and cosmic significance is established.[100] But this conversely also

---

Presence, 24–26; contrast W. D. Stacey, *The Pauline View of Man* [London: Macmillan, 1956] 137–45). However, cf. my chapter 6 for the need to distinguish the human from the divine Spirit (Rom. 8.16; 1 Cor. 2.6–16).

[95] Cf. Fee, *Presence*, 25. Although Fee thinks that 'for the most part Paul's usage can be determined with a high degree of confidence' (*Presence*, 24).

[96] In this manner Fee (*Presence*, 25) makes sense of 1 Cor. 14.32 ('the spirits of the prophets are subject to the prophets') as well as a number of other passages, and explains that they are best read as 'S/spirit'. Further, see Ellis ('Gifts', 136f.) for a number of citations from Qumran where men are described as spirits.

[97] The πνεῦμα-σάρξ discussion in Gal. 5 is a good example of this. 'As its [spirit's] opposite, σάρξ is caught up into the dualism inherent in all apocalyptic thought and is thus associated with "the world" and "the present age" which stand in contrast to the new creation. *It is this apocalyptic dualism which gives to σάρξ its negative "colouring"*: just as the present age is an evil age . . . so the flesh is at best inadequate and at worst thoroughly tainted with sin' (Barclay, *Truth*, 205; cf. S. Schulz, *Neutestamentliche Ethik* [Zürich: Theologischer Verlag, 1987] 348).

[98] Martin, *Corinthians*, 355. Both M. Dibelius (*Die Geisterwelt im Glauben des Paulus* [Göttingen: Vandenhoeck & Ruprecht, 1909] 73ff.) and his student E. Lerle ('Diakrisis Pneumaton bei Paulus' [Unpubl. PhD dissertation, University of Heidelberg, 1947]) have stressed the fact that, in the same manner as Satan can disguise himself as an angel of light (2 Cor. 11.14), so manifestations can occur that are similar to those of the Spirit but are essentially from demonic sources and powers. Dibelius sees this term as an older category of thought and claims that Paul actually thought differently (*Geisterwelt*, 75). Lerle's thesis has largely been dismissed without discussion; cf. Dautzenberg, *Prophetie*, 141. M.-A. Chevallier (*Esprit de Dieu, paroles d'hommes: Le rôle de l'Esprit dans les ministères de la parole selon l'apôtre Paul* [Neuchâtel: Delachaux & Niestlé, 1966] 190) comments that the thesis is 'décevante'.

[99] Cf. Martin, *Corinthians*, 356.

[100] With respect to the interrelationship of macro- and microcosm, Aune points out that it is a chicken-and-egg problem: 'that is, did Paul's mythological view of eschatological dualism give rise to a homologous view of human nature in which the old and the new are juxtaposed until the eschatological consummation, or did his mythological view of the structure of human nature provide confirmation for his Christian understanding of Jewish apocalyptic eschatology? Neither of these possibilities is quite satisfactory, *for the answer is probably more dialectical*' (italics mine; D. E. Aune, 'Two Pauline Models of the Person', in D. E. Aune and J. McCarthy [eds.], *The Whole and the Self* [New York: Crossroad, 1997] 107).

means that spirituality can and must be measured by the effects in the ethical realm.[101]

Ethical and Theological Sobriety

This introduces my final step. I suggest that the evaluation/interpretation of spirits is only one manner of expressing Paul's concern to examine carefully all of reality. In other words, Paul is using various types of language to denote a similar issue. Because the '*dominant theological framework*' of 1 Corinthians is 'strongly apocalyptic', Paul calls for the discernment of spirits/spiritual manifestations.[102] In other contexts the same concern/gift is clothed in a more general warning to be wary and sober in ethical and theological matters.

Hence, Paul admonishes in general terms the believers to stay awake and be sober (1 Thess. 5.6, cf. 8), come to a 'sober and right mind' (1 Cor. 15.34) and 'to think with sober judgment' (Rom. 12.3). This fits in with Paul's admonition 'to be wise in what is good and guileless in what is evil' (Rom. 16.19; cf. 1 Thess. 5.15; Gal. 5.15).[103] Watchfulness and a wise lifestyle have a spiritual purpose and dimension.

But this sobriety is also important for Paul with respect to the very heart of the gospel. Hence, throughout Galatians Paul is appealing to the church for a return to their senses so that they might realise that they are (already) turning towards the wrong gospel (1.6–10). This appeal is heightened to a biting attack in ch. 3. 'Paul speaks so scathingly because of his

---

[101] This means, for instance, observing carefully that freedom receives its allotted place in the life of the community. In 1 Cor. 8–10 Paul warns the Corinthians twice to be careful that freedom is not a stumbling block for others (βλέπετε in 1 Cor. 8.9 and 10.12). A balance between freedom and a 'loving giving up' requires reflective attention, otherwise the strong themselves will fall (1 Cor. 10.12). '[F]or legalism and libertinism are alike in that they both fail to appreciate or experience the freedom of new existence "in Christ," and so both result in a sorry end' (R. N. Longenecker, *Galatians* [WBC 41; Dallas: Word Books, 1990] 284).

[102] E. Adams, *Constructing the World* (SNTW; Edinburgh: T&T Clark, 2000) 242f. Adams contrasts 1 Corinthians with Romans where 'the dualistic aspects of Paul's apocalyptic theology are tempered by a stress on God as creator and on his faithfulness and commitment to all that he has made'. This contrast may also be explained by the different sociological contexts Paul was addressing. 'The Corinthians were involved in and committed to the larger society to a degree which, in Paul's view, compromised their participation in the life and values of the church' (*World*, 243). This concern may have led to the necessity of a gift, which other churches did not require in the same intensity.

[103] In Eph. 5.15 the church is exhorted to 'be careful (βλέπετε) then how you live, not as unwise people but as wise', and in the following verse the author shows how intricately this is bound up with the spiritual state of the cosmos and the eschatological perspective: 'Because the days are evil', the Ephesians are admonished to take advantage of the resources they have.

converts' lack of spiritual discernment in not perceiving the contradiction and imminent disaster of their own situation.'[104] Similarly, in Phil. 3.2 Paul admonishes the church to exercise extensive caution with a threefold βλέπετε, against the 'dogs, evil doers and mutilators', who probably are the same group of people.[105]

These examples show how Paul warns the believers to be ethically and theologically aware as a means of avoiding triumphalism and discovering the authentic ways of the Spirit.

Summary

My argument proposed that Paul uses various types of language to express his concern for sobriety in the matters of everyday conduct as well as with respect to matters at the heart of the gospel. The discernment of spirits is one of these expressions with a particularly apocalyptic emphasis: Paul wants to clarify that all matters require an evaluation as to their macro-cosmic significance. Hence, Paul works with various levels of reality *in order* to show the interrelationship of the discernment of salvation, ethical life and individual concerns.[106] This led to my proposal that the person gifted with discerning the spirits *will be able to establish and evaluate the macro-microcosmic link*: spiritual matters must be assessed with respect to their ethical impact; the ethical effects will in turn be explained in their cosmological significance.

---

[104] Longenecker, *Galatians*, 103.

[105] P. T. O'Brien, *The Epistle to the Philippians: A Commentary on the Greek Text* (Grand Rapids, MI: Eerdmans, 1991) 354. 'Most likely . . . at issue for them is Torah observance as evidence of Gentiles' truly belonging to God's people and therefore of their genuine obedience to Christ' (Fee, *Philippians*, 297).

On a more general note, Col. 2.8 cautions the church to be on guard against 'philosophy and empty deceit, according to human tradition'. Indeed, in this passage the human deceit is directly linked with the 'elemental spirits of the universe' (τὰ στοιχεῖα τοῦ κόσμου). The nature of the heretic 'philosophy' is very contested. For a good overview, cf. P. Pokorný, *Der Brief des Paulus an die Kolosser* (ThHK 10/1; Berlin: Evangelische Verlagsanstalt, 1987) 95–101; A. Standhartinger, *Studien zur Entstehungsgeschichte und Intention des Kolosserbriefs* (NT.S 94; Leiden: Brill, 1999) 20–7; H. Hübner, *An Philemon. An die Kolosser. An die Epheser* (HNT 12; Tübingen: Mohr/Siebeck, 1997) 94–7. Hübner argues that we cannot reconstruct the *nature* of the Colossian philosophy but we can understand the *perception* that the author of Colossians had of this philosophy: soteriology has been understood as a 'Weltanschauung' and the author is concerned that the necessary theological and Christological dimensions are missing (96).

[106] Thiselton is rather dismissive when he claims that the 'gift [of discernment] certainly concerns salvation, the church, and the world rather than relatively trivial individual experiences' (*Corinthians*, 969). The individual concerns are directly dependent on matters of salvation and church life.

But in having broadened the applicability of the gift in this manner have I not generalised too much? Does not a gift imply that it is meant only for certain people? This leads us to my final question in this chapter.

D.   The Subject of Discernment

In the following section I need to address the question of who the subject of discernment is. Who does Paul envisage as being capable of discernment? In the previous chapter we saw the whole community taking part in the ethical deliberation. However, is this also the case with discernment? What difference is there between 1 Cor. 12.10 (only a few possess the gift) and 14.29 (οἱ ἄλλοι διακρινέτωσαν)? Before turning to these passages it is necessary to see that 1 Cor. 2.6–16 precedes them. It is in that passage that Paul introduces his appeal for discernment.

There has been intense discussion about whom Paul is addressing in 1 Cor. 2.6–16.[107] By appealing to the πνευματικοί and τέλειοι is Paul referring to two types of teaching or even two levels of Christianity?[108] As G. Theissen has asked, is the relationship between the 'word of the cross' (1.18–2.5) and the message of wisdom (2.6–16) 'gradualistisch' (the latter as a development of the former) or dialectic (two different aspects of the same content)?[109] Solutions have been sought from various sources and approaches.[110] Although some see a separate or even elite group being addressed here,[111] this is not convincing. Paul's emphasis is on unity in 1 Cor. 1–4. Giving exclusive access to a superior group would contradict

---

[107]   The difficulty is the terminology which Paul only uses here: cf. σοφίαν δὲ λαλοῦμεν ἐν τοῖς τελείοις (v. 6); σοφίαν ἐν μυστηρίῳ τὴν ἀποκεκρυμμένην (v. 7); πνευματικός, σαρκικός, ψυχικός; cf. M. Widmann, '1 Cor. 2.6–16: Ein Einspruch gegen Paulus', *ZNW* 70 (1979) 44–53, for eight major terminological differences, although his conclusions are contested.

[108]   Hence, R. Scroggs ('Paul: ΣΟΦΟΣ and ΠΝΕΥΜΑΤΙΚΟΣ', *NTS* 14 [1967/68] 55) speaks of a message which is 'distinct from kerygma'. Similarly, H. Conzelmann ('Paulus und die Weisheit', *NTS* 12 [1965/66] 238–40) argues for a 'Zwei-Stufen Schema des Erkenntnisweges'; for further bibliography, see W. Willis, 'The "Mind of Christ" in 1 Corinthians 2,16' *Bib* 70 (1989) 111f.

[109]   Theissen, *Aspekte*, 340–4.

[110]   In my introductory chapter I mentioned that the Gnostic background hypothesis (Wilckens, *Weisheit*) has generally been dismissed in favour of Jewish sapiential traditions (Davis, *Wisdom*; Pearson, *Pneumatikos*; Horsley, 'Pneumatikos'). However, Brown (*Cross*) and Schrage (*Korinther* I, 244) also show the affinity with apocalyptic conceptions. Further, cf. Thiselton, *Corinthians*, 233: 'Virtually all of the "sensitive" terms were . . . part of a common religious vocabulary in the Graeco-Roman world . . .'

[111]   Cf. particularly the work of Ellis who thinks they are 'distinguished from the believers generally', namely that Paul is speaking of early Christian prophets ('Gifts', 25f.), or by Lopes, who thinks they are just the 'apostles' (A. N. G. Lopes, 'Paul as a Charismatic Interpreter of Scripture: Revelation and Interpretation in 1 Cor 2:6–16' [Unpubl. PhD dissertation, Westminster Theological Seminary, 1995] iv).

the purpose of unity.[112] Rather, Paul is using Corinthian terminology to subvert elitist attitudes.[113] Hence, Paul is calling *all* believers to become mature in their ability to discern.[114] That does not exclude the possibility of a more profound level of consciousness (as I shall still elucidate in the latter half of this book).[115] It does mean, however, that Paul is not classifying believers in categorically different classes of belief.[116] For Paul, the whole congregation is responsible for the furtherance and edification of the whole congregation.[117] There is no elite group in charge of the spiritual evaluation of the others.[118] But how then does this emphasis square with the existence of a gift?

[112] Research has recently stressed the issue of disunity in Corinth and that our text (1 Cor. 2.6–16) is to be seen as advancing Paul's plea for unity among the factions; cf. Lampe, *Ecclesiae*. Some have argued that 1 Cor. 2.6–16 achieves this through irony or polemic: Willis, 'Mind', 121; R. W. Funk, *Language, Hermeneutic, and Word of God* (New York: Harper, 1966) 300. However, whether or not, as Willis claims, all difficulties in 2.6–16 are solved by seeing the passage as a polemic against the Corinthians is questionable. I shall address this again in the following chapter.
There is a different emphasis on wisdom in 1 Cor. 1.18–2.5 and 2.6–16 but the basic objective is the same. In 2.6–16 the essential antithesis of human and divine wisdom begun in 1.18–2.5 is retained. True wisdom (as μυστήριον) is still radically different from worldly wisdom and is only revealed by the Spirit of God. Vice versa in 1.18–2.5, wisdom is not completely negative: God acted by his own wisdom (1.21) and Christ is the wisdom of God (1.24, 30). Therefore, it is not a question of contradiction between 1.18–2.5 and 2.6–16 but one of emphasis, the former more negative and the latter more positive concerning wisdom (W. Schrage, *Der erste Brief an die Korinther [1Kor 1,1–6,11]* [EKK 7/1; Neukirchen-Vluyn: Neukirchener Verlag, 1991] 268). Indeed, H.-C. Kammler (*Kreuz und Weisheit: Eine exegetische Untersuchung zu 1Kor 1,10–3,4* [WUNT 159; Tübingen: Mohr/Siebeck, 2003] 245) suggests that the messages of 1.18–2.5 and 2.6–3.4 are identical and that the distinction Paul is elaborating is an absolute one between 'Geretteten und Verlorenen'.
[113] Fee (*Presence*, 98) says that Paul uses the language of the opposition 'but filling it with his own content', which 'differs radically' from theirs.
[114] Cf. Käsemann, 'Korinther', 269: 'Jeder Christ hat für [Paul] ihn nach Röm. 8,9 den Geist und ist darum Pneumatiker'; Stuhlmacher, 'Bedeutung', 158; Lindemann, *Korintherbrief*, 74; Thiselton, *Corinthians*, 231; Bucer on 1 Cor. 2.15 quoted by Schrage, *Korinther* I, 276: '(A)lle gläubigen künden und sollen alle ding, so den glauben und gotsdienst belangen, erkennen, ortern und urteilen'. Witherington (*Conflict*, 126f.) also argues against a special elite (against E. Ellis) but for mature Christians (Witherington, *Conflict*, 122f.).
[115] Schrage (*Korinther* I, 240) argues for a 'Weisheit auf höherer Ebene mit neuen Inhalten für Fortgeschrittene'.
[116] For Paul it is an 'absolute distinction' between the 'natural man' and the one who has received the Spirit and his/her wisdom. Further, Paul contrasts the Corinthian quest to find the most advanced teacher in wisdom with his portrayal of the joint effort of himself and other teachers in building up the community together (Davis, *Wisdom*, 144).
[117] Dunn, *Jesus*, 291: '*Paul never addresses himself to a leadership group within a community* (apart from Phil. 1.1). His instructions and exhortations are generally addressed to the community as a whole.'
[118] Schürmann, 'Gnadengaben', 263; Campenhausen, *Authority*, 64.

The fact that διακρίσεις πνευμάτων is a χάρισμα, a 'gracious gift',[119] implies that not all will necessarily have the same intensity of ability to discern and that some in the congregation will particularly be known for their ability to assess, evaluate and interpret spiritual manifestations. Yet this does not mean that we need to envision a stark differentiation between this gift of discernment and the other discernment passages. For Paul it is not a contradiction to allow some 'specialists' to receive a gift and an exhortation for all to have the ability to practise that gift.[120] In other words, the existence of a gift does not preclude that the rest of the congregation cannot have the ability to 'take part' in some form or other in that gift (14.5).

With that in mind, we turn to the question of who are meant by οἱ ἄλλοι in 14.29. An impressive amount of support can be found for both the view that it is the rest of the prophets[121] or the view that it is the rest of the church.[122] Some of those proposing that it is only the prophets admit that generally Paul calls for the whole congregation to discern spiritual

---

[119] I follow Turner's (*Spirit*, 261–7) understanding that the term need not necessarily be directly connected to the Spirit or to grace nor that it need be seen as a 'short-term' event (it could even be permanent: *Spirit*, 279–85). But for the opposing views, see Dunn (*Jesus*, 199–256; particularly 253ff.) and S. Schatzmann (*A Pauline Theology of Charismata* [Peabody, MA: Hendrickson, 1987] 1–13).

[120] This is particularly evident for prophecy. As we shall note, Gordon Fee even points out that the regulation of prophecy in these verses is appealing not only to those who have the gift of prophecy, but to the whole congregation. Both in v. 24 and v. 31 he sees the 'all' referring to the whole congregation just as much as v. 1 and v. 12 are. 'This does not mean of course, that all *will* or *do* prophesy. It is simply to note that Paul's concern here is not with a group of prophets, but with the *functioning* of prophecy in the assembly' (*Presence*, 253). Indeed, Grudem himself believes that 'several of the gifts Paul mentions are simply special or "highly developed" abilities which correspond to general abilities possessed by all believers' (cited in Forbes, *Prophecy*, 266; cf. further, 269).

[121] Grosheide, *Corinthians*, 338; Lenski, *Corinthians*, 611; Ellis, 'Prophecy'; Panagopoulos, *Vocation*, 52; H. Greeven, 'Propheten, Lehrer, Vorsteher bei Paulus', *ZNW* 44 (1952–53) 6; Conzelmann, *Korinther*, 298; N. I. J Engelsen, *Glossolalia and Other Forms of Prophetic Speech According to 1 Corinthians 12–14* (Ann Arbor, MI: UMI, 1970) 170; Wolff, *Korinther*, 139; Chevallier, *Esprit*, 190f.; Hill, *Prophecy*, 133; Gillespie, *Theologians*, 162f.; Aune, *Prophecy*, 207f., 219f.; Boring, *Sayings*, 66; Robertson and Plummer, *Corinthians*, 320.

[122] Wendland, *Korinther*, 114; Lietzmann,*Korinther*, 75; Grudem, *Gift*, 60–2; Barrett, *Corinthians*, 328; Wengst, 'Zusammenkommen', 551–4; Fee, *Presence*, 252; Forbes, *Prophecy*, 265–8; Crone, *Prophecy*, 222; Wire, *Women*, 148; D. A. Carson, *Showing the Spirit: A Theological Exposition of 1 Corinthians 12–14* (Carlisle: Paternoster Press, 1995) 120. Thiselton (*Corinthians*, 1140f.) claims that in general it is the congregation as a whole but that '*apostles* and *teachers* have a special role'.

A few other positions have (legitimately) received less attention: Dautzenberg (*Prophetie*, 286) says 'alle zur Deutung befähigten', which of course leans on his interpretation of διακρίνω. Cf. E.-B. Allo, *Première épître aux Corinthiens* (Paris: Gabalda, 1956²) 370: '[C]'étaient tous ceux qui avaient le "discernement des esprits", principalement les chefs de l'assemblée'. Allo's appears to be the only position which actually refers back to the

phenomena but see an exception here on mostly co-textual grounds (that is, mainly ch. 14).[123] However, when the text is examined, no good reason can be found to limit the discernment to just the prophets. Both Grudem and Fee argue that essentially the term οἱ ἄλλοι (meaning 'someone else' or 'the others that make up the larger group') is less ambiguous than it seems. If Paul had meant the rest of the prophets, 'the more correct term' would have been οἱ λοίποι.[124] Indeed, as noted before, Fee shows that 1 Cor. 14 appeals not to a certain group of prophets but to the functioning of prophecy in the whole congregation.[125] Hence, Paul has the entire assembly in mind.[126] Moreover, Grudem also claims that it is difficult to conceive that 'teachers, administrators and other church leaders without special gifts of prophecy would sit passively awaiting the verdict of an elite group before they knew whether to accept a prophecy as genuine'.[127] Thus, finally, I can affirm that it is Paul's concern in 14.29 that the community as a whole should participate in reaching a common mind on the validity and meaning of prophecies.[128] Yet some members of the congregation may have a specific ability or intensity of the gift to discern.

gift of discernment (1 Cor. 12.10). But there is no plausible way to understand οἱ ἄλλοι as limited to those with the special gift of discernment.

[123] Dunn ('Congregation', 226) thinks 'the most natural way' is to see that 'those most experienced in the exercise of the gift (of prophecy) should bear the primary responsibility for evaluating particular prophetic utterances – no doubt, partly at least because their personal experience would have schooled them to recognise when a prophecy was outrunning the inspiration of the Spirit'. Yet in the next paragraph he partially contradicts this by saying 'that it is unlikely that he confined the process of evaluation to the prophets', because 'the implication of 1 Co 2,12–16 is precisely that *all* who have received thereby have been given an enabling to recognize and understand the gifts of God and to make a Spirit-informed judgement on matters of the Spirit (including prophecy).' He goes on to confirm this with 1 Thess. 5.20f. Finally, he tries to solve this contradiction by, to my mind, hypothetically arguing that the Corinthian church situation demanded a limit on the evaluation process. It seems his assessment of the general tendency in Paul (all should evaluate) should lead him to rethink both the primary assumption regarding οἱ ἄλλοι and his latter hypothesis. Cf. Aune (*Prophecy*, 219–21) for a similar twofold position.

[124] Fee, *Presence*, 252; cf. Grudem, *Gift*, 61.

[125] Fee, *Presence*, 252; similarly, see Crone, *Prophecy*, 222.

[126] This point is in response to those who consider the rest of the immediate co-text (especially v. 31) to be referring only to those able to prophesy and hence to be an argument that the ἄλλοι is also referring to them (cf. Hill, *Prophecy*, 133).

Further, Forbes has countered Aune's argument that 1 Cor. 14.37f. ('Anyone, who claims to be a prophet, or to have spiritual powers, must acknowledge that I am writing . . .') is evidence that the prophets discerned. He shows that Aune misses the polemic or irony against precisely the prophets or spiritual ones, since Paul is not sure whether this group will accept his words (Forbes, *Prophecy*, 267).

[127] Grudem, *Gift*, 61. Indeed as Forbes (*Prophecy*, 269) points out, it is this type of elitism that Paul is trying to counter.

[128] Wengst, 'Zusammenkommen', 554.

E.   Conclusion

In this chapter I have addressed a number of issues in my attempt to gain some insight into the nature of the gift of discernment in 1 Cor. 12.10. While in the introduction we noted that some scholars have been wary of identifying a critical attitude towards spiritual phenomena, my own work has emphasised the significance of an evaluation of all reality and in particular of spiritual manifestations. Rather than destroy the unity of the community, my own argument proposed that discernment enhances its cohesion. The whole community is responsible for the spiritual health of the whole community. Moreover, the call for discernment is wary of triumphalism in that it grounds spiritual phenomena in the concrete reality of church life by observing their ethical impact. While macrocosmic speculation is a part of Paul's theology, it is balanced by ethical sobriety. With that, spiritual discernment becomes conceptually linked with the ethical deliberation discussed in the previous chapter.

However, I have not only emphasised the evaluative aspect of discernment. Against Grudem's complete dismissal of Dautzenberg's initiative, we saw plausible linguistic and conceptual reasons for retaining an interpretative element. Hence, we observed the contours of a hermeneutical and theological act being established. This in turn seems to be consistent with the vision of Käsemann, Stuhlmacher and Beker, who understand the gift broadly as a process of theologising. But this requires more thought, and I must elaborate this in the following chapter.

At this point a summary must suffice: 'The importance of this charisma as a regulative [and signifying] force within the charismatic community can hardly be overemphasiszed.'[129]

---

[129] Dunn, *Jesus*, 236.

4

DISCERNING ALL THINGS: THE STRUCTURE OF PAUL'S EPISTEMOLOGY

A.   Introduction

ὁ δὲ πνευματικὸς ἀνακρίνει [τὰ] πάντα (1 Cor. 2.15a).

Is Paul really serious? Or is he quoting a Corinthian catch phrase?[1] Is it merely the mandate to discern all 'spiritual' knowledge or a new all-encompassing epistemological potential? In any case, this statement calls for our attention. Gordon Fee has proposed that the whole of 1 Corinthians is a spelling out of this statement.[2] My own argument will broaden this assertion: I propose that discernment reflects Paul's theologising as a whole and his expectation for the believers' comprehension of his theology.

In order to substantiate this claim we must investigate the epistemological structure of Paul's thought generally. That means studying the *formation* and *verification* of truth in his theology.[3] Further, we must arbitrate between conflicting approaches to Paul: can the truth of the gospel

---

[1] Concerns about the authorship of this passage, due to its unfamiliar terminology, should be seen within the general redaction-critical research on the integrity of 1 Corinthians. Various attempts have been made to see the letter as a composite of more than one earlier letter (famously by W. Schmithals, 'Die Korintherbriefe als Briefsammlung', *ZNW* 64 [1973] 263–88, into nine letters for 1 and 2 Corinthians). However, Thiselton, following Fee and Collins, is right that the valid concerns about integrity should only lead to partition theories if scholarship '*fails to reveal a genuine coherence*' within the letter (*Corinthians*, 39).

  For our passage this means we need to investigate how the statement of v. 15 can be integrated into a concept of discernment. How serious was Paul about this assertion? Was this 'principle' 'unthinkable' for him (R. A. Horsley, 'Wisdom of Word and Words of Wisdom', *CBQ* 39 [1977] 238), or is it rather a remarkable feature of his thought?

[2] Fee, *Presence*, 108. The issues Paul deals with in 1 Corinthians are factionalism (ch. 3), morality (ch. 5), legal issues (ch. 6), spiritual issues (chs. 12–14) and theological issues (ch. 15).

[3] The question of the truth conception underlying Paul's theology is more significant than the literature reflects. Cf. J. Murphy-O'Connor ('Truth: Paul and Qumran', in *Paul and Qumran: Studies in New Testament Exegesis* [Chicago: The Priory Press, 1968] 179–230), who has traced some development from a dynamic understanding of truth in the undisputed Pauline letters to the 'knowledge of the truth' in the Pastoral Epistles where

be nailed down to certain propositions, as O. Hofius has claimed?[4] Or is it merely the existential decision to realise a truth claim, as Bultmann and his school proposed?[5] How objective and foundational is the truth claim?

My procedure will be as follows: first I will review some proposals in recent literature concerning how Paul developed his theology. By way of contrast, I will present my own argument for a depiction of the structure, limits and scope of Paul's epistemology. Then I will delineate the vital role discernment plays in signifying and verifying meaning within the portrayed structure. Finally, this will lead us back to an understanding of 1 Cor. 2.15 which coheres with its immediate context and Paul's writings as a whole.

B.   The Question of Coherence in Paul's Theology

When attempting to find an explanation about the nature of Paul's theologising we are confronted by a broad range of questions rather than answers.[6] Did he receive his theology more or less as part and parcel of his Damascus Road conversion experience?[7] Is he extrapolating his

---

a more propositional understanding of truth appears; further, R. Bultmann, 'ἀλήθεια κτλ.', *TDNT* I, 232–51.

[4] Hofius ('Wahrheit', 29) states that proclamation and belief are unthinkable for Paul without reference to the 'truth of the gospel' (Gal. 2.5, 14), which is constituted in '*assertorischen Bekenntnissätzen*' und also in *Propositionen*' (italics mine).

[5] Accordingly, true belief in God is not a general truth ('*allgemeine Wahrheit*') which one can instrumentalise, but rather needs to be seen as continually acquired anew and growing anew ('stets neu ergriffener, neu erwachsender'; R. Bultmann, 'Die Krisis des Glaubens', in *Glauben und Verstehen: Gesammelte Aufsätze* II [Tübingen: Mohr/Siebeck, 1958] 7).

[6] J. D. G. Dunn easily illustrates the confusion still felt after the ten-year experiment and symposium on understanding/locating Pauline theology by the SBL ('In Quest of Paul's Theology. Retrospect and Prospect', in Johnson and Hay [eds.], *Theology*, IV, 96f.). Two examples illustrate the diverging understanding of theology:

i   'Paul's theology is what he thinks about the transcendent and its intervention into immanent reality' (R. Scroggs, 'Salvation History: The Theological Structure of Paul's Thought [1 Thessalonians, Philippians, and Galatians]', in J. M. Bassler [ed.], *Pauline Theology* I. *Thessalonians, Philippians, Galatians, Philemon* [Minneapolis: Fortress Press, 1991] 212).

ii   'Theology emerges as Paul listens to the doubts of others and those in his own mind, [and] reflects on essential convictions . . .' (D. M. Hay, 'The Shaping of Theology in 2 Corinthians: Convictions, Doubts, and Warrants', in D. M. Hay [ed.], *Pauline Theology* II. *1 and 2 Corinthians* [Minneapolis: Fortress Press, 1993] 155).

[7] Cf. S. Kim, *The Origin of Paul's Gospel* (WUNT 2,4; Tübingen: Mohr/Siebeck, 1981). In particular, reference is made to Gal. 1.11f., in which Paul claims that the gospel is not of a 'human source, nor was I taught it, but I received it through a revelation'. We cannot address the question of how much Paul received in his conversion and how much was deliberation *post eventum* (cf. B. Corley, 'Interpreting Paul's Conversion – Then and Now', in R. N.

theology from the Christ-event?[8] Or should his theology not be sys-
tematised at all?[9] Did Paul have 'bigger fish to fry than systematic
consistency'?[10] If so, does that imply that he did not think through his
transformation in logical categories?[11] Indeed, some agreement lies in the
fact that he is not attempting a philosophically watertight presentation of
dogmatics.[12] But that makes the question of the truth claim more pressing.
Does it lie in individual propositions or only in Paul's own experience and
its consequent interpretation? Or does it lie in the individual realisation
of the truth claim?

J. Christiaan Beker has offered an incisive proposal. He has dis-
played the genius of Pauline thought by classifying its two poles and
their interaction: 'the contingent particularity of his hermeneutic and
his sure grasp of the coherent center of the gospel' (the apocalyptic interpretation of the Christ-event).[13] Beker in fact argues that the

Longenecker [ed.], *The Road from Damascus: The Impact of Paul's Conversion on his Life,
Thought, and Ministry* [Grand Rapids, MI: Eerdmans, 1997] 1–17).

[8] L. E. Keck ('Paul as Thinker', *Int.* 47 [1993] 29) shows that 'Paul was an ex post facto
thinker. Ex post facto thinking occurs not only after an event but also because of it, and with
continual reference, explicit or implicit, to it. The event's very "happenedness" requires
thinking.' Cf. Dunn, *Theology* of Paul, 177–9; 716–29.

[9] Räisänen (*Paul*, 200ff.) writes that Paul's intuitions are sound but his thinking confused.
J. S. Vos (*Die Kunst der Argumentation bei Paulus: Studien zur antiken Rhetorik* [WUNT
149; Tübingen: Mohr/Siebeck, 2002] 172) suggests that the inconsistencies in Paul can be
understood best with respect to his persuasive strategies for different situations, although
at points Paul could be called '"sophistisch" oder "eristisch"'. For a response to Räisänen,
cf. T. E. Van Spanje, *Inconsistency in Paul?: A Critique of the Work of Heikki Räisänen*
(WUNT 2,110; Tübingen: Mohr/Siebeck, 1999) 253, and his argument that '*Paul is a
consistent theologian*'.

[10] E. P. Sanders, 'Paul', in J. Barclay and J. Sweet (eds.), *Early Christian Thought
in its Jewish Context* (Cambridge: Cambridge University Press, 1996) 117. Accordingly,
consistency should not be sought 'in genius' ('Paul', 117). 'He was a pragmatic missionary
more than a reflective theologian, though his letters reveal numerous bursts of theological
creativity and brilliance' ('Paul', 128).

[11] But see H. E. Stoessel, 'Notes on Romans 12:1–2. The Renewal of the Mind and Internalizing the Truth', *Int.* 17 (1963) 172, who claims that Romans 'represents the conclusion
of [Paul's] patient, disciplined thinking'. T. Engberg-Pedersen ('Stoicism in Philippians', in
idem, *Context*, 271) shows that Paul too expresses the result of the change he has undergone
in terms of understanding (cf. Phil. 3.8, 10).

[12] Cf. L. Gaston, *Paul and the Torah* (Vancouver: University of British Columbia Press,
1987) 5–6: 'Paul is not the first Christian dogmatic theologian, writing timeless truths about
God and the world. He is rather a pastoral theologian, saying what he thinks needs to be
said in very concrete situations'. L. E. Keck (*Paul and his Letters* [Philadelphia: Fortress
Press, 1988] 63) warns against seeing Paul's letters as 'treatises in theology'. See further
J. Bassler, 'Paul's Theology: Whence and Whither?', in Hay (ed.), *Theology II*, 6; D.
Boyarin, *A Radical Jew: Paul and the Politics of Identity* (Berkeley: University of California
Press, 1994) 85. Gooch (*Knowledge*, 10) shows that Paul lacked philosophical content in
the sense that he does not offer a complete system of thought incorporating metaphysics or
epistemology.

[13] Beker, *Paul*, 351. Beker does not look for 'one dominant symbol, "concept", or
"essence"'(*Paul*, 16) in Paul but rather for a '"deep" structure of Christian apocalyptic

'coherence-contingency method' is the '*via media* between the extremes of a purely sociological analysis and a dogmatic imposition of a specific center on Paul's thought'.[14] Beker presents Paul as the 'interpreter', his originality and creativity lying in his hermeneutic not in his 'doctrinal system'.[15] In a complex relationship of 'human mediation' and 'pneumatic immediacy' Paul brings the gospel to bear on specific issues and situations.[16] 'His hermeneutic consists in the constant interaction between the coherent center of the Gospel and its contingent interpretation.'[17] Beker goes on to show how this may be 'the most striking aspect of Paul's thought', as he is able to allow for 'a wide diversity of interpretation without sacrificing its coherent center'.[18]

Beker's position has been a helpful platform for further debate. Some argument has circled around the details of his proposal without challenging the major thrust of his argument in any significant manner.[19] Others have preferred to start from a more extensive framework. D. Patte has taken a structuralist approach and attempted to present the 'specific system of convictions which can be termed a *semantic universe*'.[20] T. L. Donaldson has followed T. Kuhn's theory of paradigm

---

and a "surface" structure of a variety of symbols' (*Paul*, 17). 'The death and resurrection of Christ in their apocalyptic setting constitute the coherent core of Paul's thought' (*Paul*, 207; cf. Beker, 'Theology', 16–18).

[14] Beker, 'Theology', 24.   [15] Beker, *Paul*, 13, cf. 351.   [16] Beker, *Paul*, 115.

[17] >Beker, *Paul*, 11.   [18] Beker, *Paul*, 17 and 108, respectively.

[19] Flemming (*Essence*, 534f.) explores the manner in which Paul 'contextualised' the gospel message and argues for an interaction of (a) 'the center' (the Christ-event), (b) 'the heart' (the meaning of the Christ-event) and (c) the 'context' in which the 'Christ event comes to fresh contextual expressions'. Cf. H. W. Boers, 'The Foundations of Paul's Thought: A Methodological Investigation – The Problem of the Coherent Center of Paul's Thought', *Studia Theologica* 42 (1988) 62: 'His attempt to think on the basis of the opposed micro-universes, the existential and the social, is the coherent center of his thought.' Davis (*Structure*, 7) states that four ideas 'remain constant and ever-present', (a) Christ's death; (b) Christ's resurrection; (c) the Christian's 'death' with Christ; (d) the Christian's resurrection with Christ. P. J. Achtemeier ('The Continuing Quest for Coherence in St. Paul: An Experiment in Thought', in Lovering and Sumney (eds.), *Theology*, 145) suggests that the coherence of Paul's theology lies at its 'generative center . . . namely the resurrection of Jesus by God's power'. He compares this with the hub of the wheel and its spokes, but sees the analogy lacking the dynamic of Paul's thought. But Paul was not a 'muddle-headed dummy'. E. Lohse ('Changes of Thought in Pauline Theology? Some Reflections on Paul's Ethical Teaching in the Context of his Theology', in Lovering and Sumney (eds.), *Theology*, 160) writes that Paul 'did not change his fundamental theological thought'; however, his theology should not be seen 'as lineal' 'but as complex and dialectical' (with reference to V. P. Furnish).

[20] Patte, *Faith*, 21: 'In this phrase, the term "universe" signifies that a system of convictions establishes a realm of reality in which the various elements of human experience are interrelated in a necessary way. The term "semantic" signifies that each element of this universe is perceived as having a specific value by comparison with the values of the other elements. An element can have the value good or evil as well as any value in between.'

shifts within scientific knowledge and has argued that Paul experienced
and explicated precisely that: a theological paradigm shift.[21] However,
neither presentation is entirely convincing. While Patte's proposal misses
the fluidity in Paul's thinking (which Beker has highlighted well), Donaldson emphasises the cognitive conversion to the detriment of Paul's
emphasis on an existential transformation.[22]

C.   Paul's Epistemology: Contingent and Comprehensive

In my own proposal I intend to adjust, sharpen and broaden Beker's thesis.
On the one hand, I mean to question the concept of his coherent centre by
bringing it more into focus. On the other hand, I wish to challenge whether
his theory is comprehensive enough. Moreover, I propose to elucidate the
role discernment plays, as it has a key function in this portrayal of Paul's
epistemology and theology.

1.   Contingency

To my mind, Beker is correct in establishing the focus of Paul's thought
in the Christ-event and highlighting Paul's role as interpreter. However,
denoting the core of the gospel as 'coherent' neglects the fact that for Paul
part of its scandal is that it is in its *very essence contingent*.[23] Although
Beker also states that the centre of Paul's theology is not 'a frozen tradition that needs casuist explication for concrete cases', he misses the
contingent (but not tangential) nature of that centre.[24] Hence, not only
is the core 'incarnated' into the 'particularity of historical occasions and
contexts', it is incarnation itself.[25] This does not mean that I wish to
ascribe a full-blown incarnation Christology to Paul. It does mean that
the ultimate revelation for Paul is found '*im Tiefsten des Irdischen . . . am*

---

[21] T. L. Donaldson, *Paul and the Gentiles* (Minneapolis: Fortress Press, 1997) 293–307.

[22] Donaldson (*Paul*, 43) does not offer a convincing case for why he has not followed
Beker more. His own usage of Kuhn is 'for utilitarian purposes'. What these are is, to my
mind, not evident. He does correctly point out that all three (Patte, Beker and himself) are
involved in finding out how Paul explicates his theology (*Paul*, 42).

[23] Cf. F. Young and D. F. Ford, *Meaning and Truth in 2 Corinthians* (Biblical Foundations
in Theology; London: SPCK, 1987) 240.

[24] Beker, *Paul*, 15 (cf. 13–18). Hence, for Beker, the centre of the gospel is only coherent
in its particularity, and the gospel ceases to be gospel unless it lights up the particular world to
which it is addressed (*Paul*, 352), but he misses the point that the Christ-event is conditional
on/subject to human actions.

[25] Beker, *Paul*, 351.

Kreuz' (1 Cor. 1–4).[26] But can we elucidate the term 'contingent' more closely?[27]

Naturally the ultimate revelation in Paul includes the resurrection, which, because it has a certain 'basicality' or fundamental status (1 Cor. 15), should maybe not be understood as a contingent event.[28] However, resurrection remains inherently dependent on incarnation and death. This dependence requires of us to rethink the centre of Paul's theology.[29] God reveals his character himself, in the form of a real person who is *vulnerable* as a slave on a cross (Phil. 2.5–11).[30] Christ becomes subject to the judgement of humanity.[31] The divine weakness is not only a historical scandal but it also opens up a continuous epistemological scandal (1 Cor. 1.18–20). If, in other words, the vulnerability of incarnation is crucial for the redemption story, its impetus is lost in Beker's coherent-contingent scheme. Why? Because the very centre of Paul's thought is an event which is dependent on the relativity of factors such as time, space and human action. Therefore, I argue, the *expression* of the theological centre of Paul's thought needs to reflect the contingent *nature* of the incarnation. What are the consequences of such an argument?

---

[26] Sellin, 'Geheimnis', 90.

[27] The term 'contingency' is naturally not Pauline, but H. Lübbe (*Religion nach der Aufklärung* [Graz: Styria, 1990²], 150ff.) shows that it is not a neologism and it stands in line with a long tradition of theological thought.

[28] Thiselton, *Corinthians*, 1218: 1 Cor. 15 offers the basis for what 'is known in theories of knowledge as a "soft" or "modest" foundationalism as against either "strong" foundationalism (Descartes) or nonfoundationalism (postmodernity). Paul agrees that many Christian beliefs are *mutually* supportive but gives a degree of primacy (ἐν πρώτοις . . . παρέλαβον . . . κατὰ τὰς γραφάς, vv.3–5).' Nevertheless, it will be my argument (cf. p. 88, where I will explain the term 'foundationalism' in more detail) that foundationalism does not do justice to the comprehensive shift in perception that Paul envisaged was necessary for true understanding.

[29] We should also note that this ultimate revelation is embedded within the story of salvation which includes the story of Israel. 'Thus, to make ethical discernments is, for Paul, simply to recognize our place within the epic story of redemption' (Hays, *Vision*, 45–6; cf. Scott, *Epistemology*, 159–276). Cf. Ehrensperger ('Reasoning') who shows how Paul inhabits scripture while at the same time he reinterprets it (further, 2 Cor. 3–4).

[30] U. B. Müller (*Der Brief des Paulus an die Philipper* [ThHK 11/1; Leipzig: Evangelische Verlagsanstalt, 1993] 103), with regard to Phil. 2.7, suggests that Paul is attempting to reveal the real personhood of the one who was originally in God's 'Gestalt'. This opposes the later tendency (such as is expressed in docetism) to see the 'Menschengestalt' only as a 'Verkleidung', or against the conclusion that in the 'Menschwerdung Gottes' humans can now become divine (D. Zeller, 'Die Menschwerdung des Sohnes Gottes und antike Religionsgeschichte', in idem [ed.], *Menschwerdung Gottes – Vergöttlichung von Menschen* [Göttingen: Vandenhoeck & Ruprecht, 1988] 175). Cf. J. D. G. Dunn, *Christology in the Making: An Inquiry into the Origins of the Doctrine of the Incarnation* (London: SCM Press, 1980) 262: Christ was thought of as '*the climactic embodiment of God's power and purpose . . . God himself reaching out to men . . . God's clearest self-expression . . .*'

[31] See Fee, *Philippians*, 217, on Phil. 2.7f.

Two major implications of this contingent centre need to be considered. They are two sides of the same coin but I shall deal with them separately: (a) Knowledge of God cannot be objectified, it requires existential appropriation; (b) Because God reveals himself in contingency, all of reality is qualified, called into question and hence requires a comprehensive reassessment. Finally, it is my thesis that these two partially antithetical aspects are reconciled through discernment.

2.   Existential Appropriation of Truth

My first point is that God's revelation in or as contingency calls into question and challenges any attempt to domesticate and objectify God in axioms and propositions.[32] On the one hand, this implies the awareness that all present understanding is of a limited and fallible nature, prone to being instrumentalised.[33] As in the Platonist tradition (and partially evident in Philo), for Paul perfect knowledge is indirect, referring to a reality beyond the perceivable world (1 Cor. 13.11–12).[34] Indeed, the attempt to domesticate God is the ultimate sin of the 'fools' (Rom. 1.22f.). Here Rom. 1.18–25 should be brought to bear on 1 Cor. 1.18–2.5. In both passages Paul resists attempts which no longer allow God to be God.[35]

On the other hand, it means the truth of the gospel can only be realised in an existential realisation, which in turn means true *knowledge is inherently*

[32] K. Niederwimmer ('Erkennen und Lieben. Gedanken zum Verhältnis von Gnosis und Agape im ersten Korintherbrief', *Kerygma und Dogma* 11 [1965] 94) claims that God cannot be made the object because man becomes the object of God. S. Vollenweider ('Weisheit am Kreuzweg. Zum theologischen Programm von 1Kor 1 und 2', in Dettwiler and Zumstein (eds.), *Kreuzestheologie*, 58) believes that the Logos of the cross calls for systematic theology and simultaneously questions any attempt to functionalise or apprehend the word.

[33] Cf. Thiselton, *Corinthians*, 1069. Voss (*Wort*, 185) depicts well the dialectic between the fact that the believer can discern everything (indirectly through Christ) and the fragmentary nature of all knowledge (*Wort*, 197).

[34] C. Senft, *La première épître de Saint-Paul aux Corinthiens* (CNT VII; Geneva: Labor et Fides, 1979) 171: 'La connaissance . . . est imparfaite, provisoire . . .'; cf. Philo, *Jos.* 16; *Spec.* 1.2. Concerning the similarity to Plato's cave in *Republic* 7.514ff, cf. Gooch, *Knowledge*, 186f. n. 13, for a nuanced comparison: 'Plato, Paul, and many others agree that mirror images, like shadows, are derivative and dependent; they do not give us real objects.' Ciholas, 'Knowledge', 195: 'Paul shares with Plato an intense desire to explain the limitations preventing man from obtaining true knowledge.'

[35] P. Lampe, 'Theological Wisdom and "Word about the Cross". The Rhetorical Scheme in I Corinthians 1–4', *Int.* 44 (1990) 123. This does not mean Paul would deny that God is absolute, but it does imply that 'any human theology is moved into a constant crisis by its own subject for discussion – by God. This subject in its power . . . constantly withdraws itself from human theology, putting up resistance against domestication' ('Wisdom', 122).

linked to ethics (cf. for instance 1 Cor. 8.1ff.; 13.2). How is this so? Young and Ford succinctly argue that, because of God's personal involvement in history, transcendence needs to be redefined. Rather than define it in spatial terms or by 'maximising' 'our ordinary notions of power, knowledge, presence etc.', 'transcendence is defined through love, through being for others. This is "the beyond in the midst", or "ethical transcendence", in a broad sense of ethics.'[36] For Paul, Jesus is at the same time the paradigm of God's self-revelation and also of true humanity (Phil. 2.5ff.).[37] It is a *paradigm of involvement* and contingency, a model for true existence.[38] As God becomes involved with humanity, so the believers must become involved with Christ and in the lives of others.[39] And this in turn qualifies epistemology.

P. Lampe has rightly pointed out that the gospel 'is delivered up to the empirical judgment of the Corinthians in spite of its revelatory character'.[40] To know is to test the cross empirically; to know is to become existentially involved. It is a knowledge which rests not on words but on Christ's power (1 Cor. 2.5). Understanding entails that 'the *knower* is changed, experiencing a drastic . . . transformation of identity'.[41] Knowing

---

[36] Young and Ford, *Meaning*, 243f.

[37] 'Jesus provided not just the pattern of humankind . . . but also the paradigm for God's self-revelation' (J. D. G. Dunn, 'Why "Incarnation"? A Review of Recent New Testament Scholarship', in S. E. Porter, P. Joyce and D. E. Orton [eds.], *Crossing the Boundaries: Essays in Biblical Interpretation in Honour of Michael D. Goulder* [Leiden: Brill, 1994] 255). 'Instead of formulating an abstract system and ignoring contingent situations or formulating an expedient Christology and ignoring matters of principle, Paul brought foundational truth into dialogue with individual problems' (S. G. Sinclair, *Jesus Christ According to Paul: The Christologies of Paul's Undisputed Epistles and the Christology of Paul* [Berkeley: Bibal Press, 1988] 142–3); for foundationalism, cf. below (C3).

[38] Pauline Christology is also an '*Existenzentwurf*', a 'Symbolsystem, in dem ein entschränktes und gesteigertes Leben möglich ist' (W. Rebell, *Christologie und Existenz bei Paulus: Eine Auslegung von 2.Kor 5,14–21* [Stuttgart: Calwer Verlag, 1992] 7). Cf. Backhaus, 'Evangelium', 9–31; on Colossians, M. Dübbers, 'Christologie und Existenz. Eine Studie zur Intention des Kolosserbriefes' 'Unpubl. PhD dissertation, University Tübingen: 2000) 299ff., for the close contact of Christology and existence/parenesis and the writer's aim to show the readers their '*existentielle Christusbestimmtheit*'.

[39] 'Because that Son has become human, other humans who are incorporated into him can become children of God . . .' (G. W. E. Nickelsburg, 'The Incarnation: Paul's Solution to the Universal Human Predicament', in B. A. Pearson [ed.], *The Future of Early Christianity: Essays in Honor of Helmut Koester* [Minneapolis: Fortress Press, 1991] 354).

[40] Lampe, 'Wisdom', 128. Lampe must be credited with an incisive argument against the propositional understanding of Schlier (see my own contention with Schlier below). Paul does not expect the Corinthians to '"swallow" or decline' the word of the cross but 'steps down from the level of fundamental theological propositions' and 'presents an *empirical attempt*' (Lampe, 'Wisdom', 126; contra Niederwimmer, 'Erkennen', 80).

[41] C. B. Cousar, *A Theology of the Cross* (Minneapolis: Fortress Press, 1990) 180. 'The cross helps no one who does not hear the word of the cross and ground his faith on that'

God then implies character formation.[42] But am I then just arguing for
a subjective experience, which will vary from expression to expression
and cannot be objectively verified?

In his extensive treatment of truth within New Testament hermeneutics, C. Landmesser makes this objection against Bultmann (who partially
follows Heidegger). Landmesser believes that to make truth an existential
category relegates logical consistency ('Konsistenz') to a secondary position. Further, such a conception of truth lacks pragmatic as well as inter-
subjective and communicable truth criteria.[43] Rather, he insists, truth must
be semantically verified because truth is dependent on language in the
same manner as the world is dependent on language ('sprachabhängig').[44]
Hence, Landmesser argues for a propositional understanding of truth.[45]
But does this reflect Paul's hermeneutics and his expectation that believers
will comprehend the gospel?[46]

(E. Käsemann, 'The Saving Significance of the Death of Jesus in Paul', *Perspectives on
Paul* [trans. M. Kohl; Philadelphia: Fortress Press, 1971] 50). Thiselton (*Corinthians*, 407)
points out that Paul attaches two meanings to truth, namely 'in contrast to falsehood' and
as it 'relates to the Christian's *identity* and a *Christian lifestyle*'. Moreover, 'early Christian
confessions embodied *both* a *cognitive truth-claiming content* . . . *and a self-involving
personal stake and personal signature* in my "*world*"' (*Corinthians*, 630; further, 276,
278 on the reception of 1 Cor. 2.6–16 by Irenaeus and Origen respectively with such an
existential view of truth). Cf. further Pedersen, 'Understanding', 31; Stoessel, 'Notes', 169:
'But since it is a theology of transformation, *this* truth must become indwelling . . .'

[42] Furnish, 'Truth', 174. H. Schlier contradicts himself. Although at one point he says that
knowledge is the existential 'Eingehen' into the whole-life-encompassing call of God ('Die
Erkenntnis nach den Briefen des Apostels Paulus', in *Besinnung auf das Neue Testament:
Exegetische Aufsätze und Verträge* II [Freiburg: Herder, 1964] 336), at an earlier point he says
God reveals himself in the kerygma which comes in the form of fixed formulas which only
require acknowledgement ('Kerygma und Sophia. Zur neutestamentlichen Grundlegung
des Dogmas', in *Die Zeit der Kirche* [Freiburg: Herder, 1956] 206–32).

[43] C. Landmesser, *Wahrheit*, 316, 318–21. He quotes an answer of Bultmann's to
K. Jaspers on the question of verification, which sums up Bultmann's position well: 'Offenbarung ist Offenbarung nur *in actu* – und *pro me*; sie wird nur in der persönlichen Entscheidung als solche verstanden und anerkannt' (Landmesser, *Wahrheit*, 317). For Bultmann,
then, the object itself is the criterion, which is unacceptable for Landmesser. Moreover,
Landmesser criticises Bultmann for believing that the uniqueness ('Einmalige') cannot be
expressed in language (*Wahrheit*, 321) and states that Bultmann's/Heidegger's identification
of truth with essence ('Eigentlichkeit') has confused the investigation of truth (*Wahrheit*,
322).

[44] Landmesser, *Wahrheit*, 106. He follows Puntel in claiming: 'No entity without intelligibility.' Cf. his reading and reception of H. Weder (Landmesser, *Wahrheit*, 418–22).

[45] 'Verhalte bzw. Propositionen sind nicht sprachliche, aber sprachabhängige Entitäten'
(Landmesser, *Wahrheit*, 106). He does not propose that these truths are eternal (*Wahrheit*,
430) nor that they are fundamentalist (*Wahrheit*, 504). His point is that they must be semantically verifiable.

[46] Landmesser's aim is to work with the same 'Wahrheitsbegriff' in the NT as in other
disciplines/sciences (*Wahrheit*, 427).

Clearly, for Paul, communicable verification is of significance. A rejection of this would invalidate his whole theological enterprise.[47] Comprehension of the gospel, as I shall argue in the next section, is paramount. Moreover, 1 Cor. 14 shows how, for Paul, allotted place, order and differentiation are important criteria for spiritual worship. A comprehensible hermeneutic is important (cf., for example, the λόγοι τῷ νοΐ in 14.19).[48] And this ordered comprehension is to some extent tied to verbal discourse.[49] However, to equate truth with semantic verification is theoretically questionable and does not cohere with Paul's overall emphasis.[50]

Truth, for Paul, is not merely assent to a proposition.[51] The contingency of the gospel cannot be encapsulated in a propositional account.[52] As

[47] Voss, *Wort*, 279; Beker, *Paul*, 10: 'The objective content and universal claim of the gospel compel Paul to give an orderly intelligible account of God's act in Christ . . . Faith in Christ, then, is never divorced from knowledge and intelligible coherence . . .' From my point of view 'objective' is not a precise enough term; cf. my discussion below.

[48] Thiselton (*Corinthians*, 1074) points this out with respect to 1 Cor. 12.4–31 and 14.26–40. Both passages include Paul's vision of discernment in worship; cf. *Corinthians*, 1162ff. (1 Cor. 14.37f.) and the importance of coherence in sifting speech.

[49] Thiselton, *Corinthians*, 1103–5; Bockmuehl, *Revelation*, 227. Moores (*Rationality*, 135) suggests that 'although the correct understanding of Paul's words is thus in a certain sense placed outside his power to promote, verbal discourse is nevertheless viewed by him as the fundamental channel of communication. It is through the power of words to convey meaning that the Spirit accomplishes its work.' 'However richly endowed by the Holy Spirit the human capacity for understanding may be, the instruments of semiosis through which understanding occurs remain those with which the limited world of our perceptions provide us' (*Rationality*, 160). While the general thrust of this is correct, it misses the fact that comprehension can take place through being as well as through semantics.

[50] On a theoretical level the paradigmatic work by Gadamer and Kuhn should make us wary of attempts to exclude the realm of being from comprehension (cf. R. B. Matlock, *Unveiling the Apocalyptic Paul. Paul's Interpreters and the Rhetoric of Criticism* [JSNT.S 127; Sheffield: Sheffield Academic Press, 1996] 329ff.). It is noteworthy that Landmesser has no discussion with Gadamer. Moreover, the attempt to link truth exclusively with speech is a remnant of the positivist school and overlooks the fact that there is 'organized, complicated and highly sophisticated thinking' which cannot be articulated in language (B. Magee, *Confessions of a Philosopher: A Journey through Western Philosophy* [London: Phoenix, 2000²] 105, cf. 86, 100, 112).

[51] Cf. C. P. Price, 'Revelation as our Knowledge of God', in J. T. Carroll, C. H. Cosgrove and E. E. Johnson (eds.), *Faith and History: Essays in Honor of P. W. Meyer* (Atlanta: Scholars Press, 1990) 314, 326; Beker, 'Theology', 18ff.; Barclay, *Truth*, 94; Voss, *Wort*, 276. The balanced view in A. C. Thiselton, *Interpreting God and the Postmodern Self: On Meaning, Manipulation and Promise* (Edinburgh: T&T Clark, 1995) 71, 104, has shifted in favour of strengthening the role of the subject in perceiving truth, which is slightly different from his argument in 'Truth, ἀλήθεια', *NIDNTT* III, 899, 901, where he was more wary of relativism.

[52] Against Hofius, 'Wahrheit', 29ff. This also means being wary of giving certain terms an absolute meaning 'by abstracting a universally applicable meaning from them' but rather observing how Paul used them (possibly differently) in specific settings, as does C. J. Roetzel (*Paul: The Man and the Myth* [Columbia: University of South Carolina, 1998] 5).

argued earlier, the contingent nature of the incarnation has consequences
for its expression(s). These expressions should not be identified with *the*
ultimate and universal meaning. 'The center of Paul's thought transcends
every instance of its expression.'[53] Rather, this centre must continually
prove itself anew (cf. 1 Thess. 1.5; 1 Cor. 4.20; Phil. 3.10).[54] And it
does this in *encounter*: God encounters humanity (Gal. 4.9; 1 Cor. 8.3).
This redefines subjectivity and objectivity. G. Ebeling speaks of a revolutionised subject–object relationship in Paul: 'Gemeint ist ein Begeg-
nungsgeschehen, das den Menschen ganzheitlich in Anspruch nimmt';
central to this encounter is the whole person.[55] Consequently, we must
reject complete objectivity, because neutrality is impossible. Knowledge
is related to the recipient and to the world he/she lives in. There is no
value-free wisdom.[56] Nevertheless, Paul need not be suspected of subjectivity because reality remains firmly rooted in God.[57]

It does mean that we can allege that God's ultimate revelation must
be embedded in 'Lebensvollzug'.[58] In 1 Thess. 2.13 Paul makes it clear
that the truth of the word is visible because it 'works' in the believers
(ἐνεργεῖται ἐν ὑμῖν). Revelation is not a theoretical statement but a mindset
(Rom. 8.6; 1 Cor. 2.16). 'Knowledge is meaningless if dissociated from

[53] Boers, 'Foundations', 61. Beker (*Paul*, 358) claims that true meaning cannot be identified with the text itself, but it has to become apparent in the text.

[54] Cf. W. Pannenberg, 'Was ist Wahrheit?', in *Grundfragen Systematischer Theologie*
(Göttingen: Vandenhoeck & Ruprecht, 1979[3]) 207f.; Thiselton, *God*, 38.

[55] G. Ebeling (*Die Wahrheit des Evangeliums: Eine Lesehilfe zum Galaterbrief*
[Tübingen: Mohr/Siebeck, 1981] 305) suggests that our scientific understanding of the
subject–object relationship will not suffice because to know God means to be known by
him. Cf. Conzelmann, 'Paulus', 240, who thinks that the content of knowledge in 1 Corinthians is to understand being as such ('das Sein schlechthin'), namely, the being of the world
of pneuma.

[56] Schrage (*Korinther* I, 277) argues that there is no value-free, neutral and objective
wisdom, but only a wisdom which is directed by God or the powers of the aeon. Everything
is qualified in one direction or the other, for or against God. But he is keen to show that this
does not imply an irrational theology (cf. Schrage, 'Verhältnis', 502). While I do not wish
to equate knowledge with virtue, virtue *is* an important factor for discerning truth. Jaquette
(*Adiaphora*, 207) states that Paul is not concerned with virtue as the moralists define the
summum bonum but that he switches their code of indifferents to suit his purposes.

[57] Young and Ford, *Meaning*, 155. As Pannenberg ('Wahrheit', 215) shows, in a theistic
framework a subjective approach to truth does not necessitate relativism. Both the Christ-
event and the Spirit (as I shall still argue) *are* objective realities (cf. Lampe, *Ecclesiae*,
110).

[58] E. Fuchs, 'Wahrheit', *RGG*[3] VI, 1515. Contra E. Käsemann, 'Zur paulinischen Anthropologie', in *Paulinische Perspektiven* (Tübingen: Mohr/Siebeck, 1972[2]) 55. Nevertheless,
some of Paul's interpreters, like Paul Tillich, have overemphasised the existential approach
(for such a criticism, cf. V. Nuovo, 'Resurrection, Realism and Truth: Reflections on Paul
Tillich and St. Paul', in G. Hummel [ed.], *Truth and History: A Dialogue with Paul Tillich*
[Berlin: W. de Gruyter, 1998] 211–26).

life and cannot be defined apart from being.'[59] This in turn implies that theory in Paul cannot be divorced from praxis, and theology is inherently related to ethics.[60] While others have shown that ethics is a necessary outworking of Paul's theology, I argue that it is an *inherent* part.[61] But this will still become clearer in the latter half of the book.

3.   Comprehensive Perception of Reality

We turn now to the second implication of God's revelation in/as contingency. Since God becomes personally involved in history, the whole understanding of history is transformed. This is where a key difference with Platonic thought becomes apparent. 'Die Unverfügbarkeit . . . der Wahrheit Gottes hängt also mit ihrer Geschichtlichkeit zusammen.'[62] Thiselton rightly writes that Pannenberg (who in turn continues the Hegelian tradition) reflects the thinking of Paul in the notion that the Christ-event is the hermeneutical key for the whole of history.[63] And indeed, not only is history as a whole transformed, but along with it the perception of reality. God's involvement in history challenges all other schemes of reality.[64] Why is this so?

Paul was motivated by a desire for the unity of reality.[65] For 'from' God and 'through' God and 'to' God are all things (Rom. 11.36). While

[59] Ciholas, 'Knowledge', 195.

[60] Cf. Scott, *Epistemology*, 155–7; Lewis, *Life*, 82. Engberg-Pedersen (*Paul*, 6) rightly refers to the Geertzian thesis that worldview ('is') and ethos ('ought') underlie a constant interchange. He goes on to show how the ethical is also an interpretation of the theological and vice versa (*Paul*, 30), and how identity and behaviour belong together (*Paul*, 327). Cf. Brown, *Cross*, 146, who states that in 1 Cor. 1–4 epistemology and ethics belong together, contra Käsemann, Beker and Martyn.

[61] For a succession of theory and praxis cf. R. Bultmann, 'γινώσκω κτλ.', *TDNT* I, 707. S. M. Ogden ('Paul in Contemporary Theology and Ethics: Presuppositions of Critically Appropriating Paul's Letters Today', in Lovering and Sumney [eds.], *Theology*, 292) differentiates between a primary level of *vital* questions regarding 'self-understanding and life-praxis' and a secondary level of critical reflection regarding '*theoretical* questions about the meaning of our answers and about the validity of the claims that we make . . .' While theology is '*oriented*' by vital questions, it is not '*constituted*' by these. This distinction does not reflect my own portrayal of Paul's theology, not even for analytical purposes.

[62] Pannenberg, 'Wahrheit', 209. At certain points, Pannenberg's distinction between Jewish and Greek truth is too simple; however, the main thrust of his argument is helpful.

[63] Thiselton (*Corinthians*, 1064f.) with reference to Pannenberg ('Wahrheit', especially 216, 219).

[64] Young and Ford, *Meaning*, 240.

[65] 'Paul was motivated by a Hellenistic desire for the One, which among other things produced an ideal of a universal human essence, beyond difference and hierarchy' (Boyarin, *A Radical Jew*, 7).

this passage is of a doxological nature, it is grounded in a Christological (1 Cor. 3.21–3; 8.6) and eschatological belief that God will be 'all in all' (1 Cor. 15.28).[66] That does not mean that Paul is a pantheist, but rather, I propose, it means macro- and microcosm are related.[67] There is no Aristotelian (or Thomist) division of reality.[68] That is to say, although revelation in Christ primarily concerns the nature of God, Paul interprets humanity and creation in the light of his theology.[69] Moreover, Paul challenges a purely individualistic interpretation, because existence is influenced by the world to which one belongs.[70] Hence, the historical Christ-event has ramifications on the whole sphere of meaning, which influences a person/community. To be in Christ has rightly been interpreted as a new horizon of meaning. A new understanding of reality (*Wirklichkeitsverständnis*) is created.[71] This is a 'realm of reality' which interrelates the experience of conversion (both the believers' and Paul's) with a comprehensible explication and a long-term transformation of perception and being (cf. 1 Cor. 3.21–3).[72] To be clear, this is not an

---

[66] For a discussion of the eschatological implications of Paul's thoughts, cf. R. Bauckham, 'Time and Eternity', in idem (ed.), *God will be All in All: The Eschatology of Jürgen Moltmann* (Edinburgh: T&T Clark, 1999) 155–226.

[67] Aune, 'Models', 105–7.

[68] Against Thiselton, *Corinthians*, 282f. Thiselton contradicts himself if he wishes to see both a Thomist interpretation of Paul and Pannenberg's as legitimate. Cf. Armstrong, 'Knowledge', 449, who argues against reading Paul in the sense of a Thomist division of truth into truths discoverable by human reason and truths revealed by faith (cf. 'Knowledge', 450).

[69] Voss (*Wort*, 178) brings this out well in his thesis on 1 Cor. 2.6–16. While the focal point of understanding the Spirit-given χαρισθέντα (2.12) is the crucified one, from that point Paul interprets all of creation and anthropology. Similarly, Healy, *Heart*, 155.

[70] Käsemann, 'Anthropologie', 53f.; Barclay, *Truth*, 200.

[71] This new understanding, as C. Strecker has stressed, is not just a cognitive but a holistic transformation of being (*Die liminale Theologie des Paulus: Zugänge zur paulinischen Theologie aus kulturanthropologischer Perspektive* [FRLANT 185; Göttingen: Vandenhoeck & Ruprecht, 1999] 209). Two different approaches rightly stress the fundamental cognitive shift:

i   For seeing the shift in terms of the sociology of knowledge, cf. Theissen, *Religion*, 29. Wolter ('Ethos', 440f.) explicitly refers back to P. Berger and T. Luckman.

ii The other approach is that of Donaldson (*Paul*) noted earlier. Cf. further, Käsemann, 'Korinther', 271; U. Schnelle, *Paulus: Leben und Denken* (Berlin: W. de Gruyter, 2003) 545, who speaks of a new '*Selbst- und Zeitverständnis*', 629. The new understanding of reality (*Wirklichkeitsverständnis*) is against Bultmann (*Glauben II*, 7), who writes against portraying belief as a '*Weltanschauung*'.

[72] Patte (*Faith*, 21) uses the terminology 'realm of reality', but without sufficiently emphasising the existential element.

epistemological meta-theory.[73] Nor will a metaphysical grammar suffice to put into words the consequences of the event.[74] But then how can we categorise Paul's theology and truth formation? Is it a foundationalist approach to truth verification?

Elements of both a modest foundationalist and coherentist approach to truth are present.[75] However, neither approach reflects the comprehensive nature of Paul's epistemology enough. As M. Westphal has argued, even a modest foundationalism is in the end a 'methodological self-purification' or 'epistemological sanctification' by unaided human efforts.[76] For Paul, no one is exempt from sin, there is no noetic innocence and hence no privileged understanding (Rom. 3.23).[77] Rather, 'as sinners we "suppress the truth"', which leads to such a distortion of rationality that a total transformation of thought and being is required.[78] It is a collapse of plausibility and truth verification which leads to the belief that only 'like can know like'.[79]

---

[73] Against Vollenweider, 'Weisheit', 43.

[74] Ebeling (*Wahrheit*, 305) writes with reference to Gal. 4.9: 'In Sachen der Gotteserkenntnis jedoch gilt vollends, daß sich unsere an der Substanzmetaphysik orientierte Grammatik als unzulänglich erweist und in Bewegung gerät. Das Gott-Erkennen gründet in einem Sich-zu-erkennen-Geben Gottes.' Cf. Keck, 'Paul', 35, who suggests that Paul is interested 'in effects not in essences'. That also means that knowledge and power should not be contrasted but belong together (cf. J. A. Fitzmyer, 'To Know him and the Power of his Resurrection [Phil 3:10]', in *To Advance the Gospel* [NTS; New York: Crossroad, 1981] 209.

[75] Foundationalism holds that reasons rest on a 'foundational structure comprised of "basic" beliefs. . . The foundational propositions, though justified, derive none of their justification from other propositions.' Coherentism, in contrast, claims that 'every belief derives some of its knowledge from other beliefs' (E. Craig [ed.], *Concise Routledge Encyclopedia of Philosophy* [London: Routledge, 2000]). As noted earlier (p. 88) in 1 Cor. 15 we find a modest foundationalism (cf. Thiselton, *Corinthians*, 1218). For a moderate coherentist approach, cf. N. Elliott, *Liberating Paul: The Justice of God and the Politics of the Apostle* (Sheffield: Sheffield Academic Press, 1995), where discerning the truth implies uncovering wrong approaches to peace, security (189), justice, faith (190) and privilege (204). Scott (*Epistemology*, 279) has also argued for a coherentist approach, although his narrative structure must be seen as distinct understanding of coherentism. To some extent coherentism and foundationalism exclude each other, although coherentism may have room for some foundational beliefs (P. D. Klein, 'Epistemology', in E. Craig [ed.], *Routledge Encyclopedia of Philosophy* III [London: Routledge: 1998] 362–5).

[76] M. Westphal, 'Taking St. Paul Seriously: Sin as an Epistemological Category', in T. P. Flint (ed.), *Christian Philosophy* (Notre Dame: University of Notre Dame Press, 1990) 218, 209, respectively. He criticises the attempts of reformed epistemology (cf. A. Plantinga and N. Wolterstorff [eds.], *Faith and Rationality: Reason and Belief in God* [Notre Dame: University of Notre Dame Press, 1983]).

[77] Westphal, 'Paul', 216.   [78] Westphal, 'Paul', 202.

[79] Theissen, *Religion*, 393f. Beker ('Theology', 20) speaks of a disclosure theory of truth.

It is this Greek principle which Paul picks up in 1 Cor. 2.6–16.[80] Only by virtue of the correct relationship of object and subject can knowledge be attained.[81] 'Consequently the sole being who is able to convey the revelation to man and open his mind to know it is God's *Pneuma*, because he comes from God.'[82] No one knows 'what is truly God's' (τὰ τοῦ θεοῦ, 2.11), except for the Spirit of God. E. Käsemann shows that as only grace can interpret grace, so only the Spirit can recognise and evaluate what is of the Spirit.[83] While Paul is not unique in applying this principle, we shall see that the Christological terms, by which he defines it, are. In other words, we still need to address the question of how Paul believes the principle is fulfilled. We shall return to that in the next Part (pp. 154–85) of this book.

4. Summary

I have so far, then, presented an overview of Paul's epistemological structure. I have argued that the centre of Paul's thought-world is the contingent gospel: God's ultimate revelation becomes subject to human actions. From this focal point (the Christ-story against the background of the salvation story) I have proposed that Paul develops the rest of his theology.[84] I have highlighted the two poles of knowledge as contingency (transcendence as ethical knowledge) and comprehensive perception (reality as a whole is qualified). Against O. Hofius, I assert that true knowledge is not merely propositional but requires existential transformation. Against Bultmann it can be said that knowledge for Paul does offer a new world-view (not only self-understanding). However, that raises the central question of how these two poles can be reconciled. How can knowledge necessarily reflect an existential realisation and a comprehensive truth-claim?

---

[80] B. E. Gärtner, 'The Pauline and Johannine Idea "To Know God" against the Hellenistic Background. The Greek Philosophical Principle "Like by Like" in Paul and John', *NTS* 14 (1967/68) 209–31. Westphal's work is not exegetical enough to pick up on this principle.

[81] Cf. Aristotle, *Nicomachean Ethics* 1155b1–8 (VIII.i.6; alternative numbering); Stuhlmacher, 'Bedeutung', 158; Sellin, 'Geheimnis', 88; J. Moltmann, *Erfahrungen theologischen Denkens: Wege und Formen christlicher Theologie* (Gütersloh: Gütersloher Verlagshaus, 1999) 139–42.

[82] Gärtner, 'Idea', 218.

[83] Käsemann, 'Korinther', 274. As Schrage points out, 'Kriterium allen Erkennens und Urteilens ist aber das Geistliche' (*Korinther* I, 269); cf. Lewis, *Life*, 68f.

[84] Again, by focal point I mean the life, death and resurrection of Christ. As mentioned earlier, that does not mean, however, that I deny the formative role of scripture in Paul's thought. But by concentrating on the Christ-event I mean to denote a centre of his thought, that which Beker calls 'core of the gospel' (*Paul*, 207).

It is here that I propose that discernment balances and partially resolves the antithesis.

D.   The Role of Discernment within Paul's Epistemology and Theology

The link between contingent particularity and comprehensive perception is established through discernment. Hence, I propose that discernment has an interpretative and a *corrective* role within the structure of Paul's thought. I will deal with these two different aspects in the following section and hence elucidate the *constitutive and creative* significance of discernment in the verification and formation of truth.

1.   The Interpretative Role

First of all, there is an *interpretative* movement. We noted the inter-pretative element of διάκρισις/διακρίνω in the previous chapter. In this manner I also understand Paul's assertion in 1 Cor. 2.13b that the Spirit aids in 'interpreting spiritual things to those who are spiritual' (πνευ-ματικοῖς πνευματικὰ συγκρίνοντες).[85] While συγκρίνω can also mean 'to compare', the meaning 'to interpret/explain' is preferable.[86] With that I follow the LXX usage and the emphasis on communication in 2.13.[87] Interpretation and explanation are necessary because the community (and the world to which it belongs) must be understood anew in the light of the Christ-event. The world must be given new significance and value. This interpretation is possible because those who have comprehended the

---

[85] It is possible to understand πνευματικοῖς as neuter or masculine (personally). Although grammatically the neuter is possible ('comparing spiritual issues with spiritual means'), I prefer the personal reading, because vv. 6 and 13 are addressed to people, and Paul's concern about their reactions to his argument is central (vv. 14f.; 3.1–3; Wolff, *Korinther*, 60). That means Paul 'is coming back "full circle" to the thought of v.6 . . . which now receives its necessary justification' (Robertson and Plummer, *Corinthians*, 47f.).

[86] Cf. Stuhlmacher, 'Bedeutung', 158; Louw and Nida, *Lexicon* I, 618. There has been an attempt to return to the 'classical' meaning of the verb, namely 'to combine' (W. C. Kaiser, 'A Neglected Text in Bibliology Discussions: I Corinthians 2:6–16', *WThJ* 43 [1981] 314). As pointed out earlier, concerning δοκιμάζω, such references to original meanings can be regarded as irrelevant if there are plausible synchronic meanings. For the other possibility, 'to compare', cf. Dunn, *Jesus*, 235; Schrage, *Korinther* I, 261f; 2 Cor. 10.12.

[87] Particularly the interpretation of dreams and enigmatic signs, cf. Gen. 40.8, 16, 22; 41.12, 13, 15; Dan. 5.7, 12, 16; F. W. Horn, *Das Angeld des Geistes: Studien zur paulinischen Pneumatologie* (FRLANT 154; Göttingen: Vandenhoeck & Ruprecht, 1992) 186; Scroggs, 'Paul', 52.

cross have the hermeneutical key to comprehend reality.[88] For analytical purposes we may differentiate here between the theological and ethical elements of this interpretative movement and deal with them separately (although we must be continually aware that they are interdependent).[89]

Within the ethical element of interpretative discernment, the lives of the believers are brought into the focus of the gospel. The contingent word of the cross is related to the concrete situation of each community.[90] The meaning of the Christ-event is *extrapolated, translated and applied* to all potentially transformative and 'problematic areas of life'.[91] In this regard, we can understand the 'articulate utterance of wisdom' and 'knowledge' (1 Cor. 12.8).[92] It is the knowledge of salvation communicated to others.[93] This communication means coming to a better understanding of God's 'Heilsdenken',[94] his 'divine plan of salvation',[95] and its particularisation for everyday lives.[96] While each individual may be the focus, those who are discerning will be aware that the actual goal is the upbuilding of the community as a whole.[97]

Moreover, the hermeneutical movement allows for theological deliberation. In 2 Cor. 5.14 Paul and the believers 'conclude' (κρίναντας τοῦτο)[98]

---

[88] Voss, *Wort*, 185– 97. There is a contradiction in Witherington, *Conflict*: whereas at one point he says that Paul is only talking about the knowledge of God (*Conflict*, 112), he otherwise says salvation 'entails the transformation of an individual spiritually, morally, and intellectually so that the person has a new worldview' (*Conflict*, 111).

[89] That also means it is not necessary to see the wisdom/mystery in 1 Cor. 2 as 'distinct from kerygma' as Scroggs suggests ('Paul', 55).

[90] Stoessel ('Notes', 168) argues for an application of kerygmatic theology to 'the personal situation'. In this sense I understand the communication which the Spirit establishes in 1 Cor. 2. Thus, the Spirit reveals (v. 10) and teaches (διδακτοῖς, v. 13) so that we can understand (ε'ιδῶμεν, v. 12; γνῶναι, v. 14), speak (λαλοῦμεν, v. 13) and discern (ἀνακρίνει, vv. 14f.). (Cf. Fee, *Corinthians*, 115; Merklein, *Korinther 1–4*, 241; Barrett, *Corinthians*, 75f.; Dunn, *Jesus*, 235f.).

[91] W. F. Orr and J. A. Walther, *I Corinthians* (AB 32; Garden City, NY: Doubleday, 1976) 166.

[92] The translation is from Thiselton, *Corinthians*, 938, since he suggests λόγος should be seen as an 'utterance with a nuance of intelligibility'.

[93] Cf. C. F. G. Heinrici, *Der erste Brief an die Korinther* (KEK 5; Göttingen: Vandenhoeck & Ruprecht, 1896[8]) 367; Allo, *Corinthiens*, 325.

[94] Wolff, *Korinther*, 62.

[95] H. H. D. Williams III, *The Wisdom of the Wise: The Presence and Function of Scripture within 1 Cor. 1:18–3:23* (Leiden: Brill, 2001) 234.

[96] J. Héring (*La première épître de Saint Paul aux Corinthiens* [Neuchâtel: Delachaux & Niestlé, 1949] 109) points out that wisdom in the LXX traditions includes moral guidance for life. Although there is much discussion in the literature about why Paul distinguishes σοφία from γνῶσις, for my purposes there is no need to observe a distinction.

[97] We may, at this point, remind ourselves of my conclusions in the preceding chapter, namely that Paul wants all to become mature and to be able to discern.

[98] The NRS offers 'because we are convinced'. My translation is from Martin, *2 Corinthians*, 128.

'that one has died for all; therefore all have died'.[99] They are deciphering the Christ-event and thinking through its theological consequences.[100] We may use the plural 'they' here because we understand that Paul is inviting his readers to 'theologize somewhat along' with him.[101] In this vein, another central concept of Paul's thought is formulated: 'For we hold (λογιζόμεθα) that a person is justified by faith apart from works prescribed by the law' (Rom. 3.28).[102] As in Rom. 6.11, 8.18 and 14.14, λογίζομαι is 'a deliberate and sober judgment on the basis of the gospel, a reasoning which is subject to the discipline of the gospel'.[103] We should be clear, however, that the 'ex post facto thinker' cannot predicate meaning in a random fashion. Rather, it means 'that one discerns meaning given with the event'.[104] In sum, this interpretative discernment is one element of Christocentric theology. The meaning of the Christ-event is established and reality is explained.[105]

2.   The Corrective Role

The other element which I wish to emphasise is the corrective role of discernment within the Pauline epistemological structure. Discernment

---

[99] There has been some discussion about whether or not Paul arrived at this conclusion at, or shortly after, his Damascus road experience (cf. P. E. Hughes, *Paul's Second Epistle to the Corinthians* [NICNT; Grand Rapids, MI: Eerdmans, 1962] 193 n. 22; M. E. Thrall, *The Second Epistle to the Corinthians* [ICC; Edinburgh: T&T Clark, 1994] 409). As Martin points out, 'we should not let the aorist tense [of κρίναντας] rule out any period of time for contemplation' (*Corinthians*, 129).

[100] The comment by Hughes (*Corinthians*, 193) that this is 'the rational ground of his [Paul's] security in Christ' is only partially helpful, since it should not be contrasted with the influence of the Spirit.

[101] Dunn, *Theology of Paul*, 211, on 2 Cor 5.14. Furnish (*2 Corinthians*, 310) correctly states that the ἡμᾶς (which is the implicit subject of κρίναντας) does not refer to Paul alone because of Paul's 'evident attempt to call upon a conviction held in common by all believers'.

[102] Yu (*Epistemology*, 298–300) shows that Paul formulated the 'doctrinal truth', 'righteousness by faith apart from the law', in the crisis over circumcision and law in Galatia. Yu does not believe that this was part of the originally revealed message of the gospel (which was 'Christ crucified') and that therefore Paul had to persuade the Galatians to accept his 'thesis' (cf. his *Epistemology*, ch. 5). See further for the interpretative development of the Christ-event my work on the mythification of the gospel in chapter 6 (pp. 163–72; also Theissen, *Aspekte*, 374ff.).

[103] C. E. B. Cranfield, *The Epistle to the Romans* I (ICC; Edinburgh: T&T Clark, 1975[6]) 315. In chapter 6 I will establish how reason and revelation are both required and need not necessarily contradict each other. Bultmann (*Theologie*, 215f.) shows the link between some instances of κρίνω, λογίζομαι and δοκιμάζω.

[104] Keck, 'Paul', 29. Indeed, as A. Schlatter writes with regard to Rom. 3.28, there is no other possibility for Paul but to think these thoughts (*Erläuterungen zum Neuen Testament* II [Calw: Verlag der Vereinsbuchhandlung, 1909] 29).

[105] Käsemann, 'Korinther', 274.

keeps a constant check on the interpretative process. That means there is a circular (or spiraling) movement between the interpretative and corrective roles: the interpretative function allows for fresh understanding, while the corrective role is concerned with the authenticity and quality of these new interpretations.[106] In this sense I understand ἀνακρίνω in 1 Cor. 2.14b and 2.15a as a 'careful evaluation', similar to my reading of διακρίνω above.[107] What does this corrective function denote?

It is of crucial importance that discernment is wary of triumphalism. The corrective role recognises the ambiguous nature of every particular contingent situation.[108] Hence, each interpretation is a discovery which involves the risk of not being authentic and possibly even including 'accommodation . . . opportunistic omissions and additions. After all, charismatic authority and apostolic insight are not synonymous with inerrancy and infallibility!'[109] For there is a distinct danger that the new comprehensive world-view, attained through understanding the Christ-event, becomes compulsive or totalitarian. If, as I have argued, only the whole is real, it is easy to lose sight of the fact that each understanding of the whole narrative is contingent.[110] On the one hand, such compulsive aspects are at points visible in Paul's 'Herrschaftsanspruch'.[111] On

---

[106] Beker ('Theology', 19) writes that the 'reciprocal relation between coherence and contingency effects a fluid relation of the coherent truth of the gospel to the various contingent situations of the moment so that the coherence of the gospel does not become a static, unalterable structure of thought'. J. L. Martyn, ('Book Review of J. C. Beker, Paul the Apostle', in *Theological Issues in the Letters of Paul* [Edinburgh: T&T Clark, 1997] 180) warns not to conceive 'the interpretative route to be a one-way street' from contingency to coherence (or vice versa, I add). But rather it should be seen as 'a movement around the *circle of contingency and coherence*, each being more sharply brought into focus as we return to it from the other' (italics mine).

[107] Louw and Nida, *Lexicon* II, 15.

[108] Broer, 'Exegese', 59–88. This is against Schrage (*Korinther* I, 269) who thinks that the point of 1 Cor. 2.6–16 is not that there is no absolute certainty ('absolute Eindeutigkeit') but only that 'like can be known by like'.

[109] Beker, 'Theology', 19. T. E. Boomershine ('Epistemology at the Turn of the Ages in Paul, Jesus, and Mark: Rhetoric and Dialectic in Apocalyptic and the New Testament', in J. Marcus and M. L. Soards [eds.], *Apocalyptic and the New Testament* [JSNT.S 24; Sheffield: Sheffield Academic Press, 1989] 149) shows (with reference to S. E. Fish) that Paul's way of knowing is presented in a 'dialectical presentation' which 'requires of its readers a searching and rigorous scrutiny of everything they believe in'; 'it does not preach the truth, but asks that its readers discover the truth for themselves'.

[110] Thiselton, *Corinthians*, 1064. Cf. Keck ('Paul', 32) who shows that Paul's holistic worldview 'requires one to grasp the constitutive character of the age as a whole'.

[111] Schrage (*Einzelgebote*, 50) shows that the renewal and 'Herrschaftsanspruch' is total in its nature. H. Ridderbos (*Paulus: Ein Entwurf seiner Theologie* [trans. E.-W. Pollmann; Wuppertal: Theologischer Verlag Rolf Brockhaus, 1970] 184–5) suggests that Pauline paresis is of a markedly totalitarian nature ('*totalitären Charakter*'). Because in Christ everything has been given, everything can also be demanded 'und zwar sowohl quantitativ und extensiv als auch qualitativ und intensiv'.

the other hand, occasionally it is the attempts, such as mine, to synthesise Paul's theology which are susceptible to the danger of compulsion, as these attempts risk losing the 'vitality and dynamism' and possibly 'complexity' and 'plurality' of Paul's thought.[112] How then can discernment balance the fact that all knowledge is tentative with the sure grasp of reality made possible in Christ?

Paul offers a helping hand in 2 Cor. 3–4. Ultimate knowledge there is expressed in the face of Christ (2 Cor. 4.6) and believers see this with 'unveiled faces' (2 Cor. 3.18). Young and Ford (following E. Levinas) argue that this is significant: faces represent 'pluralism', 'resisting all totalities' because knowledge is represented as a person, as the other, 'an alterity', that 'resists all fusion', 'all inclusion in sameness'.[113] This has implications for the corrective role of discernment.

When knowledge leads to compulsion, its truth claim is undermined. True knowledge rather leads to a transformation of power claims into a search for relationality. As in 2 Cor. 3.18, seeing the Lord implies transformation, which allows the discerning believer to understand that the summit of knowledge is not encyclopaedic knowledge, but the love of God expressed in Christ.[114] The goal is holistic comprehension which mediates between *being* (including effects, impact and relationship) and *semantic verification*.[115] Hermeneutics, then, has an ethical dimension, which include openness for the opinion of others and a concern for their integrity.[116] As L. T. Johnson stresses, each personal narrative in the community has revelatory potential.

[112] Roetzel, *Paul*, 94.

[113] Young and Ford, *Meaning*, 254. Cf. 1 Cor. 10.29 and the 'liberty' not 'to be subject to someone else's conscience'.

[114] As N. A. Dahl points out for Eph. 3.18, the summit of knowledge is not to understand the wisdom of the Creator 'but to know the love of Christ' ('Cosmic Dimensions and Religious Knowledge [Eph. 3.18]', in *Studies in Ephesians* [WUNT 131; Tübingen: Mohr/Siebeck, 2000] 381). Cf. Thompson, *Christ*, 85. Stoessel ('Notes, 171) rightly points out that the renewal of the mind implies 'an internalizing of truth' which must be 'an intensely personal and therefore demanding process'.

[115] Schlier ('Erkenntnis', 337) shows that, according to Eph. 3.16–19, the objective is to know the love of Christ which 'surpasses knowledge'. Niederwimmer ('Erkennen', 99) suggests that this knowledge transmits 'das Absolute', but knowledge does not consist of the absolute. For the interrelationship of love and knowledge, cf. C. Spicq, *Agape in the New Testament* II (St. Louis: Herder, 1965) 327.

[116] Boyarin (*Jew*, 97f.) sees both ethical and hermeneutical dimensions in the opposition of letter–Spirit in 2 Cor. 3: The 'hermeneutical and ethical moments' are 'homologous with each other'. Paul's concern that spiritual knowledge is dependent on its social realisation anticipates and precedes the modern sociological insight that the theology in Paul's letters should not be seen only as a result of Paul's theological ideas. Formative for historical processes are also 'right living' and 'proper social interaction' (Witherington, *Conflict*, xv; cf. B. Holmberg, *Paul and Power: The Structure of Authority in the Primitive Church as Reflected in the Pauline Epistles* [Lund: Gleerup, 1978]; Dunn, *Theology of Paul*, 565–71, for a helpful overview of research on the interrelationship of 'Charism and Office').

> Doubtless God knows what God is up to, and tries to get it across to us, but it takes a community time and effort – and often considerable suffering – to catch a glimpse of what that might be or how to respond to it. I have suggested that in this process *discernment* is the essential component that enables us to perceive our often ambiguous experience as revelatory, or that enables others to hear our narrative as a narrative of faith that might express the Word of God.[117]

The wisdom of finding revelation in ambiguity is crucial for the discerning believer. The key lies in the transformation of knowledge through love, a point we must return to in chapter 6.

3.   Summary

In sum, my presentation has shown the constitutive and creative role that discernment has within Paul's epistemological framework. Both the interpretative and corrective roles are crucial in developing and verifying the interpretation and application of the Christ-event. Indeed, we are now in a position to confirm E. Käsemann's comment (mentioned in the introductory chapter) that discernment is 'rechte Theologie'.[118] Or we can assert with Stuhlmacher that true Christian thinking between the death and return of Christ is to discern the spirits.[119] However, my own argument has alerted us to the fact that this thinking is not just an application of a dogmatic core to practical problems because the very centre of Paul's thought is the contingent gospel. In turn, true discernment must always also be existential transformation. But that leads us into the latter half of my book. Before moving to the second half I must attend to one final question.

E.   The Πνευματικός: Exempt from Judgement
       but not Discernment

If Paul is serious about his claim that the πνευματικός discerns everything, what about the second half of our verse: αὐτὸς δὲ ὑπ' οὐδενὸς ἀνακρίνεται

---

[117] L. T. Johnson, 'Edification as a Formal Criterion for Discernment in the Church', *Sewanee Theological Review* 39 (1996) 362. For the importance of this narrative aspect for Paul's epistemology, cf. Scott, *Epistemology*, 159–276. These personal narratives are important for any further truth claims, as Paul's life is the basis for his own knowledge claim. Cf. L. L. Welborn, 'Character and Truth in 2 Cor 1.17', *ZNW* 86 (1995) 51: 'By a massive transumption, everything that pertains to the gospel proclamation is predicated of Paul's speech as such'.
[118] Käsemann, 'Korinther', 274.   [119] Stuhlmacher, 'Glauben', 337.

(1 Cor. 2.15b)? Particularly Johan S. Vos has argued that Paul is inconsistent.[120] He is creating an immunity which contradicts those statements in which all utterances are to be tested (1 Cor. 12.10; 14.29; 1 Thess. 5.21) and creates an implicit hierarchy.[121] I propose to offer two interdependent points, which help clarify this question.

The first point is that ἀνακρίνω can be read differently in the second half of 1 Cor. 2.15. Thus, while in 2.14b and 2.15a the characteristic of the πνευματικός, as opposed to the ψυχικός, is his ability '*to evaluate carefully*', in 2.15b ἀνακρίνω can be read as '*to criticise*' or 'to judge critically'.[122] Paul is playing with the verb and the theme of judgement throughout 1 Corinthians.[123] In the latter half of this verse he is prodding the Corinthians for being judgemental 'so as to bring this clause into relationship with his apologetic self-defence in 1 Cor 4.3 and 9.3'.[124] And we should not miss the partially ironic element with which he does this.[125] Paul is using the Corinthian terminology and recontextualising it in the word of the cross. Consequently, two types of assessment are contrasted. The pneumatic person is exempt from a presumptive, negative and judgemental attitude, but careful assessment led by the Spirit will be all-encompassing.

The other important point that we should remember is that the new reality which the Christ-event has opened up for the believer is inaccessible for those outside. Hence the ψυχικός cannot understand the things of God (1 Cor. 2.15) nor is he in a position to 'judge' those under the influence of

---

[120] Vos, 'Probleem', 194–205.

[121] Vos, 'Probleem', 205. He gives three examples: in 1 Cor. 14.37–38, Paul degrades his potential opponents by calling them illusory-pneumatics; in 1 Cor 2.6–3.4, Paul claims the critical church is not rising above the level of 'fleshly people'; in Gal. 1.10–24, the apostles in Jerusalem are not more than flesh and blood.

[122] (Italics mine). There are four partially related senses as Louw and Nida (*Lexicon* II, 15) show: (i) 'study thoroughly', (ii) 'investigate in court', (iii) 'criticize', (iv) 'evaluate carefully'. Paul can use the term in a negative judgemental sense (1 Cor. 4.3; 9.3), an ambivalent manner in relation to the conscience (1 Cor. 10.25ff: with the sense 'to evaluate carefully') and parallel to ἐλέγχω in 1 Cor. 14.24, referring to 'an outsider' being evaluated by prophecy.

[123] Typically for the strong assessment/ judgement theme and polemic in 1 Corinthians, this is the only letter in which Paul uses this verb but that ten times (particularly in quite polemic sections): 1 Cor. 2.14, 15(×2); 4.3(×2), 4; 9.3; 10.25, 27; 14.24. Nevertheless, care must be taken neither to impose one meaning on all occurrences nor to amalgamate the senses of the verb.

[124] Davis, *Wisdom*, 127; Barrett, *Corinthians*, 78.

[125] Cf. R. B. Hays, 'Wisdom According to Paul', in S. C. Barton (ed.), *Where Shall Wisdom be Found? Wisdom in the Bible, the Church and the Contemporary World* (Edinburgh: T&T Clark, 1999) 119, who points out that Paul uses an 'ironic mode' by 'adopting' their 'vocabulary in order to beat them at their game'. Schrage (*Korinther* I, 264) speaks of 'gesprächsstrategische Gesichtspunkte' (cf. Thiselton, *Corinthians*, 271f.).

Christ/the Spirit. As A. Lindemann states, the point is that the πνευματικός is not delivered up to the judgement of a stranger ('Fremdurteil').[126] 'The profane person cannot understand holiness, but the holy person can well understand the depths of evil.'[127] It is probable then to assume that Paul was not declaring a general immunity for the πνευματικός but a limitation on the judgement of the ψυχικός.[128]

Finally, we may note that some tension remains: the implicit hierarchy, which Vos believes leads to an inconsistency in Paul, is balanced from within. As I shall argue in the latter half of this book, the very nature of a πνευματικός makes hierarchical thinking a contradiction in terms. Those who 'consider themselves full of the Spirit in such a way as to be beyond discipline or the counsel of others . . . are usually among those most needing such discipline'.[129] Clearly, however, as history has shown, this vision is not one easily realised and incorporates the potential for misuse and conflict. Whether or not Paul understood this sufficiently must be assessed in another study.[130]

F.   Conclusion: Discernment as Theology

Paul is serious: the πνευματικός can discern everything. However, and this is crucial, Paul uses this epistemological claim (possibly originally a Corinthian phrase) according to his own understanding and hence converts its content. Everything can be understood only in tandem with an existential transformation, which in turn must mirror the contingent nature of the gospel. Existential does not mean that only an individual realisation of truth is implied. On the contrary, Paul has a comprehensive perspective

---

[126] Lindemann, *Korintherbrief*, 73. Hence οὐδενός only refers to the ψυχικός and so the pneumatic is assessed but only by the pneumatic (Lietzmann, *Korinther*, 14f.; Schrage, *Korinther* I, 269). In that sense, the πνευματικός comes very close to the status of the apostle whose message is exempt from any human court, cf. D. Litfin, *St Paul's Theology of Proclamation: 1 Corinthians 1–4 and Greco-Roman Rhetoric* (Cambridge: Cambridge University Press, 1994) 282: 'Where they stand "in" the gospel they stand in the same power he does and their authority is the same as his.'

[127] Anonymous quote from Fee (*Corinthians*, 118); cf. Lietzmann, *Korinther*, 34: 'Nur der Herr kann den Dienst des Dieners für treu und fehlerlos erklären, nicht der Diener selbst.'

[128] Cf. Orr and Walther, *Corinthians*, 167; Allo, *Corinthiens*, 49. Dunn (*Jesus*, 235ff.) explains that the status or worth of people is not assessed.

[129] Fee, *Corinthians*, 118.

[130] Vos writes that, when both prophecy and discernment are legitimised by pneumatic authority, a 'conflict-filled reality' is not far ('Probleem', 205). This thought needs to be taken up by Systematics, and Practical Theology: How can pneumatic authority be conceptualised in a realistic manner?

on reality. However, this is qualified by the 'face of Christ', which resists propositional domestication and coercion.

My own argument has shown how discernment is the key element in resolving the tension between the contingent aspect of the revelation in Christ and its comprehensive application. I have argued for both an interpretative and an evaluative element so that the Christ-event can be understood, explained and applied to every particular situation of each community and believer. Hence, we may conclude that discernment has a creative role in Paul's theology. It is *existential theologising*, the nature of which I shall explore to a greater extent in the next section of this book.

PART III

How Can and Should True Discernment Take Place?

5

THE CONTEXT AND BACKGROUND OF PAUL

A.   Introduction

Having gained some understanding of the significance of the role of discernment within Paul's own thought and the importance he attaches to it for the community and the individual believer, we are naturally interested in how this discernment is to take place. How does Paul think that believers can discern the things that matter and are pleasing to God? I have already mentioned that the key appears to lie in the interaction of Spirit and mind. While we must still probe Paul himself as to what he could have meant by this interaction, he does not offer us an epistemological or psychological system by which we can easily go about that task. For this purpose we must investigate the context within which Paul lived and thought. Not only can the scholars and thinkers of Paul's own time illuminate our understanding of his (and his readers') conceptual framework, but also, as we shall see, in a number of cases there are strikingly similar strands of thought.

I will proceed by looking at forms of Judaism first, continuing with Philo of Alexandria, who offers a mixture of Jewish and Hellenistic thought,[1] and finally considering the Stoics. The order is methodologically significant as I acknowledge that Paul's primary 'background' allegiance was to Judaism and only the answers which cannot be found there should be sought elsewhere. However, at the end of the chapter I attempt to offer further justification for the breadth of traditions offered here.

B.   Judaism

1.   The Quest for Knowledge and Wisdom

When attempting to understand discernment within ITP Judaism, the general increased interest in knowledge and wisdom, both of a

---

[1] My classification does not propose to locate Philo outside of Judaism, but as he has been strongly influenced by Hellenism and offers more detail than his Jewish contemporaries, it is helpful to deal with his work separately.

philosophical and religious nature, should be kept in mind. On the one hand, discernment was required as Jewish thought-life was attempting to attain the same comprehensive knowledge that Hellenism appeared to have grasped. This becomes particularly evident within the wisdom tradition, where theology, anthropology and cosmology amalgamate.[2] On the other hand, there is a reaction against Greek and Roman imperialism and Jewish assimilation to their forms of knowledge. It was believed that supreme understanding, insight into the will of God, was lacking in Graeco-Roman culture.[3] Discernment was required in order to offer some critique of this culture and the correct perception of reality.[4] Moreover, philosophical speculation, it was argued, could not answer the most important questions, such as theodicy, the master plan for history and the spiritual world.

On what basis, then, was true knowledge of the world and a correct evaluation of God's saving activity to be attained? When investigating how discernment functioned in Judaism and Hellenism, there are three main areas which require thought: knowledge which is given or revealed, acquired wisdom and a third category which combines both in the form of a 'renewed heart'.

2.   The Question of Discernment

Revealed Knowledge

At the heart of the Jewish tradition, is the belief that all knowledge is set within the boundaries of the Torah.[5] That means the Torah

---

[2] Cf. *Wis.Sol.* 7.17–20 and its emphasis on comprehensive knowledge ranging from rules of logic, natural phenomena, resolution of riddles, knowledge of the past and future (for further explication, see D. Winston, 'The Sage as Mystic in the Wisdom of Solomon', in J. G. Gammie and L. G. Perdue [eds.], *The Sage in Israel and the Ancient Near East* [Winona Lake, IN: Eisenbrauns, 1990] 384).

[3] Cf. M. Hengel, *Judaism and Hellenism* I (trans. J. Bowden; London: SCM Press, 1974) 208. I use the terms 'apocalyptic' and 'wisdom' as denoting their respective traditions while acknowledging their fluidity and overlap (cf., e.g., J. I. Kampen, 'The Diverse Aspects of Wisdom in the Qumran Texts', in P. W. Flint and J. C. Vanderkam [eds.], *The Dead Sea Scrolls after Fifty Years* [Leiden: Brill, 1998] 211–42).

[4] This is particularly evident in the apocalyptic tradition, cf. C. Rowland, 'The Apocalypse: Hope, Resistance and the Revelation of Reality', *Ex Auditu* 6 (1990) 129. Discernment, particularly of revelatory activity, was a known concept in the OT: cf. Deut. 13.2–6; 18.20–22; Isa. 29.10; Jer. 14.13–16; 23.9–40; 28.8f.; Ezek. 13; 33.33; Zech. 13.3; Dunn, 'Discernment', 81.

[5] Cf. Schnabel, *Law*, 343–9. This is expressed well in *4 Ezra* 14.47: 'For in them [i.e. Torah] is the spring of understanding, the fountain of wisdom, and the river of knowledge.' Further, any form of continued revelation was intimately connected with the Torah and prophets (cf. Bockmuehl, *Revelation*, 124–6).

constitutes not only what is regarded as supreme knowledge, but it also offers the touchstone for all further insight. Moreover, true knowledge was perceived as a *gift* from God and not as a result of human achievement.[6] While this gift could be bestowed in various different manners, the crucial point is that humanity cannot discern this knowledge with its own strength.[7] That is to say, it was the Spirit that communicated matters which 'were not within the understanding of others' (Josephus, *Ant.* 10.239), that made known the 'counsel' of God (*Wis.Sol.* 9.17–18; 1QH 12.11–13) and bestowed wisdom and insight (*Sir.* 39.6). Revealed knowledge served as the texture of the theological and social 'plausibility structure' and hence was the ultimate criterion for further discernment.[8] To some extent, and in comparison with Hellenistic philosophy, this restricted the expansion of knowledge. But does the emphasis on revelation imply that the human and rational elements in discernment were not acknowledged?

Acquired Knowledge

ITP Judaism knew of the significance of education in gaining understanding[9] and the responsibility of the individual to acquire and conform to wisdom.[10] Various authors offer different perspectives on these forms of

---

[6] C. A. Newsom ('The Sage in the Literature of Qumran: The Functions of the *Maskîl*', in Gammie and Perdue [eds.], *Sage*, 375) points this out particularly for Qumran, but it applies also to the writers of the wisdom tradition, where the helplessness of the human condition in the absence of divine wisdom is accepted (cf. *Wis.Sol.* 9.13–18; Winston, 'Wisdom', 392).

[7] The Spirit communicated in the form of 'charismatic revelation', 'wisdom' or 'invasively inspired prophecy'. These categories have been developed by M. Turner, *Power from on High : The Spirit in Israel's Restoration and Witness in Luke–Acts* (Journal of Pentecostal Theology. Supplement Series 9; Sheffield: Sheffield Academic Press, 1996) 92–9. By 'charismatic revelation' he denotes a 'communication of revelatory knowledge from God' in the form of a vision, dream, or the hearing of words (*Power*, 92); by charismatic wisdom, cf. below p. 106 n. 21; by 'invasively inspired prophecy', he denotes a form of 'oracular speech' in which there is an eclipse of the rational faculties of the speaker (*Power*, 98; cf. M. Turner, 'Prophecy and Preaching in Luke–Acts', *NTS* 38 [1992] 72–6).

[8] Cf. Bockmuehl, *Revelation*, 125, who uses the term coined by sociologist Peter Berger.

[9] Dautzenberg (*Prophetie*, 120, 125) defines the conditions for the various interpretation processes in Judaism. He believes that, while the intuitive and inspired interpretation types were in high regard and seen as authoritative, this did not mean that the ability to interpret was not also based on an intellectual or educational (knowledge of tradition) foundation. He refers particularly to the 'bildungsmäßigen Voraussetzungen' for Daniel, Josephus and the study of scripture at Qumran (cf. also 43f. and 102f.).

[10] Hence there is a strong emphasis on decision and choice, cf. *T.Levi* 19.1–4: 'Choose for yourselves light or darkness, the Law of the Lord or the works of Beliar.' Moreover,

knowledge. In the *Letter of Aristeas* 255, practical and rational elements are seen as the basis for sound judgement.[11] Ben Sira, also one of the more practically minded, stresses the logical advantages of virtue over vice (*Sir.* 7.1–3; 29.11–13; 40.12–17).[12] And while the Torah and spiritual wisdom are for him the focal point, real understanding is given to the one who is devoted to study and is actively testing 'good and evil among men' (*Sir.* 39.4). Similarly, at Qumran, the teacher's authority is based not only on the revealed mysteries, but also on the fact that he is 'master of every secret of men and of every language according to their families' (CD 14.9–10).[13] Insight into the character of people was a traditional value of the wise. And while at Qumran it is given a dualistic dimension, the values on which such insight is based is spelled out clearly in a vice and virtue list (1QS 4.3–6, 9–11).[14] This in turn appears to be the basis for the evaluation of the community members by the instructor (1QS 9.12–16; 5.21–4).[15] More significantly, at Qumran it is by a process of study and deliberation that the true interpretation of the Torah was discovered (1QS 6.8–10). J. C. H. Lebram states that a similar interpretative process can be seen in the application of the post-biblical apocalypses.

there is an increasing tendency to stress the rational; cf. *4 Macc.* 1.19: '*Rational judgment is supreme over all of these* [kinds of wisdom], since by means of it reason rules over the emotions' (italics mine); Josephus, *Ant.* 1.19: 'Be it known, then, that that sage deemed it above all necessary, for one who would order his own life aright and also legislate for others, first to study the nature of God, and then having contemplated his works with the *eye of reason*, to imitate so far as possible that best of all models and endeavour to follow it' (italics mine).

[11] Similarly the answer to the question, '"What is philosophy?" . . . "To have a well reasoned assessment of each occurrence . . . and not to be carried away by impulses but to study carefully the harmful consequences of the passions . . ."'(*Letter of Aristeas* 256).

[12] Cf. J. G. Gammie, 'The Sage in Sirach', in Gammie and Perdue (eds.) *Sage*, 359. Gammie also points to the assimilationist tendency in Sirach with respect to the dietary laws ('Sage', 360f.).

[13] After meditating on the 'mystery of existence' (translation contested), 4Q417 2 I 4–8 promises: '[. . . Then you shall differentiate between] [good and evil according to his deed, for] God will spread knowledge of the foundation of truth . . .'

[14] E. Schweizer ('Gegenwart des Geistes und eschatologische Hoffnung bei Zarathustra, spätjüdischen Gruppen, Gnostikern und den Zeugen des Neuen Testaments', in W. D. Davies and D. Daube [eds.], *The Background of the New Testament and its Eschatology* [Cambridge: Cambridge University Press, 1964] 486) proposed that one of the reasons for the beginning of a dualistic framework was the need for a differentiated approach to good and evil.

[15] Cf. Newsom, 'Qumran', 377: 'The detailing of the characteristics of the spirits of truth and falsehood undoubtedly provides a guide for the formation of values in the individual community member'; *T.Ash.* 1.3–9: 'Contemplating just deeds and rejecting wickedness, the soul overcomes evil and uproots sin.'

Hence, 'by reflection and discernment [the reader of the texts] will learn to understand his own time and situation . . . and thus draw consequences out of his belief and actions'.[16] In sum, the educational and rational/reflective requirements for discernment were seen as essential elements.

A Renewed Heart

Of particular interest, however, is my third category, in which the revelatory and acquired forms are united. This is expressed in the growing conviction that true knowledge can only be attained when the whole disposition of a person is changed. And only God can achieve this. Hence, when in the *Letter of Aristeas* 236, the king asks his guests whether or not practical wisdom can be taught, the answer is: 'It is a disposition of the soul, mediated by the power of God, to accept everything of beauty and to reject its opposite.'[17] Of greater importance, of course, is the promise of a new covenant in Jer. 31.31–4 in which God's law was to be written on the people's hearts and minds. Ezekiel 36.23–8 and *Jub.* 1.22–5 take up the promise and express the future hope of an inner transformation and direct knowledge of God (due to the work of the Spirit) as the only way in which God's will can be known and practised.[18] While the objective, expressed in this hope, is not so much discernment but obedience (since God's will is known), it is still of consequence for this study. The anticipation of an immediate knowledge of God existed. An existential renewal would come: 'the re-creation of the

---

[16] J. C. H. Lebram, 'The Piety of the Jewish Apocalyptists', in D. Hellholm (ed.), *Apocalypticism in the Mediterranean World and the Near East* (Tübingen: Mohr/Siebeck, 1983) 173. It is also of interest that the author of Wisdom of Solomon refers to himself as 'ὀξὺς . . . ἐν κρίσει' (8.11).

[17] Similarly, in order to achieve self-control, the *Letter of Aristeas* continues, God must dispose 'the heart and mind' toward it and to 'show gratitude to one's parents' and cause them no pain 'is impossible unless God guides the mind toward the noblest ends' (*Aristeas* 237f.). The answer to the question of how one can be 'an attentive listener' is: 'By perceiving that all knowledge is of value, so that in the face of events a man can select one of the lessons he has heard, counteract the immediate situation and so remedy it with the guidance of God – this means that the fulfilment of our deeds comes through him' (*Aristeas* 239).

[18] For the connection of Spirit, life and new covenant in the Old Testament, cf. Hubbard, *Creation*, 113–22. This means true knowledge is connected to a change in character and the development of integrity, which is, of course, also evident in the wisdom tradition (cf., for instance, R. W. L. Moberly, 'Solomon and Job: Divine Wisdom in Human Life', in Barton, *Wisdom*, 17).

very heart of human kind' in which the epistemological faculties would be reconfigured.[19]

To some extent, foretastes of this hope were being experienced. Hence Sirach can claim that the fear of the Lord brings such obedience and character formation.[20] The Spirit was active and, in contrast to merely revelatory activity, was also known to enhance natural abilities[21] and have an ethical impact.[22] Moreover, even at its most cognitive or esoteric, revealed knowledge was experienced as transforming since, it was believed, right knowledge would lead to right behaviour.[23] It was acknowledged that revelation could form the basis for a complete '*shift in perception*' of world-view and self-understanding.[24] However, such experiences of transformation were of a limited extent.[25] To a large degree transformation and correct discernment remained the prerogative of those particularly endowed with the Spirit, those closer to perfection (cf. 1QS 4.22), who in turn mediated knowledge as best they could.[26]

3.   Conclusion

In sum, discernment was a necessary tool for ITP Judaism in the attempt to understand God's continued way with Israel. This involved a critique

---

[19] Turner, *Spirit*, 5; cf. 114ff. Cf. 1QS 4.20–3: 'Meanwhile God will refine, with his truth, all man's deeds, and will purify for himself the *configuration* of man, ripping out all spirit of injustice from the *innermost part* of his flesh . . . In this way the upright will understand knowledge of the Most High . . .' (italics mine).

[20] Cf. Gammie, 'Sirach', 359; *Sir.* 2.7–9; 15.17.

[21] Turner ('Prophecy', 73) distinguishes between 'charismatic *communication* of wisdom' (a single charismatic event, in which 'the cognition is perceived to be altered by God' thereby improving apprehension) and 'charismatic *infusion* of wisdom' ('a series of such events – virtually a process extended over time – and not necessarily consciously perceived').

[22] Cf. 1QH 17.25–6; 1QS 4.20–3; Turner, *Power*, 121–33.

[23] Cf. Brown, *Cross*, 58; Newsom, 'Qumran', 381. Bockmuehl (*Revelation*, 125) says the mysteries pertained to redemption and sanctification.

[24] Brown, *Cross*, 53. C. Rowland ('Apocalyptic, God and the World', in Barclay, *Thought*, 247) speaks of an 'epistemological rupture' quoting liberation theologians: 'that is an epistemological transformation . . . involving an ethical as well as intellectual conversion'.

[25] At Qumran, in some senses, more significant than the issue of theodicy is the question, why do the righteous sin (cf. 1QS 3.22)? The experience that even those who committed themselves to the will of God still sinned was a vexing problem, which could only be partially answered by the belief in the continued influence of evil in all people (cf. Newsom, 'Qumran', 377f.).

[26] Elliott (*Survivors*, 174) shows that knowledge served polemical ends and that, as long as the correct people, the elect, possessed the knowledge, inconsistencies would be tolerated and the content would be secondary.

of other forms of knowledge and, particularly, the process of contextu-alising revealed knowledge. C. Newsom's comment about the Qumran community applies in varied degrees to other forms of Judaism too: 'Discerning and practising the correct interpretation of the Torah is the *raison d'être* for the entire community.'[27] However, the statement also reveals the limits of discernment. While acquired, and particularly spiri-tually transformed, means of knowing were being experienced, the focal point and touchstone of all knowledge was the Torah (or the mediated interpretation of it).

For this study of Paul, it is important to note that he shares many of the basic presuppositions of this description of discernment. The need for revelation and the Spirit's role in that process (due to the basic depravity of humankind), the eschatological and dualistic framework and the hope for a re-creation of the natural faculties (resulting in a direct knowledge of God and his will), are essential boundary mark-ers of Paul's thought. We shall return later to the 'shift in perception' which the apocalyptic revelatory experience leads to, and the parenetic value which it offers. However, some questions remain open. How is the Spirit's role to be understood in its effect on natural epistemologi-cal abilities? Moreover, how can their renewal be understood? How is an apprehension of the will of God possible without a (rigid) adherence to the Torah?

It is on these questions that I hope to shed light in turning to Philo and the Stoic material.

C.   Philo of Alexandria

1.   Introduction

The concept of discernment and reflective thought has, as such, not been the object of any particular research, although it plays a central role in

---

[27] Newsom, 'Qumran', 375. Cf. 1QS 1.1ff. In a different manner this quote applies to the rabbinic traditions. As S. D. Fraade ('The Early Rabbinic Sage', in Gammie and Perdue [eds.], *Sage*, 436) points out: 'The sages and disciples who stand both behind and before such texts understood themselves to be preserving and transmitting "words of Torah", which could justify, sustain, and transform, through *rabbinic* mediation, the life of Israel ... It was especially in the continuous and collective practice of transforming Torah (both "written" and "oral") through intensively engaged, multivocal commentary as a religious act, that the sages sought to transform *themselves* into a cohesive society whose own discourse and deeds would make them worthy and capable of transforming . . . Jewish society more broadly.'

Philo's overall philosophical/theological thinking. Reflective thought and reason are essential in establishing those matters which, in Philo's view, are of significance for humankind: (inter alia) that there must be an active cause behind the world (*Op.* 8); that all existing things are the grace of God (*Quod Deus* 107); that there is a need to distinguish between the truth and the empty fancies concerning life (*L.A.* 3.157; *Agr.* 130; *Jos.* 126; cf. *Op.* 154; *Agr.* 95). In this vein Philo can claim that:

> (F)or the power to distinguish necessaries of life from refuse . . . and genuine from spurious, and a highly profitable fruitage from a root that is devoid of profit, in things yielded by the understanding, not in those which the soil puts forth, is a mark of consummate excellence.[28]

However, this process of discernment is quite ambiguous. The belief that evaluation and differentiation are important follows from the insight that deceit and concealed disguises (*Cher.* 17) obscure the authentic perception of reality. The 'great plague of the soul' is deceit (*Cong.* 18) which manifests itself in and through pleasures which have no lasting quality (*Leg.* 2), in vain fancies (*L.A.* 2.56; *Jos.* 126ff.) and ignorance (*Ebr.* 161; *Leg.* 2). But reason, and people who believe in their own competence, can also be misleading (*Ebr.* 166). Moreover, a multitude of different opinions about, and consistent changes in, one's perception of reality make the task of accurate discernment truly difficult (*Ebr.* 168–202).

How then is deception to be overcome and true knowledge attained? To answer this we encounter partially contradictory answers. Thus Philo can claim that the ultimate touchstone in finding out truth is the contemplative and philosophical mind (*Mut.* 208). On the other hand, he says that if it were not for the divine Spirit, the mind could never attain certain aspects of the truth (*Mos.* 2.265). Moreover, Philo's epistemological and psychological conceptions are at best complex.[29] He follows Platonic,[30]

---

[28] Philo, *Som.* 2.22.

[29] E. R. Goodenough (*An Introduction to Philo Judaeus* [Oxford: Basil Blackwell, 1962] 112) sees (at first sight) a 'surprising jumble of contradictions' in Philo's thoughts on the mind since he sometimes praises it, sometimes despairs of it. On the one hand, Philo describes it as divine, on the other hand calls it blind, deaf and impotent since it requires the senses for all its data.

[30] Wolfson (*Philo* II, 72) made an influential proposal that in Philo's mind Plato followed a threefold classification of knowledge: (1) sensation and opinion; (2) 'knowledge of scientific concepts formed by the mind on the basis of data ultimately furnished by sensation'; (3) 'knowledge of the incorporeal ideas attained through recollection' (also called 'philosophic frenzy'). Philo, according to Wolfson, accepted these categories, except substituting the third category with prophecy. Hence Wolfson states that Philo held the prophet to have

Aristotelian/Stoic[31] and wisdom traditions[32] in defining the lower and higher forms of knowledge. This results in some metaphysical and linguistic confusion. In other words, are the νοῦς and human πνεῦμα (and for that matter λόγος) essentially divine? Can human νοῦς and divine πνεῦμα be partially equated or should they be wholly differentiated? Indeed, is not the very essence of mind divine Spirit (*Det.* 83). It is this relationship of S/spirit and mind, of external aid and innate abilities, and how they influence discernment, which I must deal with.[33] Before doing so, I turn to Philo's epistemological framework.

2. Epistemological Framework

On the one hand, Philo is essentially a foundationalist in his approach to truth. Without acknowledgement of God, straight thinking cannot take place. Only when God is accepted as judge can one eradicate the false opinions about oneself (*Som.* 2.24). Similarly, unless the soul confesses that all actions and all progress comes from God it cannot 'live the real life' (*L.A.* 2.93). Indeed, 'only he who sets his hope on God is of the race of men which is "truly rational" (λογικῶν)'.[34] This is something of a presupposition, a sine qua non in his work and for all who want to discern correctly.

On the other hand, Philo has a coherentist tendency, in which the three objectives in life of knowing God, finding the truth and ethical purity are inseparably linked. In that sense the ethical 'war' in a person (*L.A.* 3.116–18) is part and parcel of the religious dimension.[35] Achieving a

the highest kind of knowledge. However, as I shall attempt to show, such a classification is difficult to impose on Philo.

[31] Goodenough (*Philo*, 113) believes the Aristotelian 'distinction between two minds within us, a higher and a lower' serves as the backdrop and an explanation for Philo's apparent contradictions about the different qualities and functions of the mind. However, Goodenough acknowledges that often Philo is guided more by the passages he is interpreting than by consistency.

[32] Cf. Pearson, *Pneumatikos*, 82, who sees Philo in line with what he calls 'Hellenistic-Jewish speculative mysticism', a phrase originally used by D. Georgi.

[33] There is of course a broader question about the degrees of immanence and transcendence in Philo's work, which has been answered with varying emphases resulting in, e.g., a more philosophical portrayal (Wolfson, *Philo*) or a more mystical one (E. R. Goodenough, *By Light, Light: The Mystic Gospel of Hellenistic Judaism* [New Haven, CT: Yale University Press, 1935]).

[34] Wolfson, *Philo* II, 199.

[35] The near equation in Philo between true knowledge and a pure life is the reason why it is important to overcome the passions before achieving correct discernment. It is similar to that of the Stoics (cf. J. Klausner, *From Jesus to Paul* [trans. W. Stinespring; New York: Menorah, 1943] 195; A. Strobel, *Der erste Brief an die Korinther* [Zürich: Theologischer Verlag, 1989] 63).

virtuous lifestyle can hence be described both as living in accordance to the rule of God and the law of nature (*Opif.* 3).[36] This becomes particularly evident in the manner in which Philo has linked the frames of reference of philosophy and Judaism in equating Greek virtues and the Mosaic 'laws'.[37] That is to say, when we speak of discerning the truth or coming to a clearer understanding of God or attaining ethical purity, these activities are essentially fulfilling the same purpose. In that sense, correct discernment has soteriological significance for Philo.

Moreover, while both the foundationalist and coherentist aspects are present in Philo's truth formation, we also encounter, as in Paul, the principle of 'like is known by like'. We shall return to this below (p. 118). First, however, I must elucidate the separate roles of the Spirit and the innate abilities of humans concerning discernment. Following this elucidation, I will return to the question of how mind and Spirit interrelate.

3.   Help from the Spirit

Philo's view of the divine Spirit as a cosmic force is akin to that of the Stoics. However, there is also a remarkable distinction: the divine Spirit comes from the outside and does not necessarily remain in a person (*Gig.* 28).[38] The effects of this Spirit are multiple in form.[39] I will concentrate on three types of spiritual influence in which the mind still plays an active role, and is neither transcended nor excluded.[40]

---

[36] Goodenough, *Light*, 196. To attain authentic perception one must win the battle against the enemies of that endeavour: earthly cares and civil obligations (*Spec.* 3.1–5; *Gig.* 29).

[37] N. G. Cohen, 'The Greek Virtues and the Mosaic Laws in Philo. An Elucidation of De Specialibus Legibus IV 133–135', in D. T. Runia (ed.), *The Studia Philonica Annual: Studies in Hellenistic Judaism* V (Atlanta: Scholars Press, 1993) 9–23.

[38] J. R. Levison 'Inspiration and the Divine Spirit in Philo', *JSJ* 26 (1995) 279.

[39] A number of forms of inspiration (particularly those that eclipse the mind) and the results of Spirit influence (e.g. poetic ecstasy and prophecy) lead us beyond this study. For a discussion, cf. J. R. Levison, *The Spirit in First Century Judaism* (AGJU 29; Leiden: Brill, 1997); for bibliography, Levison, 'Inspiration', 271f.

[40] I have borrowed these categories of inspiration from Levison, *Spirit*. However, they fit loosely to the categories that Turner uses more generally for Judaism; cf. the discussion earlier (pp. 102ff.). Hence, the Spirit as 'prompter' could match the 'revelatory' aspect, and the 'philosophical ascent' would fit more easily into the category of 'wisdom'. As they are only loose categories for the purposes of an overview, any such identification does not aid this study.

The Spirit as Guide

First of all, the Spirit can act as a guide or a prompter for the mind. The minds of both Moses (*Mos.* 2.264f.) and Joseph (*Jos.* 110–16), for instance, are enabled by the Spirit to understand or see something otherwise unknowable. Presumably these interpretations are inspired by Philo's own experiences, since they closely resemble his autobiographical accounts of the Spirit guiding him as a 'friend' (*Som.* 2.252; *Cher.* 27–9).[41] J. Levison has argued convincingly that the inspiration described in these instances is not ecstatic but rather rational.[42] A number of points supply evidence for this. First, the experience is described as one of being taught, as the use of the verb ἀναδιδάσκειν shows (*Som.* 2.252; *Cher.*29). Secondly, the experiences are addressed to, and linked directly with, the mind. In *Cher.* 29 Philo, having been inspired, directs the inspiration to the mind: 'O then, my mind, admit the image unalloyed of the two Cherubim . . .' Moreover, the experience leads to clearer discernment:

> Might it not have been expected, I ask, that these and like lessons would cause even those who were blind in their understanding to grow keen-sighted, receiving from the most sacred oracles the gift of eyesight, enabling them to judge of the real nature of things, and not merely rely on the literal sense?[43]

Thirdly, there is no displacement of reason nor an indication of wild or frenzied alteration such as might be expected from inspiration accounts of the Pythia or other prophets of antiquity. This is particularly worth noting with regard to the description of the inspiration of Moses. He speaks 'in his own person' (*Mos.* 2.187), in control of his mind (265).[44] The prophecy about the Sabbath does not come solely from inspiration but from his own response of amazement at the message about the manna (καταπλαγείς, 264).[45] C. Noack also emphasises this feature in his analysis of *Virt.*

[41] Levison, 'Inspiration', 299f. In a number of cases the objective of inspiration is to gain an understanding of the scriptures, but this in turn also leads to clearer discernment of reality (*Som.* 2.164) and hence the passages are applicable to my cause.

[42] Cf. Levison, 'Inspiration', 302f.; 'The Prophetic Spirit as an Angel According to Philo', *HTR* 88 (1995) 201–4.

[43] Philo, *Som.* 1.164. The reference to the Spirit comes in the following verse as the 'Sacred Guide, our prompter'.

[44] Levison, *Spirit*, 185.

[45] Levison (*Spirit*, 185) also picks up on the similarity of the depiction of the inspiration of Moses with the conception of the daemon (following Levision I use 'daemon' instead of 'demon') which indwelt Socrates in Plutarch (*De Genio Socratis* 580B–582C; 588B-589F [*Moralia* VII]). This is illuminating as it shows how Philo is able to coalesce the Jewish concept of Spirit with Graeco-Roman beliefs; cf. the discussion of this in the Stoic section below.

211–19. He speaks of a '*Hochschätzung der geschöpflichen Vernunft*', and suggests that Philo characterises belief as an '*unerschütterliches Gottesbewußtsein*' in all of his writings.[46]

The concept of the Spirit as a guide is, however, somewhat unclear in places, as it overlaps with other significant terms such as συνείδησις and ἔλεγχος. Hence, 'conviction' can come from outside as the word of God or as an angel (*Deus* 182) and can even be called 'god' (*Fug.* 212).[47] Mostly, as we shall see, the identification of what is meant is not so difficult, and conscience can be seen more as an innate ability. However, it remains to be determined whether Levison is accurate in asserting that prompting does only 'occasionally arise from within a person without divine aid, far more often the source is divine'.[48] At this point it will suffice to note the fact that inspiration can occur without eclipsing the mind, but rather by enhancing its functions.[49] This is crucial, particularly for my later comparison with Paul.

The Spirit and Philosophical Ascent

The second form of inspiration, closely linked to the first, lies in the way the Spirit aids the mind in its philosophical ascent (*Plant.* 23–5; *Gig.* 28–30; *Spec.* 3.4–5)[50]. The Spirit is the one who gives 'wisdom, understanding and knowledge' (*Gig.* 23) and who (sometimes) grants the mass of humankind a vision of God (*Gig.* 21f.).[51] Further, the Spirit helps

---

[46] C. Noack, *Gottesbewußtsein* (WUNT 2,116; Tübingen: Mohr/Siebeck, 2000) 216 and 247 respectively. Further: 'Es liegt also eine *synergistische, rationalistische Inspirations- und Ekstasedarstellung* vor' (*Gottesbewußtsein*, 217).

[47] Cf. M. E. Isaacs, *The Concept of Spirit: A Study of Pneuma in Hellenistic Judaism and its Bearing on the New Testament* (London: Heythrop College, 1976) 42; H.-J. Klauck, 'Ein Richter im eigenen Inneren: Das Gewissen bei Philo von Alexandrien', in *Alte Welt und neuer Glaube: Beiträge zur Religionsgeschichte, Forschungsgeschichte und Theologie des Neuen Testaments* (NTOA 29; Göttingen: Vandenhoeck & Ruprecht, 1994) 33–58. However, cf. the rather categorical distinction between divine Spirit, angels and voice of God in Wolfson, *Philo* II, 61.

[48] Levison, 'Inspiration', 300.

[49] In more general terms, H. Burkhardt (*Die Inspiration Heiliger Schriften bei Philo von Alexandrien* [Giessen: Brunnen Verlag, 1988]) confirms this. His thesis shows that for Philo inspiration does not happen with the exclusion of reason but rather 'als ihre Indienststellung und Begnadung mit über die Möglichkeiten empirischer und rationaler Erkenntniswege hinausführender Erkenntnis' (*Inspiration*, 221). 'Nicht von Ausschaltung der Vernunft ist also überall die Rede sondern von ihrer Verfügbarkeit für ein auf Gott ausgerichtetes Leben und Denken' (*Inspiration*, 215).

[50] The Spirit is not directly mentioned in *Spec.* 3.4f., but, based on its correspondence with *Plant.* 23–5 and because of the otherwise 'inchoate' word ἐπιθειασμόν, it is correct for Levison ('Inspiration', 291) to see the Spirit indirectly present.

[51] Cf. Levison, *Spirit*, 137–42.

a person counter the inevitable downward pressure of existential cares (*Plant.* 24–5).[52] Levison is correct that these passages are crucial in the way they call into question the Graeco-Roman concepts of philosophical ascent, in that they define the divine Spirit as a means to attaining a clear perception of the intelligible world. Nevertheless, we encounter some ambiguity again. On the one hand, Levison admits that the 'ascent of the mind' is more typically described 'without reference to the spirit'.[53] On the other hand, he can claim that 'external aid is necessary for the ascent of the mind'.[54] We will need to investigate this further below (p. 117ff.).

The Spirit and Transformation

The third category which needs to be looked at in the matter of the Spirit's influence on the mind emerges from those passages where Philo speaks of a transformation process. Often this transformation involves the attributes of ideal beauty or the ideal king. However, it also affects the mind. Hence, Philo says of Moses when he is under the influence of the Spirit: 'He therefore became another man, changed both in out-ward appearance and mind . . .' (*Mos.* 2.272). And concerning Abraham, not only do the Spirit's transforming powers affect his words (giving them 'persuasiveness') but also because of the Spirit the hearers are able to understand him (*Virt.* 217). Moreover, God may intervene and implant within people virtues, such as humanity and gentleness (*Virt.*134), or cure vice, such as cowardice (*Virt.* 26). These ethical and long-term effects of the Spirit are important alongside its punctual and revelatory functions.

In sum, we can see that the concept of the divine Spirit may be one of the key points in which Philo differs from his Hellenistic contemporaries. The importance of inspiration for an authentic perception of reality and as a means to subject the earthly forces has been noted, while the relationship with the mind's own intrinsic powers needs yet to be established. Significant for the concept of discernment has been the realisation that the Spirit's guiding, elevating or transforming powers do not exclude or eclipse rational processes; rather they enhance them.

---

[52] Again it is remarkable that inspiration and preparation are not contradictory. On the contrary, man must 'crave for wisdom and knowledge with insatiable persistence' (Levison, 'Inspiration', 293).

[53] Levison, *Spirit*, 159.   [54] Levison, 'Inspiration', 293.

4. The Innate Abilities

In the same way as the Greek philosophers before him and of his time, Philo was captivated by the mind's capabilities, particularly its ability to perceive, investigate and discern everything (*Op*. 69). The mind is given the 'high calling to decide' between 'forces drawing in opposite directions' (virtue and vice, reason and pleasure) and its choices lead either to 'fame and immortality' or a 'dishonourable death' (*Plant*. 45).[55] However, this is only possible for the 'neutral' or 'naked' mind (*L.A.* 2.53–9) which has been stripped of deceitful opinions and pleasure (*L.A.* 3.109).[56] How, then, does the mind attain this ability to choose freely and, more importantly, wisely? I have discovered three principle means by which correct evaluation takes place, all of them internal.

First of all, as mentioned in the preceding section, prompting does not take place solely by the Spirit, but there is an innate 'prompter' in all people.

> This 'man,' dwelling in the soul of each of us, is discovered at one time as king and governor, at another as judge and umpire of life's contests. Sometimes he assumes the part of witness or accuser, and, all unseen, convicts [ἐλέγχει] us from within, not allowing us so much as to open our mouth, but, holding in and curbing the tongue with the reins of conscience [συνειδότος], checks its wilful and rebellious course.[57]

The similarity with the Spirit is remarkable and yet this convictor *remains in each* individual (*Decal*. 87), in contrast to the divine Spirit (*Gig*. 28).[58] P. Bosman has warned against hasty systematisation, since the concept

---

[55] For Philo this freedom of choice is important, as God is the principle of voluntary action and not force ἀνάγκη; cf. *Som.* 2.253, and Goodenough, *Light*, 393.

[56] There is an element of belief in 'natural virtue'. Cf. Wolfson, *Philo* II, 197, who believes that Philo disagrees with both Aristotle, who believed that virtue does not depend on nature, and the Stoics, who deny that it comes through nature or through practice. However, according to my findings, the fact that some have been endowed with a predisposition for virtue does not feature prominently in Philo. Generally he believes that man 'naturally hates' virtue (*L.A.* 2.47) and he is somewhat contradictory on whether or not the prophets were originally endowed with virtue (cf. the different accounts in *Som.* 1.167 and *Abr.* 53; see my findings on Stoicism below [III, 5, D]).

[57] Philo, *Det.* 23.

[58] Cf. V. Nikiprowetzky, 'La doctrine de l'élenchos chez Philon, ses résonances philosophiques et sa portée religieuse', in *Philon d'Alexandrie* (Actes du colloques nationaux du Centre national de la recherche scientifique; Paris: 1967) 274. Klauck ('Richter', 38–41) also points to the conceptual link between ἔλεγχος and συνειδός ('Richter', 40).

of the innate prompter/conscience is fluid in Philo.[59] Indeed, there has been some discussion as to whether or not the conscience has antecedent guiding value or whether it just judges *post eventum*.[60] Clearly, the 'convicting' (*Deus*. 125, 128, 135; *Det*. 146) and 'judging' (*Op*. 128; *Fug*. 119) functions are emphasised. However, for my purposes this is an unhelpful distinction. Not only are the functions of 'king' and 'governor' mentioned earlier ambiguous enough to be able to offer both direction and correction but, more importantly, both functions in their own right are significant for discernment. Besides, an incorruptible judge (cf. *Post*. 59; *Fug*. 119) will also have some character-shaping effect that will influence all future evaluation. Moreover, when conscience is (also)[61] understood as *consciousness*, these sharp distinctions fail to be convincing.[62] This more holistic understanding of the 'guide within' as an enhancement of consciousness is particularly important for my work with Paul. In sum, Levison's claim (as presented earlier), that this internal prompter is only an occasional force, does not do justice to the significance Philo attaches to it.[63]

The second means by which correct evaluation can take place is by putting to use the intellectual and reflective capacities a person possesses.[64] In places Philo's optimism about the positive effect of reason is remarkable (particularly for a Jewish writer).[65] Hence, an active

[59] P. Bosman, *Conscience in Philo and Paul: A Conceptual History of the Synoida Word Group* (WUNT 2,166; Tübingen: Mohr/Siebeck, 2003) 175. Bosman shows that συνειδός is used with different senses in three contexts. One, it is used within the παρρησία topos where the awareness of a transgression inhibits interaction with others and freedom of speech (*Conscience*, 177ff.). Two, it becomes a 'component of the soul', as a 'universal part of the νοῦς making it possible for it to be 'neutral', 'that is, not necessarily testifying to an awareness of guilt' (*Conscience*, 183). Three, the dominant aspect of Philo's use of the word group 'is in combination with forensic terminology', namely in 'psychological processes described metaphorically as an inner court of law' (*Conscience*, 184).

[60] Cf. Klauck, 'Richter', 47, and bibliography there.

[61] I say 'also' because it could be argued that the 'incorruptible judge' and 'consciousness' are two different senses of conscience. In my work on Paul, I shall differentiate between the 'inner monitor' and 'consciousness'.

[62] R. A. Horsley ('Consciousness and Freedom among the Corinthians: 1 Corinthians 8–10', *CBQ* 40 [1978] 582), argues for the interpretation of a 'moral consciousness' whose 'function is to prevent the soul from wrong and/or to accuse and "convict" the soul of having acted unjustly'.

[63] Cf. also *Jos*. 197; *Conf*. 121; *Fug*. 131; *L.A*. 1.235–7.

[64] Cf. M. Freudenthal, *Die Erkenntnislehre Philos von Alexandria* (Berlin: S. Calvary & Co., 1891) 74: 'All diesen Kampf und Streit, den die Affekte und die Lust verursachen, können wir vermeiden, wenn wir die Sinne zügeln durch die Vernunft wenn wir diese herrschen lassen . . .'

[65] Hence, nothing in human nature is nobler than a sober mind, which penetrates in a purely intellectual manner everything, even wisdom itself (*Sob*. 3; cf. *L.A*. 3.119). While the

evaluation of arguments[66] together with a focussed contemplation are a conscious attempt to set the mind on the correct objectives and allow these in turn to shape one's value system.

A particularly good example of this is in the way Philo interprets the account of the bronze snake in Num. 21.4–9 (*L.A.* 2.79–81). Those who have been bitten by the serpents are those who have indulged in pleasure immoderately, and they can only find a cure when they *behold* and *contemplate* the bronze snake created by Moses, σωφροσύνη, which is the opposite of pleasure. It is through the contemplation (and the emphasis is on a rational act of contemplation)[67] of σωφροσύνη that a person is able to behold God and heal the soul (*L.A.* 2.81). This, then, is the answer to the snake originally encountered by Eve in the garden, which symbolises pleasure. Giving the mind such a focal point as a spiritual exercise in character formation, is something we will see in Paul too.[68]

The third aspect which is important for correct discernment is education. H. A. Wolfson points out that virtues are attained by learning and by practice.[69] Hence, Abraham had 'teaching as his guide' on the road to virtue, while Isaac was self-taught and Jacob 'relied on exercises and practisings' (*Som.* 1.168). But again, reaching virtue is not an easy education. It is devotion to continued study, practising and meditating (without intermission!; *Congr.* 24). The goal is the ability to retain and 'remember' the virtues and hence integrate them into one's character.[70]

Greek influence is obvious, Philo can use the intellectual argument against the sophists and philosophers too. Their belief that they, not God, are the cause of things (*L.A.* 3.28) is the result of unreasoned opinion. They fail to recognise that the world must have had an origin because every system needs a Creator and more: a 'protector, arbitrator, or judge' (*Op.* 11f.; cf. R. Williamson, *Jews in the Hellenistic World: Philo* [CCWJCW 1, ii; Cambridge: Cambridge University Press, 1989] 90; Klausner, *Jesus*, 190).

[66] In the tradition, which goes back to Socrates (see my quotation below [p. 121]), dialectic science can cure deceit by separating 'true argument from false' and convicting 'the plausibilities of sophistry' (*Cong.* 18). In a similar vein, Philo depicts the duty of a judge to be like that of 'a good money-changer' dividing and distinguishing 'the nature of each of the facts before him, so that genuine and spurious may not be jumbled together in confusion' (*Spec.* 4.77).

[67] As Philo's concluding remark shows: 'μόνον ἰδέτω καὶ κατανοησάτω' ('only let him look and mark well'; *L.A.* 2.81).

[68] Cf. also how the contemplation of the order of the κόσμος will lead to a law-abiding and peaceful life (*Abr.* 61). Further, the contemplative life of the Therapeutae is praised in *Cont.* as being particularly acceptable to God and giving them 'true excellence of life' (*Cont.* 90). However, this is a more mystical (*Cont.* 12) and intense example of the contemplation commended elsewhere.

[69] Wolfson, *Philo* II, 197.   [70] Cf. Horsley, 'Pneumatikos', 278.

Finally, it is important to point out the progressive aspect of the whole process of reaching the correct mindset.[71] Virtue sometimes only comes slowly and usually to the mature and older since otherwise it may overwhelm the immature recipient (*Her.* 308f.). Moreover, we find in Philo a spiral effect of discernment in which correct perception is the result of practising discernment.[72] An example of this is in the way Philo expects people to understand what things in life are *adiaphora* (such as pain, death, poverty and a desire for reputation) and how one can deny them their enslaving power. One must by diligent examination (ἐξητακὼς ἐπιμελῶς) realise that these are indifferent vicissitudes and that they stand in direct contrast to the divine things which are honoured by 'eternal order and happiness' (*Prob.* 24).[73]

In sum, we have found that there are a number of methods by which the mind can be helped to ascend and by which it is transformed from its earthly state. The inner intuitive guide acts as judge and convictor. Learning and practice are necessary, just as is putting to use the intellectual, evaluative and reflective tools a person possesses. These, in turn, will progressively aid character formation and lead the person to mature and authentic perception.

5.   The Interrelationship of Spirit and Mind

Having elaborated the separate roles that the Spirit and the mind play in discernment, I have not yet addressed the issue of their interaction and prominence. The difficulty is that Philo manages to keep two antithetical aspects in creative tension.

On the one hand, the distinction between mind and Spirit that I have argued for is an artificial one. How is this so? In the same manner as God created an incorporeal universe before creating its material counterpart (*Op. Mundi* 29, 36), so he also created a heavenly man (Gen. 1.26; *Op. Mundi* 69ff.) and an earthly man (Gen. 2.7; *Op. Mundi* 134ff.). In the heavenly man, the image of God was visible in man's rationality. Hence, the

---

[71] Cf. Freudenthal, *Erkenntnislehre*, 74: 'Die besten Waffen im Kriege gegen alle die schädlichen Einflüsse der Sinnlichkeit sind Weisheit und Tugend; sie erwerben wir stets *fortschreitend vom Sinnlichen zum Geistigen von dunkler zu reiner Erkenntnis*' (italics mine).

[72] Klausner (*Jesus*, 191) states that 'Philo demands also of man himself, that he develop in himself the good by means of discernment. And since morality and discernment are one, Philo considers ethics the most important branch of philosophy.'

[73] This is significant as it has parallels with Paul's understanding of *adiaphora* and also relates to the view of the Stoics, as I shall show below.

'source of the mind's cohesion and ability is precisely τὸ θεῖον πνεῦμα'.[74] This means that when speaking of the *essence* of heavenly mind we are speaking of Spirit (*L.A.* 1.37).[75] However, the earthly man takes part in a weaker form of divine πνεῦμα.

That means, on the other hand, that in the earthly man there *is* a distinction between innate abilities and divine Spirit.[76] Here an identification of the two should rightly be refuted as reductionism.[77] The earthly man must will himself to turn and return to the originally created image in the heavenly man. Earthly mind cannot by itself attain authentic understanding.[78] In order for this to happen, both mind and Spirit must work together *symbiotically* so that the principle of 'like is known by like' is fulfilled.[79]

[74] M. Turner, 'Spirit in Philo' (Unpubl. Paper, Aberdeen, 1991) 2. That means the essence of purified νοῦς is made of πνεῦμα (*Her.* 55), can be equated with divine πνεῦμα (*Fug.* 133) and is the copy of the divine reason (*Op.* 136; cf. Isaacs, *Spirit*, 38ff.). When speaking of τὸ θεῖον πνεῦμα, I am referring particularly to Spirit as the rational Spirit. Πνεῦμα, of course, can have a broad array of different senses ranging from 'breath' or 'wind' to 'cohesion' (*Op.* 131) to 'life-breath' (*Gig.* 10; *Op.* 67) and finally to both the 'rational' (*Det.* 83) and 'divine spirit' (*Gig.* 53).

[75] Hence true wisdom too must be seen as essentially coming from God (cf. *L.A.* 2.86–8; *Fug.* 166; *Mut.* 256ff.; Strobel, *Korinther*, 63). Divine wisdom purifies the earthly mind (*Spec.* 1.269) and that is the basis of discernment (*Op.* 154).

[76] Cf. W. Bieder, 'πνεῦμα κτλ.', *TDNT* VI, 374, who shows that Philo is not a pantheist and that there are points where the prophetic spirit takes precedence over the rational; H. Leisegang, *Der Heilige Geist: Das Wesen und Werden der mystisch-intuitiven Erkenntnis in der Philosophie und Religion der Griechen* (Leipzig: Teubner, 1919) 64f.: '... wenn es ihm [Philo] darauf ankommt, die erhabene Göttlichkeit des πνεῦμα als Weltprinzip recht deutlich zu erweisen. Dann müssen alle Philosopheme der Weltweisen hinter seiner, des Gotterfüllten, besseren Erkenntnis zurücktreten.'

[77] Therefore Isaacs (*Spirit*, 59–64) has argued against the position of A. Laurentin that πνεῦμα always is πνεῦμα θεοῦ, as it does injustice to the diversity of Philo's language. However, neither does she accept a polarisation of the senses of πνεῦμα. Isaacs argues for a *conceptual* link between the senses (excluding 'wind'; *Spirit*, 63). The key for her lies in Philo's apologetic attempt to reconcile Hellenistic and biblical thought while not attempting 'to resolve the philosophical difficulties which arise from trying to maintain both' (*Spirit*, 63). More important for him is that the spirit can be seen as both the principle of order, cohesion and reason (and as such the link between God and a person), and as the divine Spirit which only comes as the result of divine grace (*Spirit*, 64). While this mediating position is generally preferable, there is to date no real consensus on Philo's pneumatology (cf. Levison, 'Inspiration', 271ff.).

[78] There is 'nothing so shameful' as to think that the mind is the origin of comprehension since it does not even comprehend itself (*L.A.* 2.68f.; cf. E. Mühlenberg, 'Das Problem der Offenbarung in Philo von Alexandrien', *ZNW* 64 [1973] 6ff., 13f.).

[79] For the 'like is known by like principle'; cf. Gärtner, 'Idea', 213–15; *Praem.* 45f.; *Gig.* 8f.; *Mut.* 6, 56; *Mig.* 39–40; Sellin, 'Geheimnis', 87; Stuhlmacher, 'Bedeutung', 158. I say *symbiotically* because, as I have shown, Philo sees no contradiction in keeping revelation and human thinking on a continuum. This is shown also in oxymorons which he coins such as 'sober intoxication' (*Fug.* 166; *L.A.* 3.82). Further, in *Quis rerum divinarum heres sit*, to become an heir of the divine things the mind should be in a state of enthusiastic inspiration (*Her.* 70), but this liberation from the body and from speech takes place because the mind

Hence, authentic knowledge is achieved not only by God revealing himself, but also by the recipient's total reorientation of his/her natural faculties. A 'fundamental transformation of cognition' is the 'precondition of a true comprehension' of reality.[80] It is a complete emancipation, an escape (*L.A.* 3.41) from the earthly self and a process by which a person's thinking and life is offered up to God (*Her.* 74).[81] Therefore, for the principle of 'like is known by like' to be fulfilled it is important that mind and Spirit *cohere again* with one another.[82]

In sum then, while there is a distinction between divine Spirit and the mind of humans (or between revelation and thinking), this distinction should not be expressed in absolute terms.[83] Rather, I propose, it is a difference of intensity on a spectrum of divine endowment.[84] This spectrum

has learnt it 'through experience' and decided for himself to acknowledge God (*Her.* 71–3). Furthermore, it is not possible to differentiate between mind and Spirit functionally as both fulfil similar functions. Nor is a stark qualitative differentiation possible between the Spirit's role in the leaders of Israel (Abraham, Noah, Moses etc.) and in 'normal' people, as the experiences of the former are paradigmatic for the latter.

[80] Cf. H. Tronier, 'The Correspondence between Philosophical Idealism and Apocalypticism', in T. Engberg-Pedersen (ed.), *Paul beyond the Judaism/Hellenism Divide* (Louisville, KY: Westminster/John Knox Press, 2001) 171.

[81] Cf. Klausner, *Jesus*, 195. This process happens through an acknowledgement that the true explanations of things are found with God (*Mig.* 19). This means that only through an understanding of a person's οὐδένεια can he or she come to correct perception and comprehend God (*Som.* 1.60, 212; cf. *Her.* 29). This humble self-assessment is in some ways the highest form of knowledge. Cf. Betz, *Paulus*, 128; idem, 'Maxim', 104f.; *Som.* 1.60 and 212. This is significant, as it represents a marked difference to the Corinthian opposition of Paul, who may have relied on traditions of Hellenistic Judaism. This is sometimes not stressed enough; cf. Pearson, *Pneumatikos*, 39, where the difference between the Corinthians and Philonic intent is not clearly worked through. Brown (*Cross*, 163) points out that Philo would not have agreed with the use of his language at Corinth but would have subjected it to the same criticism as Paul did.

[82] In this sense Philo also has an *ethical* 'discernment of spirits': the disguise of those assuming the names of angels can be lifted if it becomes clear that they follow the path of the senses rather than virtue (*Gig.* 17). For the complex manner in which Philo distinguishes between souls, angels and demons and yet can also identify them as one reality, see Levison, *Spirit*, 140.

[83] Against Theissen, *Aspects*, 331: 'Philo says that divine Spirit and human mind cannot dwell next to each other, but Paul claims the opposite.'

[84] Cf. C. Bennema, *The Power of Saving Wisdom: An Investigation of Spirit and Wisdom in Relation to the Soteriology of the Fourth Gospel* (WUNT 2,148; Tübingen: Mohr/Siebeck, 2002) 71–83. In particular, the knowledge of God appears to be on a spectrum. To a certain extent the virtuous mindset can come to know God by itself, 'reasoning from effect to cause or from analogy' (cf. *L.A.* 3.33, 98f.; cf. *Op.* 1–12; Wolfson, *Philo* II, 83; Goodenough, *Light*, 386). But this is a limited knowledge, since to know God intimately he needs to reveal himself (cf. 'God too is His own brightness and is discerned through Himself alone, without anything co-operating or being able to co-operate in giving a perfect apprehension of His existence' [*Praem.* 45f.]; Mühlenberg, 'Offenbarung', 5, 9–18). Wolfson (*Philo* II, 148) suggests that, while the existence of God is knowable, the essence of God is not.

ranges from the mind's own abilities to the charismatic enlightenment and *visio dei*.[85]

6.   Conclusion

Philo 'defies categorisation'.[86] Precisely as such, he is of benefit to my study of Paul. While remaining firmly rooted in Judaism, he is free to borrow epistemological concepts from Hellenism to make his point. While remaining a firm believer in the transcendence of revelation, he sees the possibility and need for the individual person to progressively seek a mindset which by 'itself' can attain authentic perception. We also saw that, contra some claims, both Spirit and mind (in a significant manner) prompt, guide and help people in their fight against earthly forces and to achieve authentic perception.[87] More significantly, Spirit and reason are not considered to be mutually exclusive. Rather, the Spirit can enhance and transform reason and enable it to attain its full potential of discernment. Paul, as I shall point out in the next chapter, does not share Philo's optimism about the discerning powers of the natural faculties. Neither does he insist, however, on a sharp discontinuity between them and the revelatory functions of the Spirit. On the contrary, Paul also takes the combination of both seriously.

It is the combination of these which I am particularly interested in. Can this be described in a more detailed manner? How do virtue and

---

[85] A point that may be noted, though not explored, is that it has been argued that the apparent eviction of the mind during prophetic inspiration is *essentially* just a higher form of knowledge; cf. M. Fatehi, *The Spirit's Relation to the Risen Lord in Paul* (WUNT 2,128; Tübingen: Mohr/Siebeck, 2000) 115, who writes: 'The important point is that this highest level of knowledge is still a knowledge of the mind although in it the mind is detached from the senses and whatever they may contribute . . . So what happens is in fact not an eviction or negation of reason, but an experience in its most pure and intensive form.' His argument (based on Wolfson) is that where in *Q.G.* 3.9 the mind wanders 'beyond itself' and the intellect inspired by divine things 'no longer exists in itself', the 'itself' is the self tied to the body and the senses (116). The point is one that I have also emphasised, that as long as the mind is still caught by sensual pleasure (which equals the earthly mind) it cannot perceive correctly. *The more it is liberated the more it will see* (cf. *Q.G.* 4.90). Nonetheless, Fatehi's assertion that Philo's concept of πνεῦμα in relation to man 'is more or less a unified and coherent concept' (*Relation*, 116) is something of an overstatement.

[86] Levison, 'Inspiration', 274.

[87] Some of Levison's claims (noted earlier [pp. 112–13]) about the Spirit's role are overstatements. He also 'attributes the highest achievement of rational thought to the divine spirit' ('Prophetic Spirit', 199) and claims to find 'remarkable consistency' in Philo's understanding of 'the ways in which the spirit guides the mind to truth' (*Spirit*, 213). My research would rather support his observation that 'these two streams [rational thought and prophetic inspiration] vie for prominence and converge wildly . . . producing at times confusing whirlpools' ('Inspiration', 313).

knowledge qualify each other? Since the Stoics offer an answer, we turn to them now.

D.   The Stoics

1.   Introduction

From its very origins and by virtue of its self-definition classical Greek philosophy valued discernment.[88] Hence Plato has Socrates say,

> And the highest point of my art [κάλλιστον ἔργον] is the power to prove by every test whether the offspring of a young man's thought is a false phantom or instinct with life and truth . . . Accept, then, the ministration of a midwife's son who himself practices his mother's art, and do the best you can to answer the questions I ask. Perhaps when I examine your statements I may judge one or another of them to be an unreal phantom.[89]

Discernment is a central tool for differentiating between the real and unreal world, which in turn is the objective of Plato's enterprise. Because of epistemic vices and the limits of reason, all of reality requires uncompromising evaluation.[90] Hence, Plato describes how one inventor must

---

[88]   The definition Gooch offers of philosophy (*Knowledge*, 3) applies here: 'critical thinking and discerning knowledge'.

[89]   Plato, *Theaetetus* 150b–151c, in F. M. Cornford (trans.), *Plato's Theory of Knowledge* (London: Routledge & Kegan Paul, 1960^2) 26f.

[90]   'Immer wieder trennt der platonische Sokrates zwischen einem durch den Gesichtssinn zugänglichen und einem unsichtbaren Bereich . . . Die philosophischen Anstrengungen des Platon gelten der noetischen Erschließung der "Urbilder", die unter den sichtbaren "Abbildern" verborgen liegen. Nur wer den anstrengenden Gedankenweg mitgegangen ist, kann richtig zwischen Schein und Sein unterscheiden' (T. K. Heckel, *Der innere Mensch: Die paulinische Verarbeitung eines platonischen Motivs* [WUNT 2,53; Tübingen: Mohr/Siebeck, 1993] 18). For the danger of epistemic vices, cf. Plato, *Sophist* 230c-d-231b, where he claims that one must be rid of conceit and stubborn 'opinions' before attaining true knowledge; similarly Plutarch, *Platonicae Quaestiones* 999E (*Moralia XIII*). For the fact that reason has its limits, cf. Xenophon, *Memorabilia* 1.1.8f.: '[B]ut the deepest secrets of these matters the gods reserved to themselves; they were dark to men. You may plant a field well; but you know not who shall gather the fruits: you may build a house well; but you know not who shall dwell in it: able to command, you cannot know whether it is profitable to command: versed in statecraft, you know not whether it is profitable to guide the state: though, for your delight, you marry a pretty woman, you cannot tell whether she will bring you sorrow: though you form a party among men mighty in the state, you know not whether they will cause you to be driven from the state. [9] If any man thinks that these matters are wholly within the grasp of the human mind and nothing in them is beyond our reason, that man, he said, is irrational.'

judge the other,[91] and practitioners of geometry, astronomy and mathematics submit their work to the διαλεκτικοί.[92] Both rational and divine forms of guidance aid the process of discernment.[93] However, as we noted in chapter 3, due to the ambiguity of inspired utterances, there is a need for interpretative evaluation of such phenomena.

Moreover, there was a line of thought within Hellenism that if no possibility of measuring, no rational standard, is present, then feeling or intuitive perception (αἴσθησις) is necessary for the ability to discern correctly.[94] In this regard, Aristotle searched for a standard appropriate for each individual rather than an absolute standard, and he developed 'the mean between excess and deficiency' as the central point of his ethics.[95] This in turn can only be achieved by reasoned and reflected choosing, which in turn is that state of mind (ἕξις) which for Aristotle is the definition of ἀρετή itself.[96] This link between discernment and a virtuous state of mind is important and will be returned to below.

Due to this inheritance, the Stoics (and to a degree the Epicureans) also had reflective and rational decision making at the heart of their philosophical system. Hence Epictetus can claim

> that the greatest task of the philosopher is to test [δοκιμάζειν] the impressions [τὰς φαντασίας] and discriminate [διακρίνειν] between them and to apply [i.e. in the sense of basing action

---

[91] Plato states in a discussion about the art and invention of writing, 'one man has the ability to beget arts, but the ability to judge of their usefulness or harmfulness to their users belongs to another' (*Phaedrus* 274e).

[92] Plato, *Euthydemus* 290c. Cf. also *Cratylus* (388b and 390c) on the evaluation and questioning a dialectician carries out.

[93] Jillions ('Decision-Making', 3–4) shows how both types of guidance are discussed and yet, although they stand in tension to one another, they are not seen as mutually exclusive (with particular reference to Posidonius).

[94] W. Jaeger (*Paideia: The Ideals of Greek Culture* III [trans. G. Highet; Oxford: Basil Blackwell, 1945] 18) points out that in the treatise *On Ancient Medicine*, the author (possibly from within the Hippocratic school) suggests that, since the sick man can be hurt by eating too little or too much, 'the real doctor is recognized by his power to estimate what is appropriate for each individual case. He is the man who has the sure judgment to pick the right quantity for everyone.'

[95] Jaeger (*Paideia* III, 25) writes that Aristotle was influenced by the treatise (mentioned in the preceding footnote) in his endeavour to find a standard for each individual. Cf. Aristotle, *Ethics* 1107a4ff. (alternative numbering: II.vi.15ff.)

[96] Aristotle, *Ethics* 1106b36 (II.vi.15). Choice is defined as follows: 'Perhaps we may define it as voluntary action preceded by deliberation, since choice involves reasoning and some process of thought' (*Ethics* 1112a17 [III.ii.17]). We may also note that νοῦς, φρόνησις 'is the gift of God which enables the philosopher or statesman to be a lawgiver' (G. Bertram, 'φρήν κτλ.', *TDNT* IX, here 222; W. Jaeger, *Paideia: Die Formung des Griechischen Menschen* III [Berlin: W. de Gruyter, 1947] 303f., 342).

upon only such impressions that have been tested and found to be trustworthy] none that has not been tested.[97]

Moreover, the best gift which Zeus has given humanity (even in comparison to life) is the faculty which can make use of all other faculties and skills by testing them, judging them and estimating 'the value of each'.[98] Learning true discernment is a lifelong task, a struggle, 'for rational mastery'.[99]

While this explains the centrality of discernment in Hellenistic thought, it also raises a number of questions. For one thing, there is the central question of my thesis: how can one acquire this discernment? Secondly, how can I introduce into my discussion of discernment a philosophical process of discernment, one that emphasises the rational to the apparent exclusion of the spiritual? Indeed, how can we compare two systems of thought, which appear to have different starting and finishing points?[100] I propose that the answer to both sets of questions lies in the particular manner in which the Stoics linked discernment to a fundamental perceptual shift, a new understanding of oneself and the world around. We will look at a number of different elements of such a transformed perspective, but the framework of such a shift has recently been explored by Troels Engberg-Pedersen.

2.   A New Self-Understanding

The Model

Having studied both Stoic and Pauline thought structures, Engberg-Pedersen has found that underlying the 'anthropology' and 'ethics' of

[97] Epictetus, *Discourses* 1.20.7. Cf. 2.12.20.

[98] Epictetus, *Discourses* 2.23.5f. This he calls the 'faculty of moral purpose' (προαιρετική; 2.23.9). Further, the final good is a life in which one has learnt to apply the knowledge of what is in agreement and consistent with nature by *selecting* those things in accordance and *rejecting* those contrary. Cf. Cicero, *De Finibus* 3.31.

[99] Meeks, *World*, 47, concerning Musonius Rufus.

[100] It has of course been argued (with partial justification) that the Stoic framework of thought was so different that it has little bearing on Paul. The abstract intellectualism, the optimistic view of humanity's capabilities and the teleological motivations (of reaching the good in this life) have been primary concerns and appear to set Paul a world apart (cf. S. K. Stowers, 'Paul on the Use and Abuse of Reason', in Balch, *Greeks*, 253–86; M. Strom, *Reframing Paul: Conversations in Grace and Community* [Downers Grove, IL: InterVarsity Press, 2000] 49–50; P. F. Esler, 'Paul and Stoicism: Romans 12 as a Test Case', *NTS* 50 [2004] 106–24).

both a similar pattern can be found, which he has depicted in the following model.[101]

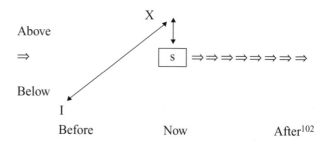

The main emphasis lies in the 'change that may occur in the perception
of individuals of their own identity' and their 'I'-centred concerns (the
I-level) to a state in which that individual sees him- or herself as part of
a 'social "We"' with new concerns; namely, fulfilling the desires of that
'We' (the S-level).[103] This change in self-understanding comes about
when the individual is 'struck' by something exterior (for Paul this is
God/Christ and for the Stoics this is reason) but with which the individual
can identify and can see him- or herself *'belonging'* to (which is the X-
level). Consequently, this has the result of bringing the individual to the
S-level. This is due to the 'specific content of what the individual has
identified with at the X-level' which is 'an understanding of oneself as
one among the others, one of *all* those who *share* in participating in X'.[104]

---

[101] Engberg-Pedersen, *Paul*. The model is primarily one that works on an anthropological or ethical level, and Engberg-Pedersen separates these from the theological level for
'analytical purposes'. But in both his introduction (*Paul*, 6) and conclusion (*Paul*, 295) he
stresses the unity of theology and ethics in Paul, and his essential goal is to see how the
model works for the whole of Paul (*Paul*, 44). With respect to the model, he points out
that it has no independent value. 'Rather it functions as a map of reading the two bodies
of thought in their *own* particularity' (*Paul*, 33). In addition, it brings some order to the
complex bodies of thought.

[102] This is a slightly simplified copy of the model in Engberg-Pedersen, *Paul*, 34.

[103] Engberg-Pedersen, *Paul*, 34. The author is aware of the objections of reading individualism into antiquity, but he is at pains to show that this individual understanding of
people is genuinely present and is not a modernisation of the past (*Paul*, 65).

[104] Engberg-Pedersen, *Paul*, 35. The fact that each arrow is pointing both upwards and
downwards is significant in that the individual is both 'struck' by something and is 'stretching
upwards' towards it. I will clarify these movements below in more detail.

The model has three different but interrelated dimensions:

1.   There is a social and 'political' aspect, which attempts to capture the basic
      community orientation of both Paul and the Stoics.
2.   The moral dimension is that to be outside this new group is to live in 'sin' or the
      'flesh' (Paul) or in 'moral stupidity', vice and the 'resulting errors' (Stoics).

This model has been sharply criticised as being both too complex,[105] too simple,[106] not differentiated enough[107] and, particularly, not doing justice to Paul's apocalyptic framework.[108] Especially this latter point is a significant critique. Indeed, in the following chapter on Paul I will only appropriate elements of Engberg-Pedersen's work and *not* the whole model. However, for the purposes of an overview of *Stoic* material the model is beneficial. It offers a helpful introduction into Stoic thought as a whole (although even here I shall offer a critique). That means, further, that although I acknowledge the existence of various schools within Stoicism, a coherent picture does emerge because there 'was extensive agreement between individual Stoics'.[109] Moreover, while elsewhere only certain elements of Stoic teaching are compared with Paul, Engberg-Pedersen's work attempts a structural comparison. Here, as in Paul, we find ethics at the heart of epistemology; in both frameworks of thought theory and practice belong inseparably together, since truth requires ethical change (and conformity with the veracity).[110] But I will elucidate this further here.

3. The 'moral psychological' feature is that the new state (guided by the Spirit [Paul] or by reason [Stoics]) is basically a cognitive and not a desiderative matter. Desire is involved but it is secondary and dependent on the new understanding. Moreover, the new state is the necessary precondition for actions (Engberg-Pedersen, *Paul*, 37–9).

[105] C. Hoegen-Rohls ('Rezension: T. Engberg-Pedersen, Paul and the Stoics', *BZ* 46 [2002] 141–3) shows this particularly in the matter of the further differentiation of the model in the Pauline section of Engberg-Pedersen, *Paul*.
[106] M. Bockmuehl, 'Book Review of Paul and the Stoics by Troels Engberg-Pedersen', *Studies in Christian Ethics* 15 (2002) 128–32.
[107] Esler ('Paul', 108–14) criticises Engberg-Pedersen for not pointing out the differences enough between Stoicism and Paul's thought. He argues that Engberg-Pedersen's focus on the deep structure of Stoic and Pauline thought misses the actual moral detail and the 'realities of everyday life' ('Paul', 110). However, to my mind, Engberg-Pedersen's comparison is of benefit. Although the differences need to be stressed, in order to understand Paul and his ethics better we need to study the structure of his thought as well as the details.
[108] J. L. Martyn, 'De-apocalypticizing Paul: An Essay Focused on Paul and the Stoics by Troels Engberg-Pedersen', *JSNT* 86 (2002) 61–102.
[109] D. Sedley, 'Stoicism', in E. Craig (ed.), *Routledge Encyclopedia of Philosophy* IX (London: Routledge, 1998) 141–61, here 144. Engberg-Pedersen (*Paul*, 46) takes as the basic text for his discussion Book III of Cicero's treatise *De finibus bonorum et malorum*, which, according to him, represents fairly well the Chrysippean ethics. Generally the Chrysippean ethics appear to be the theoretical framework with which even late Stoicism works. Moreover, Cicero's 'account is the most systematic one and . . . he brings out better than any others certain features of Stoic ethics that are at the heart of the I⇒X⇒S model' (*Paul*, 46; cf. A. A Long, *Hellenistic Philosophy: Stoics, Epicureans, Sceptics* [London: Duckworth, 1974] 185). However, we should be wary of making the Stoic theory completely homogeneous (cf. Adams, *World*, 52).
[110] Cf. H. G. Link, 'Wahrheit', in L. Coenen and K. Haacker (eds.), *Theologisches Begriffslexikon zum Neuen Testament* II (Wuppertal: Brockhaus, 2000) 1835f. Link shows how both the Stoa and Paul emphasise the conformity of the individual life with the truth. Cf. Epictetus, *Discourses* 1.17.14; R. Wallace and W. Williams, *The Three Worlds of Paul of*

The overall framework of Stoic thought is a striving for the τέλος, εὐδαιμονία.[111] Εὐδαιμονία is not, as is commonly misunderstood, simply an individualistic concept. Even Aristotelian 'eudaimonistic theory' allows for 'other-regardedness' and altruism, and the Stoics develop this further.[112] Stoics describe the attainment of the τέλος in a manner that is conceptually similar to a conversion. Engberg-Pedersen divides the whole process of the conversion into two stages of οἰκείωσις i and ii.[113] The first is the change (in the model) from I to X and the second is the complete shift from I to S via X.

Concerning οἰκείωσις I, the starting point, I-level, is 'love of the self' with the concerns and world-perception centred on the individual and subjective.[114] The necessary change (I to X) comes in the way the individual understands (hence a cognitive emphasis) him/herself and the world

---

Tarsus (London: Routledge, 1998) 126: 'Ethics was the centre of both systems [Stoicism and Epicureanism], and in each case was supported by an elaborate structure of physics, cosmology and epistemology. Both schools believed that there was a single goal which was the aim of all activity, and whose achievement constituted the supreme fulfilment of human nature. Both regarded it as intolerable that the achievement of this goal should be at the mercy of fate or chance, or should be dependent on anything but the individual's unfettered choices, and consequently both regarded the individual's internal state as all-important, and his (or her . . .) external circumstances as insignificant.' Nevertheless, Wallace and Williams state that 'it was with Stoicism, rather than Epicureanism that both Jews and Christians wished to associate themselves' (*Worlds*, 129). The authors presume that this was due to 'the Epicurean doctrine that the world is not divinely created or governed, coupled probably with the feeling that an association with the moral seriousness of Stoicism rather than the apparent hedonism of Epicureanism was a safer strategy . . . for respectability . . .' (*Worlds*, 131).

The intricate link of ethics with theoretical knowledge is a significant difference between Aristotle and the Stoics. That means for the Stoics, in contrast to Aristotle, moral, practical knowledge (φρόνησις) is not different from theoretical knowledge (σοφία; Engberg-Pedersen, *Paul*, 49).

[111] From the start, Engberg-Pedersen (*Paul*, 49) clarifies that the basic objectives of Paul and Stoicism (which relied heavily on the Aristotelian τέλος, εὐδαιμονία) were different in vital areas. For instance, for the Stoics the ultimate good was only 'this worldly', which stands in sharp contrast to Pauline eschatology. The more obvious distinction, that Paul was not really concerned with 'happiness', is, according to the author, not true since 'he too was thinking about the general shape of the best form of human living . . .'(*Paul*, 47). We may add a further distinction, namely a very different concept and explanation of the existence of evil (cf. L-S I:332–33).

[112] Engberg-Pedersen, *Paul*, 51.

[113] Engberg-Pedersen (*Paul*, 54) translates οἰκείωσις as 'familiarisation' (but to my mind 'appropriation' is better). Hence the change or conversion is 'essentially the result of a development in the understanding of one's own identity (who and what the self is) with a concomitant change in the perception of what particular things "belong" or are "alien" to one'.

[114] Engberg-Pedersen, *Paul*, 54, with respect to Cicero, *De Finibus* 3.16. Cf. Diogenes Laertius 7.85: 'An animal's first impulse, say the Stoics, is to self-preservation, because nature from the outset endears it to itself . . .' The Stoics' starting point is always the new-born creature or, more specifically, the child and its impulses.

around him/her. The individual 'grows up' and learns that it is not a particular object through which one can attain happiness, but only by '*using one's reason* for the purposes for which it is designed, that is, for reaching *truth about* the world'.[115] It is a change from subjectivity to objectivity in which everything is related to the objective perspective of rationality itself. It is a view of the world 'from above', a view which will allow him/her to assess and understand the world correctly.[116] Expressed differently, the 'wise man' understands that his 'good' lies not at the I- but at the X-level. Having understood and grasped that and decided to conform to the level of 'rationality', he or she is led to a new valuation of everything.[117]

So far the individual will only relate his/her new perspective to him/herself, primarily as a detachment from the world and the self-regarding attitude. Οἰκείωσις ii is the next step, although it is immediately dependent on the first.[118] The identification with reason results in seeing oneself as part of a whole:

> They believe that it is relevant to the matter discussed to see that it happens by nature that children are loved by their parents. From this starting point we derive and explain the universal community of the human race. This must be clear already from the shape and

[115] Engberg-Pedersen, *Paul*, 59, with reference to Cicero, *De Finibus* 3.21 (trans. here from L-S I:360f.; II:356f.): 'At this point [having learnt to select and reject things consistent and in full accordance with nature], for the first time that which can be truly called good begins to be present in a man and understood. For a man's first affiliation is towards those things which are in accordance with nature. But as soon as he has acquired understanding, or rather, the conception which the Stoics call *ennoia*, and has seen the regularity and, so to speak, the harmony of conduct, he comes to value this far higher than all those objects of his initial affection; and he draws the rational conclusion that this constitutes the highest human good which is worthy of praise and desirable for its own sake. Since that good is situated in what the Stoics call *homologia* ("agreement" will be our term for this, if you don't mind) – since it is in this, then, that that good consists to which everything is the means, that good which is the standard of all things, right actions and rectitude itself, which is reckoned the only good, though later in origin, is the only thing desirable through its intrinsic nature and value, whereas none of the first objects of nature is desirable for its own sake.'
[116] Engberg-Pedersen, *Paul*, 65f. It is the ability 'to judge that everything that may happen to a man is beneath one' (64; cf. Cicero, *De Finibus* 3.25; Marcus Aurelius, *Meditations* 7.48; 9.30). Further, Engberg-Pedersen (*Paul*, 58) shows how *homologia* 'conformity' is the τέλος which is basically the same thing as 'life in accordance with nature', 'moral virtue and virtuous acts' and 'wisdom' (*Paul*, 66).
[117] For texts on valuation, particularly on finding out what matters, cf. L-S I: 354–9; II: 349–55 (particularly no. 58A, Diogenes Laertius 7.101–3; 58B, 7.104–5; 58C, Stobaeus 2.79.18–80.13).
[118] Engberg-Pedersen says that the move to the S-level is 'in fact already logically contained in the one from I to X' (*Paul*, 67). This is a further similarity for him between Paul and the Stoics, as the identification with 'Christ' or 'reason', respectively, necessitates the final step to S.

members of the body, which by themselves make it clear that nature has arranged for the procreation of offspring. Nor could it be mutually consistent that nature should not want offspring to be procreated and should not take care that the offspring be loved . . . Therefore, just as it is evident that we shrink from pain by nature, so it is clear that we are impelled by nature itself to love those to whom we have given birth. From this arises a natural, shared attachment of man to man, so that just because he is a man, a man must be considered not alien by another man.[119]

It is notable that this regard for the others should be essentially 'natural'. 'All parts of the universe are related to one another by the *pneuma* which pervades them.'[120] From this it follows *naturally* that the universe 'is a city or state of which both men and gods are members, and each of us is part of this universe'.[121] However, this view of the world is not 'natural' to all men. It is the wise man, the one who has obtained both the basic virtues of 'magnanimity' and 'justice', who is brought the whole way from I to S, from self to a regard for others.[122] Finally, it is not just a care for others which is expressed here, but a preference for the common over the personal advantage and a genuine sense of community.[123] As Long and Sedley put it, 'the distinction between altruism and egoism collapses into a single beneficial relation of mutual betterment'.[124]

The New Valuation and Discernment

Having gained an overview of the model for a new self-understanding and how this transforms the valuation of the individual, it is helpful to recap and expand this in its significance for my concept of discernment.

Discernment is linked to one's valuation and perception of the world. In the primary stages, whilst still immature, the basis for this is the self's (egocentric) needs.[125] As people align themselves with the divine mind,

---

[119] Cicero, *De Finibus* 3.62–63 (trans. Engberg-Pedersen, *Paul*, 67).

[120] Long, *Philosophy*, 163.   [121] Cicero, *De Finibus* 3.64.

[122] Engberg-Pedersen, *Paul*, 70.

[123] Long, *Philosophy*, 61; cf. Cicero, *De Finibus* 3.64; Stobaeus 2.101.21–102.3: 'All goods are common to the virtuous, and all that is bad to the inferior. Therefore a man who benefits someone also benefits himself, and one who does harm also harms himself' (in L-S I:373; II:372, no. 60P).

[124] L-S I:377.

[125] 'In other words, *perspective understood as sheer descriptive viewpoint implies valuation.*' 'Thus according to the Stoics the genuine basis for valuation is the self or the I as providing an unchangeable viewpoint from which everything else is seen, and valuation itself is a function of things being seen *from* that viewpoint as (descriptively) belonging or

and their impulses with the preordained good, a complete transformation takes place. For one thing, the individual realises that in aligning him/herself with reason he or she receives a critical faculty which can scrutinise everything else.[126] More importantly though, the entire perspective changes: the thoughts of the individual will be enriched and clarified in such a manner that the objects and people around the individual will be seen in a completely different light.[127] There is also a transformation of the affective aspects of the person: 'Aus Lust entsteht Freude, aus Begierde Wille, aus Furcht Vorsicht . . .';[128] and hence the virtuous mindset develops. The emphasis on mindset is important, as it is not so much the acquisition of single virtues, but rather a change in the *whole disposition and moral attitude* of the person.[129] Hence, the result is a comprehensive knowledge of good and bad rather than just individual correct decisions. Finally, the transformation integrates others and the whole of society into the individual's world-view. The individual is able to free him- or herself from self-centredness in understanding that what is good for the community will also be good for the individual, and, in acting in accordance with that knowledge, he/she finds the true 'self'.[130] The impact on decision making is extensive:

> Thus even his evaluative judgments . . . are no longer based on his perception of himself as a particular individual with whom he stands in a special, favored relationship. Rather, he has given up his individual identity markers as the basis for evaluation,

being alien' (T. Engberg-Pedersen, *The Stoic Theory of Oikeiosis: Moral Development and Social Interaction in Early Stoic Philosophy* [Aarhus: Aarhus University Press, 1990] 71).

[126] Epictetus, *Discourses* 4.7.40: 'Consider what this thing [reason, your 'governing principle'] is which you possess, and where it has come from, the thing which utilizes everything else, submits everything else to the test, selects and rejects.'

[127] J. Annas, *Hellenistic Philosophy of Mind* (Oxford: University of California Press, 1992) 82: 'There is a sense in which we are seeing the same things, but there is also a sense in which we are seeing them for the first time.' Two people can look at the same object and the more knowledgeable one will see *more*, for instance: 'one observer merely sees a tree; the other, who knows more, sees a silver birch' (*Philosophy*, 81).

[128] Vollenweider, *Freiheit*, 69.

[129] L-S I:383: The four virtues, prudence, moderation, courage and justice, had been widely acknowledged to be inseparable, 'alternative characterizations of a single state of mind, knowledge of good and bad' (cf. A. Dihle, *Die Vorstellung vom Willen in der Antike* [Göttingen: Vandenhoeck & Ruprecht, 1985] 72).

[130] Cf. Seneca, *Epistulae* 95.52: '[A]ll that you behold, that which comprises both god and man, is one – we are the parts of one great body'; Vollenweider, *Freiheit*, 43: 'worin der Mensch sich aus der Verstrickung in seine egozentrischen Vorstellungen und Triebe löst und sein wahres Selbst im Horizont des Ganzen, im Einklang mit der Weltdurchwaltung Gottes gewinnt'. However, the community spirit does not mean that the self is denigrated, rather self-love and love of the neighbour are identical (cf. Vollenweider, *Freiheit*, 53–8).

finding instead his identity in what belongs to all human beings, namely, their rationality.[131]

The Various Movements

Engberg-Pedersen explains that εὐδαιμονία contains two movements. This is depicted in the model by the fact that the arrows are both moving 'upwards' and 'downwards'. The 'upwards movement' represents the ordering of one's life in order to attain a single, comprehensive grasp (of the τέλος). The 'downwards movement' represents the 'practical deliberation' which allows particular decision making to be done '*in the light of such a single grasp*'.[132] These two movements are interdependent. 'How one will order one's immediate ends and how one will decide in particular situations are questions the answers to which will influence one another.'[133] It is vital to see the connection here (particularly for discernment) between the overall framework of the person's thought-world and his or her individual decisions. However, some additional comments are required, which Engberg-Pedersen does not offer.

First of all, in the 'downwards movement' Engberg-Pedersen deliberately does not incorporate 'any explicit *action* initiated from above', as his model is primarily anthropological and ethical and working from *below*.[134] However, it is worth mentioning that Stoicism does have a 'downwards movement' which is not from *below*. There is a sense in which knowledge is imparted to humankind through the air by means of the cosmic πνεῦμα, which not only permeates everything but is the vehicle of divine intelligence.[135] As K. Reinhardt puts it:

> das Umgebende, die Luft, ist nun selbst wie mit einem geistigen, geheimnisvollen Fluidum erfüllt, das in den Menschen dringt und einströmt; dies, dies ist Erkenntnis: Überströmen aus dem Makrokosmus in den Mikrokosmus.[136]

Hence, the correspondence between microcosm and macrocosm is attained not only by the individual conforming to god (i.e. reason, nature), but also by 'the figurative inundation of the microcosm by the

---

[131] Engberg-Pedersen, 'Stoicism', 271.   [132] Engberg-Pedersen, *Paul*, 49.

[133] Engberg-Pedersen, *Paul*, 50.   [134] Engberg-Pedersen, *Paul*, 35.

[135] L-S I:282; II:280 (no. 47F, Galen. *On Bodily Mass* 7.525.9–14; 47O, Diogenes Laertius 7.138–9).

[136] K. Reinhardt, *Kosmos und Sympathie: Neue Untersuchung über Poseidonios* (Munich: C. H. Beck, 1926) 199.

macrocosm'.[137] Although, without doubt, it is very different to the Pauline vision of the Spirit's activity, it is significant to note that there is more to the Stoic concept of change than simply the individual's effort.[138]

Secondly, Engberg-Pedersen does not explain in detail how the 'upwards movement' functions. Especially in the matter of discernment, there are a number of aspects that are of particular interest. To these we must turn now.

The 'Upwards Movement'

We will look at three relevant factors which assist the 'upwards movement': (1) the role of choice; (2) the role of observation and imitation; and (3) how the 'god in you' helps.

With regard to the first, the Stoics believed that εὐδαιμονία is essentially a matter of choice. In fact, according to Epictetus προαίρεσις, moral choice, is the only thing that is under human control and 'all other things [externals which we have no influence over] are nothing to us'.[139] This explains why for him the 'principle task in life is this: distinguish matters and weigh them one against another . . .'[140] In a sense this is the first step then in attaining the earlier-mentioned new self-understanding. It means to realise that external things are 'neither good nor evil but indifferent because they are not subject to one's moral control'.[141] The individual

---

[137] B. E. Gärtner, *The Areopagus Speech and Natural Revelation* (trans. C. H. King; ASNU 21; Uppsala: Almqvist & Wiksell, 1955) 107f.; cf. Gärtner, 'Idea', 210f.

[138] Epictetus (*Discourses* 2.16.42) brings out both the anthropological and divine sides well: '"Use me henceforward for whatever Thou wilt; I am of one mind with Thee; I am Thine; I crave exemption from nothing that seems good in Thy sight; where Thou wilt, lead me; in what raiment Thou wilt, clothe me". . .'

[139] Epictetus, *Discourses* 1.25.1.

[140] Epictetus, *Discourses* 2.5.4; cf. Jaquette, *Adiaphora*, 55, for further comment. For the fact that this choosing is not a single affair but a continuous process, cf. L-S I:357; II:354 (no. 58K, Stobaeus 2.76.9–15: 'Diogenes [of Babylon] represented the end as: reasoning well in the selection and disselection of things in accordance with nature . . . and Antipater to live continuously selecting things in accordance with nature and disselecting things contrary to nature. He also frequently rendered it thus: to do everything in one's power continuously and undeviatingly with a view to obtaining the predominating things which accord with nature').

[141] Jaquette, *Adiaphora*, 56. Jaquette also clarifies that the things not under the moral agent's control are 'everything that is not our doing' such as the body, its parts, possessions, parents, siblings, children, country, property, reputation, office. There is more differentiation among the Stoics than the earlier statement appears to allow. In their further assessment they give all the 'indifferent' objects some ranking. For instance, although health and wealth are in themselves 'indifferent' they have 'preferred' status in comparison with their opposites. But this ranking was not accepted by Aristo, who saw everything between vice and virtue as equally indifferent (cf. L-S I: 357–9 for discussion).

must realise that he or she is in control of his/her 'moral purpose' and that he/she must put this to use since '[j]udgments determine the value of things and motivate a person's actions'.[142] In sum, this requires of philosophers to start with themselves, examining themselves rigorously[143] and beginning to understand how they fit into 'the divine scheme of things'.[144]

Secondly, but tied closely to the first point, deliberate observation and reflection on the world are important. These lead to knowledge and, when practised, to virtue.[145] As Seneca points out, the knowledge of virtue is not innate, nor is it acquired by chance. Rather,

> [w]e believe that it is inference due to observation, a comparison of events that have occurred frequently; our school of philosophy hold that the honourable and the good have been comprehended by analogy.[146]

He then goes on to list numerous examples of how truth is deduced analogically; for instance, bodily health leads one to understand that mental health exists. However, observation has also taught that reality is complex, and that things related in appearance may in fact be 'at odds with one another'.[147] This in turn leads the Stoics to conclude that only the most perfect sage must be imitated, one who is 'consistent in all his actions, not only sound in his judgement but trained by habit to such an extent that . . . he cannot help acting rightly'.[148] While observation may be open to the relativism of people's experiences, imitation of the sage is not.[149] Of course, the Stoics were not alone in emphasising the

---

[142] Jaquette (*Adiaphora*, 56) with reference to Epictetus, *Discourses* 2.5.8. Cf. Long, *Philosophy*, 176, who refers to Chrysippus, saying that passions are 'false judgements'.

[143] Cf. Epictetus, *Discourses* 3.2.9–18; Gärtner, *Areopagus*, 107f.

[144] A. J. Malherbe, *Moral Exhortation: A Greco-Roman Sourcebook* (Philadelphia: Westminster Press, 1986) 36. It is remarkable, though, how the Stoics (particularly Cicero, Seneca, Epictetus) have changed the Delphic maxim, ΓΝΩΘΙ ΣΑΥΤΟΝ, under the influence of Posidonius. Betz ('Maxim', 475–7) shows how the older meaning of '"Know yourself" as "Know you are mortal"' is taken as an injunction to know 'one's own inner divine self' ('Maxim', 477). This stands in stark contrast to Paul (and Philo) who clearly does not see salvation as the 'potentially divine man' realising 'his divinity' ('Maxim', 484). However, cf. how Plutarch understands it in the traditional manner (in Betz, *Paulus*, 128).

[145] Practice and παιδεία lie at the heart of the Stoic attainment of virtue; cf. Epictetus, *Discourses*, 4.1.111, who speaks of 'practice from morning to evening'. Further see Vollenweider, *Freiheit*, 43.

[146] Seneca, *Epistulae* 120.4. Cf. Cicero, *De Finibus* 3.62–3.

[147] Seneca, *Epistulae* 120.8–9.   [148] Seneca, *Epistulae* 120.10.

[149] Long, *Philosophy*, 202: 'The Stoics tried to avoid the problems of relativism by setting up the sage as a paradigm and giving detailed descriptions of his disposition and of the kinds of the things that he does. Imitation of the sage . . . cannot ensure virtue, but it can certainly set a man on the right road to secure it.'

significance of this as it links in with the broader concept of 'mimesis' in Graeco-Roman thought.[150] In sum, it is important to have an intellectual focus, a paradigm, which attracts the attention of the individual and by observation and imitation of which character and values are formed.[151]

The third aspect which assists the 'upward movement' is perhaps best summed up in what Seneca called 'the god in you':

> We do not need to uplift our hands towards heaven, or to beg the keeper of a temple to let us approach his idol's ear as if in this way our prayers were more likely to be heard. God is near you, he is with you, he is within you [prope est a te deus, tecum est, intus est]. This is what I mean, Lucilius: a holy spirit indwells within us, one who marks our good and bad deeds, and is our guardian. As we treat this spirit, so are we treated by it.[152]

This 'god' illustrates well the Stoic concept of panentheism and can be conceptually linked to other terms of Stoic and Hellenistic thought such as the tradition of the δαίμων of Socrates or the guardian, *custos*, or even the concept of *conscientia*.[153] Moreover, all have some bearing on discernment. While the precise nature of the δαίμων which indwelt Socrates remained (even at the time) unclear and keenly debated,[154] Theocritus,

---

[150] E. A. Castelli (*Imitating Paul: A Discourse of Power* [Louisville, KY: Westminster/John Knox, 1991] 59–87) gives an overview of the role of aesthetic, cosmological, ethical mimesis and the imitation of God. At points her study is etymologically driven (cf. *Paul*, 60, 75) and she searches primarily for the term rather than the concept. However, it is important to understand that 'the imitation of a teacher or a model in the educational systems of Greco-Roman antiquity and in the ethical positions of both pagan and Jewish writers is a fundamental category' with the prospect that 'the pupil who imitates well will function best in the society for which he is being trained' (*Paul*, 85).

[151] D. E. Aune ('Human Nature and Ethics in Hellenistic Philosophical Traditions and Paul: Some Issues and Problems', in Engberg-Pedersen [ed.], *Context*, 305–12) describes the popular philosophical *commentatio mortis* theme. Through intellectual focus the philosopher 'practices death', 'a turning away from the encumbrances of physical life that impede the life of the soul' ('Nature', 308) and accepts 'the challenge to live in this world in a way approximating postmortem conditions as far as possible' ('Nature', 309). Aune believes that this may be the basis of Paul's use of the death-metaphor for ethical behaviour. Important for our purposes is the fact that there is a *cognitive appropriation* of the concept of death (more generally in Hellenism, or Christ's death in Paul) as the basis for ethical change.

[152] Seneca, *Epistulae* 41.1f.; cf. H.-J. Klauck, *The Religious Context of Early Christianity: A Guide to Graeco-Roman Religions* (trans. B. McNeil; SNTW; Edinburgh: T&T Clark, 2000) 367, for discussion.

[153] Cf. H.-J. Klauck, '"Der Gott in dir" (Ep 41.1): Autonomie des Gewissens bei Seneca und Paulus', in *Welt*, 16–19. J. N. Sevenster (*Paul and Seneca* [NT.S 4; Leiden: Brill, 1961] 89) points out that the guardian, *custos*, is a metaphor for the conscience and that conscience belongs to the divine elements in man.

[154] Cf. Levison, 'Prophetic Spirit', 201, 204, who explains that the interest was due to the fact that both Plato and Xenophon believed that the daemon was the primary reason for

in Plutarch's *De Genio Socratis*, showed the value of this being for discerning the path to virtue:

> Very well ... but what, my dear sir, do we call Socrates' sign?
> ... [F]or exactly as Homer has represented Athena as 'standing at' Odysseus' 'side in all his labours,' so Heaven seems to have attached to Socrates from his earliest years as his guide in life a vision of this kind which alone 'Showed him the way, illumining his path' in matters dark and inscrutable to human wisdom, through the frequent concordance of the sign with his own decisions, to which it lent a divine sanction.[155]

The Stoics demythologise and develop this being to some extent: *everyone* now has a guardian, and its authority and significance are extended.[156] It becomes the voice which whispers 'into the deafened ear' and the guardian who 'pluck[s] us continually by the ear'[157]. And (more often denoted by the term *conscientia*) it can now also be equated with a moral self-consciousness.[158] Indeed, the conscience becomes the highest authority against which one's conduct is measured.[159] However, even the conscience does not guarantee correct conduct. People must continuously

---

which Socrates was sentenced to death. However, it remained unclear whether it was to be understood generally as 'the divine' or as a 'daemonic being'. Levison points to Xenophon's attempt to conform the daemon to the state gods, hoping to refute the charge that Socrates rejected the state religion, and in this venture Xenophon refers to it as a god (Levison, 'Prophetic Spirit', 204). The author of *Theages* calls the daemon a 'voice' without naming the source of the voice (Levison, 'Prophetic Spirit', 204). Cf. also how the concept is used in Galen (*De Placitis Hippocratis et Platonis* vv. 469–76) quoting Posidonius: 'The cause of the emotions, that is, of inconsistency and of the unhappy life, is not to follow in everything the daimon in oneself, which is akin and has a similar nature to the one which governs the whole universe, but at times to deviate and be swept along with what is worse and beast-like' (in I. G. Kidd and L. E. Edelstein [eds.], *Posidonius* I. *The Fragments* [Cambridge: Cambridge University Press, 1972] 170 [Frag. 187]; I. G. Kidd [ed.], *Posidonius* III. *The Translation of the Fragments* [Cambridge: Cambridge University Press, 1999] 248 [Frag. 187]).

[155] Plutarch, *De Genio Socratis* 580 C-D (*Moralia* VII). The being does not seem to initiate decisions (cf. Levison, 'Prophetic Spirit', 202) but it is not clear how affirming it is. Plutarch claims that this voice offers 'divine sanction', but Cicero (*De Divinatione* 1.122–4) has Socrates say that it never urges him on, but often holds him back (cf. Klauck, 'Gott', 18, for discussion).

[156] Cf. Klauck, 'Gott', 18.

[157] Seneca, *Epistulae* 94.59, and 55, respectively; cf. Sevenster, *Paul*, 88.

[158] Cf. Klauck, 'Gott', 22ff.; idem, *Context*, 369f. Hence, according to Seneca, sleep is troubled by a bad conscience (*Epistulae* 105.8) and it torments those whose crimes are not discovered (*Epistulae* 97.15f.).

[159] Cf. Seneca, *De Vita Beata* 20.4: 'Nothing shall I ever do for the sake of opinion, everything for the sake of my conscience. Whatever I shall do when I alone am witness I shall count as done beneath the gaze of the Roman people.'

evaluate and cross-examine themselves, taking the 'part, first of accuser, then of judge, last of intercessor', against oneself.[160]

I have then, in sum, described three important elements (choice, imitation and an inner voice) of the 'upwards movement' towards εὐδαιμονία. Clearly, these are not to be taken separately but rather together they depict some aspects of how the individual could be transformed. As with Philo, it is noteworthy that discernment leads to discernment. Hence, particularly the first two elements, choice and reflective observation (leading to imitation), are essentially discerning elements. This is the spiral effect in which truth is only discerned progressively and in which true discernment presupposes certain choices, reflections and the adherence of the inner voice. Put differently, discernment requires a virtuous mindset, but that can only be attained by taking certain 'discerned' steps. However, this opens up an important question: Is progression really a Stoic concept? Is εὐδαιμονία not an 'all-out', either/or affair?

In the following section I will deal with this question along with another tension, that of the autonomy of the wise man. Both of these issues we have already, or will still to some extent, encounter in Paul.

3.   Tensions within the System

First of all, then, we may deal with the possibility of progression. Engberg-Pedersen explains that generally for the Stoics (and for Paul) reaching the τέλος is 'an all or nothing affair', in which the individual is *'taken over'* from something outside and accordingly gives him- or herself up.[161] 'The Stoics offer a complete world picture and in a sense, as they themselves observed, one must swallow the whole thing or none of it.'[162] This means that only those who have grasped the good can be called σοφός, all others are μωροί, even those who are on the way.[163] Nevertheless, this is not the whole picture. The person who has grasped the one insight that matters (that the 'things that are in accordance with nature' are to be selected and their opposites to be rejected) is *basically* wise.[164] He may still need to learn more, expound and develop the insight, and more importantly understand what it means in concrete situations. In other words, he has grasped what matters, 'but perhaps not *quite* so'.[165] Expressed within the

---

[160] Seneca, *Epistulae* 28.10. Cf. Klauck, *Context*, 370, for discussion.
[161] Engberg-Pedersen, *Paul*, 40, cf. 36.   [162] Long, *Philosophy*, 208.
[163] Engberg-Pedersen, *Paul*, 70.
[164] Cicero, *De Finibus* 3.20; cf. L-S I:394; II:389 (no. 63A, Stobaeus 2.75.16–27.); Engberg-Pedersen, *Paul*, 71.
[165] Engberg-Pedersen, *Paul*, 71. Cf. Long, *Philosophy*, 188, for how the progression is a part of the Stoic system of thought.

framework of the 'upward movement', the person has chosen to conform to reason, has begun to observe, imitate and listen to his/her inner voice. Moreover, even when the end is grasped, it remains a constant process of reconsidering and reorienting oneself towards reason.[166] While the details will vary, this tension between progression and undivided grasp is particularly relevant to Paul, as my reflections in the following chapter will show.[167]

The second tension within the Stoic system, which we may address briefly, is between the wise person's autonomy as judge of good and evil and his or her social, altruistic perspective.[168] The ultimate reference point and obligation is to the 'transcendent norm', reason or nature: 'One must obey one's father – so long as one understands that *real* obedience means to follow nature'.[169] Hence the individual's relationships may ultimately be jeopardised if these call into question the basic belief structure. Moreover, the sage's judgement cannot seriously be called into question by anyone, as the sage has proven superiority by mastering the most difficult enemies (passions, emotions etc.). In a sense, this person requires no one. He/she has attained self-sufficiency.[170] There is an otherworldly aspect to such a position which stands in awkward tension with community life and which is reminiscent of the πνευματικός in 1 Cor. 2.14–16.

Thus, the Stoic system had its inconsistencies, and it is notable that some of them are in their nature similar to Paul's.[171] A further difficulty with Stoicism is its intellectualism.[172] In contrast to Plato, there is no room

---

[166] Cf. Vollenweider, *Freiheit*, 43: '*Freiheit* [or the τέλος] *ist nicht statischer Habitus, sondern ereignet sich ständig neu im Rückbezug auf den universalen Logos . . .*'.

[167] Engberg-Pedersen (*Paul*, 40) points out that in both Paul and the Stoics any sense of simultaneity (for instance in Paul the 'already-but not yet') should still be seen as something temporary, that will be overcome.

[168] Meeks, *World*, 51, with reference to Musonius Rufus.   [169] Meeks, *World*, 51.

[170] Malherbe, *Exhortation*, 37, citing Dio Chrysostom, *Oration* 49.8–11.

[171] There is a further underlying tension which deserves more attention. The Stoics believed both in the freedom of choice, particularly in the freedom of the sage, and on the other hand in fate, which governs and predetermines even the details of the world cycle. This presented a problem for their ethics, as the Epicureans pointed out. Chrysippus attempted to solve it by separating causal determination from necessitation by maintaining a 'notion of counterfactual possibility', something which amounts to *opportunity* (L-S I:393). In more general terms they believed that morality 'belongs first and foremost to the entire cosmic plan. It is from there that it filters down to individual human lives . . . sliding from the notion of fate, through increasingly moral concepts, to individual responsibility' (L-S I:394). Hence, the cosmic providence is worked out by means of human decisions and actions (cf. Adams, *World*, 58, for literature). This issue has been brought to bear on 1 Cor. 8–9 (Malherbe, 'Determinism', 231–55) but not to my knowledge on Rom. 9–11. Although indirectly applicable to discernment, it cannot be dealt with here.

[172] Cf. Long, *Philosophy*, 175; Annas, *Philosophy*, 82; L-S I:319: 'The world-soul is rational or intelligent through and through.'

for the irrational. Although for Paul, as we shall see, correct behaviour is also linked to correct knowledge, his insistence on (particularly) love as the basis for knowing will offer a broader picture.

4.   Conclusion

We have followed the philosophical enterprise from Plato onwards in its endeavour to differentiate between real and unreal, necessary and unnecessary and can see how analysis and evaluation linked to a virtuous mindset (Aristotle) became indispensable tools – so much so that 'discernment' is the most significant part of their work (Socrates, Epictetus). It is, however, the Stoics who have particularly caught our attention. Their insistence that there must be a change in one's self-understanding, a transformed perception of oneself, others and the world, as the key for discernment is a crucial accomplishment. As the individual is transformed, so is his or her valuation: from self-centred to a regard for others; from childish to mature; from subjective to objective.[173] Correct discernment is then based on a *change in disposition*, and, because of this and the conformity with the divine (with reason and nature), a comprehensive knowledge of good and bad is possible. The alignment of the individual's mind with the divine, of the microcosm with the macrocosm, is the realisation of the Greek principle 'like is known by like'.[174] I have also pointed out that there are 'discerned elements' that form part of the process of achieving εὐδαιμονία. The three elements, choice, imitation and the inner voice, are examples of how discernment leads to discernment in an upward spiral. Finally, we were able to see how the resulting system of 'true wisdom' has its similarities with progression (I will deal with this further) and pneumatic status in Paul.

   In sum, although the differences need to be considered, this philosophical approach of a new self-understanding and transformed value system as the basis for correct discernment will be invaluable in understanding the concept of the renewed mind in Paul. The 'grasp of the whole' of the gospel and the progression to understanding what that implies in the believer's life is a key to discernment.

---

[173] The movement to an objective position distinguishes to some extent the Stoics from Paul's epistemology (in view of the preceding chapter where I argued for a transformed understanding of objectivity and subjectivity in Paul). However, what is similar is how a change in viewpoint allows for a comprehensive reassessment of reality.

[174] Cf. Diogenes Laertius 7.88: 'And this very thing constitutes the virtue of the happy man and the smooth current of life, when all actions promote the harmony of the spirit dwelling in the individual man with the will of him who orders the universe'; Gärtner, 'Idea', 210f.

E.   The Combination of Traditions

My quest for the process of discernment has led us to study and, indeed, focus on Philo and the Stoics rather than mainline Judaism. The reason for this lies in the lack of anthropological and epistemological detail in Judaism and the helpful material and models that Philo and the Stoics offered. However, does this justify my focus sufficiently? A number of further points clarify my position.

For one thing, in the first century AD a sharp distinction should be avoided generally between Hellenism and Judaism, and specifically between Stoicism and those Jews open to Greek thought. M. Hengel points out that Stoic thought exerted particular influence in the region of Palestine and Phoenicia as it was not only the dominating Hellenistic philosophy of the day, but also had a significant interdependent relationship with Semitic thought.[175] Indeed, Paul's own education in Tarsus may have been strongly influenced by Hellenistic-Stoic thought.[176] This makes a mixture of thought-worlds for Paul not only possible, but (to some extent) probable.[177]

Such a mixture is exemplified in Philo, who eclectically mixed various traditions.[178] Because of this mixture it has been difficult to classify his enterprise precisely, either as a '*de facto* Middle Platonist' or a 'Platonizing expositor of scripture'.[179] He himself may have not recognised such labels at all, as he presumably saw himself as an adherent of the Mosaic school.[180] Therefore, while accepting the uniqueness of Paul's theology,

---

[175] Hengel (*Judaism*, 87f.) points out that Zeno and Chrysippus were Semites and that Stoicism was influenced by Semitic thought. Moreover, the traditions were mixed eclectically (104).

[176] J. Murphy-O'Connor, *Paul: A Critical Life* (Oxford: Clarendon Press, 1996) 46–51.

[177] This seems a weakness of F. Philip, *The Origins of Pauline Pneumatology* (WUNT 2,194; Tübingen, Mohr/Siebeck, 2005) 225f., who rightly emphasises the importance of Jewish thought but does not consider enough the levels of mixture with Stoic concepts.

[178] 'Philo was by no means the only figure who attempted to demonstrate the unity of oriental and occidental thought: Chaeremon, Plutarch, and Numenius all undertook the same enterprise' (G. E. Sterling, 'Platonizing Moses: Philo and Middle Platonism', in Runia [ed.], *Philonica*, 110).

[179] D. T. Runia, 'Was Philo a Middle Platonist? A Difficult Question Revisited', in idem (ed.), *Philonica*, 125. Runia shows that Philo was not a Middle Platonist. Because of his Jewish tradition which colours his whole framework there are accents in his work 'that a Middle Platonist would immediately recognize as foreign to his "school of thought"' (139; cf. Levison, 'Prophetic Spirit', 207).

[180] T. H. Tobin ('Was Philo a Middle Platonist? Some Suggestions', in Runia [ed.], *Philonica*, 150) makes the helpful differentiation of an 'emic' (internal structures of a particular system) and an 'etic' (analysis of 'phenomena considered in relation to predetermined general concepts') analysis. Accordingly in 'emic terms' Philo would not have been a Middle Platonist because he saw himself as an interpreter of Jewish scriptures and

it is important to see that it was not uncommon for a Jewish scholar of the day to utilise philosophical concepts of Hellenism without necessarily identifying with its complete plausibility structure.

Finally, it is not so much a question of direct dependence by Paul on Philo or any one of the Stoics, but rather the fact that they exemplify and witness to traditions and patterns/structures of thought which were debated more broadly.[181] Moreover, using terminology or concepts from various traditions need not even be a completely conscious act.

That is to say, in sum, there is no historical objection to the plausibility of a Jewish/Christian thinker sharpening inchoate elements of his thinking (such as anthropology and epistemology), which were not addressed directly by his own tradition, with other concepts.[182] However, whether or not the proposed concepts help us to make sense of the essence of Paul's thought needs still to be examined.[183]

F.   Conclusion

I have searched for an answer to my question: How did people in Paul's context believe true discernment could occur? What epistemological and anthropological models would Paul have conceived of as standing behind the concepts of the 'renewed mind' and 'the mindset of the Spirit'?

I established a number of particular aspects of how the various authors believed true discernment could be attained. Important common aspects were prompting (both exterior and innate), focussed contemplation of the correct objectives, and evaluative thinking. These combined to form an upward spiral in which practising discernment leads *progressively* to clearer discernment.

More important for this study was the interrelationship of innate or acquired possibilities of discernment and those that are given by the Spirit.

belonging to the Mosaic school. However, in 'etic terms' one could call him a Middle Platonist since he 'reflects so many of the basic positions associated with the more general category of Middle Platonism'.

[181] Sterling ('Wisdom', 382) states concerning the way in which Philo elucidates the anthropology of the Corinthians: 'We should not think of Philo as the source of these traditions, but as our major witness to them.' Further, see the discussion ('Wisdom', 382f.) of how the Corinthians and finally Paul may have come into contact with Jewish sapiential and Philonic traditions.

[182] Aune ('Models', 90) says that Paul's anthropology is not explicable from Judaism alone, nor can one other influence be identified, but rather Paul borrows in an 'ad hoc manner' from various traditions that served his 'more central ethical concerns'.

[183] Consequently D. T. Runia (*Philo in Early Christian Literature: A Survey* [Minneapolis: Fortress Press, 1993] 72) warns against understanding the terminological similarity as evidence of conceptual congruity.

Judaism's hope for an eschatological gift, a 'new heart', appears to be a significant basis of Paul's thinking. But there is little specification of the mechanics of this Jewish vision. Philo, on the other hand, has a high view of both the Spirit and the mind (the virtuous mindset, educated, liberated and transformed). He does not set them in antithesis but sees both *together* as the means for an authentic perception of reality.

Moreover, we observed how the Stoics combined a 'shift in perspective' (which we also observed within apocalyptic Judaism) with a form of ethical transformation. True discernment is linked with a comprehensive new valuation: only through a new perception and a new understanding of self, others and the world will authentic evaluation of reality be possible. That means a person must be 'converted' from an individual to a social perspective; the individual must be aligned with the divine and then knowledge of good and evil can be attained.

Both the detail and comprehensive picture will in some aspects be decisively different for Paul, but these concepts and models offer essential building blocks to begin understanding his thought better.

6

HOW DOES PAUL BELIEVE TRUE DISCERNMENT CAN AND SHOULD TAKE PLACE?

A.   Introduction

We enter the last but not least part of this inquiry into the Pauline view of discernment. The main task I have set myself here is to understand how Paul believed true discernment could and should take place. My previous work on the objects of discernment led us to see that the focus of research must be on the interrelationship of the Spirit and the mind. How are we to describe this relationship? Can it be expressed in epistemological and psychological categories? Or must we use metaphysical terminology? It will be my argument to show that a coherent answer can only be attained when we look at the juncture of Spirit and mind. While in chapter 2 we saw that Paul calls this juncture the renewed mind (Rom. 12.2) or the 'mind of Christ' (1 Cor. 2.16; and I shall add here the 'mindset of the Spirit' [Rom.8.6]), we need to find out what the nature of this juncture is and how it compares with the conceptions of Paul's intellectually diverse yet fertile context.

In order to address these questions and set out my own argument we must first follow a lead Pauline scholarship has given us. Thus, we turn first to the question of criteria for discernment and, through this, return briefly to the more general issue of normativity (law, external norms) and its relationship to decision making. This more formal approach we can then use as a backdrop to my dominant concern with the epistemological questions regarding the interrelationship of mind and Spirit.

B.   The Question of Criteria and External Norms

Criteria as the basis for discernment have been proposed mainly with respect to διάκρισις πνευμάτων (1 Cor. 12.10). Just as this gift has often been limited to the testing of the spiritual manifestations (or just prophecy), so in 1 Cor. 12–14 the scope of the criteria is similarly restricted.[1] The criteria may be summed up as follows.

1. The norm of former revelation: earlier kerygmatic or apostolic traditions are to be the test for all new charismatic expressions. This is also called the Christological criterion (or even confession) and is often linked to 1 Cor. 12.2f.: 'No one speaking by the Spirit of God ever says "Let Jesus be cursed!" and no one can say, "Jesus is Lord" except by the Holy Spirit'.[2]

2. The test of love: this is not only a test of the nature of a charism but also of the character and motivation of the ones performing the ministry.[3] It is argued that, as Paul has placed 1 Cor. 13 between chs. 12 and 14, so he places love as the control over the charisms in recognition of the fact that they can be exercised in 'a selfish and uncaring manner'.[4]

3. The edification and benefit of the community (οἰκοδομή) (1 Cor. 8.1; 10.23; 14): for some this is the clearest test. Only those expressions of faith that edify the others are to be allowed within the congregation.[5]

It is undeniable that these criteria are focal points within Paul's discussion of the charisms and we will return to them, from a different approach, later.[6] However, for my purposes a number of problems remain and some new questions are raised. For one, I have argued that the gift of discerning spirits is not only for prophecy or charisms, but also incorporates the evaluation of ethical and soteriological issues. How do these three criteria work there? Secondly, the discussion about tradition and the

---

[1] I have mentioned the significant work done by Dunn on the three criteria already in my introduction (cf. *Jesus*, 223ff., 233–6; 'Discernment', 79–96; 'Congregation', 201–36; *Theology*, 594–8).

[2] This is important particularly for those who see the gift of διάκρισις πνευμάτων only for the charisms (cf. Hahn, 'Charisma', 440) or just for prophecy. It is seen as a 'rule of thumb' (Dunn, *Jesus*, 234). As in Rom. 12.6, κατὰ τὴν ἀναλογίαν τῆς πίστεως, Schrage (*Korinther* III, 157) believes an 'inhaltliche Prüfung' is intended. Cf. also Chevallier, *Esprit*, 190; Gillespie, *Theologians*, 162f.

[3] Love is often also seen very generally as a reliable moral guide, cf. J.-P. Lémonon, 'Le discernement dans les lettres pauliniennes', *Lumière et Vie* 252 (2001) 28: 'En toutes circonstances la charité est un critère sûr lors d'une décision.'

[4] Dunn, *Theology of Paul*, 596. Martucci ('Diakriseis', 470f.) sees 'service et charité' as the only criteria. For Hahn ('Charisma', 442f.) ἀγάπη is the eschatological criterion, as it will not end in this world, in contrast to the charisms.

[5] For a lengthy discussion, cf. Johnson, 'Edification', 362–72; also L. T. Johnson, 'Holiness as a Material Criterion for Discernment in the Church', *Sewannee Theological Review* 39 (1996) 373–84. But for him holiness as a criterion has a 'remarkable convergence' with Paul's notion of edification (375).

[6] To some degree they fit into Paul's broader principles, too. Dunn has helpfully augmented his discussion of criteria for discernment with his broader and differentiated discussion of how to recognise the 'Spirit as the Spirit of Christ' (*Theology*, 433) and how the Spirit must bear the marks of the cross (*Theology*, 494–6).

Christological criterion is itself contested. It links in with the debate about the centre and coherence of Paul's thought mentioned in chapter 4.[7] More importantly, and against Dunn's assumption, only very straightforward ethical and theological issues can adequately be solved by the application of the basic confession 'Jesus is Lord'.[8] It is not in any way helpful for questions of more precise ethical or theological concern. Similarly, and thirdly, the question is whether or not any process of decision making can sufficiently and helpfully be explained by the application of (fairly imprecise) criteria.[9] Dunn has clearly acknowledged this problem. As he points out, the application of the confession should not be seen as a clear-cut standard, but rather as a 'dialectical process' which involves the 'community's careful and sensitive use of the criteria'.[10] This process is described as follows:

1.   The dialectic of liberty is the arbitration between the mandate of the community to call for conformity and the individual's right not to conform.[11]

2.   The dialectic of revelation is the 'recognition that in some instances past revelation will be normative, in others that past revelation will have to be regarded as superseded'.[12]

---

[7] To be sure the Christological focus and theological criterion are important. Particularly the *Rezeptionsgeschichte* is worthwhile studying here (for a brief overview, cf. S. Chan, *Spiritual Theology: A Systematic Study of the Christian Life* [Downers Grove, IL: Inter-Varsity Press, 1998] 217ff.). While Chan shows that for both Ignatius and Edwards the theological criterion is the ultimate test, both clearly interpreted these in their own manner. In the matter of the use of tradition(s), I noted earlier (pp. 27–35) Paul's own (partially apparently eclectic) choosing and disregarding of norms for his communities, which in turn *required* discernment.

[8] Not only is the interpretation of the verse very contested (cf. Thiselton,*Corinthians*, 918–27, for a discussion of the twelve [*sic*] distinct explanations to account for the phrase ἀνάθεμα'Ιησοῦς), but also its value as a test for discernment, cf. Dautzenberg, *Prophetie*, 146; Fee, *Presence*, 157. K. Maly ('1Kor 12,1–3, eine Regel zur Unterscheidung der Geister?', *BZ* 10 [1966] 82–95) says the verse is not a 'pastorale Faustregel' for discernment because as such it would be 'ein wenig primitiv' ('1Kor 12,1–3', 95).

[9] Käsemann ('Korinther', 275) claims that the discernment of spirits cannot be effected according to stark principles because the Spirit cannot be appropriated into human volition or 'Maßstäbe'. Cf. Claußen, 'Frage', 31: 'Diese Kriterien [the above three] sind vernunft-gemäß anwendbar. Und doch sind sie so allgemein, daß es oft zu einem schwierigen und zeitraubenden Prozeß der Urteilsbildung gekommen sein mag . . .' For a similar discussion in a more systematic work, cf. Chan, *Theology*, 201, who shows that 'knowing God's will' 'is more than just the scientific application of principles to particular situations'. Similarly, cf. H. W. Owen, 'Some Philosophical Problems in Christian Ethics', in G. R. Dunstan (ed.), *Duty and Discernment* (London: SCM Press, 1975) 3. Lerle (*Diakrisis*, 101) rightly shows that the gift of discernment is a more complex phenomenon than the mere application of criteria to a given situation.

[10] Dunn, 'Discernment', 91–95.   [11] Dunn, 'Discernment', 92.

[12] Dunn, 'Discernment', 93.

3.   Finally, the dialectic of authority involves the balance of author-
       ity between the apostle, the community, those manifesting a
       particular gift and the 'ministry' itself.[13]

But this brief description shows that the criteria *require* discernment
rather than providing us with a clearer view of how decision making can
function.[14]

Here we encounter the same result we observed in my discussion of
the law and of norms in chapter 2. There, too, my conclusion was that
the various traditions *require* discernment rather than offering a definitive
guideline. Moreover, I asked whether Paul's vision is not one of an internalised law, which can actually fulfil its demand. However, we need to
be aware that this question has been overshadowed by a development in
scholarship which has anachronistically read into Paul a concept of ethical autonomy and 'Selbstgesetzgebung'.[15] The counter-reaction against
this has, in turn, re-emphasised external law in a problematic manner,
in part because there is an incorrect perception of (mutually exclusive)
alternatives between, on the one hand, the Spirit and the law and, on
the other, reason and the law. Dunn, for instance, *contrasts* external law
with an internal 'direct and immediate apprehension of the divine will':[16]
'[T]he alternative to dependence on written formulations is a charismatic
immediacy of dependence on God.'[17] This means Spirit activity is more
or less reduced to charismatic spontaneity or an 'inward compulsion'.[18]

---

[13] Dunn, 'Discernment', 94f.   [14] Dunn, 'Discernment', 91.

[15] Cf. R. Hasenstab (*Modelle paulinischer Ethik: Beiträge zu einem Autonomie-Modell
aus paulinischem Geist* [Mainz: Matthias-Grünewald Verlag, 1977], 206), who says ἀγάπη
gives καρδία, νοῦς and συνείδησις their 'Autonomiefunktion' and makes a 'Sich-selbst-
Gesetz-Sein' possible. Schrage (*Einzelgebote*, 10 n. 12) is right to assume Kant's concept
of autonomy as the motivating force behind the 'Selbstgesetzgebung', which was taken up
by Protestant scholars as an opposition to any type of casuistic or authoritarian ethics (cf.
Goppelt, *Theologie*, 28).

[16] Dunn, *Theology of Paul*, 647; cf. similarly (at least from his argument) Schrage,
Einzelgebote, 11.

[17] Dunn, *Romans 9–16*, 717, with regard to 12.2 but also in reference to 6.4; 7.6; 8.4.
The contrast of external and internal norm is also important in Dunn, *Theology of Paul*,
647–9, 668f. However, Dunn is very much aware of the dangers of enthusiasism (*Theology
of Paul*, 432f.) or of overemphasising the spontaneous element (*Theology of Paul*, 558). He
sees the need for spiritual maturity and 'life-style' (*The Theology of Paul's Letter to the
Galatians* [Cambridge: Cambridge University Press, 1993] 107). But, to my mind, he does
not sufficiently correlate this with the circumcised heart, partly because he sees the need
for retaining the law as an ethical boundary marker.

[18] Dunn, *Jesus*, 225: '*The distinctive element in Paul's ethics is the charismatic recognition of God's will and the inward compulsion of love.*' It means that, while Dunn is aware of
the difficulty of a criterion such as love being applied to each individual case, the alternative
he sees is 'the inner compulsion of God's Spirit' (*Jesus*, 224). While he is aware that the

But does this not miss a central point? Cannot the Spirit create a long-term change of disposition, which *internalises* the demand of the law in such a manner that a stark contrast of external and internal norm becomes superfluous?[19] On the other hand, Schnabel relegates the use of reason for discerning the will of God to a near irrelevant position, since the external 'binding norms' are sufficient.[20] But does this respect Paul's position that 'everything' is to be discerned (1 Cor. 2.14f.)? Moreover, does such a de-ontological view of Pauline ethics take into account enough the role of the renewed human faculties?[21]

We must address these issues in section D of this chapter by probing Paul for a more comprehensive view of ethics in which external norms are more fully integrated into internal change. And in order to do that we must turn to a further understanding of how mind and Spirit work together.

C.   Spirit versus Mind

When we ask how scholarship understands the relationship of Spirit and mind concerning discernment, we get an unclear picture at best. This is demonstrated well in the various assessments of how διακρίνω in 1 Cor. 12.10 and 14.29 might function. While Aune can state that (for 14.29) we should envisage 'a fully rational procedure',[22] J. Friedrich

renewed mind of Rom. 12.2 is the 'inward reality of a circumcised heart', this becomes manifest in '*spontaneous* knowledge of God's will' (*Galatians*, 107; my italics). Schrage (*Einzelgebote*, 163–7), on the other hand, is careful not to identify the Spirit's activity with the spontaneous, but while in *Einzelgebote* he attaches much weight to the external directives of Paul, in 'Verhältnis' (his later work) the role of the renewed mind is stressed.

[19] The criticism is expressed well by Thiselton (*Corinthians*, 937, 942), but not with respect to external norms as I have done (cf. my further discussion in the following section on the Spirit). We should also note that we do not need to *exclude* the criteria from the decision-making process, as does Lerle (*Diakrisis*, 88): 'Gäbe es ein Kriterium der Geisterscheidung, so wäre die Diakrisis kein Charisma mehr. Was durch Anwendung eines Kriteriums ausgeführt wird, dazu ist keine besondere, allein durch den Geistesbesitz gegebene Fähigkeit notwendig.'

[20] Schnabel, *Wisdom*, 332: 'This means that the searching reason of the Christian is not [!] particularly relevant for the substantiation of Christian moral behaviour, since it never provides the final word in questions of Christian life-style, nor cancels or invalidates God's norms and commandments nor is it relevant for discerning and deciding basic moral questions, as these have been decided already in God's eternally valid revelation. The believer's reason is relevant for questions of minor importance and for deciding how [not whether!] the binding norms are to be realized' (for a critique, cf. Pate, *Reverse*, 415–20).

[21] Schnabel (*Wisdom*, 330) recognises that it is significant that the mind is renewed, but he then, to my mind, contradicts this earlier remark in giving the mind only a role of 'minor importance' in ethics (332).

[22] Aune, *Prophecy*, 219. Cf. A. R. Hunt, *The Inspired Body: Paul, the Corinthians, and Divine Inspiration* (Macon, GA: Mercer University Press, 1996) 125–7, who writes

believes rational evaluation misses the point and would fail.[23] Robertson and Plummer are sure that 'an intuitive discernment is implied, without the application of tests'.[24] Some are more comprehensive. Dunn, for instance, sees 'a process of evaluation which involved both what we might call "straight thinking" and "common sense" on the one hand and sensitivity to the inspiration of the Spirit on the other'.[25] It is remarkable, however, that all of these positions seem to imply a contrast between the Spirit's and the mind's role.[26] In the broader discussion, this dualism is sharpened by an anachronistic discussion of faith versus reason and the supernatural versus the natural.[27] This has, among other effects, led to an attack of the 'primacy of the rational' in Pauline exegesis,[28] or to attempts to set theological and historical readings in antithesis.[29] The problem for these scholars is that the Spirit (or scripture) is subject to judgement by

more generally about Paul's view of inspiration in contrast to that of Philo, Plutarch and Josephus. He points to Paul's 'insistence on the superiority of rational, nonecstatic behaviour and communication'; see my critique of this contrast on pp. 163–72.

[23] Friedrich, 'προφήτης', 855. Bultmann (*Theologie*, 484) says that the σοφία of 1 Cor. 2 comes from the Spirit and is not a product of rational thought.

[24] Robertson and Plummer, *Corinthians*, 267.

[25] Dunn, 'Congregation', 225; similarly Schrage, *Korinther* III, 156: 'Die διάκρισις ist ebenso geistgewirkt wie die Prophetie und darum auch nicht einfach Sache des common sense oder der menschlichen Vernunft, sosehr diese darin involviert ist.'

[26] This is further demonstrated by Kleinknecht ('πνεῦμα', 344ff.), who shows that the evaluation of spiritual phenomena is not (as in Plato's description of the Delphic oracle) through the νοῦς, φρόνησις and the dialectic method but through the gift of God's own Spirit. Further, he comments that the real Pauline πνευματικός thus takes the place of the Platonic φιλόσοφος. It is not clear what Schrage (*Korinther* III, 157) means practically by the Spirit being the actual subject of διάκρισις nor by his comment that in majority resolutions one must assume that Paul believed, 'daß der Geist selbst die Wahrheit durchsetzen wird' (*Korinther* III, 452).

[27] Cf., for instance, Cerfaux, *Christian*, 512ff., who defines ἐπίγνωσις in the captivity epistles as the 'supernatural penetration into the mysteries of Christ' and differentiates it categorically from faith (which is the foundation of Christians). J. T. Forestell ('Christian Perfection and Gnosis in Philippians 3,7–16', *CBQ* 18 [1956] 133) speaks of attaining moral and intellectual 'supernatural perfection'. See also the discussion in Armstrong, 'Theory', 438–52; V. Warnach, 'Ratio und Pneuma', in L. Scheffczyk, W. Dettloff and R. Heinzmann (eds.), *Wahrheit und Verkündigung* I (Munich: Schöningh, 1967) 429–48; Ciholas, 'Knowledge', 188–201.

[28] S. Summers ('"Out of my Mind for God": A Social-Scientific Approach to Pauline Pneumatology', *JPT* 13 [1998] 77–106) has made a plea for a more 'experientially rooted understanding of the Spirit' (with 'power, energy and drama'; 'Mind', 105) and a recognition that Paul 'could claim to be "out of his mind for God" as part of his normative Christian experience' ('Mind', 106).

[29] Cf. Healy, *Heart*, 8–10, who in her section on methodology states that she does not want to eliminate the historical and conceptual analysis, but 'since what is mediated by the text are divine realities, they are in principle accessible only by faith' (*Heart*, 9). It is intriguing that E. Käsemann ('Der Ruf zur Vernunft', in *Kirchliche Konflikte* I [Göttingen: Vandenhoeck & Ruprecht, 1982] 119) laments the neglect of implementing 1 Cor. 14's view of reason in modern church life (against 'enthusiastische Äußerungen' and 'Verzückungen'). Summers, on the other hand, assumes that 'many commentators on Pauline texts seem to

merely human means. This leads some to nearly eliminate the role of the discerning community.[30]

This leaves us with an unconvincing opposition of reason versus 'spiritual' faith. We must ask whether or not this does justice to Paul. Does he see the Spirit and mind in complete antithesis? To acquire a better understanding I must first give a definition of what I mean by 'Spirit' and 'mind' and an overview of their significance.

1.   The Spirit

For Paul the role of the Spirit for attaining true knowledge is decisive: the Spirit is '*the absolutely essential constituent*', norm and power of the new Christian life.[31] As in *Wis. Sol.* 9.14–18 the Spirit is the reliable guide to all divine wisdom.[32] And the Spirit is fundamental for authentic discernment (1 Cor. 2.6–16).[33] However, what does this mean epistemologically? If the Spirit is both '*detective and judge*', does this not eliminate the need for human mediation?[34] Moreover, does 'pneumatic epistemology' necessitate that knowledge comes 'in immediate intuition'?[35] Apparently, we need some further differentiation here.

have no personal experience of these dramatic manifestations, or exhibit little interest in exploring them' ('Mind', 78).

[30] So Schnabel, *Wisdom*, 332, 338–42. However, for seeing an important role of reason, cf. Käsemann, 'Ruf', 119: 'Nötiger als fromme Erlebnisse und himmlische Entzückungen hat die Christenheit in ihren Versammlungen wie ihrem weltlichen Gottesdienst die Vernunft.'

[31] Fee, *Presence*, 898. Cf. Therrien, *Discernement*, 269, who says it is the 'element constitutif', 'principe dynamique' and the norm. Turner (*Spirit*, 116–19) shows that Paul appeals and alludes to the tradition of Jer. 31 and Ezek. 36 in 1 Thess. 4.7f. and 2 Cor. 3. U. Schnelle (*Neutestamentliche Anthropologie* [Neukirchen-Vluyn: Neukirchener Verlag, 1991] 58) writes: 'Der Geist ist Kraft (ἐν πνεύματι) und Norm (κατὰ Πνεῦμα) des neuen Lebens. Der Geist ermöglicht, daß der Christ bleiben kann, was er schon geworden ist.'

[32] Cf. Davis, *Wisdom*, 106. Even in Rom. 12.2, where the Spirit is missing, Paul presupposes the pneumatic existence of Rom. 8, so, rightly, Therrien (*Discernement*, 269).

[33] Hofius ('Wahrheit', 30f.) suggests that the truth of the gospel can be '*verkündigt, entfaltet* und *erklärt*' with 'Vernunft', but it cannot be verified by rational means because that is only possible by the power of the Spirit. Cf. J. Reiling, 'Wisdom and Spirit', in T. Baarda, A. Hilhorst, G. P. Luttikhuizen and A. S. van der Woude (eds.), *Text and Testimony* (Kampen: Kok, 1988) 200–11; Hahn, 'Charisma', 431 n. 47: 'So schafft der Geist Gottes Zugang zu Dimensionen, die der Vernunft des natürlichen Menschen verschlossen sind . . .'

[34] Beker, 'Theology', 19. As noted in the introductory chapter, Beker of course sees the need for human mediation.

[35] Yu, *Epistemology*, 206. Yu is not always completely clear as to what he means by pneumatic epistemology. While he is right to say it is an 'expression of Paul's belief in God as the ultimate source and the fundamental revealer of truth in the light of his Christian experience of the Spirit' (*Epistemology*, v), does this necessitate 'immediate intuition'? He does see other possibilities of truth formation (*Epistemology*, 7) but does not explain them. (Cf. Stuhlmacher, 'Bedeutung', 157ff.)

First of all we can contrast Paul's understanding of divine πνεῦμα with that of Stoicism. Paul is not a panentheist.[36] For him God's Spirit comes from *extra nos* as a transcendent power indicating God's 'otherness and holiness, in contradistinction from the "world"'.[37] That means there is a sharp distinction between pneumatic and human existence.[38] It is not a flowing continuum.[39] But does this mean that the presence of the Spirit is incompatible with or should necessitate an eviction (or even destruction) of the human spirit and its natural faculties?[40]

---

[36]   Cf. my Context chapter (5) where I showed that πνεῦμα, as the Stoics saw it, permeated the whole world and humankind. Hence, the divine Spirit was for them ontologically related to man's spirit. M. Pohlenz ('Paulus und die Stoa', in K. H. Rengstorf [ed.], *Das Paulusbild in der neueren deutschen Forschung* [Darmstadt: Wissenschaftliche Buchgesellschaft, 1964] 537) believes that the Pauline Spirit has nothing to do with the Stoic πνεῦμα.

[37]   Thiselton, *Corinthians*, 260; cf. J. Weiß, *Das Urchristentum* (Göttingen: Vandenhoeck & Ruprecht, 1917) 396; Bultmann, *Theologie*, 155. But cf. Aune, who is not wholly consistent. In, 'Models' (113 n. 20) he thinks the '*pneuma tou theou* (1 Cor.2:11), is equivalent to the *nous kyriou* . . . and the *nous Christou* (1 Cor.2:16); that is, in conventional philosophic parlance, the *nous* is the divine portion of the *psyche*'. In 'Nature' (300 n. 18) he says it is not clear whether the human spirit is infused with the divine Spirit. Schrage (*Korinther* I, 258), on the other hand, is very severe in refuting any link, since there is a total 'Inkommensurabilität' between man's and God's πνεῦμα. Whether or not, as he says, there is no direct contact, no bridge, no relation or consubstantiality between the two, seems to me somewhat stark, but cf. further my comments below (section D).

[38]   Sterling ('Wisdom', 355–84) writes that Paul counters the view of the Corinthians that pneumatic existence is an ontological possibility and a constituent element of human nature. Meier (*Mystik*, 253) shows that the immanence of the Spirit always remains the presence of the Other in humans (cf. Voss, *Wort*, 177). However, I would not agree with Thiselton (*Corinthians*, 1107) that for Paul 'spirituality' is never a disposition, in view of my argument (and indeed Thiselton's own argument) that true spirituality includes habituation and stance and consequently is *partially* a disposition.

[39]   However, I should not force the distinction between Spirit and spirit into an ontological dualism. This is true concerning the origin of the human spirit and its Christian destiny. With regard to the former, Paul, unlike Philo, is not concerned to comment about the tradition that all creation has received God's Spirit (Gen. 2.7; cf. S. Vollenweider, 'Der Geist Gottes als Selbst der Glaubenden', *ZThK* 93 [1996] 176 n. 52; but in contrast R. B. Hoyle, *The Holy Spirit in St. Paul* [London: Hodder and Stoughton, 1927] 239). But we should remember that for him the 'Spirit is preeminently "the Spirit of life," the "life-giver"' (Dunn, *Theology of Paul*, 429; cf. 260–4; Hubbard, *Creation*, 120–2). Concerning the Christian destiny, cf. Theissen, *Aspects*, 373 n. 8: 'If the Christian can become "one Spirit" with the Lord (1 Cor. 6:17), then excessively sharp distinctions disappear.'

[40]   This is the impression one receives when reading Stuhlmacher ('Bedeutung', 159, 161), who repeatedly states that people have to be made 'zunichte'; cf. O. Moe, 'Vernunft und Geist im Neuen Testament', *Zeitschrift für Systematische Theologie* 11 (1934) 353. But see Vollenweider, 'Geist', 183f., who attempts to define Paul's pneumatology in differentiating it from two other models: (1) mantic inspiration in which the divine suspends and replaces the 'Ichinstanz'. But for Paul: 'Der eingehende göttliche Geist ersetzt also nicht das Ich als Erlebnis- und Verhaltenszentrum des geschichtlichen Menschen, sondern er durchdringt es. Zugespitzt formuliert: *Das Pneuma handelt nicht anstelle unser selbst, sondern als unser Selbst*'; (2) a Gnostic discontinuity between true spiritual and false worldly reality which have no relationship (184). Similarly, cf. K. Stalder, *Das Werk des*

The following research shows that such an incompatibility is not given.

On a general note, it has rightly been pointed out that Paul stands in a tradition in which revelation is not an objective entity external to any human participation.[41] D. O. Via has done well to explicate this point in showing how the human capacity *constitutes* revelation in actively receiving it.[42] More specifically, this translates well into another significant point about the role of human mediation. Spirit activity has rightly been proposed to be on a 'spectrum of experience'.[43] This spectrum may range from invasive experiences to a less directly traceable character change or from highly charged emotional to more subtle rational forms.[44] It is crucial to understand, however, that a more habituated or intellectual form of spirituality does not mean that there is *less* spiritual involvement than in spontaneous manifestations. Such a position (as I mentioned earlier [chapter 6, section B]) reflects a false identification

Geistes in der Heiligung bei Paulus (Zürich: EVZ -Verlag, 1962) 492, who suggests that something new and 'Fremdes' comes into the 'Personzentrum' but this does not imply a split personality.

[41] This is also one of the central points in D. Lührmann, *Das Offenbarungsverständnis bei Paulus und in paulinischen Gemeinden* (Neukirchen-Vluyn: Neukirchener Verlag, 1965) 164, who speaks rightly of revelation as a 'Heilshandeln Gottes am Menschen', although his work still sees Paul in distinction to Gnostic influence (cf. Goppelt, *Theologie*, 365ff.). Cf. H. Hübner, *Biblische Theologie des Neuen Testaments* I (Göttingen: Vandenhoeck & Ruprecht, 1990) 177, who shows that revelation in Paul (analogous to the OT) is not an objective 'Depositum', which can exist without the recipient. To be sure, I understand that 'revelation' is a very fluid term in Paul and requires accurate definition; cf. R. E. Sturm, 'An Exegetical Study of the Apostle Paul's Use of the Word Apokalypto/Apokalypsis. The Gospel as God's Apocalypse' (Unpubl. PhD dissertation, Union Theological Seminary, 1985) 251ff., who argues for an 'apocalyptic epistemology', by which he means an 'eschatological way of perceiving and understanding' which is expressed both in 'having a "renewed mind" and being "known by God"'.

[42] D. O. Via (*The Revelation of God and/as Human Reception in the New Testament* [Harrisburg, PA: Trinity Press International, 1997] 57–65) writes this with reference to Paul. But see also his general conclusion: 'Word as content and power does not become the self-disclosure of God unless it is actively received by human beings through the merging of their specific human understanding of reality with the content of the word. The factor of human reception makes a constitutive contribution to the form and content of the revelation. Human reception is not a clear transparency on to the pure word of God' (*Revelation*, 192f.).

[43] Dunn, *Theology of Paul*, 430. Noting the Spirit's influence as being on a spectrum appears to me to be a broader understanding than when he characterises it mainly as charismatic spontaneity or 'inward compulsion' (*Jesus*, 225; see chapter 6 section B). It is not clear whether the broader understanding (found in *Theology*) is a development of his earlier work (found in *Jesus*). In any case, the former does more justice to Paul than the latter.

[44] This corresponds with my research on how Judaism saw various types of Spirit activity and hence distinguished between 'charismatic *communication* of wisdom', 'charismatic *infusion* of wisdom' and invasive revelation (Turner, 'Prophecy', 73).

of spontaneity with Spirit-involvement and 'a dualistic *Deus ex machina* worldview'.[45] Nor should we assume that more invasive ('ecstatic') experiences imply *more* spiritual input and *less* human mediation.[46] Not only can an altered state of consciousness leave the recipient some amount of control,[47] but also, more importantly, no experience is 'wholly "raw"'.[48] To constitute any experience as such (even if complete loss of control were primarily given), some sort of 'conceptualisation' is involved. This in turn depends on a certain amount of perception and interpretation.[49] In other words, the whole spectrum of Spirit activity requires some form of human mediation.

It is clear, then, that we need to consider more closely the 'human' side of the equation. What is its role and how significant is it? For the primary locus of this mediation, in the matter of discernment and understanding, we turn to the mind (Rom. 12.2).

2.   Reason and the Mind

When we attempt to portray the role of the faculty that understands and reasons in Paul, we are confronted by two basic questions.

The first question arises out of a basic dialectic which we find in Paul. On the one hand, we encounter Paul's disappointment (and partial despair) in relation to reason. While reason may lead to some form of *knowledge about* God, it has not brought about the required *acknowledgement* (Rom.

---

[45] Thiselton, *Corinthians*, 943; further cf.: 'Such gifts as *teaching* and *critically evaluating* can hardly be "spontaneous," but are *habits* of *trained judgment* marked precisely by a *continuity* of the Spirit's *giving as a process over time* (cf. Rom 12:7–8; 1 Cor 12:27; Eph 4:11).' Dunn (*Theology*, 427) in another context is aware of this and seeks to be careful to 'not allow experience to be too easily played off against rationality or "religious experience" to be defined by or limited to the extraordinary'.

[46] The term 'ecstatic' has rightly been shown to be too crude, hence I use 'invasive' to denote an external influence which affects the awareness in such a manner that it can (in varying degrees) lead to a loss of self-control and possibly be against the will of the recipient (following Grudem, *Gift*, 150f.; cf. Forbes, *Prophecy*, 53–6; Turner, *Spirit*, 200–4).

[47] Cf. Aune, *Prophecy*, 20–1, 34. B. J. Malina and J. J. Pilch (*Social Science Commentary on the Book of Revelation* [Minneapolis: Fortress Press, 2000] 249) show that altered states of consciousness as the basis for receiving revelations may be more 'normal' than apparent. This is because they break with the 'fixed and stable state of ordinary consciousness' which is developed in a certain culture's plausibility structure. My discussion below (pp. 163–72) develops this.

[48] Dunn, *Theology of Paul*, 427.

[49] Horn, *Angeld*, 14–15, 20; cf. H. Räisänen, *Neutestamentliche Theologie?* (Stuttgart: Verlag Katholisches Bibelwerk, 2000) 104. Thiselton (*Corinthians*, 1112) points to the 'well-established' psychological phenomenon of how critical reflection 'raises our consciousness from an alpha' to a beta state, which would be a helpful avenue to explore, but he does not offer any substantiation.

1.18–32).[50] While it may have the right intentions, it has not brought about the required fulfilment of the law (Rom. 7.7–25).[51] And a solution to the human plight does not lie in conforming to reason alone or in becoming more 'reasonable'.[52] On the other hand, we encounter Paul's heavy reliance on rationality. His own argument is highly dependent on being *reasonable*,[53] he is keen that his listeners understand his message,[54]

[50] 'Die Erkenntnis Gottes ist verleugnet, wenn sie nicht seine Anerkennung ist' (Bultmann, *Theologie*, 214). This phrase sums up in a nutshell Paul's point in Rom. 1.18–32, which has been unnecessarily complicated by debates about natural revelation. Fitzmyer (*Romans*, 274) is right to respect the fact that Paul allows for some form of general knowledge of God and hence we need not overreact, importing into Paul a post-enlightenment fear of a substitution of natural religion for Christian revelation. Paul is not concerned about such a debate and therefore does not specify the issue (cf. Schrage, 'Verhältnis', 497). He merely follows a common religious axiom that God has made himself known (cf. *Wis.Sol.* 13.1–9; Dunn, *Theology of Paul*, 91) in order to set up his actual point of showing that all are without excuse, his 'geistesgeschichtliches Pauschalurteil' (Haacker, *Römer*, 49). Cf. G. Bornkamm ('Glaube und Vernunft bei Paulus', in K. H. Rengstorf [ed.], *Das Paulusbild in der neueren deutschen Forschung* [Darmstadt: Wissenschaftliche Buchgesellschaft, 1964] 599) who points out that this type of knowledge is only the beginning and not the goal for Paul. K. Kertelge ('"Natürliche Theologie" und Rechtfertigung aus dem Glauben', in *Grundthemen paulinischer Theologie* [Freiburg: Herder, 1991] 159) shows that we need not think of a complete and exclusive contrast between the '"natürliche Theologie" des heidnisch-philosophischen Umfeldes' and the gospel.

[51] This is true if one understands the 'I' of the section as referring to a more individual account (cf. Theissen, *Aspects*, 190–201) or as a rhetorical element to involve the readers (cf. W. G. Kümmel, *Römer 7 und die Bekehrung des Paulus* [Leipzig: Hinrichs'sche Buchhandlung, 1929]). However, it seems difficult to understand the passage as a description of the continued reality of a Christian, since, as I will argue, the renewal of the mind by the Holy Spirit changes the perspective fundamentally (contra, e.g., Dunn, *Romans* I, 387; see Haacker, *Römer*, 142 n. 7, for further bibliography).

[52] Against Bornkamm, 'Glaube', 612: 'Der Ruf, vernünftig und besonnen zu sein, ist darum für Paulus gleichbedeutend mit der Forderung der Erneuerung des Sinnes . . . (Röm 12, 2)'; cf. Schnelle, *Anthropologie*, 124.

[53] There have rightly been a number of attempts to dispel the 'myth of Paul the non-thinker' (Betz, *Galatians*, xiv). Bornkamm ('Glaube', 610) points out that Paul is not ashamed to explain his thoughts using 'Vernunftgründe'. D. Kemmler (*Faith and Human Reason: A Study of Paul's Method of Preaching as Illustrated by 1–2 Thessalonians and Acts 17, 2–4* [NT.S 40; Leiden: Brill, 1975] 206) concludes his investigation of 1 Thessalonians with the assessment that Paul was concerned to 'anchor the "gospel" in the νοῦς of the Thessalonians'. M. Theobald ('Glaube und Vernunft. Zur Argumentation des Paulus im Römerbrief', in *Studien zum Römerbrief* [WUNT 136; Tübingen: Mohr/Siebeck, 2001] 417–32) argues that Paul's deliberative argument is carried out in a disciplined manner and is of a high argumentative quality and that he is concerned for a 'vernünftige, an konsensfähigen Instanzen, Kriterien, Erfahrungen und Deutungen orientierte Bewahrheitung des Evangeliums' ('Glaube', 429f.). Cf. Moores, *Rationality*, 1: 'For Paul the truth of the gospel of Christ was not to be understood by dodging the logical riddles with which it confronts us.' Moores believes Paul's approach is out of line with the Greek tradition, since it was not 'his aim to stimulate detached intellectual enquiry in anything like the Socratic tradition'. Moores goes on to attempt a vindication of Paul's argument by showing that some of Paul's arguments fit the analytical description of 'fuzzy logic' (*Rationality*, 2).

[54] Cf. Bornkamm, 'Glaube', 607: 'Wieder ist deutlich, daß die reale, natürliche Lebenssituation, in der die Hörer der Botschaft sind, für Paulus alles Gewicht hat. Sie soll von den

and an important criterion for proper worship is that it is conducted in an intelligible manner.[55] Moreover, as Schlatter points out, does not Paul insist that we cannot serve God truly if we do not understand his will and concur with it?[56] Hence we must clarify the question: how can reason be of benefit for discernment if it is such an ambivalent phenomenon? Or put differently, how can the Spirit affect understanding in such a manner that it can regain a prominent role in Paul's theology?

The second set of questions that arises is of a more conceptual nature. It is based on a distinction between νοῦς as 'a constellation of thoughts and assumptions which makes up the consciousness' and as the 'rational faculty'.[57] Primarily, this distinction is helpful. The former category broadens our scope of research from looking only at the 'organ of thought' to what has rightly been described as a 'mind-set', which includes consciousness, 'disposition' and 'character'.[58] This does more justice to Paul's anthropology, which is not strictly systematic,[59] and to a more conceptual approach, which recognises that for Paul rationality, intentionality, volition and consciousness belong together.[60]

However, the distinction becomes problematic when νοῦς as 'rational principle' is excluded from Paul on the basis of a more-or-less theological argument. How is this so? Liberal idealism (pre 1920s) attempted to read into Paul the Greek usage of the mind as a divine

Glaubenden in Christus neu *verstanden* werden.' Betz ('Problem', 199) points out that for Paul the Christian religion is a reasonable and enlightened religion. Jewett (*Terms*, 373f.) shows Paul's concern about the Galatians being torn away from their 'reasonable state of mind'.

[55] Käsemann, 'Ruf', 120. He regards the appeal for intelligible worship in 1 Cor. 14 as a 'hohe Lied' of 'Vernunft'.

[56] Schlatter, *Erläuterungen*, 149. Cf. further Schrage, *Einzelgebote*, 168.

[57] Jewett, *Terms*, 367, 451, respectively. The differentiation as such is an advance on the work by J. Behm ('νοέω κτλ.', *TDNT* IV, 958f.), who offers four distinctions ('disposition'; 'practical reason'; 'understanding'; 'thought/judgment/resolve') and which Jewett rightly compresses to two.

[58] Jewett, *Terms*, 362. Brown (*Cross*, 146) says 'the *mind reflects the orientation of the whole self toward or away from God*'.

[59] Aune, 'Models', 108: 'Paul's anthropology exhibits variety and inconsistency' because anthropology is not his central concern, but H. D. Betz ('The Concept of the "Inner Human Being" [ὁ ἔσω ἄνθρωπος] in the Anthropology of Paul', *NTS* 46 [2000] 315–41) points out that 'inconsistency may indicate complexities' ('Concept', 328). In any case, Paul allows for considerable overlap between νοῦς and καρδία (e.g. 2 Cor. 3.14f., where νοήματα [v. 14] are the equivalent of καρδία [v. 15]; cf. Martin, *Corinthians*, 69). Schrage ('Verhältnis', 492) shows that the 'Vernunftbegriffe' are '*pars pro toto*', which show the person as a whole from one aspect.

[60] Hence I take into consideration Paul's other noetic language (as shown in chapter 1) such as φρονέω (e.g. Rom. 12.3, 16; 14.6; 15.5; Phil. 2.2, 5; 3.15, 19; 4.2, 10; cf. Dunn, *Theology of Paul*, 75).

link ('Anknüpfungspunkt').[61] In reaction to this, scholarship has become overly reticent to give the mind, as an independent agent, a role in the believer's new life (apparent also above [chapter 6, section B] in the alleged difference to Spirit/faith).[62] This leads Jewett to reject the understanding of the 'strictly individual mind' which has 'the power of judgement and decision which the Greek idea supposes'.[63] But is this distinction stringent? If we accept that for Paul the mind is not the divine link in humans, does this mean we need to completely reject the mind as 'the rational principle'?[64] If the Spirit is required to transform human understanding, will this only involve the thoughts alone (as Jewett would have it) or more holistically affect rationality?[65] Moreover, has the reaction against so called 'Greek' thought been a fair representation of it or, at least partially, been an over-reaction against the idealistic tradition?[66]

In sum, I see that neither the Spirit alone nor the mind's innate abilities suffice to offer a comprehensive solution to achieving true discernment. My own argument proposes to look at the juncture of the two. But how can we describe this juncture? Do the two work together, do they co-exist or

---

[61] Jewett (*Terms*, 358–67) gives a helpful history of research, although his results are difficult, partly because he still accepts a crude antithesis between Greek and Jewish thought (cf. *Terms*, 362). Moreover, his indebtedness to the Gnostic influence hypothesis (*Terms*, 377) and the dissection of the Corinthian letters is confusing at best. R. Reitzenstein (*Die hellenistischen Mysterienreligionen* [Leipzig: B. G. Teubner, 1910] 165) is a prominent example of the *religionsgeschichtliche* School. He identifies νοῦς with πνεῦμα and sees it as the divine 'Fluidum' which is granted humans to make them πνευματικός.

[62] Jewett (*Terms*, 359) speaks of a 'violent rejection' of the liberal position which is evident in the reluctance to speak of mind at all. For example, with regard to 1 Cor. 2.16b, ἡμεῖς δὲ νοῦν Χριστοῦ ἔχομεν, Conzelmann (*Korinther*, 94) makes mind the equivalent of πνεῦμα, while Barrett (*Corinthians*, 78) thinks the 'matter is obscured by the introduction of the word *mind*' and Wilckens (*Weisheit*, 87ff.) pays no attention to the verse. The same reticence is visible concerning Rom. 12.2 (for examples, cf. Schrage, *Einzelgebote*, 164 n. 5). Stuhlmacher ('Glauben', 337 n. 1) warns in a general manner against an identification of human understanding with the Pauline concept of νοῦς. We will return below to the problem of Paul following the LXX here rather than the Hebrew text.

[63] Jewett, *Terms*, 387, 378, respectively.

[64] Paul would surely not agree with Seneca's belief that, 'Reason . . . is nothing else than a portion of the divine spirit set in a human body' (*Epistulae* 66.12). Nevertheless, Schrage ('Verhältnis', 496) shows clearly that, while Paul does not see reason as divine, still the 'rational principle' is addressed and active (495–8). Cf. further below (pp. 163–72).

[65] Jewett (*Terms*, 378, 387) is very keen on maintaining this difference, although in his conclusion he seems to mix in some of the supposed Greek thought which he is so wary of, when he sees the νοῦς as the 'agent of rational discernment and communication' (*Terms*, 450). It seems inevitable that the whole of rationality is changed, not only the thoughts. Thiselton follows this differentiation but not generally the negation of reason (*Corinthians*, 275).

[66] Moe ('Vernunft', 354) rightly shows how dialectic theology has overreacted so that the mind is reduced in such a manner, 'daß es eigentlich unverständlich bleibt, wie Gott sich überhaupt dem Menschen offenbaren kann'.

amalgamate? I suggest looking at four particular aspects of this juncture. Specifically I will look at the role of choice, the question of direct guidance by the Spirit and the conscience, the interrelationship of rationality and revelation, and finally dispositional change. These four aspects will serve as windows onto understanding the relationship of mind and Spirit more closely. We should note from the start, though, that discernment is not just the result of this juncture, but discerning elements will be part of the process, a point to which we shall return at the end.

D.   The Juncture of Mind and Spirit

1.   To Choose or to Be Chosen

The first aspect to be looked at is the interrelationship between the role of human choice and God's choosing. What do I mean by this? The reservation about reason, which we encountered earlier (section B), expresses itself here again in stressing that the 'new creation and one's place in it' is only 'God's sovereign act of election apart from any human decision'.[67] The reasons for this position are pluriform and we cannot adequately address them here.[68] However, to my mind, they present a solution to a tension which Paul himself does not attempt to resolve. This is particularly evident in the fact that Paul can portray his conversion experience both

---

[67] Brown, *Cross*, 149, with reference to J. L. Martyn, 'Apocalyptic Antinomies in Paul's Letter to the Galatians', *NTS* 31 (1985) 410–24. Cf. Schrage, *Einzelgebote*, 164f., who is keen to show that the renewal is no 'Akt des Nous und also kein Akt der Selbstbesinnung ... wie in der Stoa, sondern an ihm geschehene Umformung'. Further, see Käsemann, *Römer*, 218; C. H. Cosgrove, *The Cross and the Spirit: A Study in the Argument and Theology of Galatians* (Macon, GA: Mercer University Press, 1988) 192: 'Existential participation in Christ's death *happens* to Paul; witness his passive formulations (2 Cor 1:6; 4.11; cf. 1 Thess 2:14).' Cosgrove emphasises that life 'attached to the Crucified' 'lies outside the control and calculation of believers' (*Cross*, 194).

[68] This is partially due to an irritation with the strong emphasis on the freedom of choice from Kant onwards, developing in the existentialist tradition and thereafter visible in Bultmann's work. In this regard, see the somewhat (to my mind) exaggerated discrepancy that is portrayed between Paul and Kant in H. W. Cassirer, *Grace and Law: St. Paul, Kant, and the Hebrew Prophets* (Grand Rapids, MI: Eerdmans, 1988) chs. 2 and 4, where he wishes to see Paul's idea of morality as diametrically opposed to Kant's (where the 'ought' means one 'can'). Sometimes the language is more reminiscent of Kant than Paul; cf. F. J. Leenhardt, *L'épître de Saint Paul aux Romains* (Geneva: Labor et Fides, 1981²) 173, who speaks of the imperatives in Rom. 12.2 as 'véritables impératifs catégoriques'. However, while Bultmann (*Theologie*, 337f.) emphasises the decision of the individual, he also says that the new will ('Wollen') is founded in the πνεῦμα which in turn finds its source not in humanity but in the divine 'Heilstat'.

as a divine vocation (Gal. 1.15f.) and as a process of actively deciding and learning (Phil. 3.7ff.).[69]

Two further aspects also highlight the important role of decision. On the one hand, choice is important in the manner of reacting to the Christ-event (or its communication). This involves an evaluative and interpretative process in which the individual[70] recognises the experiences of conversion and Paul's words as part of God's action with him or her.[71] The other aspect of choice, which we should note, is the conscious opening up to the transforming powers of the Spirit.[72] This becomes particularly clear in the double imperative in Rom. 12.2: μὴ συσχηματίζεσθε τῷ αἰῶνι τούτῳ, ἀλλὰ μεταμορφοῦσθε... Both imperatives can be translated best by emphasising the consent on the part of the believer: '[S]top allowing yourselves to be conformed . . . let yourselves be transformed.'[73] That is, the emphasis is on active reception rather than a passive uncontrollable operation.[74] And it is this receptive attitude which stands in creative

---

[69] Cf. Theissen, *Aspects*, 153, who shows that in Phil. 3.7ff., through a triple ἡγεῖσθαι, Paul 'emphasizes this judgment [what he considers a gain and what a loss] as his own evaluation'; cf. also Frenschkowski, *Offenbarung* I, 377 n. 149, who points to the same paradox in Phil. 2.12f.: 'Therefore . . . work out your own salvation with fear and trembling; for it is God who is at work in you, enabling you both to will and to work for his good pleasure.'

[70] I recognise the need to be careful about emphasising in Paul's thought the individual over against the community as a whole and will justify my frequent use of individual below (p. 185).

[71] Cf. Via, *God*, 58: 'The hearing-reception of the gospel is an act of understanding and evaluation. In 1 Thess 2:13 Paul commends the Thessalonians because receiving the word of God that they heard from him, they accepted it not as human word but as the word of God that it truly is'; similarly Tronier, 'Correspondence', 184–6. Scroggs ('Being', 179) writes of deliberate 'world-switching'.

[72] Cranfield (*Romans* II, 607) points out in relation to Rom. 12.2 that, 'while this transformation is not the Christians' own doing but the work of the Holy Spirit, they nevertheless have a real responsibility in the matter – to let themselves be transformed, to respond to the leading and pressure of God's Spirit'. Cf. Dunn, *Theology of Paul*, 497: 'In every moral decision there was a choice to be made, for the flesh or for the Spirit. Conversion is every day.'

[73] Cranfield, *Romans* II, 607. Cranfield also points out that the present imperative 'may be used to indicate that an action already happening is to continue indefinitely [transformation], and in a prohibition to indicate that an action which is happening is to stop [conforming to this world]'. As συσχηματίζεσθε is a 'deponent' verb, it can be translated as having an active voice (since it has no active form in its outward spelling), which would confirm the proposal of J. Buchegger, *Erneuerung des Menschen: Exegetische Studien zu Paulus* (TANZ 40; Tübingen: Francke, 2003) 186, concerning these two verbs: 'Es scheint, als ob von der Umgestaltung ein Imperativ gebildet werden kann, während "Erneuerung" immer nur im Passiv steht . . .'

[74] Voss (*Wort*, 276) differentiates 'Rezeptivität von Passivität'; similarly, Young and Ford (*Meaning*, 250) speaks of 'receptivity without passivity'. The emphasis is important

tension with the other side of the equation:[75] God's choosing of humanity/believers.[76]

Much can be said about the importance of God's initiating role within Paul's theology. I wish to highlight one central element. In both 1 Cor. 8.3 and Gal. 4.9 Paul (apparently)[77] explains that true knowledge only comes when and because God knows one.[78] This 'being known by God' is nearly synonymous with 'being chosen by him'.[79] And, this is crucial, it is *loving* knowledge. God's choosing and knowing is expressed in the pouring out of his love into the hearts of the believers (Rom. 5.5). God does not know of or about the believer, but knows in an acknowledging, affirming and accepting sense.[80] This is important as the believers *experience* that real knowledge (and consequently discernment) is in direct correspondence with the manner in which one has been loved and in turn can love.[81] Consequently, knowledge is not defined by understanding propositions or accumulating data. True knowledge is rather placed within a nexus of renewed relationality and orientation of the whole self towards God.[82] Love is not only a criterion but also the *prerequisite*

---

as it is somewhat different to other passages, where the will is given by God (Phil 2.13) and knowledge is bestowed as a result of the apostle's prayer (cf. Eph. 1.13, 17f.; 3.18) or at least is not as clearly linked to an active reception (cf. Eph. 4.23, although see the performative language of 1 Cor. 2.16; Col. 3.10).

[75] The tension is expressed well by U. Krömer ('Wachsende Erkenntnis und christliche Vollendung in paulinischer Sicht', in J. Tenzler [ed.] *Wirklichkeit der Mitte: Beiträge zu einer Strukturanthropologie* [Freiburg: Adler, 1968] 648), who differentiates between 'Erkenntnis als die lebendige, spannungsgeladene Einheit der beiden Pole menschlicher Wesensart, nämlich der rezeptiven, vom Eindruck bestimmten Seite . . . und der produktiven, vom Antrieb bestimmten Seite . . .'

[76] Whether or not this just refers to a predestined group or whether Paul had a broader vision for all of humanity cannot be answered here. To be sure, Paul, like the Stoics, saw no inconsistency between forms of pre-destination and free human choice (cf. Engberg-Pedersen, *Paul*, 296f.).

[77] As so often in Paul the text is so short, that we have to make an academic guess at what Paul left out; cf. Thiselton, *Corinthians*, 626f., for a full discussion of the ellipsis in 1 Cor. 8.3 and how this fits in with Gal. 4.9.

[78] For the centrality of this principle in Pauline theology, cf. J. Dupont, *Gnosis: la connaissance religieuse dans les épîtres de Saint Paul* (Louvain: E. Nauwelaerts, 1949) 51–105. 'Faith's knowledge of God derives from *being known by God*, whose electing love both calls faith into being and animates it for obedience in love . . .' (Furnish, 'Truth', 176).

[79] Héring, *Corinthiens*, 64.

[80] Cf. J. Weiß, *Der erste Korintherbrief* (KEK 5; Göttingen: Vandenhoeck & Ruprecht, 1977[9]) 218; Voss, *Wort*, 224. Moreover, Sturm, *Study*, 252ff.: 'Hearing the gospel is an apocalyptic encounter between God and humanity' (*Wort*, 252) which is 'dynamically invasive' (*Wort*, 254).

[81] Spicq, *Agape* II, 267: 'If in heaven we shall know even as we are known . . . we can say that here on earth we know as we have been loved.'

[82] Cf. Bultmann, 'γινώσκω', 709.

of authentic Christian knowing.[83] This requires more attention below (pp. 176–7).

For now I can summarise as follows. We have examined the juncture of mind and Spirit in the close interdependence of human and divine initiative. Moreover, this is not reduced to singular acts of decision making but is best understood as a *'constant interplay* between the grace of God and the work of the believer'.[84] While we encountered a similar emphasis on choice of a distinct, exclusive and unitary good, particularly in the Stoics,[85] we have seen that Paul makes a significant contribution in his understanding of 'being chosen' and in equating it with loving knowledge. This, in turn, not only implies an existential encounter (as opposed to purely noetic knowledge), but also exemplifies in an ontological manner how true knowledge works.[86]

2.   The Spirit and the Conscience: Coercive Guides?

Through my next window I aim to investigate the juncture of the Spirit and innate faculties with respect to guidance. Does Paul have a clear concept of direct guidance by the Spirit or by the conscience? If not, what replaces it?

Spirit Guidance or Consciousness?

In the matter of Spirit guidance, common points of reference are the 'leading of the Spirit' (Rom. 8.14; Gal. 5.18) or the 'words' of 'wisdom' and 'knowledge' (1 Cor. 12.8). Some commentators, such as Dunn and Käsemann, are keen to see a charismatic, even ecstatic, tradition behind

---

[83] Cf. P. D. Gardner, *The Gifts of God and the Authentication of a Christian: An Exegetical Study of 1 Corinthians 8–11* (Lanham, MD: University Press of America, 1994) 187ff.; Thiselton, *Corinthians*, 626.

[84] Barclay, *Truth*, 227. This 'accords with his complex understanding of faith as response, reception, trust, decision *and* obedience'. Of course, both indicative and imperative are the consequence of God's mercy.

[85] S. K. Stowers ('Does Pauline Christianity Resemble a Hellenistic Philosophy?', in Engberg-Pedersen [ed.], *Judaism*, 89) offers this as a legitimate point of comparison with those Hellenistic philosophers (Stoics, Epicureans, Sceptics, Cynics) who had 'mutually exclusive attitudes toward life' in contradistinction to, e.g., Aristotle's philosophy, which 'rejected the idea of a unitary good' but rather followed 'a balanced accommodation' of different values. Cf. Tronier, 'Correspondence', 172, who shows how Philo basically sees the 'acquisition of the blessed and happy life' as 'an interpretative event'.

[86] I use 'ontological' as opposed to 'deontological' (e.g. the law) and do mean 'ontic' as an infusion (contra Spicq, *Agape* II, 320). Cf. further Krömer, 'Erkenntnis', 649, who speaks of a 'Betroffenwerden' by revelation (further see, Voss, *Wort*, 224).

the phrase the 'leading of the Spirit'.[87] And Dunn generally sees scope in Paul's writings for charismatic individual guidance.[88] Others, such as G. Fee, rule this out: '[T]his phrase has no connotation either of "ecstasy" or "Spirit seizure," on the one hand, or of "guidance" in the sense of direct help for the details of one's life, on the other.'[89] These scholars point to the misuse of Pauline terminology throughout history for experiences of illuminism, which cannot be *conceptually* linked with Paul.[90]

Where does this leave us? On the one hand, we need not be too exclusive about this. Paul, like early Christianity[91] and forms of Judaism and Hellenism,[92] knew of experiences of individual leading and revelation.[93]

---

[87] Käsemann (*Römer*, 218) points out that it is not the free moral decision nor a weak form of 'being led' but a 'getrieben werden' by the Spirit. Cf. Dunn, *Galatians*, 104: 'When used in connection with the Spirit, the verb "led" implies the sense of being constrained by a *compelling inner force*, or of surrendering to a powerful inner compulsion . . . Here, evidently, the understanding of the Spirit is of a power which works like a deep-rooted passion or *overmastering compulsion*' (italics mine). Similarly, cf. Cosgrove, *Cross*, ix, who emphasises the 'enthusiastic' and not only the 'noetic' understanding of the Spirit. Finally, I. de la Potterie ('Le chrétien conduit par l'Esprit dans son cheminement eschatologique [*Rom* 8,14]', in L. De Lorenzi [ed.], *The Law of the Spirit in Rom 7 and 8* [Rome: St. Paul's Abbey, 1976] 209–28) suggests that the exodus story lies behind the vocabulary of guidance.

[88] While Dunn's definition of guidance as '*assured conviction regarding God's will in matters of ethical conduct and decision*' does not, for me, necessitate spontaneity or an enthusiastic state of mind, he is keen to demonstrate precisely this (*Jesus*, 222). Cf. Healy, *Heart*, 150, who speaks of 'direct guidance' as 'a normal, if not frequent, phenomenon' for Paul.

[89] Fee (*Presence*, 563) does not want to see a link here with the 'popular phrase, "the leading of the Spirit," meaning that a certain decision, conscious or unconscious, was the result of the Spirit's guidance' (*Presence*, 563 n. 264). He has in mind rather an ethical transformation through the Spirit, which has resemblance with the type of dispositional change that I wish to describe below (pp. 172–85).

[90] Cf. T. Dubay, *Authenticity: A Biblical Theology of Discernment* (San Francisco: Ignatius Press, 1997²) 81–95, who gives a good, although semi-popular, account. Concerning the λόγος σοφίας and γνώσεως (1 Cor. 12.8), cf. Thiselton, *Corinthians*, 943: 'This is different from popular assumptions about "flashes of insight" into this or that particular situation', but rather a '*trained, habituated disposition, shaped and nourished by the Holy Spirit for the use at the moment of God's choice.*' Dunn, also, is aware of the dangers of subjectivity and illuminism (*Galatians*, 107).

[91] Often the descriptions in Acts are used as evidence, cf. 8.29; 10.19; 13.2; 16.6 ('being forbidden by the Holy Spirit to preach the word in Asia') in Healy, *Heart*, 150; or 5.1–11 (Peter's perception of the lies of Ananias and Sapphira) in Thiselton, *Corinthians*, 969.

[92] See my descriptions in chapter 5, particularly the voice guiding Socrates in Plutarch, *De Genio Socratis*, 580C–D (*Moralia* VII). Cf. further, Turner, *Spirit*, 6–10 and Meier, *Mystik*, 264, who gives examples of divine coercion. Moreover, as I pointed out, Philo's teaching on direct guidance is not theoretical but is based on his own experience.

[93] Healy (*Heart*, 150) correctly points to 2 Cor. 12.1 and the 'mysteries' revealed to Paul. Cf. Frenschkowski, *Offenbarung* I, 381, who believes that Paul knew the elementary experience of enthusiasts of a dichotomy of states of consciousness and he could speak of an 'obligation' to preach the gospel (1 Cor. 9.16).

Nevertheless, as I have already pointed out, revelation should not be characterised exclusively as immediate or spontaneous.[94] And in any case, we should not see this as the '*distinctive element*' in Paul's ethics or theology.[95] On the contrary, I wish to place the emphasis elsewhere. As Schrage puts it, πνεύματι ἄγεσθαι does not mean being driven automatically in a certain direction but rather means letting oneself be led *consciously* and *responsibly*.[96] Hence, the Spirit's role is seen as reinforcing, building and expanding consciousness.[97]

This can be further explained as an opening up to the Spirit's power to expand the consciousness into areas that are otherwise inaccessible.[98] As well as the Christological restructuring of perceived reality (which I shall deal with below [pp. 178–85]), a helpful avenue to explain the expansion of consciousness is the access to the pre-conscious and pre-cognitive. Theissen explains how access (through the Spirit) to the unconscious has revelatory and transforming effects, as it is an 'unveiling' of both 'conflicting' and 'integrative' tendencies.[99] The former is a confrontation with

---

[94] In addition to my notes (chapter 6, section B) earlier I might add: the verb ἀποκαλύπτω is 'neutral with respect to the strength and clarity of the revelation' and can be seen as the 'firm conviction gradually etched on the mind' (Turner, 'Gifts', 12). Furthermore, those passages which clearly speak of a revelatory process in which a mystery is revealed are not the norm nor, with respect to the experience of 2 Cor. 12.1–10, the basis of his apostleship or of his belonging to Christ (A. T. Lincoln, '"Paul the Visionary": The Setting and Significance of the Rapture to Paradise in II Cor xii:1–10', *NTS* 25 [1979] 204–20). Frenschkowski (*Offenbarung* I, 377) notes that Paul never placed the ecstatic-visionary experiences on the same level as the Easter experiences.

[95] Dunn (*Jesus*, 225) with respect to ethics. Spicq (*Agape* II, 329) argues along a similar route to Dunn's: 'At this level, judgments are made more by instinct than by rational lucidity' because the 'Christian knows and senses' what God's will is. Therrien (*Discernement*, 177) is far more balanced and may be right that αἴσθησις has a '*caractère intuitif*' in Phil. 1.9f.

[96] Schrage, *Einzelgebote*, 167. This dimension is alluded to in Dunn, *Galatians*, 107; Healy, *Heart*, 167: 'permanent disposition of openness to and reliance on the Spirit'.

[97] Goppelt (*Theologie*, 450) speaks of the Spirit's 'bewußtseinsbildende Kraft'. E. Dirscherl (*Der Heilige Geist und das menschliche Bewußtsein: Eine theologiegeschichtliche Untersuchung* [Würzburg: Echter Verlag, 1989] 196), in his section on Paul, speaks of a transformation of consciousness which, following Theissen, he calls a 'Bewußtseinserweiterung' leading to new 'Denken', 'Handeln', 'Erfahren' and 'Verhalten'. Noack (*Gottesbewußtsein*, 3) offers a definition of 'consciousness' as that centre of perception and experience which constitutes meaning. It is hence the structuring and reflecting perception/conception of reality: it encompasses the understanding and construction of reality.

[98] Here the Spirit has a hermeneutical function, 'relating sema[n]tic and noetic fields', as Moores (*Rationality*, 135) puts it. Theissen (*Aspects*, 373) explains further: 'They have opened their individual spirits to the more comprehensive Spirit of God. Only now does "what no eye has seen and no ear heard, what has entered the heart of man" (1 Cor 2.9) become accessible to them. Only as transformed do they become receptive to new impulses, reinforcements, and models.'

[99] Theissen, *Aspects*, 395ff. The 'unveiling' is based on his *psychodynamic* interpretation of 2 Cor. 3–4 where the veil 'symbolizes a boundary between the consciousness and

the 'aggressive power' of normative systems, 'censors' and 'compulsive standards', which can be of a spiritual, sociological or psychological origin.[100] And these are replaced by the integrative aspect, which is a restructuring of the 'human interior' according to the 'archetypal' model of Christ acting as a 'healing power'.[101] Accordingly, I argue that Spirit guidance takes place when the innermost 'presupposition pools' of the believers are healed and/or activated, leading to a more authentic perception of both the self and others. This in turn is an integral part of a holistic understanding of soteriology and fundamental for character formation and maturation.

Conscience and Consciousness

If, then, Paul does not develop a concept of direct guidance by the Spirit, what about his references to the conscience? Is he influenced by the Philonic and Stoic uses of the term? And if so, does he attach the same significance to it? Recent scholarship has given the concept detailed attention, to which we may refer at this point.[102]

There is some agreement that for Paul συνείδησις did not have direct revelatory quality or was in any sense the/a *vox dei*.[103] Furthermore, we should not take the word as the basis for a singular concept. Paul can use

unconsciousness' which is eliminated in Christ (*Aspects*, 143). The psychodynamic is only one of three interpretation models Theissen uses. I address the other two, the *cognitive* and *learning* models in a more indirect manner below (pp. 163–71 and 172–84, respectively).

[100] Theissen, *Aspects*, 142–53, with respect to 2 Cor. 3.4–4.6, and 373–86, with regard to 1 Cor. 2.6–16. His understanding of the role of the law as such an 'aggressive norm' is in part problematic, as he has not balanced it with the new perspective on Paul.

[101] Theissen, *Aspects*, 150–3. He shows that access to the unconscious has transforming effects since 'the veil of Moses' also concealed the true counterpart to the aggressive norm of the law – 'the true splendor of Christ that shines in the interior of human beings' and transforms them into his image (2 Cor. 3.18; 4.3; *Aspects*, 150). 'As image, Christ reveals not only the Deity but also man . . . in psychodynamic terms, we could say that as the image of the goal of true humanity, Christ takes the place of the punishing superego' (*Aspects*, 152).

[102] Cf. Rom. 2.15; 9.1; 13.51; 1 Cor. 8.7, 10, 12; 10.25, 27, 28, 29; 2 Cor. 1.12; 4.2; 5.11; Bosman, *Conscience*, 1–48; 191–275; R. Schnackenburg, *The Moral Teaching of the New Testament* (London: Burns & Oates, 1969[5]) 287–95; and other authors cited in this section.

[103] Cf. C. A. Pierce, *Conscience in the New Testament* (London: SCM Press, 1955) 13–20. Pierce may be somewhat reactionary in attempting to categorically distance Paul from Stoic thought here, but the terminological similarity should, of course, not be used as the basis for introducing the Stoics' pantheistic worldview which they combined with the concept. See further Jewett, *Terms*, 460 (who argues that the συνείδησις has 'a purely human function'); W. Schrage, *Der erste Brief an die Korinther (1Kor 6,12–11,16)*, (EKK 7/II ; Neukirchen-Vluyn: Neukirchener Verlag, 1995) 257; Thiselton, *Corinthians*, 641.

the term in different but related senses.[104] For one, there is the sense of an autonomous witness in which the controlling element is emphasised (Rom. 2.15; 9.1).[105] P. Bosman speaks of an 'inner monitor' 'which registers the states of the inner person and reports on them in an impartial and reliable manner'.[106] But this should not be read in an absolute manner as an infallible judge nor as a form of natural revelation (in the dogmatic sense).[107] That is to say, it does not have so much a normative but more a testing function.[108] Consequently, while at points there is an overlap with the semantic scope of νοῦς,[109] the locus of normative thinking is in the mind and not in the conscience.[110] Likewise, the *mind* is the fulcrum point of renewal (Rom. 12.2).

The other sense of συνείδησις is 'self-awareness' or 'consciousness'.[111] This is an awareness of one's own strengths, weaknesses and limits

---

[104] Cf. Jewett, *Terms*, 459; Thiselton, *Corinthians*, 642, and contra H.-J. Eckstein, *Der Begriff Syneidesis bei Paulus* (WUNT 2,10; Tübingen: Mohr/Siebeck, 1983) 311. Eckstein sees the term used 'einheitlich' with various nuances.

[105] Paul clearly appropriates aspects of the Hellenistic-Jewish tradition which I showed in my work on Philo earlier (pp. 114–17), where he can be 'witness', 'accuser', 'governor' or even 'king'; cf. Schrage, *Korinther* II, 258: 'also vom Wollen und Tun eigentümlich unabhängige Instanz'; Jewett, *Terms*, 459.

[106] Bosman, *Conscience*, 265.

[107] Here there is a difference to Philo's incorruptible judge or the Stoics' view that the conscience is the highest authority, as I portrayed earlier (pp. 114–17). However, I also showed that for Seneca it is not a guarantee for correct conduct, and hence 'finality' (of conscience) should not be overemphasised as the distinguishing point between Paul and the Stoics (contra Sevenster, *Paul*, 101). Pierce (*Conscience*, 13–20, 111–30) rightly points out that the term should not be identified with the post third-century AD notion of a knowledge of a moral law or with the way it is used in modern ethical theory (cf. Thiselton, *Corinthians*, 644).

[108] Schrage, *Korinther* II, 258 (who claims this for the Stoics, too); Eckstein, *Begriff*, 314. Against J. Gnilka, *Paulus von Tarsus: Apostel und Zeuge* (HThK.S 6; Freiburg: Herder, 1996) 208: 'Das Gewissen ist das dem Menschen – jedem Menschen – in das Herz geschriebene Gesetz . . . Dabei ist an das Sittengesetz zu denken, vielleicht in erster Linie an den Dekalog' (so also U. Wilckens, *Der Brief an die Römer [Röm 1–5]*, [EKK 6/I; Neukirchen-Vluyn: Neukirchener Verlag, 1978] 139).

[109] Jewett (*Terms*, 459) thinks that in 2 Cor. 4.2; 5.11 it is 'fully identical with νοῦς; it is the agent of rational discernment . . .'

[110] Eckstein, *Terms*, 314f. Cf. Bultmann, *Theologie*, 217, who states that while νοῦς has an inherent intentionality, the conscience only reflects and evaluates those intentions.

[111] This has been argued particularly for the use in 1 Cor. 8 by P. W. Gooch, '"Conscience" in 1 Corinthians 8 and 10', *NTS* 33 (1987) 244–54; Gardner, *Gifts*, 44–46; Horsley, 'Consciousness', 574–89. Horsley shows that this sense is also related to the ἔλεγχος concept in Philo (582).

Against, Bosman (*Conscience*, 2) who understands this sense as a 'modern conceptualisation'. However, Bosman differentiates Paul's concept of conscience from Philo's in arguing that there is a shift towards neutrality. 'The tendency towards neutrality, already notable in Philo, becomes established in Paul's συνείδησις.' To my mind, the sense 'consciousness' does justice precisely to the emphasis on neutrality.

(1 Cor. 8) leading to a stronger inner consonance.[112] But it is also see-ing oneself in relation to others,[113] having an understanding of one's own 'identity' as different from others.[114] This is important since this makes συνείδησις less a moral category and rather an indicator of pre-serving one's own integrity and, importantly, that of others.[115] Rather than emphasising the freedom and 'rights' of individuals, it is a respect for the integrity of each member of the community.[116] And this respect in turn is the basis of love, which allows some to give up their 'rights' for the sake of the more vulnerable in the community.[117]

How, then, can we conclude this section on guidance? We have seen that Paul was aware of direct discernment through the Spirit and knew of a guiding power within humans. Both may include intuitive and immediate elements. But rather than a 'mechanical' or 'automatic' form of guidance (be it from outside or inside), my own argument emphasised that for Paul it is important *that the whole person is strengthened in consciousness.* That means there is an expansion of awareness concerning previously inaccessible areas and also with respect to the believer's own person-hood. To my mind, such an understanding of guidance is more congruent (than that of those who argue for direct guidance) with Paul's empha-sis on maturity, as it is based on a deeper, more coherent and long-term comprehension of identity and spiritual experience.

---

[112] Cf. J. M. Gundry-Volf, 'Conscience', *DPL*, 155.

[113] Gardner, *Gifts*, 45; Seneca, *De Vita Beata*, 20.4: 'Nothing shall I ever do for the sake of opinion, everything for the sake of my conscience. Whatever I shall do when I alone am witness I shall count as done beneath the gaze of the Roman people.'
It is also noteworthy that Paul uses σύνοιδα in 1 Cor. 4.4 to describe his relationship to God.

[114] Gooch, 'Conscience', 250.

[115] Schrage (*Korinther* II, 258) says that the decision based on the conscience takes the whole person into account. Cf. C. Maurer, 'σύνοιδα κτλ.', *TDNT* VII, 914: 'Thus συνείδησις is not to be defined as a power of religious and moral evaluation or the like which can be detached from man. It is man himself aware of himself in perception and acknowledgment in willing and acting.'

[116] Thiselton, *Corinthians*, 644. One could of course object that in 1 Cor. 10.29b Paul refers to his own integrity rather than of the other person but this difficult passage requires careful thought. Thiselton, *Corinthians*, 788–92 offers an overview of the six major inter-pretations and follows D. F. Watson. The brief summary of this discussion is of general importance for the understanding of freedom: 'At one level the Christian is free: it is not other people's judgments, as such, which should determine one's own. On the other hand, always to ask about the impact or effect on the self-awareness . . . . of *the other* must play a part in the believer's decision about how the *freedom* which God has granted is to be *constructively used*' (792f.).

[117] Contra Thiselton, *Corinthians*, 644, who speaks of the basis as a restraint 'by self-discipline', I emphasise respect as the basis of love which gives a more natural impulse for the giving up of rights.

3.   Relating Reason and Revelation

We turn now to the relationship of rationality and revelation. If, as I
pointed out earlier (pp. 35–43), human mediation requires some form of
renewal, we must clarify what this implies. That is, how does the gospel
through the Spirit affect rationality? My thesis proposes that an essential
twofold distinction of the Spirit's effect on cognition can be found in
1 Cor. 1–2. The primary influence is at first sight deconstructive and is
portrayed in 1.18–25. The second is a more positive, constructive aspect,
described in 2.6–16. The latter aspect depends on the former.[118]

Deconstruction of Perceived Reality

Concerning the more negative effect, Paul confronts Corinthian conven-
tion with a serious affront: the cross. Graeco-Roman honour and shame
culture revolved around public recognition in which acclaim from others
became more important than authenticity. And the constant search for
status turned into a legitimisation of the manipulative appropriation of
others for one's own purposes.[119] Corinth was no exception to this; on the
contrary: 'Corinth was a city where public boasting and self-promotion
had become an art form.'[120] The cross disrupted this consensus reality in
a particularly dramatic manner: the symbol of ultimate rejection, subjec-
tion and humiliation was declared the locus of revelation, reconciliation
and liberation.[121] Hence, those confronted by the λόγος τοῦ σταυροῦ

---

[118] Brown (*Cross*, 19) writes that Paul's word of the cross has a performative effect
corresponding to J. L. Austin's speech-acts theory. The two sections I have described are,
for Brown, two acts 'in the dramatic performance of the text' (*Cross*, 29).

[119] S. M. Pogoloff (*Logos and Sophia: The Rhetorical Situation of 1 Corinthians*
[SBL.DS 134; Atlanta: Scholars Press, 1992] 7–196) shows how the Corinthians concerned themselves not with truth but with applause and success. Moreover, he sees Paul not
rejecting rhetoric as such but 'the cultural values wedded to it' and working with a 'rhetoric
of status reversal' (*Logos*, 121). This work on the rhetorical aspects of the Corinthian
dilemma is interconnected with sociological research which has shown that the problems
in the church were tied to the social stratification of Corinthian society (cf. G. Theissen,
'Soziale Schichtung in der korinthischen Gemeinde. Ein Beitrag zur Soziologie des Hellenistischen Urchristentums', in *Studien zur Soziologie des Urchristentums* [WUNT 19;
Tübingen: Mohr/Siebeck, 1989³] 231–71). Thiselton (*Corinthians*, 40) sums up the issue:
'*Concerns about self-promotion, the psychological insecurity generated by status inconsistency, competitive pragmatism, and the radical pluralism . . . all encouraged concerns
about "high status" as "people of the Spirit who were gifted" within a Christian subculture
with its own autonomous value system.*'

[120] Witherington, *Conflict*, 8.

[121] The cross was a severe σκάνδαλον 'in both an *epistemic* sense (the cross defines
in what reality consists) and in a *salvific* sense (the cross defines the pathway to life and
well-being)' (Thiselton, *Corinthians*, 158). Cf. Voss, *Wort*, 87ff., for how the cross affects
Jews and Greeks differently (1 Cor. 1.18).

had to experience a process which can be described as intense cognitive dissonance. Such dissonance is an intense cognitive conflict, which forces one 'either to defend the received system of interpretation through reinforcement of elements consonant with it or to restructure it to such an extent that originally dissonant elements appear as consonant in a more comprehensive or transformed framework'.[122]

In other words, only rejection or a complete 'world switch' can follow. Such a 'world switch' entails a 'radical perceptual shift' where '*everything* is viewed differently, oneself, others, society, the past, and the future'.[123] It implies an 'epistemological revolution'.[124]

Important for us is that revelation as expressed here is a revolution of the understanding but without denigrating the mind's functions. How is this possible? On the one hand, although there is a rupture of 'normal' thinking, noetic perception is involved 'throughout the entire process'.[125] Cultural selectivity and plausibility structures shape the characteristic and habitual patterns of mental consciousness. A complete break with these will be perceived and experienced as a break with everything that is 'reasonable', but it is and remains a *noetic* affair.[126] The mind is never switched off.[127] And this fact in turn does not belittle the totality of the perceptual shift. In other words, the mind is not only repaired.[128] It is not a release from some partial inefficiency or a development of present knowledge.[129] There is a complete break with the old way of thinking to make way for a new order, a new grammar of thought.[130] In fact,

[122] Theissen, *Aspects*, 387. Cf. Brown, *Cross*, 157, and her further depiction of how cognitive dissonance works (n. 13).

[123] Scroggs, 'Being', 170.

[124] Hays, 'Wisdom', 113: 'The cross becomes the starting point for an epistemological revolution, a *conversion of the imagination*. For anyone who grasps the paradoxical logic of this text [1 Cor. 2], the world can never look the same again.' Yu (*Epistemology*, 304) speaks of the Spirit as a 'perception-transforming power'.

[125] Scroggs ('Being', 170) is correct on this point. That does not mean 'abstract, intellectual processes' but rather a change in self- and world-awareness which is, as I shall argue, quite existential.

[126] It is important to understand that such an altered state of consciousness (ASC) can appear to disregard rationality (and hence be interpreted as a negation of reason) but it is *only* a collapse of ordinary consciousness which is based around a certain culturally defined consensus reality; cf. Malina and Pilch, *Revelations*, 249. Voss (*Wort*, 276) says the cross interprets us *precisely as* we are thinking and understanding.

[127] Moe, 'Vernunft', 361; Voss, *Wort*, 12.   [128] Schrage, 'Verhältnis', 498.

[129] This is the impression one can get from *Wis. Sol.* 9, from Betz ('Grundlagen', 201), who speaks of a release from the mind's inefficiency, and from V. P. Furnish ('Theology in 1 Corinthians', in Hay [ed.], *Theology* II, 67), who says that 'their faculties for critical thought and reasoned action are *informed* and *guided* by the wisdom of the cross' (italics mine).

[130] Stuhlmacher ('Bedeutung', 159) says that the believers are released from a 'verblendeten und untüchtigen Verstand' and are 'zu einem neuen Denken befreit'. 'Our

such a radical shift in perception and awareness will affect not only a person's cognition, but also his/her valuation and intentionality.[131] This implies and necessitates an ethical change, which I must attend to later (pp. 172–85).

For now I can summarise that I begin to understand why Paul can speak of two types of wisdom, which are mutually exclusive without requiring a displacement of the noetic functions nor any form of ontic change in a person.[132] It is, rather, a new framework of thought, a new perception of reality as a whole, which leads to a radical restructuring of 'self-understanding'.[133] It is a 'reconfiguration' of the convictional world, which is no less dramatic than Paul's own conversion experience.[134] But it remains a thoroughly cognitive experience.[135] This in turn begins to show how true discernment is based on a very intricate mix of revelation and cognition. But so far I have concentrated more on the deconstructive effect. Paul does not leave it at that as we see when we turn to 1 Cor. 2.6–16.

knowledge will not simply be filled in: it will be changed.' This comment by Gooch (*Knowledge*, 147) is with respect to the eschatological fulfilment of knowledge in 1 Cor. 13 but to my mind it shows the direction Paul is also taking in 1 Cor. 1–2. Knowledge is not just pieced together but transformed.

[131] Scroggs, 'Being', 170: 'A new self is created because a new world is being entered, because of a change in the perception of reality.' Rowland ('Apocalyptic', 247) shows that such an 'epistemological rupture' leads to a transformation 'involving ethical as well as intellectual conversion'.

[132] Cf. Merklein, *Korinther 1–4*, 242, who rightly opposes any ontic dualism between the ψυχικός and the πνευματικός in 1 Cor. 2.13f. However, against this position, cf. D. J. Lull, *The Spirit in Galatia* (SBL.DS 49; Chico, CA: Scholars Press, 1980) 197: 'For Paul, the Spirit brings a real *structural* change in the believer's existence, and not merely a change of "self-understanding".'

[133] Engberg-Pedersen (*Paul*, 289ff.) shows convincingly that this is also one of Paul's aims in Romans.

[134] Donaldson (*Paul*, 297) shows how Paul's own 'foundational cognitions' were reconfigured 'around a new center', Christ (293–307). He highlights the balance of 'continuity and discontinuity. On the one hand, paradigms are sharply disjunctive and discontinuous [because they reject a theory in favour of a new one incompatible with the first] . . . Yet, at the same time, there is continuity . . . Many old observations, cognitions, and even convictions are carried over, but organized and understood with respect to a new structure' (304).

[135] Tronier ('Correspondence', 168) makes a case that the old dichotomy of faith and reason with respect to Paul cannot be maintained. 'Paul's ideas of faith, revelation, and the soteriological state of being united with Christ refer to a mode of perception with a particular rationality that is linked to a certain idea of cosmology.' For example, Paul's confrontation in 1 Corinthians has a 'distinctly cognitive content' ('Correspondence', 182) with an inherent rationality in the argument ('Correspondence', 185). Contra J. F. M. Smit ('"What is Apollos? What is Paul?" In search for the Coherence of First Corinthians 1:10–4:21', *NT* 44 [2002] 231–51), who claims that the rejection of σοφία λόγου does not attack rhetoric as such but human reasoning.

Learning a New Reality

The construction of the new reality is clearly dependent on 'the presence and power of another actor': the Spirit.[136] But does this necessitate the eviction of cognitive apprehension? On the contrary: in a similar manner to Philo, Paul describes inspiration in distinctly rational categories in 1 Cor. 2.6–16. The believers are taught (v. 13: διδακτοῖς) and hence made able to know (v. 12: ἵνα εἰδῶμεν; cf. vv. 14, 16: γινώσκω), interpret (v. 13: συγκρίνω) and evaluate (vv. 14f.: ἀνακρίνω).[137]

Furthermore, it is not by chance that Paul says 'we have the νοῦς of Christ' (v. 16): Paul wishes to denote that the Spirit brings about a new Christocentric rationality.[138] This fits with the broader picture in Paul. In 2 Cor. 4.6, the light of the gospel comes in the form of *knowledge* of the glory of God.[139] And this corresponds to the reason why for Paul the primary ethical and spiritual appeal is a new thinking (Rom. 8.5; 12.1f.; cf. Eph. 4.23).[140] As K. Stalder repeatedly points out, it is the mark of the Spirit that it leads the believers themselves to know and discern.

[136] Brown, *Cross*, 165. The introduction of the Spirit in 1 Cor. 2 should not make us believe that the proclamation of the cross in 1 Cor. 1 excluded the presence of the Spirit as Paul clarifies in 2.4: 'My speech and my proclamation were not with plausible words of wisdom, but with a demonstration of the Spirit and of power.'

[137] Theissen, *Aspects*, 365: 'conferral of the divine Spirit makes one capable of knowledge, understanding, and recognition'. Cf. Gooch, *Knowledge*, 47, who shows that on the basis of 1 Cor. 1–4 one cannot 'deprecate reason or . . . banish it from the domain of theology'.

[138] Paul, in his quotation of Isa. 40.13, follows the unusual LXX reading, which uses νοῦς instead of the Hebrew רוח. Wolff (*Korinther*, 62 n. 220) speaks of the 'Vernunft Gottes' in 1 Cor. 2.16a and Brown (*Cross*, 141) sees an intended 'shift in meaning', but follows Jewett in referring to 'a constellation of thoughts'.

[139] Cf. Via, *God*, 55–7. 'Paul speaks of *gospel* and *knowledge* interchangeably as the means of access to the reality of God. Notice the parallelism between the important chain of words in [2 Cor.] 4:4 and 4:6. Illumination-*gospel*-glory parallels illumination-*knowledge*-glory' (*God*, 66).
The link between intellectual illumination and the Spirit's activity is further explored in Ephesians. There the Spirit reveals (3.5), but does this so that the *believers* might 'know' (1.9; 3.3–5) and have 'insight' and 'wisdom' (1.8: ἐν πάσῃ σοφίᾳ καὶ φρονήσει). Cf. P. Pokorný, *Der Brief an die Epheser* (ThHK 10/2; Leipzig: Evangelische Verlagsanstalt, 1992) 64, who shows that, while insight and wisdom are not autonomous gifts, their introduction here shows that an appropriation of the gospel was important also as a 'Voraussetzung richtigen Denkens' and for the 'Überwindung der intellektuellen Entfremdung'. For the fact that the insight and wisdom is to be seen as that of the believers, cf. R. Schnackenburg, *Der Brief an die Epheser* (EKK 10; Neukirchen-Vluyn: Neukirchener Verlag, 1982) 55. Further, for the emphasis on the believers' knowledge, compare Cerfaux, *Christian*, 512ff; Phil. 1.9; Col. 1.9; Phm. 6.

[140] Betz, 'Grundlagen', 200: 'Paulus stellt damit . . . unübersehbar heraus, daß der Intellekt eine große Rolle bei der Erfüllung der ethischen Aufgabe spielt.' Schrage (*Einzelgebote*, 165) rightly points out that it is important to see that Rom. 12.1f. is the heading of Paul's parenesis. The transformation of the believer is foremost a renewal of *reason* (*Einzelgebote*, 164). Moreover, he says this renewed thinking cannot be substituted with any amount of 'Tun, Glauben und Beten'. At the same time, Schrage is always keen to keep

> Dabei ist es nicht etwa so, daß eigentlich nur der Heilige Geist in uns Gott erkännte. Das Wunderwerk des Heiligen Geistes besteht vielmehr darin, daß er uns dazu bringt, daß wirklich *wir selbst* Gott in Christus erkennen, an ihn glauben, von ihm wissen und *von dieser Erkenntnis her denken, urteilen, und entscheiden* können.[141]

Hence, rather than a displacement or eviction of the rational functions, we can speak of their enhancement and enlightenment.[142] How the Spirit accomplishes this can be elucidated with the following three points.

First, the Spirit shows that the break with the old plausibility structure is a liberation: 'The ability to see reality in an entirely different way means freedom'.[143] How is this so? For the Corinthians this means that the coercive norms of the honour and shame culture no longer needed to control their lives. What follows is a release from a status-dominated life that led to performance anxiety, arrogance and social stratification.[144] Additionally, there is release from the far greater hubris (which lies below the surface of the external problems) of the creatures confusing themselves

---

the balance. The renewal does not come as an act of νοῦς, as a 'becoming reasonable', but something that *happens* to it (*Einzelgebote*, 164).

[141] Stalder, *Werk*, 487 (final italics mine); cf. further 80, 83ff., 491, 493. Moreover, this emphasis on understanding is not reduced to certain forms of inspiration (for instance, the words of knowledge and wisdom in 1 Cor. 12.8) but it is central to how Paul understands true epistemology. Hence one need not distinguish between the 'word of knowledge' and the formulation of the gospel as Thiselton (*Corinthians*, 943) rightly points out against Bittlinger (*Gifts*, 30–2; cf. Dunn, *Jesus*, 217).

[142] 'For Paul the human mind is heightened in its activity rather than overpowered or idle in receiving divine revelation' (Healy, *Heart*, 150). Cf. Frenschkowski, *Offenbarung* I, 381, who points to the lack of 'enthusiastic' terminology and the 'rationalen Grundtenor seines Denkens' (*Offenbarung* I, 383). Theissen (*Aspects*, 331) points out that there is no 'unbridgeable contradiction between human reason and divine Spirit'. Compare further, Voss, *Wort*, 13; Hunt, *Body*, 127: 'Paul does not divorce the cognitive element from the spiritual activity and communication of Christians; rather rational human cognition plays a vital role.' Further, Moores (*Rationality*, 1) says that for Paul the illumination by the Holy Spirit does not dispense with the need for reflection. Rather the 'human capacity for exercising critical judgement' is 'sharpened and directed by the Holy Spirit'.

[143] Theissen, *Aspects*, 392: 'Seen retrospectively, abrupt dissonances can have liberating effects because they necessitate restructuring and open new perspectives' (*Aspects*, 387). Liberation is of course a marked feature of Romans, Galatians and 2 Corinthians. 'For freedom Christ has set us free. Stand firm, therefore, and do not submit again to a yoke of slavery' (Gal. 5.1; cf. 2 Cor. 3.17; Dunn, *Theology of Paul*, 388; Gnilka, *Paulus*, 250–2).

[144] With that idea I take up a point of Thiselton's (*Corinthians*, 13) in understanding the honour-shame culture in epistemological categories. The emphasis in such a culture does not lie on '*individual moral failure*' but on '*corporate and social lack of honor*' (*Corinthians*, 187). But the 'abolition of the performance principle' is an important liberating step in both (R. Scroggs, 'The Heuristic Value of Psychoanalytic Model in the Interpretation of Paul', *Zygon* 13 [1978] 152).

with the Creator (1 Cor. 1.21; Rom. 1.25).[145] At this point the cross
liberates the self from its ultimate deceit: it need not and cannot constitute true meaning, relationship and understanding by its own means.[146]
But through the catharsis of utter meaninglessness in the cross, the self
can experience a new consonance within the 'new world' created by the
Spirit.[147] This leads me to my second point.

The Spirit clarifies and deepens the meaning of the new plausibility
structure. In chapter 4 we observed that discernment has an interpretative
function. Here it is important to see that the Spirit aids this signifying
role by opening up the full dimensions of the Christ-event leading to a
'more comprehensive horizon of meaning'.[148] On the one hand, the Spirit
brings the cross to its full relevance: it is not *just* a historical event, but
through the Spirit has continued and cosmic significance.[149] On the other
hand, the cross defines the knowledge that is given by the Spirit. The cross
is the 'hermeneutical key' and the focal point of the new epistemology.[150]
True spiritual knowledge is therefore neither knowing κατὰ σάρκα nor
is it simply knowing κατὰ πνεῦμα: J. L. Martyn proposes that authentic knowledge for Paul is knowing κατὰ σταυρόν (cf. 2 Cor. 5.16).[151]
Cruciform knowledge in turn implies that the believers cannot 'plot their
progress' towards God 'by way of greater knowledge . . . or more exalted
mystical experiences' as these only enhance elitism.[152] On the contrary,
the cross entails a surrender of individualistic status seeking so that true
relationality can follow. Hence, progress is measured by the intensity of

[145] V. P. Furnish, *The Theology of the First Letter to the Corinthians* (Cambridge: Cambridge University Press, 1999) 38–42.
[146] Voss (*Wort*, 275f., 294) sees the epistemological effects of sin in limiting reason and
making it believe it can constitute meaning and a relationship to God by itself and hence
giving itself a false soteriological significance (*Corinthians*, 287).
[147] Pedersen ('Understanding', 11) speaks of 'existential deliverance'.
[148] Theissen, *Aspects*, 388.
[149] Sturm, *Study*, 251: 'Here [knowing Christ crucified] one knows the full cosmic dimension of the suffering and conflict that one is in, even as one also knows, through the resurrection hope, the final outcome, the ultimate sovereignty or triumph of God.' Cf. Voss,
Wort, 87; Theissen, *Aspects*, 374–9.
[150] Merklein, 'Weisheit', 383; Voss, *Wort*, 15, 195; Cousar, *Theology*, 180. That the cross
is also the qualification of wisdom in Colossians and Ephesians is argued by F.-J. Steinmetz
('Die Weisheit und das Kreuz', *Geist und Leben* 2 [1999] 112–26).
[151] Martyn ('Epistemology', 285) has offered this argument for 2 Cor. 5.16: the opposite
of knowing κατὰ σάρκα is knowing κατὰ σταυρόν and not κατὰ πνεῦμα as might be
expected. To be sure 2 Cor. 5.16 is very contested (as is the Gnostic hypothesis Martyn
works with, but his work is also based on 1 Cor. 2.6–16 and offers a good general definition
of Pauline epistemology.
[152] Johnson, 'Edification', 366. Cf. Horn, *Angeld*, 262ff., who argues the more traditional
line that Paul is formulating an 'antienthusiastische' position.

edification and unity within the community.[153] Here again we see that true knowledge becomes dependent on a change of orientation, intentionality and life ethos; a point we must return to (pp. 172–85).[154] For now it is crucial to see that the Spirit through the cross brings discernment into direct interdependence with both a true understanding of Christology and a correct practice of ecclesiology.[155]

Finally, I can elucidate the third aspect of how the Spirit affects rationality. It leads to a more mature interaction with reality. Again, we encountered in chapter 4 the corrective role of discernment and, again, we can observe that the Spirit aids this movement this time by creating an 'openness to that which is new and different' and at the same time a stronger awareness of the necessity for testing.[156] This duality of openness and the need for testing is expressed in 1 Thess. 5.19–21: 'Do not quench the Spirit . . . but test everything'. With regard to the openness, rather than revealing a closed system of thought, the Spirit allows for an openness of results and the possibility of trial and error.[157] Concerning the need for testing, there is a new wariness of triumphalism.[158] As mentioned before (p. 68), reality seen through the cross leads to a sobriety and realism which require that critical assessment takes place.[159] As Käsemann points out,

---

[153] 'For Paul sociology is indicative of theology' (S. Grindheim, 'Wisdom for the Perfect: Paul's Challenge to the Corinthian Church [1 Corinthians 2:6–16]', *JBL* 121 [2002] 690). Cf. Hays, *Vision*, 197f.; Johnson, 'Edification', 380ff.; Lull, *Galatians*, 196. Brown (*Cross*, 166) rightly points out that the 'mind of Christ' in 1 Cor. 2.16 is defined by the call for unity, ἐν τῷ αὐτῷ νοΐ καὶ ἐν τῇ αὐτῇ γνώμῃ, in 1.10.

[154] G. Haufe ('Das Geistmotiv in der paulinischen Ethik', *ZNW* 85 [1995] 191) shows accurately how the Spirit's unfolding of the Christ-event not only leads to knowledge of the same but also *intrinsically* leads to a praxis which corresponds to it: 'Die erkenntnismäßige Entfaltung des Heilsgeschehens ruft nach Entsprechung in der Lebensführung des Christen.'

[155] Johnson, 'Edification', 380: 'Reading through this passage [1 Cor. 2.12f.] we find ourselves moving from christology to ecclesiology to discernment along a single axis.'

[156] Stowers ('Paul', 260) shows well how 1 Cor. 1–4 criticises such a lack of openness (cf. Hays, *Vision*, 27).

[157] Betz ('Grundlagen', 201) rightly points out that the new ethical conduct is not just a given but that it has to be *discovered* 'und zwar durch Nachforschung'. Moreover, as we noted in chapter 2, there is a strong element of independence (not from the community but from the world). In this sense it is possible to read the fact that the πνευματικός is not judged by anyone (1 Cor. 2.14f.) and is able to judge everything: he is independent of the compulsive standards of the world and the negative powers that reign over it.

[158] Dunn (*Theology*, 432f.) points out how farsighted Paul was in saying that even the experience of the Spirit required testing. Cf. E. Käsemann, 'Gottesdienst im Alltag der Welt', in *Exegetische Versuche und Besinnungen* II (Göttingen: Vandenhoeck & Ruprecht, 1964) 200f., who speaks of 'unablässiger kritischer Unterscheidung'.

[159] E. Lohse, 'Das Evangelium für Juden und Griechen', *ZNW* 92 (2001) 181: 'Durch diese nüchterne Sicht der Welt, wie sie das Evangelium eröffnet, wird die Fähigkeit zu kritischem Wägen und Prüfen geweckt und geschärft.' Stuhlmacher ('Glauben', 348) correlates διάκρισις πνευμάτων with a 'Nüchternheit' which keeps hope aglow in the painful

the Spirit does not only give wisdom and gifts, the Spirit also makes one critical of wisdom and gifts.[160] Moreover, the release from the confines of status seeking allows the community to 'raise questions, offer objections, and make alternative recommendations that are themselves subject to the testing of the other members' without impinging on the honour of the fellow seekers.[161]

Recapitulation

In concluding this section we see how Paul portrays a strategy to reunite the Corinthian factions. True knowledge and spirituality, both of which the Corinthians desired, are dependent on authentic relationships. These relationships can only be experienced if and when the value system attached to the honour and shame culture is radically restructured.[162] I proposed that the Spirit, who deconstructs the previous plausibility structure of the believer and aids the mind in learning a new liberated reality, brings about this process of transformation. The liberated reality is the basis of new community life.

Regarding the relationship of mind and Spirit, the renewed mind (Rom. 12.2) and the 'mind of Christ' (1 Cor. 2.16) imply an epistemological change in which both Spirit and mind are active. While the Spirit is the prerequisite for true knowledge, it becomes active without eclipsing the function of the mind. My thesis proposes that this means that the Spirit 'transfigures' the mind: it revolutionises the basis on which the mind works by liberating it and placing it within a new perception of reality.[163] Hence we can speak of spiritual reasoning: a '*ratio*', or '*cognitio*

---

realities of an ending world. Schrage (*Einzelgebote*, 170) says the Christian is now able to discover *through critical questioning, sifting and testing* what the will of God is due to the renewal of his evaluative faculties. In this manner he also understands the λογίζεσθε of Phil. 4.8. Cf. further Conzelmann, *Grundriß*, 202, who shows that this testing has both theoretical and practical elements.

[160] Käsemann, 'Korinther', 274. To my mind, an example of this is seen in Paul's own openness to have the gospel he has received verified and evaluated by the apostles in Jerusalem (Gal. 2.2).

[161] Fredrickson, 'Ethics', 120. Fredrickson offers insight into how important the communal aspect of testing is ('Ethics', 115–29), but he does not relate this to an honour/shame culture.

[162] Cf. Käsemann, 'Korinther', 276; Dunn, *Jesus*, 223; Theissen, *Aspects*, 386.

[163] Cf. R. M. Liddy, *Transforming Light: Intellectual Conversion in the Early Lonergan* (Collegeville, MN: Liturgical Press, 1993) 198f., who presents a similar concept concerning intellectual, moral and religious conversion with reference to K. Rahner but uses the term 'sublation' instead of our 'transfiguration'. Both terms are not ideal, however. To 'transfigure' the mind should not be read as a Gnostic concept but is meant to express a new *foundation* of thought.

spiritualis'.[164] This coheres with my work on Philo, where I observed the vision of a symbiosis of Spirit and mind.[165]

At this point we need to return to the questions about reason which we encountered in the first part of this chapter (pp. 150–3).

First, how can reason be of benefit if it is of such an ambivalent nature as Rom. 7.7–25 would have us believe? My research has offered a way forward. If reason is attached to an understanding of the world which values the honour and shame of the creature more than the Creator, it is flawed in such a manner that it is of no (soteriological/ethical) use. Only through the epistemological rupture of accepting Christ on the cross can liberation and revaluation take place. These in turn give reason its intended rational capability and perceptiveness.

My second question at the beginning of this chapter was concerned with the extent to which the mind is affected in the process of trans-formation. Does the renewal affect only the constellation of thoughts (as Jewett would have it) or does it, in a comprehensive manner, affect rationality as a whole?[166] From my argument in this section, it is impos-sible to divorce the two notions, as the old and new perceptions have an extensive effect on the whole grammar of thought. Hence, rationality as a whole is embedded in a particular grasp of reality.[167] The new grasp on reality has occasionally been misinterpreted as portraying a mystical or extra-cognitive epistemology.[168] I have shown that the world switch is

---

[164] Ambrosius and Piscator, respectively, as quoted by Schrage, *Korinther* I, 270. Cf. J.-C. Kim, 'Der gekreuzigte Christus als geheimnisvolle Weisheit Gottes – Exegetische Studien zu 1 Korinther 2,6–16' (Unpubl. PhD dissertation, University of Tübingen, 1987) 174: 'Im νοῦς Χριστοῦ erfahren wir die Externität des Geistes (extra nos) und die Internität seines Wirkens (in nobis) zugleich . . . Die menschliche Vernunft ist das zugleich rezeptive und aktive Subjekt des pneumatischen Erkennens.'

[165] In this sense I understand τὴν λογικὴν λατρείαν ὑμῶν in Rom. 12.1 as 'true worship' (Moo, *Romans*, 752) which acknowledges both the spiritual and rational dimension of worship (Wilckens, *Römer* III, 6; Schrage, 'Verhältnis', 498). It is a 'logical expression of his creatureliness properly understood, and lived out' (Dunn, *Romans 9–16*, 712).

[166] Jewett, *Terms*, 378, 387.

[167] Cf. K. Maly, *Mündige Gemeinde* (Stuttgart: Verlag Katholisches Bibelwerk, 1967) 47, who states that believers receive the 'Vernunft, Verstand' of Christ. Schrage ('Verhältnis', 498, 506) points out that we need not think believers have become more intelligent but neither do they only receive a new 'Sinn' or 'Gesinnung' because it is a new 'Denken'. On the other hand, it is not helpful to favour the rational principle and to sharply differentiate this from the constellation of thoughts; cf. Sanday-Headlam, *Romans*, 354: 'By this renewal the intellectual or rational principle will no longer be a νοῦς σαρκός (Col. ii.18), but will be filled with the Spirit and coincident with the highest part of human nature (1 Cor.ii.15,16).' Further: 'The result of this purification is to make the intellect, which is the seat of moral judgement, true and exact in judging on spiritual and moral questions.'

[168] Against Healy (*Heart*, 13), who speaks of a 'mystical life', and Merklein (*Korinther*, 244), who is similarly unclear.

a thoroughly cognitive process and requires the presence of the rational faculties *but* in a new paradigm of thinking. Following a short excursus, I will elucidate this new paradigm further.

Excursus: Relating Greek and Jewish Thought

We should be wary of insisting on a stark distinction between Greek and Jewish thought on reason (implied by Jewett).[169] While the epistemological rupture is often (rightly) compared with an apocalyptic perceptual shift,[170] it is wrongly contrasted with Greek thought. Paul's critique of the Corinthians' manipulative use of reason ending in conceit and distorted relationships is not dissimilar to the criticism of epistemic vices by Plato, the Stoics and Philo.[171] They, too, saw the need of radically abandoning common conceptions of the true and the good to become truly wise.[172] Neither is it legitimate to see Paul's concept of the Spirit's enhancing rationality as unique. My work on Philo showed that this is not the case.[173] The difference, however, is that for Paul the restructuring of reality is not according to the ultimate τέλος of reason or law, but according to the person of Christ. Hence, the 'like is known by like' principle is not fulfilled by transcending human finitude but by acknowledging the contingency of humanity and being reconciled with the Creator.[174]

4.   New Valuation and Disposition: Internalising the Christ-event

I have repeatedly noted that we need to study further the interrelationship of epistemological and ethical change. Not only did the 'radical perceptual shift', developed earlier, implicate some alteration of valuation, but in chapter 4 we observed how true knowledge *requires* dispositional change. Now, clearly ethical change in Paul is a multi-dimensional phenomenon

---

[169] For such a dichotomy between Greek and Hebrew conceptions of knowledge, cf. Forestell, 'Perfection', 128, who refers back to Dupont (*Gnosis*). See Lémonon, 'Discernement', 26.

[170] Cf. Rowland, 'Apocalyptic', 247.

[171] Cf. my previous chapter; Stowers, 'Paul', 259f.; Plato, *Sophist* 230C–231B; Plutarch, *Platonicae Quaestiones* 999E (*Moralia* XIII); J. T. Fitzgerald, *Cracks in Earthen Vessels: An Examination of the Catalogues of Hardships in the Corinthian Correspondence* (SBL.DS 99; Atlanta: Scholars Press, 1988) chs. 3–4; Pogoloff, *Logos*, 7–196, particularly 27–30; B. Winter, *Philo and Paul among the Sophists* (MSSNTS 96; Cambridge: Cambridge University Press, 1997) 1–15, 111–202; Thiselton, *Corinthians*, 12–16

[172] Stowers, 'Paul', 260; Seneca, *Epistulae*, 71.7.

[173] Contra, Dupont, *Gnosis*, 170; Theissen, *Aspects*, 331, 364f.; Hunt, *Body*, 142ff.; Healy, *Heart*, 150 (who follows Dupont, Theissen and Hunt). Strom (*Paul*, 111) even concludes that Paul has a 'distinct perspective on rationality'.

[174] Cf. Stowers, 'Paul', 284–6; Horn, *Angeld*, 273.

(on which I have shed some light in chapter 2).[175] Hence, we must distil out the elements relevant to the question of how discernment can function correctly. In other words, we must ask not only how the 'new creation' is brought about but also how this is related to attaining true knowledge. Moreover, we encounter the same question noted at the beginning of this chapter: is character change the condition for discernment or vice versa?

Our answers can be derived from a compressed description of the Christian ethos as τὸ φρόνημα τοῦ πνεύματος (Rom. 8.6).[176] While it is my argument that this 'mindset of the Spirit' is the equivalent of the renewed mind (Rom. 12.2) and the 'mind of Christ' (1 Cor. 2.16), I concentrate on the first phrase because it serves as a window on the ethical (and literal) juncture of mind and Spirit.[177] I turn first to the effects and role of πνεῦμα and then to why Paul signifies the new life as a φρόνημα.

The Role of the Spirit in Ethical Change

For Paul the Spirit is the sine qua non of the new life.[178] Not the individual but the πνεῦμα is ultimately responsible for the new set of attitudes of the 'cruciform' character:[179] 'The *pneuma* facilitates the transforming of the

[175] For a comprehensive, although somewhat systematics-oriented, overview of the motivations on which Pauline ethics are founded, cf. Merk, *Handeln*, 240ff., for summary; further, Furnish, *Theology*, 112–206.

[176] Cf. Backhaus, 'Evangelium', 28ff.; Schnelle, *Paulus*, 634, for the significance of φρονέω in Paul's ethics and theology.

[177] I use the term 'ethos', since it denotes the amalgamation of cognitive and social identity and, furthermore, shows a shift in Pauline ethics away from the laborious debate about the relationship of 'imperative' and 'indicative' to a more comprehensive understanding in which the objectification of personal and social identity *necessitates* some form of praxis (cf. particularly Wolter, 'Identität', 61–89). U. Wilckens (*Der Brief an die Römer [Röm 6–11]* [EKK 6/II ; Neukirchen-Vluyn: Neukirchener Verlag, 1980] 130) expresses this correctly in connection with Rom. 8.5f.: 'Es gibt kein *Sein* des Menschen, das nicht seine Wirklichkeit im *Handeln* hat, das also nicht den Charakter zielbestimmter Handlungsintention (φρονεῖν) hat.' For an overview of how prominent the indicative-imperative debate has been, cf. Willis, 'Bibliography', 306–19.

[178] Pfeiffer (*Einweisung*, 241) shows the intricate link between the 'Lebendigkeit' of the believers and the life-creating force of the Spirit in Paul (further Barclay, *Truth*, 106–45).

[179] M. J. Gorman, *Cruciformity: Paul's Narrative Spirituality of the Cross* (Grand Rapids, MI: Eerdmans, 2002) 49: 'For Paul, cruciformity cannot be attributed to human effort. There is a power at work . . . [which] enables the narrative of the cross to be retold and relived. This power is, for Paul, the Spirit of God . . .' (Similarly cf. B. Witherington, III, *Paul's Narrative Thought World: The Tapestry of Tragedy and Triumph* [Louisville, KY: Westminster/John Knox Press, 1994] 299).

human *nous* to the *nous tou Christou*.'[180] In other words, the Spirit translates the Christ-event into the lives of believers by empowering them
to live in a similar manner. And this is for Paul the fulfilment of the
eschatological promise of the new covenant (Jer. 31–33; Ezek. 36.26f.)
in which an immediate apprehension of God's will would become possible because the *inner* person has been renewed: a 'new creation' is
brought about.[181] But can we explain this process in more detail?[182] The
most helpful avenue of enquiry for my purposes is the investigation of
the interrelationship of Spirit, love and understanding.[183] This matrix of
Pauline thought is described in its interdependence by Fee: 'Not only
does the mind renewed by the Spirit lead one to understand that love
must rule over all, but only by such a renewed mind may one determine
how best to love.'[184] We noted earlier (pp. 156–7) that the love the Spirit
gives is for Paul the prerequisite of true knowledge. Because this love
is Christologically defined, it helps us to see how the Spirit transforms
the character of believers (not only their cognition) and how this in turn
affects knowledge.[185] Three aspects should be highlighted.

[180] A. R. Brown, 'Paul's Apocalyptic Word of the Cross: Perception and Transformation
in 1 Corinthians 1–2' (Unpubl. PhD dissertation, Columbia University, 1990) 260 (my
italics instead of her underlining).

[181] Cf. Hubbard, *Creation*, 113–22, who uses this background and the nexus of Spirit,
life and newness as the constellation of ideas to explain καινὴ κτίσις (2 Cor. 5.17; Gal. 6.15).
'If the mind of the flesh is death, the mind of the Spirit is *life* [Rom. 8.8] . . . As in Ezekiel,
God's δικαίωμα (v. 4) is finally kept through the enabling (δύναμαι, vv. 7–8) power of the
Spirit within (vv. 9, 11). Paul makes this point again in verse 10: "The Spirit *is life* through
righteousness"' (*Creation*, 121).

[182] This question is often left open. Hence, Brown (*Word*, 276) says: 'of course it is
impossible to say how such transformation really happens'. Or it is explained in language
which is somewhat circular; cf. Frenschkowski, *Offenbarung* I, 384, who says that the means
of appropriation of revelation are pneumatic: 'die dem einzelnen *pneumatisch* zugeeignet
und von ihm *pneumatisch* ergriffen wird' (italics mine).

[183] To speak of love as the medium of the Spirit's activity is to recognise that the 'Wesen'
of the Spirit is defined by love (cf. Gnilka, *Paulus*, 264). The interrelationship of Spirit,
love and understanding is the most helpful avenue for understanding the new creation, but
the apocalyptic dimension is another significant one. Cf. J. L. Martyn, *Galatians* (AB 33A;
New York: Doubleday, 1998) 532, who believes that vice and virtue (Gal. 5.19–23) are
'without exception effected by the two warring powers, the Flesh and the Spirit'. But the
apocalyptic element should not lead to a negative view of creation as this element can also
mean 'recreation' (cf. Adams, *World*, 201f.).

[184] Fee, *Presence*, 878. Cf. Rom. 5.5; Spicq, *Agape* II, 267: 'Our knowledge is a discovery
made by a love arising from God's initial charity'. Further, cf. Schürmann, 'Gnadengaben',
261; Dunn, *Jesus*, 224.

[185] As Hays (*Vision*, 202) rightly points out, to speak of love as such as the focal point
of ethics is unsatisfactory, since Pauline love is an interpretation of a concrete image, the
cross. While Söding (*Liebesgebot*, 272) thinks love is the criterion of authentic Christian behaviour, he shows how it must be incorporated within and understood from the

First, the Spirit's power is not merely an impersonal forcefield, but it works also according to an inherently personal and relational paradigm.[186] V. Rabens notes an important and neglected aspect of Pauline theology that ethical transformation occurs in the 'intimate relationship' with God and with other believers.[187] Just as the original motivation of the Christ-event was relational (revelation of God's *innermost being*),[188] so also the goal of the Spirit's work is relational (adoption into God's family).[189] This consequently means that each believer is personally addressed and not (as in the ancient concept of order) just integrated as a part into the whole.[190] The Spirit's transforming power cannot become effective unless it links into the personal 'stories' of the believers.[191] Consequently, true discernment is dependent on the development of personhood. There is no true knowledge independent of the one who understands.[192]

Christ-event so that the believers 'in der Nächstenliebe dem Heilswillen Gottes entsprechen können und mit dem proexistenten Jesus Christus gleichförmig werden'.

[186] With that I do not mean to denote the personhood of the Spirit as much as the paradigm according to which it works, but contrast Horn, *Angeld*, 407, who explains that Paul gives the πνεῦμα the function, 'diese ἀγάπη τοῦ Θεοῦ den Glaubenden *persönlich* zu übereignen' (italics mine; cf. Fee, *Presence*, 845; V. Rabens, 'The Development of Pauline Pneumatology: A Response to F. W. Horn', *BZ* 43 [1999], 177f.). Hubbard (*Creation*, 127f., 235) argues for a '*pneumatological restoration*' instead of an '*ontological transformation*'.

[187] V. Rabens, 'Transforming Relationships: The Spirit's Empowering for Religious-Ethical Life According to the Apostle Paul' (Unpublished paper, 18th British New Testament Conference, 2000), 10–16; idem, 'Coming Out: "Bible-Based" Identity Formation in 2 Corinthians 6:14–7:1', in U. Rembold and R. G. Czapla (eds.), *Gotteswort und Menschenrede: Die Bibel im Dialog mit Wissenschaften, Künsten und Medien* (JIG 73; Bern: Lang, 2006), 48 n. 29, 65f.

[188] Voss (*Wort*, 276) points out that the λόγος τοῦ σταυροῦ is not a 'Positum' or a fixed entity of thoughts and sentences which can be controlled wilfully, but rather it is '(Selbst) Vergegenwärtigung'. Cf. Thiselton, *Corinthians*, 257, who explains 'the depths of God' in 1 Cor. 2.10: 'God is "grounded in" nothing beyond his own selfhood. Today we might speak of the Spirit's revealing God's *inmost heart*, which gives precisely the christological focus toward which Paul is working in 2:16.'

[189] Cf. Rom. 8.29; Dunn, *Theology of Paul*, 424. This is also exemplified by the fact that love for Paul is parallel to righteousness and 'lack of righteousness is due to lack of love. Both expressions assume the biblical idea of man being created in God's image' (Pedersen, 'Understanding', 25).

[190] 'Die *Liebe* nimmt sich des Einzelnen an, statt es nur im Sinn des antiken Ordnungs-gedankens als Teil in das Ganze zu integrieren (Kap. 13)' (S. Vollenweider, 'Viele Welten und ein Geist', in *Horizonte neutestamentlicher Christologie* [WUNT 144; Tübingen: Mohr/Siebeck, 2002] 212). Cf. Therrien, *Discernement*, 269, who believes that the fact that the Spirit 'lives' in us means a 'merveilleuse intimité' which respects the personality of the individual and the transcendence of the divine (also Healy, *Heart*, 150ff.).

[191] Cf. Johnson, 'Edification', 371.

[192] This is argued well by Voss (*Wort*, 14), who says that the central question posed by the cross is the one of the integrity of the person who is seeking to understand. One cannot watch from a neutral or distanced position, rather one will be questioned as to the presuppositions which one brings to understanding. 'Paulus macht klar, daß es kein

Secondly, the Spirit's transforming activity is of a *holistic* nature. This means that the fact that the Spirit mediates its power through love counters ethical solutions which are superficial or which distort the message of the cross. With respect to the latter, only love can transform the cross from a symbol of 'self-emptying sacrifice' or 'obsessive self-humiliation' to become the locus of authentic humanity.[193] In the matter of the former, love curtails the threat of a rationalised ethical system.[194] For Paul rationality must be integrated into the total transformation of the person.[195] This includes emotion, volition and motivation, that which drives and compels a person to be that particular person.[196] But this is only possible when the believer takes part in the divine love, when he/she is 'intellectually and affectively permeated with it'.[197] Accordingly, spiritual discernment will entail a comprehensive 'Lebensbewegung'.[198]

Finally, we must note the *integrative* role of love in the Spirit's transforming activity on both the vertical and horizontal level of relationships. On the horizontal level, Thiselton lucidly shows that Paul understood (as postmodern and 'critical theorists' have explicated) that,

Verstehen gibt unabhängig von dem Menschen, der etwas zu verstehen sich anschickt . . .' (*Wort*, 281; similarly cf. Young and Ford, *Meaning*, 253).

[193] Brown, *Cross*, 153. This aspect of authenticity deserves more careful research which I cannot offer here. But for Paul there is a balance between emptying oneself (as Christ did, Phil. 2) and finding one's authentic vocation (Rom. 12.3). It is important that humility should not be interpreted as 'docility' or 'servile mediocrity' (Thiselton, *Corinthians*, 1057) but rather as a correct self-assessment (cf. R. Y. K. Fung, *The Epistle to the Galatians* [NICNT; Grand Rapids, MI: Eerdmans, 1988] 290f., with regard to Gal. 6.4). Cf. Col. 2.18.

[194] This threat is more apparent within Stoic ethics (cf. J. Gnilka, *Der Philipperbrief* [HThK 10/3; Freiburg: Herder, 1976^2] 52; Engberg-Pedersen, *Paul*, 288).

[195] Dunn, *Theology of Paul*, 74. Dunn's work has been helpful in showing that the affective aspects are not an additum to Paul's theology but that the role of experience is a presupposition of Paul's communication with his churches as they have experienced grace through the Spirit as something which embraces the totality of life (cf. *Jesus*, 200ff., 327ff.). Moreover, Paul does not follow the Platonic tradition of giving the inner person a higher status than the outer person (Betz, 'Concept', 334) and he keeps them firmly connected, as both require eschatological redemption. In that way he offers a 'decisive contribution to ancient anthropology' ('Concept', 340).

[196] Cf. Therrien, *Discernement*, 292. Schrage ('Verhältnis', 486, 491f.) argues for an integration of emotional and volitional elements.

[197] Spicq, *Agape* II, 329; cf. 327: 'Charity understands that the immensity of Christ's love surpasses it on all sides so that it can never adequately comprehend it. In fact Christian maturity consists in this awareness.' 'Agape opens the intelligence and gives it the acuteness it needs to understand something of the divine mystery' (*Agape* II, 328). Further, see Eph. 1.18; 3.16f.; 4.18.

[198] Kim, *Christus*, 172: 'Pneumatisches Erkennen ist nicht nur eine intellektuelle Leistung, sondern zugleich ein Herzensakt, d.h. eine ganzheitlich persönliche Lebensbewegung.'

virtually every action and stance bears some relationship to the power interests of the self, or to one's peer group. Genuine love . . . alone *decenters* the[se] power 'interests' . . . and in recentering them in the Other (primarily in God, but also in the other person) disengages from self-interest. Only now can truth emerge as disengaged from a power agenda. . . Love, Paul says, has discovered *integrity* . . .[199]

That means only love can bring the egalitarian vision of community to fruition because only love can level the differences of race, status and gender.[200] At this point we may note the reception of Pauline theology in Col. 3.10f. There the author shows how this egalitarianism is the identity marker of the *renewed knowledge* of the new self.[201] Understanding, according to this portrayal, is linked to the new formation of community life.

However, again, for Paul this is only possible because the vertical relationship between God and the believer has been defined and transformed by God's love (Rom. 5.5–8).[202] And (a point scholarship has missed) this love is the key for the fulfilment of the 'like is known by like' principle.[203] Because God has poured out his love, the disparity of the believers' position is compensated. God can now be known because the believer is transformed through love so as to be enabled to perceive God.[204]

---

[199] Thiselton, *Corinthians*, 1055. In other words, the earlier mentioned holistic nature of the Spirit's activity translates into a holistic perception of others enabling undivided relationship. Söding, *Liebesgebot*, 270, speaks of 'ganzheitliche Hinwendung' which leads to 'umfassender Gemeinschaft'.

[200] Cf. Johnson, 'Holiness', 383; Wolter, 'Identität', 84ff..

[201] 'Do not lie to one another, seeing that you have stripped off the old self with its practices and have clothed yourselves with the *new self*, which is being *renewed in knowledge* according to the image of its creator. In that renewal there is *no longer Greek and Jew, circumcised and uncircumcised, barbarian, Scythian, slave and free;* but Christ is all and in all!' (Col. 3.9–11). For the dependence of the egalitarian possibility on the new self and the fact that this links in with Gal. 6.15; 3.27f., cf. M. Wolter, *Der Brief an die Kolosser. Der Brief an Philemon* (ÖTK 12; Gütersloh: Gütersloher Verlagshaus, 1993) 181 (further, in comparison to Col. 3.9–11, note 1 Cor. 12.12f.). Scroggs ('Being', 180) shows how, rather than making people blind, love offers the truest and most penetrating understanding of the other. 'Paul means that love frees the mind so that more accurate perception of the other can happen' (cf. similarly Therrien, *Discernement*, 273).

[202] So, correctly, Voss, *Wort*, 243. Fee (*Presence*, 498) explains how the context of Rom. 5.5 shows that 'Christ's dying for the helpless – sinners *all* (Jew and Gentile alike) – demonstrates God's *impartiality* toward Jew and Gentile alike' (my italics).

[203] For instance, neither Voss (*Wort*, 176f.) nor Thiselton (*Corinthians*, 258f.) pick this up, although both see the significance of 1 Cor. 13 for understanding 1 Cor. 2.

[204] 1 Cor. 13 is thus the explication of the hermeneutical key (the cross) and hence of spiritual discernment in 1 Cor. 1–2.

In sum, we have further explored (in a development of chapter 4) how the renewal of knowledge of the believers is contingent on, and conditioned by, the transformation of their character. That means we understand in more detail why and how true discernment is an existential process.[205] Knowledge cannot be separated from the knower. Furthermore, my argument has shown that love cannot be seen merely as an exterior criterion for decision making (against the positions portrayed in the introduction of this chapter). Love must be an integrated part of the life orientation of the believer.

I have also pointed to the interdependence of love and knowledge. Love is rightly often presented as the ultimate qualifier of knowledge.[206] And love not only controls knowledge, but also gives it character and depth.[207] Nevertheless, we must also remember that love without knowledge remains 'blind und taub'.[208] That is why the apostle prays that 'your love may overflow more and more with knowledge and full insight' (Phil. 1.9). Discernment is thus as much a 'connaissance cordiale' as it is an 'amour clairvoyant'.[209]

Pauline Ethics as a Mindset

Now we may turn to why it is significant that Paul can sum up the Christian life as a spiritual φρόνημα. It highlights the cognitive and intentional aspects as well as the internalised normativity of Pauline ethics, three points which I will take in turn here.

First, we should note that, as Engberg-Pedersen rightly shows, Paul's parenesis is an undertaking that addresses the *understanding*.[210]

---

[205] Cf. Young and Ford, *Meaning*, 253; Furnish, 'Truth', 176; Pedersen, 'Understanding', 31.

[206] O. Wischmeyer (*Der höchste Weg: Das 13. Kapitel des 1. Korintherbriefes* [StNT 13; Gütersloh: Gütersloher Verlagshaus, 1981] 68) says that not γνῶσις but ἀγάπη is the right 'christliche Lebensform'. And Bultmann ('γινώσκω', 710) thinks love, not knowledge, signifies the relationship with God.

[207] H. Schlier ('Über die Liebe. – 1 Kor. 13', in *Die Zeit der Kirche* [Freiburg: Herder, 1956] 187) shows that love reveals whether inspiration and intuition have 'Kraft' 'etwas Wirkliches zu sagen'.

[208] Käsemann, 'Ruf', 126. Knowledge as such is not criticised by Paul but only its soteriological significance (Wischmeyer, *Weg*, 69).

[209] Therrien, *Discernement*, 173, 264, respectively; cf. Fee, *Philippians*, 98–100. As Ephesians 3.18f. puts it, the believers are to 'comprehend' and 'know' 'the love of Christ' which in turn 'surpasses' their knowledge.

[210] Engberg-Pedersen, *Paul*, 168. But 'addressed to the understanding' does not mean it is 'intellectualist'. Cf. Söding, *Liebesgebot*, 273, who suggests that Paul founds the 'Liebesgebot' not on a matter of 'Zwang', but on 'Einsicht' so making it plausible for his addressees.

Engberg-Pedersen's point is that, rather than conceptualising the new life of the believer solely in substantial categories (as an infusion or a 'substantive takeover'), it can also be seen as a change in self-understanding.[211] 'It is all a matter of growth in understanding through an application of what one *already* knows.'[212] It means that the process from conversion to an appropriation of the Christ-event is from one state of understanding to another.[213] Furthermore, only when a *comprehensive* grasp of this event is attained can the correct praxis follow.[214] Hence, as in the ethical tradition of the Stoics, virtue is a state of mind.[215] This also implies that thinking is a tool by which thinking is renewed and by which the new values are appropriated.[216]

And this leads us to my second point, that is, why φρόνημα sums up Paul's ethical concern well: it denotes a mindset.[217] The mind is not neutral or in some manner free of valuation.[218] For Paul, thinking is

[211] Engberg-Pedersen, *Paul*, 250. Similarly Haufe ('Geistmotiv', 191) claims that the opposition of flesh and Spirit as opposing powers is a 'Grundorientierung' which cannot be separated from the person's understanding.

[212] Engberg-Pedersen, *Paul*, 109. But the following may exaggerate the point somewhat: 'For St. Paul, knowledge is the ideal to be sought in the full life of a Christian' (Forestell, 'Perfection', 127, with reference to Dupont, *Gnosis*, 528).

[213] Panagopoulos ('Prophetie', 28) believes that, although the church has all knowledge and wisdom in the Spirit, it still needs explaining.

[214] Engberg-Pedersen, *Paul*, 216, 281–92; cf. Söding, *Liebesgebot*, 273.

[215] Engberg-Pedersen, *Paul*, 165. Moreover, he claims that first addressing the 'understanding' and not the 'will' (which follows) is similar to Stoic moral psychology (*Paul*, 168). Even for Esler ('Paul', 124), who highlights the differences between Pauline and Stoic thought, 'a striking feature of Paul's presentation that may derive from his interaction with Stoicism is the extent to which he stresses the rational basis underlying the attitudes and behaviour he recommends'.

[216] K. Barth (*The Epistle to the Romans* [trans. E. C. Hoskyns; Oxford: Oxford University Press, 1933] 436f.) rightly warns that we cannot 'exhort men to participate in pure thought'. However, Barth adds, when we recognise 'that the final meaning of our temporal existence lies in our questioning as to its meaning, then it is that we think the thought of eternity – in our most utter collapse. For the vast ambiguity of our life is at once its deepest truth. And moreover, when we *think this thought, our thinking is renewed*' (italics mine). Cf. A. Schlatter, *Gottes Gerechtigkeit: Ein Kommentar zum Römerbrief* (Stuttgart: Calwer Verlag, 1991[6]) 334, who says that, in order to find the will of God, believers must ask with the 'gesammelten, angestrengten Arbeit ihres Denkens'. In comparison with Rom. 7.23–25, where the mind was not able to effect good, is the liberating power which the Spirit adds to the equation (introduced in Rom. 8.1) which makes thinking fruitful again (and the crucial transition and epistemological rupture of the cross; cf. Fee, *Presence*, 822).

[217] Cf. C. K. Barrett, *A Commentary on the Epistle to the Romans*, (London: A. & C. Black, 1973[5]) 157, who says φρόνημα is to 'be determined by the Spirit . . . *to have one's gaze focused upon* . . . to have one's mind set'. Fitzmyer (*Romans*, 488) writes that it is 'the way one thinks and desires'; contra T. J. Deidun (*New Covenant Morality in Paul* [Rome: Biblical Institute Press, 1981] 233) who speaks of 'christian instinct'.

[218] Cf. Schrage, 'Verhältnis', 492; A. Schlatter, *Der Brief an die Römer* (Stuttgart: Calwer Vereinsbuchhandlung, 1928) 151. While Bultmann (*Theologie*, 212) may see νοῦς as neutral,

inherently linked to intentionality, and this in turn determines the actions. How can this intentionality be changed? Engberg-Pedersen shows how Paul's letters are intended to exhort the believers to replace the τέλος of their previous thinking (their egocentricity) with Christ.[219] The τέλος is what one identifies with in such a manner that it is completely normative and something which one follows because one *wants* to. This change of τέλος is achieved by linking the whole self into the Christ-story and hence identifying completely with Christ.[220] P. Lampe refers here to the results of psychoanalytical studies which have shown how powerful such a process of identification (as opposed to merely imitation)[221] is with respect to the restructuring of the self.

> They [psychoanalysts] clearly distinguish between mere imitation and authentic identification. What is the difference? The imitator only displays the behavior of the model person. The one who *identifies* with the model, on the other hand, also adopts the model's motivations. She or he assumes the model's role by taking over the goals and emotions that are expressed in the role. Acquiring the *motivations, goals* and *emotions* which are connected with a behavior – these are the key words that characterize genuine identification as opposed to imitation.[222]

---

the renewal of the same is for him a renewal of intentionality ('Absicht'). Cf. further 1 Cor. 1.10; Col. 3.2 (τὰ ἄνω φρονεῖτε); 2 Cor. 10.5 (taking captive πᾶν νόημα); 11.3 (φθαρῇ τὰ νοήματα ὑμῶν).

[219] Engberg-Pedersen, *Paul*, 238, 280f. Stoessel ('Notes', 167) rightly states that the renewal of the mind is *both* the renewal of attitude *and* renewed theological foundations.

[220] To be sure Engberg-Pedersen does not wish to deny the fact that it is the Spirit which generates the new τέλος and which is ultimately responsible (*Paul*, 161), but the question is how we should understand it and hence his argument that it is appropriated by identification. This identification is bifocal, focussing on the Christ-event (more in Galatians) and the 'culminating event' (more in Philippians) as is argued by J. P. Sampley ('Reasoning from the Horizons of Paul's Thought World. A Comparison of Galatians and Philippians', in Lovering and Sumney [eds.], *Theology*, 114–31).

[221] 1 Cor. 11.1: 'Be imitators of me, as I am of Christ.' The value of imitation is contested, famously so by E. Käsemann ('Kritische Analyse von Phil. 2, 5–11', in *Versuche* I, 51–95), who believes that what is at stake is not an ethical example because obedience is not effected through an example but only through the word.

[222] P. Lampe, 'Identification with Christ. A Psychological View of Pauline Theology', in T. Fornberg and D. Hellholm (eds.), *Texts and Contexts: Biblical Texts in their Textual and Situational Contexts* (Oslo: Scandinavian University Press, 1995) 937. This clarifies what has traditionally been explained in theological terms: 'Das Leben Christi wird vielmehr durch den Glauben in mein Leben integriert, so daß alles, was ich lebe, zu geglaubtem Leben wird, und alles, was ich glaube, zu gelebtem Glauben' (Ebeling, *Wahrheit*, 209).

I suggest that this is implied when Paul, in 2 Cor. 3.18, speaks of beholding (κατοπτρίζομαι) the glory of the Lord and hence being transformed.[223] More importantly, it is clearly explicated in Phil. 2.5: Τοῦτο φρονεῖτε ἐν ὑμῖν ὃ καὶ ἐν Χριστῷ Ἰησοῦ.[224] On the one hand, this means the 'I' will be dead in the sense that there is a 'complete restructuring of a person's self-understanding': the basis of fleshly desires and all that with which the believer previously wished 'to *identify normatively*' is left behind.[225] On the other hand a new life is received by adopting a new character and disposition: Christ's love, humility and regard for others are internalised into a new manner of thinking and a new ethos.[226] A new identity is appropriated in which 'the boundaries of self' are exchanged 'in favour of concepts such as coinherence, exchange, mutual indwelling and living for others'.[227] This amounts to a reflective transformation which encompasses the believer's whole existence: *it is existential theologising.*[228]

And with that we come to my third point. Paul tends towards a virtue ethic in which the solution to the human plight (not being able to do what is right) is found where the problem began, *intra nos* and not *extra*

---

[223] Turner, *Spirit*, 116; cf. Wright, *Climax*, 191. F. Back (*Verwandlung durch Offenbarung bei Paulus* [WUNT 2,153; Tübingen: Mohr/Siebeck, 2002]) writes that the transformation is the sign that not only Paul but all Christians receive a 'göttliche Botschaft' (201).

[224] Kemmler (*Faith*, 206f.) shows how the φρονεῖν effects the translation of the gospel into everyday life. Brown (*Cross*, 145) shows how in both 1 Cor. 2.16 and Phil. 2.5–11 'the cross event is closely associated with a state of mind'. It is to be 'cognitively identified with Christ's death on the cross', 'to have a cruciform mind', it is 'both internal and experiential', it '*reflects the orientation of the whole self toward or away from God*' (146); cf. Eph. 4.20–3; Col. 3.9–11. Dunn (*Theology of Paul*, 194) speaks of the 'intensity of dedication and application in living out the life of Christ . . .'

[225] Engberg-Pedersen, *Paul*, 164 and 147, respectively; cf. Rom. 6.1–11; Lampe, 'Identification', 939.

[226] Hubbard (*Creation*, 103) shows how, in Rom. 6.1–11, Paul uses initiatory symbolism to stress 'ritual suffering (death, burial, crucifixion with Christ), empowerment ("so that we might walk in the newness of life," v.4), and transformation ("alive to God," v.11)'. Cf. W. F. Murphy, 'The Pauline Understanding of Appropriated Revelation as a Principle of Christian Moral Action', *Studia Moralia* 39 (2001) 371–409, who shows how in Rom. 12.1ff and Ephesians (particularly 4.20–4) the Christ-event is appropriated so that the believer is transformed and ethics receives a Christological foundation.

[227] Young and Ford, *Meaning*, 251. To what degree the death of the 'I' is a loss of previous identity is contested and would require a more detailed study. While Stuhlmacher ('Glauben', 337 n. 1.) argues for a 'Zunichtemachen der Person', J. Lambrecht thinks that it does not imply a loss of personal identity but only the 'profound idea of unity with Christ' ('Transformation in 2 Corinthians 3,18', in J. Lambrecht and R. Bieringer [eds.], *Studies on 2 Corinthians* [Leuven: Leuven University Press, 1994] 305).

[228] And with that I pick up a line of thought which I left open at the end of chapter 4, where I concluded that Paul expects of the believers existential theologising. I have now explored what that means. It is a process of thought which identifies with Christ and appropriates his values into character and mind.

nos.[229] Thus, Paul expresses his belief in the fulfilment of the Spirit-mediated new heart (of Jeremiah and Ezekiel),[230] and he reflects the concern of ancient Greek ethical tradition, which sees the need for internalisation as the condition for actually fulfilling ethics.[231] Such an internalisation does not mean that the Torah has been completely abrogated.[232] It does, however, mean that there is a shift in the conceptualisation of normativity.[233] Internalising the will of God is attaining a 'certain *inner state of mind* . . . that ensures that he [the believer] actually does what he knows needs doing because he (now) wishes to do it for himself'.[234] This means that the demand of the law corresponds authentically with the will of the believer.[235] As noted in chapter 2, this coheres with Paul's understanding that the fundamental will of God is the 'Christomorphic life' and with

[229] Cf. Barclay, *Truth*, 231; Theissen, *Aspects*, 367f., for intrinsically motivated love. Hubbard (*Creation*, 185, 227, 232, 236) suggests throughout that 'Paul's new-creation motif should be interpreted in light of the internal-external antithesis' (*Creation*, 236). 'Contrasted with the outward state of circumcision or uncircumcision, new creation should be related to the inner dynamic of the Christian life, which is precisely where Paul locates the work of the Spirit (Rom. 2.28–9; 5.5; 8.9–11, 23; 1 Cor. 6.19; 2 Cor. 1.22; 3.3: Gal. 4.6)' (*Creation*, 227). This means that for Hubbard the traditional link with the new heavens and earth, while not 'inconceivable', is not given, and the emphasis is on the anthropological transformation (*Creation*, 185; cf. Engberg-Pedersen, *Paul*, 165–9).

[230] While, as we saw in chapter 2, there is disagreement about the continued relationship with the law, there is agreement that the Christ-event, through the Spirit, brings about the new covenant; cf. Hafemann, *Paul*, 429–36; P. Stuhlmacher, *Paul's Letter to the Romans* (Edinburgh: T&T Clark, 1989) 121: Paul 'teaches and shows how the breakthrough of the new revelation and spiritual internalisation of the instruction of God promised in Jer. 31:31ff comes about in and through Christ and how this instruction is then followed by Christians in the power of the Spirit!'

[231] This is described by Engberg-Pedersen (*Paul*, 232–55) by showing that, as in the ethical tradition, Paul argues that the problem with the law is that it cannot sufficiently address the actual problem of ethics, the 'weakness of the will' (ἀκρασία; *Paul*, 232f.). Paul's unique Christological formulation of the solution remains visible, however, in his belief that the 'internal disharmony and dissociation' (*Paul*, 232) can only be left behind through the Christ-event and radical faith therein. If believers '*see themselves as* having been taken over by God, Christ and the spirit . . . [then they] have gone over completely to an altogether new kind of total directedness towards God . . . They no longer identify at all with that [egocentricity] and will never allow it a role as the locus of normativity' (*Paul*, 252).

[232] My argument in chapter 2 showed that there is no evidence for a complete abrogation of the law but only for a *selective appropriation*.

[233] As noted in chapter 2, Thielmann (*Paul*, 243) claims that the 'Mosaic Law is absorbed by the gospel'. This more nuanced position reflects Horn's: 'Weder ersetzt der Geist das Gesetz als Lebensordnung noch kann man das Gesetz über den Umweg wiedereinführen – auch nicht als tertius usus legis' (*Angeld*, 374).

[234] Engberg-Pedersen, *Paul*, 215. 'Internalisation is a matter of coming to want to do something for oneself' (214). Cf. Gathercole, 'Law', 46.

[235] Engberg-Pedersen, *Paul*, 254: 'God's will has now been completely internalized in such a way that the Christ-believer wills that for him- or herself alone.'

that a restoration of the *imago dei*.[236] Therefore, the emphasis is on the transformation of the whole person and not on an adherence to individual duties, criteria or norms.[237] Such a position neither makes Paul antinomian, because the norm is there, only internalised,[238] nor does it amount to subjectivism,[239] because the Christomorphic life is in its essence oriented towards others generally and the community in particular. Finally, it is not a 'Gesinnungsethik' because it necessitates that one does what one believes.[240] Having said that, it should be noted that the internalisation of the gospel does give the new creation a certain amount of autonomy from other external norms.[241] It cannot be autonomous from God but, as already argued in chapter 2, it *is* liberated to be able to assess and

[236] Hays, *Vision*, 46. Cf. Witherington, *Thought*, 299; Pedersen, 'Understanding', 25–32. Hubbard (*Creation*, 235) rightly emphasises the anthropological dimension while realising that this implies a communal orientation. See N. A. Dahl, 'Christ, Creation and the Church', in Davies and Daube (eds.), *Background*, 439, who stresses the corporate aspect of new-creation more but (with regard to Col. 3.10 and Eph. 4.24) also says that the emphasis is on the 'fundamental conviction, that what is realized in the Church, the new creation, is in harmony with the original will of God the Creator'.

[237] Schrage (*Einzelgebote*, 49ff.) believes that Paul does not envision an array of individual deeds or 'Gehorsamsleistungen' but rather that God's claim is on the whole person which incorporates the believer's self-understanding (Rom. 6.11), heart (Rom. 6.17), θέλειν und ποιεῖν (2 Cor. 8.10), πνεῦμα (1 Cor. 14.15), ψυχή (1 Thess. 5.23) and σῶμα (1 Cor. 6.13). Further cf. Fee, *Presence*, 697; Barclay, *Truth*, 231: 'By summing up Christian morality in a list of "virtues" (the fruit of the Spirit) Paul lays a significant emphasis on the *character* of the moral actor – rather than, for instance, the enumeration of his *duties* . . . His concern is for the fundamental direction of a person's life . . .'

[238] Cf. Sonntag, ΝΟΜΟΣ, 300, who speaks of a 'νόμος -freie Norm'.

[239] Deidun (*Morality*, 186) puts the situational aspect of Paul's ethics like this: 'Paul would undoubtedly agree with the "situationist" that love is all that matters and that whatever is not loving is not right; but he would want to add – and only for the sake of love – that whatever is not right is not loving.'

[240] Söding, *Liebesgebot*, 270; Wolter, 'Identität', 61–89; Hubbard, *Creation*, 103; contra the concern of Schrage, *Einzelgebote*, 11ff.

[241] Vollenweider, *Freiheit*, 403: 'Paulus bindet die Glaubenden nicht an die – allenfalls purgierte – Tora zurück, sondern verweist sie an das Gottes Willen erschliessende Wahrnehmungspotential der Liebe. Paulinische Ethik hat insofern einen eigentümlichen Zug zur "*Autonomie*" . Dabei verzichtet er sowenig wie die Stoiker auf konkrete Paränese, die sich aus dem reichen Schatz menschlicher Erfahrungen wie Überlieferungen nährt, will aber das Gebotene nicht im Gebot festgeschrieben wissen.' Paul holds the believers 'zu verantwortlicher Selbstbestimmung an, für deren Grenzen die Liebe sensibilisiert.' Hasenstab (*Modelle*, 25) has argued that a historical-critical study of Paul will not offer clear support for an 'Autonomiekonzept' as modern ethics understands it. However, he claims that a theological study of the concept of κλῆσις in Paul could be the starting point of an 'Autonomie-Modell aus paulinischem Geist'. My own work offers support for such a differentiated approach, although I stress that the internalised demand of the law distinguishes the Pauline believer from the modern concept of 'Sich-selbst-Gesetz-sein'.

evaluate the efficacy and validity of norms/traditions. The renewed mind is the locus of this liberty.[242]

Summary

We have investigated the final juncture of mind and Spirit by investigating the meaning of the φρόνημα τοῦ πνεύματος (which is the equivalent of the renewed mind and the 'mind of Christ'). My argument proposed that discernment is dependent on a *dispositional change*. Paul realises that true decision making is related to a change of intentionality and valuation. This can only happen when both mind and character are shaped by the Christ-event. This means, however, that Christ's love does not serve merely as an example, but becomes an integral part of the character. Furthermore, we have explored what it means to do *existential theologising*. On the one hand, ethical change is effected through spiritual understanding. On the other, authentic discernment requires that the whole person be transformed. That is to say, the renewal of the person is the focal and starting point of true knowledge.

The dispositional appropriation of the Christ-event corresponds to the results in chapter 4, where we discovered the inherent link for Paul between theology and ethics. As was brought out by my work on the Stoics, true knowledge is only possible when virtue is appropriated in lifestyle and mindset. In Paul, however, this receives a Christological focus.

With that in mind we may return to the questions of criteria and norms addressed at the beginning of the chapter. Paul wants the recipients of his letters to understand and internalise the normative values exemplified in the Christ-event. This encompasses the three mentioned criteria (love, edification and the Christological norm, see section B) and more comprehensively the will of God. I have suggested that this does not remain merely an external point of reference, but is integrated into the lives of the believers. The Spirit transforms the human faculties in such a manner that the believer can now understand what the will of God is and also *wants* to do it. This means that the Spirit effects a long-term dispositional change, which does not allow for a contrast between Spirit and law (as I showed Dunn tends towards). Furthermore, the understanding of the believer is involved throughout the transformation, so that we cannot relegate it to a sideline position (as I showed Schnabel does).

---

[242] Longenecker, *Paul*, 182: 'Throughout Paul's discussions of liberty, this factor of the mind of Christ as applied by the Spirit reappears as the distinguishing feature in the direction of Christian liberty.'

E.   Remaining Questions

Before concluding this chapter I must attend to two questions which my investigation has not addressed sufficiently. For one, I must offer some justification for my heavy emphasis on the individual as opposed to the more corporate dimension of Paul's theology. Secondly, I may reiterate the issue of discernment as both the condition and result of the juncture of mind and Spirit.

1.   Corporate versus Individual

I have quite consistently argued that the starting point of Paul's theology lies in the individual. But is this not reading an anachronistic individualism into Paul? To be sure, we need to be aware of this tendency in scholarship, which was exemplified by Bultmann's position of describing the new 'self-understanding' only at the individual level.[243] This has rightly been criticised as missing the social and even cosmic dimension of Paul's theology.[244] However, recent research has found the correct balance by pointing out that, while the goal of the new existence is distinctly communitarian, the starting point is the individual.[245] In other words, Paul understands that it is idealistic to speak of altruism if the individual is still bound in selfishness and has not internalised the will to be other-regarded.[246] This does not mean that the process of change

---

[243] Bultmann (*Theologie*, 332–41) argues well for the change in self-understanding, but it is not evident that this incorporates the social dimension: 'Das neue Selbstverständnis . . . ist das der *Freiheit*, in der der Glaubende die ζωή und damit sich selbst gewinnt' (*Theologie*, 332).

[244] For such a criticism cf. Käsemann, 'Gottesdienst', 198–202; Barclay, *Truth*, 194–9; Lull, *Spirit*, 197. This reflects, of course, a broader problem of one's general worldview. While ancient Mediterranean thinking operated in a more or less collectivist paradigm, Western twentieth/twenty-first-century thought is inherently individualistic, which has considerable implications for anthropology and sociology (cf. B. J. Malina and J. H. Neyrey, *Portraits of Paul* [Louisville, KY: Westminster/John Knox Press, 1996] 1–18, 225–31).

[245] It is remarkable that, although Hubbard and Engberg-Pedersen are concentrating on two different backgrounds, Judaism and Stoicism respectively, both demonstrate that the focus is on the individual but the ultimate goal is social integration (cf. Fee, *Presence*, 696; Dunn, *Theology of Paul*, 534–6; Engberg-Pedersen, *Paul*, 294 and Hubbard, *Creation*, 129, 233). P. Eckstein (*Gemeinde, Brief und Heilsbotschaft: Ein phänomenologischer Vergleich zwischen Paulus und Epikur* [Herders Biblische Studien 42; Freiburg: Herder, 2004] 351f.) argues that the balance is given more clearly in Paul than in Epicurean literature, where the final goal is the personal peace of the soul.

[246] Engberg-Pedersen, *Paul*, 275: '[Paul] was precisely interested in the proper prerequisite *for* external and social behaviour. And in the best ancient philosophical style that interest led him to think about inner attitudes.' Malina and Neyrey (*Portraits*, 224f.) show well that, while in collectivist cultures people are socialised to think in a group-oriented

is solely individual.[247] But it does mean that true community can only happen when each individual experiences (through the catharsis of the cross) the release from a status- and performance-dominated life.

2.   A Spiral of Discernment

We noted from the start that the juncture of Spirit and mind is not only the foundation of discernment, but that there are elements of discernment which condition the juncture. Therefore, as observed in my work on Philo and the Stoics, we see again that discernment leads to discernment. The renewed mind is both the product of certain discerning actions (choice, reflection, identification) and the requirement for true perception.[248] Rather than thinking that this makes the argument circular, I propose to think of the process as a spiral. This means that true knowledge is ever increasing, dynamic and defined by *continuous growth*.[249] This should not, however, lead to an elitist understanding of discernment.[250] On the contrary, it is static knowledge that is not open to correction and discussion. The very essence of the Pauline vision of maturity is to

manner, that does not yet denote the *quality* of their orientation. Hence, even collectivist cultures 'can be styled self-centered' (and individualistic cultures altruistic). Moreover, he states that Paul's own background as a Pharisee was more self-centred ('"no mixture" ideology') which, to my mind, may help to explain the immensity of his shift as a believer to an other-centred orientation (*Portraits*, 226). Similarly, Engberg-Pedersen differentiates between formal and substantial individualism (*Paul*, 7).

[247] The opposite is true, since unity is the means by which one understands God. Hence Hunt (*Body*, 141–4) believes that there is no exclusive access to the mind of God, because it is a communal search. We should also not underestimate the role of the community in impressing and creating a new plausibility structure on and for the believer through teaching and common rituals, such as baptism (cf. Therrien, *Discernement*, 267; Eph. 4.20 ['learning Christ']). Hays (*Vision* 35f.) writes that the surrender and renewal in Rom. 12.2 is communal and that Paul's view is of a 'corporate sacrifice'.

[248] Hence, Therrien (*Discernement*, 304, following Cullmann) is right that Christian ethics is also the result of correct discernment or, put differently, the effects of the Spirit can be seen in true discernment. Voss (*Wort*, 193 n. 593) speaks of a circle, but seeks to make a similar point when he points out that the Spirit-given revelation is both the condition for Christian proclamation as well as its goal.

[249] Cf. Col. 1.10: αὐξανόμενοι τῇ ἐπιγνώσει τοῦ Θεοῦ; Schrage, 'Verhältnis', 501. Scroggs ('Being', 181) argues against a 'spontaneous' process but for one of 'struggle and growth' (cf. Therrien, *Discernement*, 271). Barclay (*Truth*, 227) speaks of 'peculiarly dynamic terms' contra Strom, *Paul*, 154, who is correct in saying that Paul does not follow the ideal of an individual's progress towards perfection, but that does not mean that this led Paul to 'dispense with progress as such'.

[250] Forestell ('Perfection', 133) can be understood to propose this when he writes that charity 'embraces both the moral and the intellectual perfection of man, in the supernatural order'.

understand that one is not perfect and requires correction.[251] Further-more, a spiral clarifies that attaining true discernment is not a linear, mono-causal process but that Spirit and mind are both active in varying degrees around the axis of Christ. Nevertheless, and finally, some tension remains (similar to that which we saw in my work on the Stoics) between a 'total directedness towards God', a once and for all affair, and a process of continual learning and appropriating this grasp of the Christ-event.[252]

F.   Conclusion

In this chapter my thesis proposed to look through four different windows on the juncture of mind and Spirit. I may now summarise my results in a more concise form concerning how true evaluation can take place.

An important result of my work is that I argued that we cannot set the roles of mind and Spirit in opposition. The Spirit's presence is a condition for true knowledge. But it does not evict the natural faculties. On the contrary, as in Philo, it enhances them. The Spirit, by means of the cross, brings about an epistemological crisis and sets rationality on a new basis. This means that, while at the beginning I emphasised the discontinuity of Spirit and mind, we must also see that the restoration of the *imago dei* achieves a continuity without resolving the tension between transcendence and immanence. Therefore, a symbiosis of mind and Spirit is effected, which respects the individual in the whole scope of his/her personhood and which retains the otherness of the Spirit. This symbiosis I called the renewed mind or 'mindset of the Spirit', which is the equivalent of the 'mind of Christ'.

Another important aspect of my argument was that I described the junc-ture of mind and Spirit without using metaphysical categories. We saw that the new existence is also a new *self-understanding*, which necessitates a new perception of God, others and the world. The renewed mind then can be adequately described as a new basis of rationality, consciousness

---

[251] Cf. Maly, *Gemeinde*, 48. F. W. Beare (*A Commentary on the Epistle to the Philippians* [London: A. & C. Black, 1969^2] 130) suggests that perfect can 'only mean "conscious that we are not perfect"' and following Luther he points out that 'the nature of a Christian does not lie in what he has become, but in what he is becoming'. Compare, further, Thiselton, *Corinthians*, 624, 941; Dunn (*Theology of Paul*, 631), following his own changed version of Pindar, writes: 'Become what you are becoming'.

[252] Engberg-Pedersen, *Paul*, 232. The dialectic is picked up in a different manner by Wolff (*Korinther*, 54): 'Der τέλειος ist also der christlich Bewährte . . . Das aber gilt prinzipiell nicht für eine besondere Gruppe von Christen, sondern für jeden Glaubenden aufgrund des Geistbesitzes . . .' Voss (*Wort*, 194) thinks Paul is 'unfreiwillig esoterisch'.

and valuation. The believer is relocated into a new sphere of meaning, and his perception of the world revolutionised.

I called this relocation a 'world-switch'. The individual is liberated from the coercive norms of status and performance orientation so as to be able to seek the good of others. This means that reconciliation with the Creator includes a renewed relationality. The mark of true knowledge is that it edifies the community. This implies that the quality of knowledge and the quality of relationships are dependent on one another.

My investigation also suggested that Paul, in line with certain Jewish and Greek traditions, followed a new conceptualisation of normativity. In identifying with Christ, a new self-understanding is appropriated, the believer's valuation and intentionality are renewed, and God's will is internalised. Hence, discernment is primarily related to an existential renewal. Spirituality is a long-term dispositional change. This may include intuitive moments but will not be exclusively defined by these. Rather it is 'a stance of heart and will', a new mindset.[253]

Finally, I argued that for Paul, as in the Stoic tradition, the principle of 'like is known by like' is linked with ethical transformation. True decision making requires a comprehensive life orientation. However, Paul makes the Christ-event the decisive focal point of the new life. This means that true knowledge is exemplified and made possible because of God's initiating love. Therein lies the ultimate key for knowing God and for true discernment.

---

[253] Thiselton, *Corinthians*, 223.

PART IV

Conclusion

7

RECAPITULATION AND IMPLICATIONS FOR THEOLOGY

My study began with a broad introduction into contemporary questions, which require discernment. Before addressing these questions below I need to summarise my conclusions. We set out by learning that Käsemann, Stuhlmacher and Beker place discernment at the heart of Paul's theology without clearly substantiating their claim. My thesis provides the evidence for these claims. I argue that discernment is *existential theologising* in which the 'renewed mind' (or 'mind of Christ' or 'mindset of the Spirit') takes on a constitutive role in constructing and verifying meaning. How does my work substantiate the basis for this assertion? In a brief overview I recapitulate the results of my thesis before returning to offer a summary of the contribution of this work. Finally, I will present some thoughts on the implications this study will have for theological deliberation in our time.

A.   Recapitulation

Before focussing on the conceptual study of discernment I needed to review previous research which concentrated only on certain terms. Hence in separate sections I touched upon ethical and spiritual discernment, connected with δοκιμάζω and διακρίνω/διάκρισις respectively. At the same time I argued for their interdependence. With respect to ethical discernment I underlined its significance within Paul's ethics. My argument showed that the norms and traditions which were part of Paul's plausibility structure *required discernment*. For example, rather than concluding that the law offers a sufficient and binding standard, I argued for a form of wisdom which is anthropologically centred. The renewed mind selects, validates and applies the norms and commandments applicable to the lives of believers. Moreover, in linking discernment with the renewed mind I realised that ethical discernment is inherently connected to Paul's Christological orientation. Ethical life must be evaluated on the basis of a Christologically formed ethos (identity and behaviour).

With respect to spiritual discernment I attempted to gain some insight into the nature of the gift of discernment in 1 Cor. 12.10. While I noted that some scholars were against identifying a critical attitude towards spiritual phenomena, my own work emphasised the significance of an evaluation of all of reality. This study argues that, instead of destroying the unity of the community, discernment enhances its cohesion. I maintained that discernment shows how the entire community is responsible for the spiritual health of the community. The link to ethical discernment has been firmly established, as spiritual phenomena must form an integral part of the concrete reality of church life, and by observing their ethical impact, spiritual manifestations can be assessed. Hence, macrocosmic contemplation, while being a part of Paul's theology, is balanced by ethical sobriety.

However, I not only emphasised the evaluative aspect of discernment, I saw plausible reasons for retaining an interpretative element and outlined this in chapter 4. It was here that I became aware of the constitutive and creative role that discernment has within Paul's epistemological framework. As the Christ-event is explored and explained, meaning is established and corrected for each particular situation. However, this is not the application of a dogmatic core to specific circumstances because, for Paul, the gospel itself is of a contingent nature, resisting objectification and requiring existential appropriation. In other words, discernment dynamically balances the fact that all knowledge is tentative, with the fact that Paul believes that the gospel offers the key to a comprehensive grasp of reality. This comprehensive perspective, however, can only be attained with the background of an individual realisation of the meaning extrapolated from the Christ-event, which leads me into the latter half of this study.

The question as to how true knowledge can be attained is the topic of the second half of my book. Here we paused to regard Paul's intellectual context. We encountered profound speculation on how discernment can function, authentic discernment being a gift that was much sought after. Judaism supplied us with a rudimentary understanding of revealed and acquired forms of knowledge. Furthermore, it provided a vision of how true discernment is linked to the eschatological 'new heart'. By looking to Philo, we were able to perceive in more detail how Spirit and mind function together. While these cannot be equated in the earthly person, their symbiosis is required to attain true knowledge. Both Spirit and mind guide, prompt and educate the person seeking liberating knowledge. Important for this study of Paul was the discovery that the Spirit can enhance rationality and need not displace the mind in revelation. Finally, we looked to the Stoics as they too regarded discernment as one of their most important arts. Here, true understanding is linked to a change in self-understanding and to ethical transformation. This shift in perspective also implies a new understanding of others and the world. A person is 'converted' from an individual to a social value system. The new valuation is crucial in transforming decision making.

In returning to Paul, we saw that here, too, we needed to study the juncture of mind and Spirit, as neither can attain true knowledge on its own. I proposed to look through four different windows at this juncture. The first window regarded the interrelationship of choice on the part of the believer and being chosen by God. While divine and human initiative are best seen as a *'constant interplay'*,[1] I proposed that the believer learns authentic knowledge in his/her being encountered in divine love. The second window considered the roles of guidance by the Spirit and the conscience. While both included intuitive and immediate elements, I emphasised that it is important that the whole person be strengthened in consciousness. In other words, it is important that believers become more aware of their strengths, weaknesses and limits (1 Cor. 8) leading to a stronger inner consonance. This means that guidance is an aid for the development of selfhood, of coherent identity and for a long-term grasp of spiritual experience. The third window looked out upon the interrelationship of revelation and reason. We encountered a critique of rationality, which is confined to a plausibility structure captivated by status and manipulation. By means of the cross this reality is disqualified, liberating the mind, giving new meaning and a mature (open but critical) attitude. Hence, a complete 'world-switch' takes place, which, while being a noetic process throughout, is a comprehensive new perception of reality. The fourth window clarified this comprehensive grasp in showing that true discernment must be part of a *dispositional* change. The 'mind-set of the Spirit' (Rom. 8.5f.) signifies the pneumatological and cognitive process of appropriating and internalising the Christ-event into character and mind. A renewal of intentionality and valuation takes place, which makes it possible for the believer to *want* to do the will of God.

B.   Conclusion

This study provides the first conceptual investigation into discernment in the Pauline writings, and by placing discernment at the heart of his epistemology we have gained new insight into the nature of Paul's theology.

---

[1] Barclay, *Truth*, 227.

My argument shows that, in establishing and correcting (ethical and theological) meaning, extrapolated from the Christ-event, *the renewed mind* (or 'mind of Christ' or 'mindset of the Spirit') *has a creative function* within Paul's theology and the lives of the believers. It has this creative function in linking the contingent interpretation of the Christ-event with a comprehensive perception of reality.

Two further features are of particular significance. First of all, I asserted that *knowledge is linked with ethics*. Because 'like is known by like', authentic discernment requires the transformation of the whole person. In addition, this transformation is an objective of discernment. That is to say, the renewal of the believer is the starting and focal point of true knowledge. Secondly, we observed the need for an *interaction of human mediation and divine revelation*. Both Spirit and mind must be at work symbiotically in order for authentic discernment to take place. Hence, the Spirit effects a noetic 'world-switch', which is the revolutionised understanding of self, others, God and the world.

C.   Implications for Contemporary Theological Deliberation

Finally we should return to the questions addressed at the beginning of this study regarding the need for discernment in our day and age. Does my research offer any advice for issues concerning theology today? Can we address matters so diverse as globalisation or biotechnology or the Spirit's guidance for everyday life? Does Paul shed light on the need for evaluation in both secular and ecclesiastical contexts in today's world? To my mind Paul does offer some helpful insight.

For one, the discernment of spirits, presented here, is a vision of communities that are enabled to perceive both the micro and macro level of existence. Paul expects the Christ-event to liberate the new communities for *independent forms of discernment*. This implies a new possibility of and responsibility for evaluating matters of individual and social concern, moral and political issues anticipated by communities.[2] It is important to note, however, that Paul was keen on putting ethics into a fundamentally new perspective of reality, which challenges strands of theological scholarship, in which dogmatics and ethics have increasingly been

---

[2] Here a discussion with legal and political research on Paul will be highly beneficial, cf. B. Blumenfeld, *The Political Paul: Justice, Democracy and Kingship in a Hellenistic Framework* (JSNT.S 210; Sheffield: Sheffield Academic Press, 2001); M. Konradt, *Gericht und Gemeinde: Eine Studie zur Bedeutung und Funktion von Gerichtsaussagen im Rahmen der paulinischen Ekklesiologie und Ethik im 1 Thess und 1 Kor* (Beihefte zur Zeitschrift für die neutestamentliche Wissenschaft 117; Berlin: W. de Gruyter, 2003).

separated.[3] Paul would surely question these approaches and ask: Can ethics be discussed without an understanding of what constitutes reality? And, on the other hand, are dogmatics without application not hollow and do they not miss the crucial point of the incarnation? Will both ethics and dogmatics not become meaningless if they are not incorporated into a paradigm of love, a paradigm that seeks authentic self-understanding, a genuine regard for others and a relationship to the Divine?

Secondly, my work will have implications *for our approach to understanding reality*.[4] Paul would seem to challenge two sorts of epistemological attitudes evident today. On the one hand, I argue, Paul would be sceptical of the indiscriminate faith in the power of reason that some enlightenment scholars have pursued. On the other hand, and possibly more surprisingly, Paul would be wary of those who, in a reaction against modernity, have emphasised the need for charismatic, intuitive and spontaneous 'guidance by the Spirit'. Rather, it is the difficult path in searching for a symbiosis of Spirit and mind that should be followed. This implies challenging those plausibility structures, which undermine, shame or instrumentalise the dignity of individuals and their communities. Since this approach is very concerned about the conditions on which reason operates, a natural analogy could lie in virtue epistemology, which has attempted to evaluate knowledge according to its underlying values.[5] However, such an epistemology might be misconstrued to be the prerogative of the elite. That would contradict the very heart of Paul's thinking: understanding the truth is possible for *all* who have been touched by the love of God.

Thirdly, Paul's concern about the conditions for ethical reasoning has been related to recent philosophical debates about the nature of decision making and the relationship of reason and tradition. J. Habermas, for instance, constructed a social theory that seeks to set out the communicative conditions ('kommunikative Vernunft') under which moral norms

[3] Some scholars to which this criticism applies may be noted: T. Rendtorff, *Ethics I. Basic Elements and Methodology in an Ethical Theology* (trans. K. Crim; Philadelphia: Fortress Press, 1986); M. Honecker, *Einführung in die Theologische Ethik: Grundlagen und Grundbegriffe* (Berlin: de Gruyter, 1990). Both have attempted to keep dogmatic difficulties out of the ethical discussion. W. Pannenberg, *Systematische Theologie* I (Göttingen: Vandenhoeck & Ruprecht, 1988) 7, on the other hand, eliminates ethics from his Systematic Theology.

[4] Further research must of course still be done on Paul's epistemology generally and his concept of truth more specifically. My work is only a stepping stone for ongoing discourse on Paul. For instance, in-depth comparison is necessary with his Hellenistic and Jewish context as well as with, for instance, Johannine epistemology (cf. Bennema, *Power*).

[5] Cf., for instance, W. J. Wood, *Epistemology: Becoming Intellectually Virtuous* (Leicester: Apollos, 1998).

may be discerned rather than defining those moral norms a priori.[6] My research confirms D. G. Horrell's assumption that there is a parallel here in Paul as concerns the shift of emphasis from specific ethical norms to 'the construction of communities' and the conditions within which a new appreciation of what is right and wrong can be attained.[7] Paul's understanding of ethics does open up the possibility of discerning crucial questions owing to a transformation of the perception of reality and the change this brings about in the manner of dealing with others. However, optimistic visions of emancipated human communities, which achieve procedural consensus in discourse ethics (as Habermas would have it), have been criticised by others, since they neglect the need for ethics to be based in virtues, traditions and communities.[8] Paul would also, no doubt, be wary about such optimism. This tension beween communitarian and procedural ethics raises a difficult question for the possibility of globalised consensus. Can ethics be reasonably accessible for all, or will they always be traditionally tied to certain aspects of virtue, religion and *Weltanschauung*. Paul offers no easy answer. He points to the tension between an inclusive universal perspective and a communitarian moral framework. Is there a solution to this tension?

This brings me to my final point. My work has attempted to emphasise the need for understanding the contingency of the incarnation. God presents himself as a vulnerable 'slave'. This contingency, I argue, has implications for the humility with which we approach our own and other interpretations of truth. Ultimate reality is neither presented in an easily accessible framework of propositional accounts nor can God be domesticated in certain accounts of metaphysics. Understanding ultimate reality is possible only in comprehending what love is, and love can only be understood by loving. The dialectics of universal perspectives and communitarian morality will require more thought because living together in an increasingly interdependent world is dependent on a deeper appreciation of what it means to discern the spirits of antagonism on the one side and respect for identity and difference on the other.

---

[6] J. Habermas, *Erkenntnis und Interesse* (Frankfurt a.M.: Suhrkamp, 1994[11]); idem, *Theorie des kommunikativen Handelns*, 2 Volumes (Frankfurt a.M.: Suhrkamp, 1987[4]).

[7] D. G. Horrell, 'Restructuring Human Relationships. Paul's Corinthian Letters and Habermas's Discourse Ethics', *Expository Times* 110 (1999) 321–5.

[8] A. MacIntyre, *After Virtue: A Study in Moral Theory* (London: Duckworth, 1985[2]); M. Walzer, *Thick and Thin: Moral Argument at Home and Abroad* (Notre Dame: University of Notre Dame Press, 1990). These authors belong to the school of communitarianism.

BIBLIOGRAPHY

A.   Reference Works and Sources

Translations and numbering of Philo, Josephus, Greek and Latin authors, if not stated otherwise, were taken from T. E. Page, E. Capps, W. H. D. Rouse, L. A. Post and E. H. Warmington (eds.), *The Loeb Classical Library* (Cambridge, MA: William Heinemann).

Aland, K., Black, M., Martini, C. M., Metzger, B. M. and Wikgren, A. (eds.), *Novum Testamentum Graece* (Stuttgart: Deutsche Bibelgesellschaft, 1993²⁷).

Bauer, W., *A Greek–English Lexicon of the New Testament and Other Early Christian Literature* (trans. and ed. W. F. Arndt, F. W. Gingrich and F. W. Danker; Chicago: University of Chicago Press, 1979²).

Balz, H. and Schneider, G. (eds.), *Exegetical Dictionary of the New Testament* I–III (Grand Rapids: Eerdmans, 1993).

BibleWorks 4.0 – The Premier Biblical Exegesis and Research Program (Big Fork, MT: Hermeneutika Bible Research Software, 1999).

Brown, C. (ed.), *New International Dictionary of New Testament Theology* I–IV (Exeter: Paternoster Press, 1975; 1976; 1978; 1986).

Cornford, F. M. (trans.), *Plato's Theory of Knowledge* (London: Routledge & Kegan Paul, 1960²).

Craig, E. (ed.), *Concise Routledge Encyclopedia of Philosophy* (London: Routledge, 2000).

Routledge Encyclopedia of Philosophy (London: Routledge: 1998).

Danker, F. W. (ed.), *A Greek–English Lexicon of the New Testament and Other Early Christian Literature* (Chicago: University of Chicago Press, 2000³).

Hawthorne, G. F. and Martin, R. P. (eds.), *Dictionary of Paul and his Letters* (Leicester: InterVarsity Press, 1993).

Galling, K. (ed.), *Die Religion in Geschichte und Gegenwart. Handwörterbuch für Theologie und Religionswissenschaft* (Tübingen: Mohr/Siebeck, 1962³).

Kidd, I. G. (ed.), *Posidonius* III. *The Translation of the Fragments* (Cambridge: Cambridge University Press, 1999).

Kidd, I. G. and Edelstein, L. E. (eds.), *Posidonius* I. *The Fragments* (Cambridge: Cambridge University Press, 1972).

Kittel, G. and Friedrich, G. (eds.), *Theological Dictionary of the New Testament* (trans. G. W. Bromiley; Grand Rapids, MI: Eerdmans, 1964; 1971).

Long, A. A. and Sedley, D. N. (eds.), *The Hellenistic Philosophers* I. *Translations of the Principal Sources with Philosophical Commentary*; II. *Greek and Latin*

Texts with Notes and Bibliography (Cambridge: Cambridge University Press, 1987).

Liddell, H. G. and Scott, R., *A Greek–English Lexicon* (Oxford: Clarendon Press, 1958⁹).

Louw, J. P. and Nida, E. A., *Greek–English Lexicon of the New Testament* I–II (New York: United Bible Societies, 1988).

Martinez, F. G., *The Dead Sea Scrolls Translated* (trans. W. G. E. Watson; Leiden: Brill, 1994).

Moulton, J. H., Howard, W. F. and Turner, N., *A Grammar of New Testament Greek* II (Edinburgh: T&T Clark, 1923).

Rahlfs, A., *Septuaginta* I–II (Stuttgart: Württembergische Bibelanstalt, 1952⁵).

Wise, M., Abegg, M. and Cook, E., *The Dead Sea Scrolls* (London: Harper, 1996).

B.   Other Literature

Achtemeier, P. J., 'The Continuing Quest for Coherence in St. Paul: An Experiment in Thought', in E. H. Lovering, Jr and J. L. Sumney (eds.), *Theology and Ethics in Paul and his Interpreters: Essays in Honor of Victor Paul Furnish* (Nashville: Abingdon Press, 1996) 132–45.

Adams, E., *Constructing the World* (SNTW; Edinburgh: T&T Clark, 2000).

Allo, E.-B., *Première épître aux Corinthiens* (Paris: Gabalda, 1956²).

Annas, J., *Hellenistic Philosophy of Mind* (Oxford: University of California Press, 1992).

Armstrong, C. B., 'St. Paul's Theory of Knowledge', *Church Quarterly Review* 154 (1953) 438–52.

Arnold, C. E., *Ephesians: Power and Magic. The Concept of Power in Ephesians in Light of its Historical Setting* (MSSNTS 63; Cambridge: Cambridge University Press, 1989).

Powers of Darkness (Leicester: InterVarsity Press, 1992).

Asciutto, L., 'Decisione e liberta in Cristo. Δοκιμάζειν in alcuni passi di S. Paolo', *Rivista di Teologia Morale* 3 (1971) 229–45.

Aune, D. E., 'Human Nature and Ethics in Hellenistic Philosophical Traditions and Paul: Some Issues and Problems', in T. Engberg-Pedersen (ed.), *Paul in his Hellenistic Context* (Edinburgh: T&T Clark, 1994) 291–312.

'Two Pauline Models of the Person', in D. E. Aune and J. McCarthy (eds.), *The Whole and the Self* (New York: Crossroad, 1997) 89–114.

Prophecy in Early Christianity and the Ancient Mediterranean World (Grand Rapids, MI: Eerdmans, 1983).

Back, F., *Verwandlung durch Offenbarung bei Paulus* (WUNT 2,153; Tübingen: Mohr/Siebeck, 2002).

Backhaus, K., 'Evangelium als Lebensraum. Christologie und Ethik bei Paulus', in U. Schnelle and T. Söding (eds.), *Paulinische Christologie: Exegetische Beiträge. Hans Hübner zum 70. Geburtstag* (Göttingen: Vandenhoeck & Ruprecht, 2000) 9–31.

Barclay, J., *Obeying the Truth* (SNTW; Edinburgh: T&T Clark, 1988).

Barr, J., *The Semantics of Biblical Language* (Oxford: Oxford University Press, 1961).

Barrett, C. K., *A Commentary on the First Epistle to the Corinthians* (London: A. & C. Black, 1971²).

A Commentary on the Epistle to the Romans (London: A. & C. Black, 1973[5]).
Barth, K., *The Epistle to the Romans* (trans. E. C. Hoskyns; Oxford: Oxford University Press, 1933).
Bassler, J., 'Paul's Theology: Whence and Whither?', in D. M. Hay (ed.), *Pauline Theology* II. *1 and 2 Corinthians* (Minneapolis: Fortress Press, 1993) 3–17.
Bauckham, R., 'Book Review of E. J. Schnabel, Law and Wisdom', *Expository Times* 98 (1986–87) 54.
'Time and Eternity', in idem (ed.), *God Will Be All in All: The Eschatology of Jürgen Moltmann* (Edinburgh: T&T Clark, 1999) 155–226.
Baumert, N., 'Charisma und Amt bei Paulus', in A. Vanhoye (ed.), *L'apôtre Paul: personalité, style et conception du ministère* (Leuven: Leuven University Press, 1986) 203–28.
'Zur "Unterscheidung der Geister"', *ZKTh* 111 (1989) 183–95.
Beare, F. W., *A Commentary on the Epistle to the Philippians* (London: A. & C. Black, 1969[2]).
Behm, J., 'νοέω κτλ.', *TDNT* IV, 947–1016.
Beker, J. C., *Paul the Apostle: The Triumph of God in Life and Thought* (Philadelphia: Fortress Press, 1984).
'Recasting Pauline Theology: The Coherence-Contingency Scheme as Interpretive Model', in J. M. Bassler (ed.), *Pauline Theology* I. *Thessalonians, Philippians, Galatians, Philemon* (Minneapolis: Fortress Press, 1991) 15–24.
Belleville, L. L., *2 Corinthians* (Leicester: InterVarsity Press, 1996).
Bennema, C., *The Power of Saving Wisdom: An Investigation of Spirit and Wisdom in Relation to the Soteriology of the Fourth Gospel* (WUNT 2,148; Tübingen: Mohr/Siebeck, 2002).
Bertram, G., 'φρήν κτλ.', *TDNT* IX, 220–35.
Betz, H. D., *Der Apostel Paulus und die sokratische Tradition* (Tübingen: Mohr/Siebeck, 1972).
'The Concept of the "Inner Human Being" (ὁ ἔσω ἄνθρωπος) in the Anthropology of Paul', *NTS* 46 (2000) 315–41.
'The Delphic Maxim ΓΝΩΘΙ ΣΑΥΤΟΝ in Hermetic Interpretation', in *Hellenismus und Urchristentum: Gesammelte Aufsätze* I (Tübingen: Mohr/Siebeck, 1990) 92–111.
Galatians (Philadelphia: Fortress Press, 1979).
'Humanisierung des Menschen: Delphi, Plato, Paulus', in *Hellenismus und Urchristentum: Gesammelte Aufsätze* I (Tübingen: Mohr/Siebeck, 1990) 120–34.
'Das Problem der Grundlagen der paulinischen Ethik (Röm 12,1–2)', in *Paulinische Studien: Gesammelte Aufsätze* III (Tübingen: Mohr/Siebeck, 1994) 184–205.
Bieder, W., 'πνεῦμα κτλ.', *TDNT* VI, 368–75.
Bittlinger, A., *Gifts and Graces* (London: Hodder & Stoughton, 1967).
Blumenfeld, B., *The Political Paul: Justice, Democracy and Kingship in a Hellenistic Framework* (JSNT.S 210; Sheffield: Sheffield Academic Press, 2001).
Böcher, O., *Das Neue Testament und die dämonischen Mächte* (Stuttgart: Katholisches Bibelwerk, 1972).

Bockmuehl, M., *Jewish Law in Gentile Churches: Halakhah and the Beginning of Christian Public Ethics* (Edinburgh: T & T Clark, 2000).
Revelation and Mystery (WUNT 2,36; Tübingen: Mohr/Siebeck, 1990).
'Book Review of T. Engberg-Pedersen, Paul and the Stoics', *Studies in Christian Ethics* 15 (2002) 128–32.
Boers, H. W., 'The Foundations of Paul's Thought: A Methodological Investigation – The Problem of the Coherent Center of Paul's Thought', *Studia Theologica* 42 (1988) 55–68.
Bonnard, P., 'L'intelligence chez Saint Paul', in *L'évangile hier et aujourd'hui: Mélanges offerts au Professeur Franz-J. Leenhardt* (Geneva: Labor et Fides, 1982) 13–24.
Boomershine, T. E., 'Epistemology at the Turn of the Ages in Paul, Jesus, and Mark: Rhetoric and Dialectic in Apocalyptic and the New Testament', in J. Marcus and M. L. Soards (eds.), *Apocalyptic and the New Testament* (JSNT.S 24; Sheffield: Sheffield Academic Press, 1989) 147–67.
Boring, M. E., *Sayings of the Risen Jesus: Christian Prophecy in the Synoptic Tradition* (MSSNTS 46; Cambridge: Cambridge University Press, 1982).
Bornkamm, G., 'Glaube und Vernunft bei Paulus', in K. H. Rengstorf (ed.), *Das Paulusbild in der neueren deutschen Forschung* (Darmstadt: Wissenschaftliche Buchgesellschaft, 1964) 591–612.
'Lord's Supper and Church in Paul', in *Early Christian Experience* (trans. P. L. Hammer; London: SCM Press, 1969) 123–60.
Bosman, P., *Conscience in Philo and Paul: A Conceptual History of the Synoida Word Group* (WUNT 2,166; Tübingen: Mohr/Siebeck, 2003).
Boyarin, D., *A Radical Jew: Paul and the Politics of Identity* (Berkeley: University of California, 1994).
Broer, I., 'Fundamentalistische Exegese oder kritische Bibelwissenschaft? Anmerkungen zum Fundamentalismusproblem anhand des paulinischen Offenbarungsverständnisses', in J. Werbick (ed.), *Offenbarungsanspruch und fundamentalistische Versuchung* (Freiburg: Herder, 1991) 59–88.
Brown, A. R., *The Cross and Human Transformation: Paul's Apocalyptic Word in 1 Corinthians* (Minneapolis: Fortress Press, 1995).
'The Cross and Moral Discernment-2', *Doctrine and Life* 47, 4 (1997) 284–90.
'Paul's Apocalyptic Word of the Cross: Perception and Transformation in 1 Corinthians 1–2' (Unpubl. PhD dissertation: Columbia University, 1990).
Buchegger, J., *Erneuerung des Menschen: Exegetische Studien zu Paulus* (TANZ 40; Tübingen: Francke, 2003).
Bultmann, R., 'ἀλήθεια κτλ.', *TDNT* I, 232–51.
'γινώσκω κτλ.', *TDNT* I, 689–718.
'Die Krisis des Glaubens', in *Glauben und Verstehen: Gesammelte Aufsätze* II (Tübingen: Mohr/Siebeck, 1958) 1–19.
'Das Problem der Ethik bei Paulus', *ZNW* 23 (1924) 123–40.
Theologie des Neuen Testaments (Tübingen: Mohr/Siebeck, 1968[6]).
Der zweite Brief an die Korinther (KEK 6; Göttingen: Vandenhoeck & Ruprecht, 1976).
Burkhardt, H., *Die Inspiration Heiliger Schriften bei Philo von Alexandrien* (Giessen: Brunnen Verlag, 1988).
Caird, G. B., *Principalities and Powers: A Study in Pauline Theology* (Oxford: Clarendon Press, 1956).

Calvin, J., *The First Epistle of Paul the Apostle to the Corinthians* (trans. J. W. Fraser; Edinburgh: Saint Andrew Press, 1960).

Campenhausen, H von, 'Zur Auslegung von Röm 13: Die dämonistische Deutung des ἐξουσία-Begriffes', in W. Baumgartner, O. Eissfeldt, K. Elliger and L. Rost (eds.), *Festschrift Alfred Bertholet zum 80. Geburtstag* (Tübingen: Mohr/Siebeck, 1950) 97–113.

    Ecclesiastical Authority and Spiritual Power (trans. J. A. Baker; London: A. & C. Black, 1969).

Carr, W., *Angels and Principalities* (MSSNTS 42; Cambridge: Cambridge University Press, 1981).

Carson, D. A., *Showing the Spirit: A Theological Exposition of 1 Corinthians 12–14* (Carlisle: Paternoster Press, 1995) 120.

    'Summaries and Conclusions', in D. A. Carson, P. T. O'Brien and M. A. Seifrid (eds.), *Justification and Variegated Nomism* I. *The Complexities of Second Temple Judaism* (WUNT 2,140; Tübingen: J. C. B. Mohr/Siebeck, 2001) 505–48.

Cassirer, H. W., *Grace and Law: St. Paul, Kant, and the Hebrew Prophets* (Grand Rapids, MI: Eerdmans, 1988).

Castelli, E. A., *Imitating Paul: A Discourse of Power* (Louisville, KY: Westminster/John Knox, 1991).

Cerfaux, L., *The Christian in the Theology of Paul* (London: Geoffrey Chapman, 1967).

Chan, S., *Spiritual Theology: A Systematic Study of the Christian Life* (Downers Grove, IL: InterVarsity Press, 1998).

Charry, E. T., 'The Grace of God and the Law of Christ', *Int.* 57 (2003) 34–44.

Chevallier, M.-A., *Esprit de Dieu, paroles d'hommes: Le rôle de l'Esprit dans les ministères de la parole selon l'apôtre Paul* (Neuchâtel: Delachaux and Niestlé, 1966).

Ciholas, P., 'Knowledge and Faith: Pauline Platonisms and the Spiritualization of Reality', *Perspectives in Religious Studies* 3 (1976) 188–201.

Claußen, C., 'Die Frage nach der "Unterscheidung der Geister"', *ZNT* 8 (2001) 25–33.

Cohen, N. G., 'The Greek Virtues and the Mosaic Laws in Philo. An Elucidation of De Specialibus Legibus IV 133–135', in D. T. Runia (ed.), *The Studia Philonica Annual: Studies in Hellenistic Judaism* V (Atlanta: Scholars Press, 1993) 9–23.

Conzelmann, H., *Der erste Brief an die Korinther* (KEK 5; Göttingen: Vandenhoeck & Ruprecht, 1981[2]).

    Grundriß der Theologie des Neuen Testaments (Tübingen: Mohr/Siebeck, 1976).

    'Paulus und die Weisheit', *NTS* 12 (1965/66) 231–44.

Corley, B., 'Interpreting Paul's Conversion – Then and Now', in R. N. Longenecker (ed.), *The Road from Damascus: The Impact of Paul's Conversion on his Life, Thought, and Ministry* (Grand Rapids, MI: Eerdmans, 1997) 1–17.

Cosgrove, C. H., *The Cross and the Spirit: A Study in the Argument and Theology of Galatians* (Macon, GA: Mercer University Press, 1988).

Cothonet, E., 'Les prophètes chrétiens comme exégètes charismatiques de l'écriture', in J. Panagopoulos (ed.), *Prophetic Vocation in the New Testament and Today* (NT.S 45; Leiden: Brill, 1977) 77–107.

Cotterell, P. and Turner, M., *Linguistics and Biblical Interpretation* (Downers Grove, IL: InterVarsity Press, 1989).

Cousar, C. B., *A Theology of the Cross* (Minneapolis: Fortress Press, 1990).

Cranfield, C. E. B., *The Epistle to the Romans* I (ICC; Edinburgh: T&T Clark, 1975⁶).

The Epistle to the Romans II (ICC; Edinburgh: T&T Clark, 1983³).

Crone, T. M., *Early Christian Prophecy* (Baltimore, MD: St Mary's Press, 1973).

Cullmann, O., *Christ and Time: The Primitive Christian Conception of Time and History* (trans. F. V. Filson; London: SCM Press, 1962²).

Der Staat im Neuen Testament (Tübingen: Mohr/Siebeck, 1961²).

Dahl, N. A., 'Christ, Creation and the Church', in W. D. Davies and D. Daube (eds.), *The Background of the New Testament and its Eschatology* (Cambridge: Cambridge University Press, 1964) 422–43.

'Cosmic Dimensions and Religious Knowledge (Eph. 3.18)', in *Studies in Ephesians* (WUNT 131; Tübingen: Mohr/Siebeck, 2000) 365–81.

Dautzenberg, G., 'Botschaft und Bedeutung der urchristlichen Prophetie', in J. Panagopoulos (ed.), *Prophetic Vocation in the New Testament and Today* (NT.S 45; Leiden: Brill, 1977) 145–57.

'Prophetie bei Paulus', in *Prophetie und Charisma, Jahrbuch für biblische Theologie* 14 (1999) 55–70.

'Zum religionsgeschichtlichen Hintergrund der διακρίσεις πνευμάτων (1 Kor 12:10)', *BZ* 15 (1971) 93–104.

Urchristliche Prophetie: Ihre Erforschung, ihre Voraussetzungen im Judentum und ihre Struktur im ersten Korintherbrief (BWANT 104; Stuttgart: Kohlhammer, 1975).

Davis, C. A., *The Structure of Paul's Theology: 'The Truth which is the Gospel'* (Lewiston, NJ: Mellen Biblical Press, 1995).

Davis, J. A., *Wisdom and Spirit: An Investigation of 1 Corinthians 1.18–3.20 against the Background of Jewish Sapiential Traditions in the Greco-Roman Period* (Lanham, MD: University Press of America, 1984).

Davis, S. K., *The Antithesis of the Ages: Paul's Reconfiguration of Torah* (CBQ.MS 33; Washington, DC: Catholic Biblical Association, 2002).

Deidun, T. J., *New Covenant Morality in Paul* (Rome: Biblical Institute Press, 1981).

Dibelius, M., *Die Geisterwelt im Glauben des Paulus* (Göttingen: Vandenhoeck & Ruprecht, 1909).

Dihle, A., *Die Vorstellung vom Willen in der Antike* (Göttingen: Vandenhoeck & Ruprecht, 1985).

Dirscherl, E., *Der Heilige Geist und das menschliche Bewußtsein: Eine theologiegeschichtliche Untersuchung* (Würzburg: Echter Verlag, 1989).

Donaldson, T. L., *Paul and the Gentiles* (Minneapolis: Fortress Press, 1997).

Dubay, T., *Authenticity: A Biblical Theology of Discernment* (San Francisco: Ignatius Press, 1997²).

Dübbers, M., 'Christologie und Existenz: Eine Studie zur Intention des Kolosserbriefes' (Unpubl. PhD dissertation, University of Tübingen, 2000).

Dunn, J. D. G., *Christology in the Making: An Inquiry into the Origins of the Doctrine of the Incarnation* (London: SCM Press, 1980).

'Discernment of Spirits – A Neglected Gift', in W. Harrington (ed.), *Witness to the Spirit* (Dublin: Irish Biblical Association, 1979) 79–96.

Jesus and the Spirit (London: SCM Press, 1975).

'Prophetic "I"-Sayings and the Jesus Tradition: The Importance of Testing Prophetic Utterances within Early Christianity', *NTS* 24 (1977–78) 175–98.

'In Quest of Paul's Theology. Retrospect and Prospect', in E. E. Johnson and D. M. Hay (eds.), *Pauline Theology* IV. *Looking Back, Pressing On* (Atlanta: Scholars Press, 1997) 95–115.

'Responsible Congregation (1 Cor. 14.26–40)', in L. de Lorenzi (ed.), *Charisma and Agape (1 Kor. 12–14)* (Rome: Abtei von St Paul vor den Mauern, 1983) 201–36.

Romans 1–8 (WBC 38A; Dallas: Word Books, 1988).

Romans 9–16 (WBC 38B; Dallas: Word Books, 1988).

The Theology of Paul the Apostle (Edinburgh: T&T Clark, 1998).

The Theology of Paul's Letter to the Galatians (Cambridge: Cambridge University Press, 1993).

'Why "Incarnation"? A Review of Recent New Testament Scholarship', in S. E. Porter, P. Joyce and D. E. Orton (eds.), *Crossing the Boundaries: Essays in Biblical Interpretation in Honour of Michael D. Goulder* (Leiden: Brill, 1994) 235–56.

Dupont, J., *Gnosis: la connaissance religieuse dans les épîtres de Saint Paul* (Louvain: E. Nauwelaerts, 1949).

Ebeling, G., *The Truth of the Gospel: An Exposition of Galatians* (trans. D. Green; Philadelphia: Fortress Press, 1985).

Die Wahrheit des Evangeliums: Eine Lesehilfe zum Galaterbrief (Tübingen: Mohr/Siebeck, 1981).

Eckstein, H.-J., *Der Begriff Syneidesis bei Paulus* (WUNT 2,10; Tübingen: Mohr/Siebeck, 1983).

Eckstein, P., *Gemeinde, Brief und Heilsbotschaft: Ein phänomenologischer Vergleich zwischen Paulus und Epikur* (Herders Biblische Studien 42; Freiburg: Herder, 2004).

Ehrensperger, K., 'Scriptural Reasoning – the Dynamic that Informed Paul's Theologizing' (Seminar Paper, British New Testament Conference, September 2003) 1–12.

Elliott, M. A., *The Survivors of Israel: A Reconsideration of the Theology of Pre-Christian Judaism* (Grand Rapids, MI: Eerdmans, 2000).

Elliott, N., *Liberating Paul: The Justice of God and the Politics of the Apostle* (Sheffield: Sheffield Academic Press, 1995).

Ellis, E. E., *Prophecy and Hermeneutic in Early Christianity* (WUNT 18; Tübingen: Mohr/Siebeck, 1978).

'Prophecy in the New Testament Church – and Today', in J. Panagopoulos (ed.), *Prophetic Vocation in the New Testament and Today* (NT.S 45; Leiden: Brill, 1977) 46–57.

'"Spiritual" Gifts in the Pauline Community', *NTS* 20 (1973/74) 128–44.

'"Wisdom" and "Knowledge" in I Corinthians', in *Prophecy and Hermeneutic in Early Christianity* (WUNT 18; Tübingen: Mohr/Siebeck, 1978) 45–62.

Engberg-Pedersen, T., *Paul and the Stoics* (Edinburgh: T&T Clark, 2000).

'Stoicism in Philippians', in idem (ed.), *Paul in his Hellenistic Context* (Edinburgh: T&T Clark, 1994) 256–90.

The Stoic Theory of Oikeiosis: Moral Development and Social Interaction in Early Stoic Philosophy (Aarhus: Aarhus University Press, 1990).

Engelsen, N. I. J., *Glossolalia and Other Forms of Prophetic Speech According to 1 Corinthians 12–14* (Ann Arbor, MI: UMI, 1970).

Esler, P. F., 'Paul and Stoicism: Romans 12 as a Test Case', *NTS* 50 (2004) 106–24.

Evans, C. F., 'Romans 12.1–2: The True Worship', in L. De Lorenzi (ed.), *Dimensions de la vie chrétienne (Rm 12–13)* (Rome: Abbaye de S. Paul h.l.m., 1979) 7–33.

Farnell, F. D., 'The Gift of Prophecy in the Old and New Testament', *Bibliotheca Sacra* 149 (1992) 387–410.

Fascher, E., *Prophētēs: Eine sprach- und religionsgeschichtliche Untersuchung* (Gießen: Töpelmann, 1927).

Fatehi, M., *The Spirit's Relation to the Risen Lord in Paul* (WUNT 2,128; Tübingen: Mohr/Siebeck, 2000).

Fee, G. D., *The First Epistle to the Corinthians* (Grand Rapids, MI: Eerdmans, 1987).

God's Empowering Presence (Peabody, MA: Hendrickson, 1994).

Paul's Letter to the Philippians (NICNT; Grand Rapids, MI: Eerdmans, 1995).

Finsterbusch, K., *Die Thora als Lebensweisung für Heidenchristen: Studien zur Bedeutung der Thora für die paulinische Ethik* (Göttingen: Vandenhoeck & Ruprecht, 1996).

Fitzgerald, J. T., *Cracks in Earthen Vessels: An Examination of the Catalogues of Hardships in the Corinthian Correspondence* (SBL.DS 99; Atlanta: Scholars Press, 1988).

Fitzmyer, J. A., 'To Know him and the Power of his Resurrection (Phil 3:10)', in *To Advance the Gospel* (NTS; New York: Crossroad, 1981) 202–17.

Romans (AB 33; New York: Doubleday, 1993).

Flemming, D., 'Essence and Adaptation: Contextualisation and the Heart of Paul's Gospel' I–II (Unpubl. PhD dissertation, University of Aberdeen, 1987).

Forbes, C., 'Pauline Demonology and/or Cosmology? Principalities, Powers and the Elements of the World in their Hellenistic Context', *JSNT* 85 (2002) 51–73.

'Paul's Principalities and Powers: Demythologising Apocalyptic?', *JSNT* 82 (2001) 61–88.

Prophecy and Inspired Speech in Early Christianity and its Hellenistic Environment (WUNT 2,75; Tübingen: Mohr/Siebeck, 1995).

Forestell, J. T., 'Christian Perfection and Gnosis in Philippians 3,7–16', *CBQ* 18 (1956) 123–36.

Fraade, S. D., 'The Early Rabbinic Sage', in J. G. Gammie and L. G. Perdue (eds.), *The Sage in Israel and the Ancient Near East* (Winona Lake, IN: Eisenbrauns, 1990) 417–36.

Fredrickson, D., 'Pauline Ethics: Congregations as Communities of Moral Deliberation', in K. L. Bloomquist and J. R. Stumme (eds.), *The Promise of Lutheran Ethics* (Minneapolis: Fortress Press, 1998) 115–29.

Frenschkowski, M., *Offenbarung und Epiphanie* I. *Grundlagen des spätantiken und frühchristlichen Offenbarungsglanbens* (WUNT 2,79; Tübingen: Mohr/Siebeck, 1995).

Freudenthal, M., *Die Erkenntnislehre Philos von Alexandria* (Berlin: S. Calvary & Co., 1891).

Friedrich, G., 'προφήτης κτλ.', *TDNT* VI, 781–861.

Fuchs, E., 'Wahrheit', *RGG³* VI, 1515–17.

Fung, R. Y. K., *The Epistle to the Galatians* (NICNT; Grand Rapids, MI: Eerdmans, 1988).

Funk, R. W., *Language, Hermeneutic, and Word of God* (New York: Harper, 1966).

Furnish, V. P., *2 Corinthians* (AB 32A; New York: Doubleday, 1984).

'Theology in 1 Corinthians', in D. M. Hay (ed.), *Pauline Theology* II. *1 & 2 Corinthians* (Minneapolis: Fortress Press, 1993) 59–89.

Theology and Ethics in Paul (Nashville: Abingdon Press, 1968).

The Theology of the First Letter to the Corinthians (Cambridge: Cambridge University Press, 1999).

'Where is "The Truth" in Paul's Gospel?', in E. E. Johnson and D. M. Hay (eds.), *Pauline Theology* IV. *Looking Back, Pressing On* (Atlanta: Scholars Press, 1997) 161–78.

Gammie, J. G., 'The Sage in Sirach', in J. G. Gammie and L. G. Perdue (eds.), *The Sage in Israel and the Ancient Near East* (Winona Lake, IN: Eisenbrauns, 1990) 355–72.

Gardner, P. D., *The Gifts of God and the Authentication of a Christian: An Exegetical Study of 1 Corinthians 8–11* (Lanham, MD: University Press of America, 1994).

Gärtner, B. E., *The Areopagus Speech and Natural Revelation* (trans. C. H. King; ASNU 21; Uppsala: Almqvist & Wiksell, 1955).

'The Pauline and Johannine Idea "To Know God" against the Hellenistic Background', *NTS* 14 (1967/68) 209–31.

Gaston, L., *Paul and the Torah* (Vancouver: University of British Columbia Press, 1987).

Gathercole, S. J., 'A Law unto themselves: The Gentiles in Romans 2.14–15 Revisited', *JSNT* 85 (2002) 27–49.

Where is Boasting? Early Jewish Soteriologiy and Paul's Response in Romans 1–5 (Grand Rapids, MI: Eerdmans, 2002).

Gillespie, T. W., *The First Theologians: A Study in Early Christian Prophecy* (Grand Rapids, MI: Eerdmans, 1994).

Gnilka, J., *Paulus von Tarsus: Apostel und Zeuge* (Freiburg: Herder, 1996).

Der Philipperbrief (HThK 10/3; Freiburg: Herder, 1976²).

Göbel, C., *Griechische Selbsterkenntnis: Platon-Parmenides-Stoa-Aristipp* (Stuttgart: Kohlhammer, 2002).

Gooch, P. W., '"Conscience" in 1 Corinthians 8 and 10', *NTS* 33 (1987) 244–54.

Partial Knowledge: Philosophical Studies in Paul (Notre Dame: University of Notre Dame Press, 1987).

Goodenough, E. R., *An Introduction to Philo Judaeus* (Oxford: Basil Blackwell, 1962).

By Light, Light: The Mystic Gospel of Hellenistic Judaism (New Haven, CT: Yale University Press, 1935).

Goppelt, L., *Theologie des Neuen Testaments* (Göttingen: Vandenhoeck & Ruprecht, 1991³).

Gorman, M. J., *Apostle of the Crucified Lord: A Theological Introduction to Paul and his Letters* (Grand Rapids, MI: Eerdmans, 2004).

Cruciformity: Paul's Narrative Spirituality of the Cross (Grand Rapids, MI: Eerdmans, 2002).

Goulder, M. D., 'ΣΟΦΙΑ in 1 Corinthians', *NTS* 37 (1991) 516–34.

Greeven, H., 'Propheten, Lehrer, Vorsteher bei Paulus', *ZNW* 44 (1952–53) 18–29.

Grindheim, S., 'Wisdom for the Perfect: Paul's Challenge to the Corinthian Church (1 Corinthians 2:6–16)', *JBL* 121 (2002) 689–709.

Grosheide, F. W., *Commentary on the First Epistle to the Corinthians* (London: Marshall, Morgan & Scott, 1954²).

Grudem, W., *The Gift of Prophecy in 1 Corinthians* (Washington, DC: University Press of America, 1982).

'A Response to Gerhard Dautzenberg on 1 Cor. 12.10', *BZ* 22 (1978) 253–70.

Grundmann, W., 'δόκιμος κτλ.', *TDNT* II, 255–60.

Gundry-Volf, J. M., 'Conscience', *DPL*, 153–56.

Gunkel, H., *The Influence of the Holy Spirit* (Philadelphia: Fortress Press, 1979).

Haacker, K., *Der Brief des Paulus an die Römer* (ThHK 6; Leipzig: Evangelische Verlagsanstalt, 1999).

Habermas, J., *Erkenntnis und Interesse* (Frankfurt a.M.: Suhrkamp, 1994¹¹).

Theorie des kommunikativen Handelns, 2 Volumes (Frankfurt a.M.: Suhrkamp, 1987⁴).

Hafemann, S. J., *Paul, Moses, and the History of Israel* (WUNT 81; Tübingen: Mohr/Siebeck, 1995).

Hahn, F., 'Charisma und Amt', *ZThK* 76 (1979) 418–49.

Haldimann, K., 'Kreuz – Wort vom Kreuz – Kreuztheologie. Zu einer Begriffs- differenzierung in der Paulusinterpretation', in A. Dettwiler and J. Zum- stein (eds.), *Kreuzestheologie im Neuen Testament* (WUNT 151; Tübingen: Mohr/Siebeck, 2002) 1–26.

Hasenstab, R., *Modelle paulinischer Ethik: Beiträge zu einem Autonomie-Modell aus paulinischem Geist* (Mainz: Matthias-Grünewald Verlag, 1977).

Haufe, G., 'Das Geistmotiv in der paulinischen Ethik', *ZNW* 85 (1995) 183–91.

Hay, D. M., 'The Shaping of Theology in 2 Corinthians: Convictions, Doubts, and Warrants', in D. M. Hay (ed.), *Pauline Theology* II. *1 & 2 Corinthians* (Minneapolis: Fortress Press, 1993) 135–55.

Hays, R.B., *The Moral Vision of the New Testament: A Contemporary Introduction to New Testament Ethics* (Edinburgh: T&T Clark, 1997).

'The Role of Scripture in Paul's Ethics', in E. H. Lovering, Jr and J. L. Sumney (eds.), *Theology and Ethics in Paul and his Interpreters: Essays in Honor of Victor Paul Furnish* (Nashville: Abingdon Press, 1996) 30–47.

'Wisdom According to Paul', in S. C. Barton (ed.), *Where Shall Wisdom be Found? Wisdom in the Bible, the Church and the Contemporary World* (Edinburgh: T&T Clark, 1999) 111–23.

Healy, M., '"What the Heart of Man Has not Conceived": A Theological Approach to 1.Cor 2:6–16' (Unpubl. PhD dissertation, Pontifical Gregorian University, 2000).

Heckel, T. K., *Der innere Mensch: Die paulinische Verarbeitung eines platonis- chen Motivs* (WUNT 2,53; Tübingen: Mohr/Siebeck, 1993).

Heinrici, C. F. G., *Der erste Brief an die Korinther* (KEK 5; Göttingen: Vanden- hoeck & Ruprecht, 1896⁸).

Hengel, M., *Judaism and Hellenism* I (trans. J. Bowden; London: SCM Press, 1974).

Der Sohn Gottes: Die Entstehung der Christologie und die jüdisch-hellenistische Religionsgeschichte (Tübingen: Mohr/Siebeck, 1975).

Héring, J., *La première épître de Saint Paul aux Corinthiens* (Neuchâtel: Delachaux & Niestlé, 1949).

Herr, T., *Naturrecht aus der kritischen Sicht des neuen Testaments* (Munich: Schöningh, 1976).

Hill, D., 'Christian Prophets as Teachers or Instructors in the Church', in J. Panagopoulos (ed.), *Prophetic Vocation in the New Testament and Today* (NT.S 45; Leiden: Brill, 1977) 108–30.

New Testament Prophecy (London: Marshall, Morgan & Scott, 1979).

'On the Evidence for the Creative Role of Christian Prophets', *NTS* 20 (1974) 262–74.

Hoegen-Rohls, C., 'Rezension: T. Engberg-Pedersen, Paul and the Stoics', *BZ* 46 (2002) 141–43.

Hofius, O., '"Die Wahrheit des Evangeliums". Exegetische und theologische Erwägungen zum Wahrheitsanspruch der paulinischen Verkündigung', in *Paulusstudien* II (WUNT 143; Tübingen: Mohr/Siebeck, 2002) 17–37.

Holmberg, B., *Paul and Power: The Structure of Authority in the Primitive Church as Reflected in the Pauline Epistles* (Lund: Gleerup, 1978).

Holtz, T., *Der erste Brief an die Thessalonicher* (EKK 13; Neukirchen-Vluyn: Neurkirchner Verlag, 1986).

Honecker, M., *Einführung in die theologische Ethik: Grundlagen und Grundbegriffe* (Berlin: de Gruyter, 1990).

Hooker, M. D., 'Interchange in Christ and Ethics', *JSNT* 25 (1985) 3–17.

Horn, F. W., *Das Angeld des Geistes: Studien zur paulinischen Pneumatologie* (FRLANT 154; Göttingen: Vandenhoeck & Ruprecht, 1992).

Horrell, D. G., '"No Longer Jew or Greek." Paul's Corporate Christology and the Construction of Christian Community', in D. G. Horrell and C. M. Tuckett (eds.), *Christology, Controversy and Community: New Testament Essays in Honour of D. R. Catchpole* (NT.S. 99; Leiden: Brill, 2000) 279–302.

'Restructuring Human Relationships. Paul's Corinthian Letters and Habermas's Discourse Ethics', *Expository Times* 110 (1999) 321–25.

Horsley, R. A., 'Consciousness and Freedom among the Corinthians: 1 Corinthians 8–10', *CBQ* 40 (1978) 574–89.

'Pneumatikos versus Psychikos: Distinctions of Status among the Corinthians', *HTR* 69 (1976) 269–88.

'Wisdom of Word and Words of Wisdom', *CBQ* 39 (1977) 224–39.

Hoyle, R. B., *The Holy Spirit in St. Paul* (London: Hodder & Stoughton, 1927).

Hubbard, M. V., *New Creation in Paul's Letters and Thought* (MSSNTS 119; Cambridge: Cambridge University Press, 2002).

Hübner, H., *An Philemon. An die Kolosser. An die Epheser* (HNT 12; Tübingen: Mohr/Siebeck, 1997).

Biblische Theologie des Neuen Testaments I (Göttingen: Vandenhoeck & Ruprecht, 1990).

Das Gesetz bei Paulus (Göttingen: Vandenhoeck & Ruprecht, 1980^2).

Hughes, P. E., *Paul's Second Epistle to the Corinthians* (NICNT; Grand Rapids, MI: Eerdmans, 1962).

Hunt, A. R., *The Inspired Body: Paul, the Corinthians, and Divine Inspiration* (Macon, GA: Mercer University Press, 1996).

Isaacs, M. E., *The Concept of Spirit: A Study of Pneuma in Hellenistic Judaism and its Bearing on the New Testament* (London: Heythrop College, 1976).

Jaeger, W., *Paideia: Die Formung des griechischen Menschen* III (Berlin: W. de Gruyter, 1947).

    Paideia: The Ideals of Greek Culture III (trans. G. Highet; Oxford: Basil Blackwell, 1945).

Jaquette, J. L., *Discerning what Counts: The Function of the Adiaphora Topos in Paul's Letters* (SBL.DS 147; Atlanta: Scholars Press, 1995).

Jewett, R., *Paul's Anthropological Terms: A Study of their Use in Conflict Settings* (AGJU 10; Leiden: Brill, 1971).

Jillions, J., 'Decision-Making and Divine Guidance: Greco-Roman, Jewish and Pauline Views' (Seminar Paper, SBL Conference, July 2003) 1–14.

Johnson, L. T., 'Edification as a Formal Criterion for Discernment in the Church', *Sewanee Theological Review* 39 (1996) 362–72.

    'Holiness as a Material Criterion for Discernment in the Church', *Sewanee Theological Review* 39 (1996) 373–84.

Kaiser, W. C., 'A Neglected Text in Bibliology Discussions: I Corinthians 2:6–16', *WThJ* 43 (1981) 301–19.

Kammler, H.-C., *Kreuz und Weisheit: Eine exegetische Untersuchung zu 1Kor 1,10–3,4* (WUNT 159; Tübingen: Mohr/Siebeck, 2003).

Kampen, J. I., 'The Diverse Aspects of Wisdom in the Qumran Texts', in P. W. Flint and J. C. Vanderkam (eds.), *The Dead Sea Scrolls after Fifty Years* (Leiden: Brill, 1998) 211–42.

Käsemann, E., *An die Römer* (HNT 8a; Tübingen: Mohr/Siebeck, 1980[4]).

    'Gottesdienst im Alltag der Welt', in *Exegetische Versuche und Besinnungen* II (Göttingen: Vandenhoeck & Ruprecht, 1964) 198–202.

    '1 Korinther 2, 6–16', in *Exegetische Versuche und Besinnungen* I (Göttingen: Vandenhoek & Ruprecht, 1965[4]) 267–76.

    'Kritische Analyse von Phil. 2, 5–11', in *Exegetische Versuche und Besinnungen* I (Göttingen: Vandenhoek & Ruprecht, 1965[4]) 51–95.

    'Der Ruf zur Vernunft', in *Kirchliche Konflikte* I (Göttingen: Vandenhoeck & Ruprecht, 1982) 116–27.

    'The Saving Significance of the Death of Jesus in Paul', in *Perspectives on Paul* (trans. M. Kohl; Philadelphia: Fortress Press, 1971) 32–59.

    'Zur paulinischen Anthropologie', in *Paulinische Perspektiven* (Tübingen: Mohr/Siebeck, 1972[2]) 9–61.

Keck, L. E., *Paul and his Letters* (Philadelphia: Fortress Press, 1988).

    'Paul as Thinker', *Int.* 47 (1993) 27–38.

Kemmler, D., *Faith and Human Reason: A Study of Paul's Method of Preaching as Illustrated by 1–2 Thessalonians and Acts 17, 2–4* (NT.S 40; Leiden: Brill, 1975).

Kertelge, K., '"Natürliche Theologie" und Rechtfertigung aus dem Glauben', in *Grundthemen paulinischer Theologie* (Freiburg: Herder, 1991) 148–60.

Kilner, J. F., 'A Pauline Approach to Ethical Decision-Making', *Int.* 44 (1989) 366–79.

Kim, J.-C., 'Der gekreuzigte Christus als geheimnisvolle Weisheit Gottes – Exegetische Studien zu 1 Korinther 2,6–16' (Unpubl. PhD dissertation, University of Tübingen, 1987).

Kim, S., *The Origin of Paul's Gospel* (WUNT 2,4; Tübingen: Mohr/Siebeck, 1981).

—— *Paul and the New Perspective: Second Thoughts on the Origin of Paul's Gospel* (WUNT 140; Tübingen: Mohr/Siebeck, 2002).

Klauck, H.-J., '"Der Gott in dir" (Ep 41.1): Autonomie des Gewissens bei Seneca und Paulus', in *Alte Welt und neuer Glaube: Beiträge zur Religionsgeschichte, Forschungsgeschichte und Theologie des Neuen Testaments* (NTOA 29; Göttingen: Vandenhoeck & Ruprecht, 1994) 11–31.

—— *1. Korintherbrief* (NEB; Würzburg: Echter Verlag, 1984).

—— *The Religious Context of Early Christianity: A Guide to Graeco-Roman Religions* (trans. B. McNeil; SNTW; Edinburgh: T&T Clark, 2000).

—— 'Ein Richter im eigenen Inneren: Das Gewissen bei Philo von Alexandrien', in *Alte Welt und neuer Glaube: Beiträge zur Religionsgeschichte, Forschungsgeschichte und Theologie des Neuen Testaments* (NTOA 29; Göttingen: Vandenhoeck & Ruprecht, 1994) 33–58.

Klausner, J., *From Jesus to Paul* (trans. W. Stinespring; New York: Menorah, 1943).

Klein, P. D., 'Epistemology', in E. Craig (ed.), *Routledge Encyclopedia of Philosophy* III (London: Routledge: 1998) 362–65.

Kleinknecht, H., 'πνεῦμα κτλ.', *TDNT* VI, 332–59.

Konradt, M., *Gericht und Gemeinde: Eine Studie zur Bedeutung und Funktion von Gerichtsaussagen im Rahmen der paulinischen Ekklesiologie und Ethik im 1 Thess und 1 Kor* (Beihefte zur Zeitschrift für die neutestamentliche Wissenschaft 117; Berlin: W. de Gruyter, 2003).

Kremer, J., *Der erste Brief an die Korinther* (RNT; Regensburg: Friedrich Pustet, 1997).

Krömer, U., 'Wachsende Erkenntnis und christliche Vollendung in paulinischer Sicht', in J. Tenzler (ed.), *Wirklichkeit der Mitte: Beiträge zu einer Strukturanthropologie* (Freiburg: Adler, 1968) 648–54.

Kümmel, W. G., *Römer 7 und die Bekehrung des Paulus* (Leipzig: Hinrichs'sche Buchhandlung, 1929).

Lambrecht, J., 'Transformation in 2 Corinthians 3,18', in J. Lambrecht and R. Bieringer (eds.), *Studies on 2 Corinthians* (Leuven: Leuven University Press, 1994) 295–306.

Lamp, J. S., *First Corinthians 1–4 in Light of Jewish Wisdom Traditions* (Studies in the Bible and Early Christianity 42; Lampeter: Edwin Mellen Press, 2000).

Lampe, G. W. H., 'Church Discipline and the Epistles to the Corinthians', in W. R. Farmer, C. F. D. Moule and R. R. Niebuhr (eds.), *Christian History and Interpretation: Studies Presented to John Knox* (Cambridge: Cambridge University Press, 1967) 337–61.

Lampe, P., 'Ad ecclesiae unitatem: Eine exegetisch-theologische und sozialpsychologische Paulusstudie' (Unpubl. Habilitationsschrift Bern, 1989).

—— 'Identification with Christ. A Psychological View of Pauline Theology', in T. Fornberg and D. Hellholm (eds.), *Texts and Contexts: Biblical Texts in their Textual and Situational Contexts* (Oslo: Scandinavian University Press, 1995) 931–43.

—— 'Theological Wisdom and "Word about the Cross". The Rhetorical Scheme in I Corinthians 1–4', *Int.* 44 (1990) 117–31.

Lang, F., *Die Briefe an die Korinther* (NTD 7; Göttingen: Vandenhoeck & Ruprecht, 1986).

Lebram, J. C. H., 'The Piety of the Jewish Apocalyptists', in D. Hellholm (ed.), *Apocalypticism in the Mediterranean World and the Near East* (Tübingen: Mohr/Siebeck, 1983) 171–210.

Leenhardt, F. J., *L'épître de Saint Paul aux Romains* (Geneva: Labor et Fides, 1957; 1981[2]).

Leisegang, H., *Der Heilige Geist: Das Wesen und Werden der mystisch-intuitiven Erkenntnis in der Philosophie und Religion der Griechen* (Leipzig: Teubner, 1919).

Lémonon, J.-P., 'Le discernement dans les lettres pauliniennes', *Lumière et Vie* 252 (2001) 23–31.

Lenski, R. C. H., *St. Paul's First and Second Epistles to the Corinthians* (Minneapolis: Augsburg Publishing House, 1963).

Lerle, E., 'Diakrisis Pneumaton bei Paulus' (Unpubl. PhD dissertation, University of Heidelberg, 1947).

Levison, J. R., 'Inspiration and the Divine Spirit in Philo', *JSJ* 26 (1995) 271–323.
'The Prophetic Spirit as an Angel According to Philo', *HTR* 88 (1995) 189–207.
The Spirit in First Century Judaism (AGJU 29; Leiden: Brill, 1997).

Lewis, J. G., *Looking for Life: The Role of 'Theo-Ethical Reasoning' in Paul's Religion* (JSNT.S 291; London, T&T Clark, 2005).

Liddy, R. M., *Transforming Light: Intellectual Conversion in the Early Lonergan* (Collegeville, MN: Liturgical Press, 1993).

Lietzmann, D. H., *An die Korinther* I–II (supplemented by W. G. Kümmel; HNT 9; Tübingen: Mohr/Siebeck, 1969[5]).

Lincoln, A. T., '"Paul the Visionary": The Setting and Significance of the Rapture to Paradise in II Cor xii:1–10', *NTS* 25 (1979) 204–20.

Lindemann, A., 'Die biblischen Toragebote und die paulinische Ethik', in *Paulus, Apostel und Lehrer der Kirche* (Tübingen: Mohr/Siebeck, 1999) 91–114.
Der erste Korintherbrief (HNT 9,1; Tübingen: Mohr/Siebeck, 2000).

Link, H. G., 'Wahrheit', in L. Coenen and K. Haacker (eds.), *Theologisches Begriffslexikon zum Neuen Testament* II (Wuppertal: Brockhaus, 2000).

Litfin, D., *St Paul's Theology of Proclamation: 1 Corinthians 1–4 and Greco-Roman Rhetoric* (Cambridge: Cambridge University Press, 1994).

Lohse, E., *Der Brief an die Römer* (KEK 4; Göttingen: Vandenhoeck & Ruprecht, 2003).
'Changes of Thought in Pauline Theology? Some Reflections on Paul's Ethical Teaching in the Context of his Theology', in E. H. Lovering, Jr and J. L. Sumney (eds.), *Theology and Ethics in Paul and his Interpreters: Essays in Honor of Victor Paul Furnish* (Nashville: Abingdon Press, 1996) 146–60.
'Das Evangelium für Juden und Griechen', *ZNW* 92 (2001) 168–84.

Long, A. A., *Hellenistic Philosophy: Stoics, Epicureans, Sceptics* (London: Duckworth, 1974).

Longenecker, R. N., *Galatians* (WBC 41; Dallas: Word Books, 1990).
Paul, Apostle of Liberty (Grand Rapids, MI: Baker Book House, 1977).

Lopes, A. N. G., 'Paul as a Charismatic Interpreter of Scripture: Revelation and Interpretation in 1 Cor 2:6–16' (Unpubl. PhD dissertation, Westminster Theological Seminary, 1995).

Lübbe, H., *Religion nach der Aufklärung* (Graz: Styria, 1990[2]).

Lührmann, D., *Das Offenbarungsverständnis bei Paulus und in paulinischen Gemeinden* (Neukirchen-Vluyn: Neukirchener Verlag, 1965).

Lull, D. J., *The Spirit in Galatia* (SBL.DS 49; Chico, CA: Scholars Press, 1980).

MacIntyre, A., *After Virtue: A Study in Moral Theory* (London: Duckworth, 1985²).

Magee, B., *Confessions of a Philosopher: A Journey through Western Philosophy* (London: Phoenix, 2000²).

Malherbe, A. J., 'Determinism and Free Will in Paul: The Argument of 1 Corinthians 8 and 9', in T. Engberg-Pedersen (ed.), *Paul in his Hellenistic Context* (SNTW; Edinburgh: T&T Clark, 1994) 231–55.

    The Letters to the Thessalonians (AB 32B; New York: Doubleday, 2000).

    Moral Exhortation: A Greco-Roman Sourcebook (Philadelphia: Westminster Press, 1986).

Malina, B. J. and Neyrey, J. H., *Portraits of Paul* (Louisville, KY: Westminster/John Knox Press, 1996).

Malina, B. J. and Pilch, J. J., *Social Science Commentary on the Book of Revelation* (Minneapolis: Fortress Press, 2000).

Maly, K., '1Kor 12,1–3, eine Regel zur Unterscheidung der Geister?', *BZ* 10 (1966) 82–95.

    Mündige Gemeinde (Stuttgart: Verlag Katholisches Bibelwerk, 1967).

Martin, R. P., *2 Corinthians* (WBC 40; Waco, TX: Word Books, 1986).

Martucci, J., 'Diakriseis Pneumatōn (1 Co 12,10)', *Eglise et Théologie* 9 (1978) 465–71.

Martyn, J. L., 'Apocalyptic Antinomies in Paul's Letter to the Galatians', *NTS* 31 (1985) 410–24.

    'Book Review of J. C. Beker, Paul the Apostle', in *Theological Issues in the Letters of Paul* (Edinburgh: T&T Clark, 1997) 176–81.

    'De-apocalypticizing Paul: An Essay Focused on Paul and the Stoics by Troels Engberg-Pedersen', *JSNT* 86 (2002) 61–102.

    'Epistemology at the Turn of the Ages: 2 Corinthians 5:16', in W. R. Farmer, C. F. D. Moule and R. R. Niebuhr (eds.), *Christian History and Interpretation: Studies Presented to John Knox* (Cambridge: Cambridge University Press, 1967) 269–87.

    Galatians (AB 33A; New York: Doubleday, 1998).

Marxsen, W., *'Christliche' und christliche Ethik im Neuen Testament* (Gütersloh: Gütersloher Verlagshaus, 1989).

Matera, F. J., *New Testament Ethics: The Legacies of Jesus and Paul* (Louisville, KY: Westminster/John Knox Press, 1996).

Mathewson, M. D., 'Moral Intuitionism and the Law Inscribed on our Hearts', *JEThS* 42 (1999) 629–43.

Matlock, R. B., *Unveiling the Apocalyptic Paul: Paul's Interpreters and the Rhetoric of Criticism* (JSNT.S 127; Sheffield: Sheffield Academic Press, 1996).

Maurer, C., 'σύνοιδα κτλ.', *TDNT* VII, 898–919.

Meeks, W. A., 'The Circle of Reference within the Pauline Community', in D. L. Balch, E. F. Ferguson and W. A. Meeks (eds.), *Greeks, Romans, Christians* (Minneapolis: Fortress Press, 1990).

    The Moral World of the First Christians (Philadelphia: Westminster Press, 1986).

Meier, H.-C., *Mystik bei Paulus: Zur Phänomenologie religiöser Erfahrung im Neuen Testament* (TANZ 26; Tübingen: Francke, 1998).

Merk, O., *Handeln aus Glauben: Die Motivierungen der paulinischen Ethik* (Marburg: Elwert, 1968).

Merklein, H., *Der erste Brief an die Korinther Kapitel 1–4* (ÖTK 7/1; Gütersloh: Gütersloher Verlagshaus Gerd Mohn, 1992).

'Der Theologe als Prophet. Zur Funktion prophetischen Redens im theologischen Diskurs des Paulus', *NTS* 38 (1992) 402–29.

'Die Weisheit Gottes und die Weisheit der Welt (1Kor 1,21)', in *Studien zu Jesus und Paulus* (WUNT 43; Tübingen: Mohr/Siebeck, 1987) 376–84.

Michel, O., *Der Brief an die Römer* (KEK 4; Göttingen: Vandenhoeck & Ruprecht, 1978⁵).

Moberly, R. W. L., 'Solomon and Job: Divine Wisdom in Human Life', in S. C. Barton (ed.), *Where Shall Wisdom be Found? Wisdom in the Bible, the Church and the Contemporary World* (Edinburgh: T&T Clark, 1999) 3–18.

Moe, O., 'Vernunft und Geist im Neuen Testament', *Zeitschrift für Systematische Theologie* 11 (1934) 351–91.

Moltmann, J., *Erfahrungen theologischen Denkens: Wege und Formen christlicher Theologie* (Gütersloh: Gütersloher Verlagshaus, 1999).

Moo, D. J., *The Epistle to the Romans* (NICNT; Grand Rapids, MI: Eerdmans, 1996).

Moores, J. D., *Wrestling with Rationality in Paul: Romans 1–8 in a New Perspective* (MSSNTS 82; Cambridge: Cambridge University Press, 1995).

Mühlenberg, E., 'Das Problem der Offenbarung in Philo von Alexandrien', *ZNW* 64 (1973) 1–18.

Müller, U. B., *Der Brief des Paulus an die Philipper* (ThHK 11/1; Leipzig: Evangelische Verlagsanstalt, 1993).

Prophetie und Predigt im Neuen Testament (StNT 10; Gütersloh: Gütersloher Verlagshaus, 1975).

Murphy, W. F., 'The Pauline Understanding of Appropriated Revelation as a Principle of Christian Moral Action', *Studia Moralia* 39 (2001) 371–409.

Murphy-O'Connor, J., *Paul: A Critical Life* (Oxford: Clarendon Press, 1996).

'Truth: Paul and Qumran', *Paul and Qumran: Studies in New Testament Exegesis* (Chicago: The Priory Press, 1968) 179–230.

Newsom, C. A., 'The Sage in the Literature of Qumran: The Functions of the Maskîl', in J. G. Gammie and L. G. Perdue (eds.), *The Sage in Israel and the Ancient Near East* (Winona Lake, IN: Eisenbrauns, 1990) 373–82.

Nickelsburg, G. W. E., 'The Incarnation: Paul's Solution to the Universal Human Predicament', in B. A. Pearson (ed.), *The Future of Early Christianity: Essays in Honor of Helmut Koester* (Minneapolis: Fortress Press, 1991) 348–57.

Niederwimmer, K., 'Erkennen und Lieben. Gedanken zum Verhältnis von Gnosis und Agape im ersten Korintherbrief', *Kerygma und Dogma* 11 (1965) 75–102.

Nikiprowetzky, V., 'La doctrine de l'élenchos chez Philon, ses résonances philosophiques et sa portée religieuse', in *Philon d'Alexandrie* (Actes du colloques nationaux du Centre national de la recherche scientifique; Paris: 1967) 253–75.

Noack, C., *Gottesbewußtsein* (WUNT 2,116; Tübingen: Mohr/Siebeck, 2000).

Nuovo, V., 'Resurrection, Realism and Truth: Reflections on Paul Tillich and St. Paul', in G. Hummel (ed.), *Truth and History: A Dialogue with Paul Tillich* (Berlin: W. de Gruyter, 1998) 211–26.

O'Brien, P. T., *The Epistle to the Philippians: A Commentary on the Greek Text* (Grand Rapids, MI: Eerdmans, 1991).

'Principalities and Powers: Opponents of the Church', in D. A. Carson (ed.), *Biblical Interpretation and the Church: Text and Context* (Exeter: Paternoster Press, 1984) 110–50.

Ogden, S. M., 'Paul in Contemporary Theology and Ethics: Presuppositions of Critically Appropriating Paul's Letters Today', in E. H. Lovering, Jr and J. L. Sumney (eds.), *Theology and Ethics in Paul and his Interpreters: Essays in Honor of Victor Paul Furnish* (Nashville: Abingdon Press, 1996) 289–305.

Orr, W. F. and Walther, J. A., *I Corinthians* (AB 32; Garden City, NY: Doubleday, 1976).

Owen, H. W., 'Some Philosophical Problems in Christian Ethics', in G. R. Dunstan (ed.), *Duty and Discernment* (London: SCM Press, 1975) 1–8.

Panagopoulos, J., 'Die urchristliche Prophetie', in idem (ed.), *Prophetic Vocation in the New Testament and Today* (NT.S 45; Leiden: Brill, 1977) 1–32.

Pannenberg, W., *Systematische Theologie* I (Göttingen: Vandenhoeck & Ruprecht, 1988).

'Was ist Wahrheit', in *Grundfragen Systematischer Theologie* (Göttingen: Vandenhoeck & Ruprecht, 1979³) 202–22.

Pate, C. M., *The Reverse of the Curse: Paul, Wisdom and the Law* (WUNT 2,114; Tübingen: Mohr/Siebeck, 2000).

Patte, D., *Paul's Faith and the Power of the Gospel: A Structural Introduction to the Pauline Letters* (Philadelphia: Fortress Press, 1983).

Pearson, B. A., *The Pneumatikos-Psychikos Terminology in 1 Corinthians* (Missoula, MT: Scholars Press, 1973).

Pedersen, S., 'Paul's Understanding of the Biblical Law', *NT* 44 (2002) 1–34.

Penna, R., 'Dissolution and Restoration of the Relationship of Law and Wisdom in Paul', in *Paul the Apostle* II. *Wisdom and Folly of the Cross* (trans. P. Wahl; Collegeville, MN: Liturgical Press, 1996) 135–62.

'The Problem of the Law in Paul's Letters', in *Paul the Apostle* II. *Wisdom and Folly of the Cross* (trans. P. Wahl; Collegeville, MN: Liturgical Press, 1996) 115–34.

'Problems of Pauline Morality: The Present State of the Question', in *Paul the Apostle* II. *Wisdom and Folly of the Cross* (trans. P. Wahl; Collegeville, MN: Liturgical Press, 1996) 163–73.

Penney, J., 'The Testing of New Testament Prophecy', *JPT* 10 (1997) 35–84.

Pfeiffer, M., *Einweisung in das neue Sein: Neutestamentliche Erwägungen zur Grundlegung der Ethik* (Gütersloh: Gütersloher Verlagshaus, 2001).

Philip, F., *The Origins of Pauline Pneumatology* (WUNT 2,194; Tübingen: Mohr/Siebeck, 2005).

Pierce, C. A., *Conscience in the New Testament* (London: SCM Press, 1955).

Plantinga, A. and Wolterstorff, N. (eds.), *Faith and Rationality: Reason and Belief in God* (Notre Dame: University of Notre Dame Press, 1983).

Pogoloff, S. M., *Logos and Sophia: The Rhetorical Situation of 1 Corinthians* (SBL.DS 134; Atlanta: Scholars Press, 1992).

Pohlenz, M., 'Paulus und die Stoa', in K. H. Rengstorf (ed.), *Das Paulusbild in der neueren deutschen Forschung* (Darmstadt: Wissenschaftliche Buchgesellschaft, 1964).

Pokorný, P., *Der Brief an die Epheser* (ThHK 10/2; Leipzig: Evangelische Verlagsanstalt, 1992).

Der Brief des Paulus an die Kolosser (ThHK 10/1; Berlin: Evangelische Verlagsanstalt, 1987).

Potterie, I. de la, 'Le Chrétien conduit par l'Esprit dans son cheminement eschatologique (*Rom* 8,14)', in L. De Lorenzi (ed.), *The Law of the Spirit in Rom 7 and 8* (Rome: St. Paul's Abbey, 1976) 209–28.

Price, C. P., 'Revelation as our Knowledge of God', in J. T. Carroll, C. H. Cosgrove and E. E. Johnson (eds.), *Faith and History: Essays in Honor of P. W. Meyer* (Atlanta: Scholars Press, 1990) 313–34.

Rabens, V., 'Coming Out: "Bible-Based" Identity Formation in 2 Corinthians 6:14–7:1', in U. Rembold and R. G. Czapla (eds.), *Gotteswort und Menschenrede: Die Bibel im Dialog mit Wissenschaften, Künsten und Medien* (JIG 73; Bern: Lang, 2006) 43–66.

'The Development of Pauline Pneumatology: A Response to F. W. Horn', *BZ* 43 (1999), 161–79.

'Transforming Relationships: The Spirit's Empowering for Religious-Ethical Life According to the Apostle Paul' (Unpublished paper, 18th British New Testament Conference, London, 2000).

Räisänen, H., *Neutestamentliche Theologie?* (Stuttgart: Verlag Katholisches Bibelwerk, 2000).

Paul and the Law (WUNT 29; Tübingen: Mohr/Siebeck, 1983).

Rebell, W., *Christologie und Existenz bei Paulus: Eine Auslegung von 2.Kor 5, 14–21* (Stuttgart: Calwer Verlag, 1992).

Reid, D. G., 'Satan, Devil', *DPL*, 862–67.

Reiling, J., 'Wisdom and Spirit', in T. Baarda, A. Hilhorst, G. P. Luttikhuizen and A. S. van der Woude (eds.), *Text and Testimony* (Kampen: Kok, 1988) 200–11.

Reinhardt, K., *Kosmos und Sympathie: Neue Untersuchung über Poseidonios* (Munich: C. H. Beck, 1926).

Reitzenstein, R., *Die hellenistischen Mysterienreligionen* (Leipzig: B. G. Teubner, 1910).

Rendtorff, T., *Ethics I. Basic Elements and Methodology in an Ethical Theology* (trans. K. Crim; Philadelphia: Fortress Press, 1986).

Richardson, P., *Paul's Ethic of Freedom* (Philadelphia: Westminster Press, 1979).

Ridderbos, H., *Paulus: Ein Entwurf seiner Theologie* (trans. E.-W. Pollmann; Wuppertal: Theologischer Verlag Rolf Brockhaus, 1970).

Rissi, M., 'κρίνω', *EDNT* II, 318–21.

Robertson, A. and Plummer, A., *First Epistle of St. Paul to the Corinthians* (Edinburgh: T&T Clark, 1955²).

Roetzel, C. J., *Judgement in the Community: A Study of the Relationship between Eschatology and Ecclesiology in Paul* (Leiden: Brill, 1972).

Paul: The Man and the Myth (Columbia: University of South Carolina, 1998).

Rosner, B. S., *Paul, Scripture and Ethics* (AGJU 22; Leiden: Brill, 1994).

Rowland, C., 'The Apocalypse: Hope, Resistance and the Revelation of Reality', *Ex Auditu* 6 (1990) 129–44.

'Apocalyptic, God and the World', in J. Barclay and J. Sweet (eds.), *Early Christian Thought in its Jewish Context* (Cambridge: Cambridge University Press, 1996) 238–49.

Runia, D. T., *Philo in Early Christian Literature: A Survey* (Minneapolis: Fortress Press, 1993).

'Was Philo a Middle Platonist? A Difficult Question Revisited', in idem (ed.), *The Studia Philonica Annual: Studies in Hellenistic Judaism* V (Atlanta: Scholars Press, 1993) 112–40.

Russell, J. B., *The Devil: Perceptions of Evil from Antiquity to Primitive Christianity* (Ithaca, NY: Cornell University Press, 1977).

Sampley, J. P., 'Reasoning from the Horizons of Paul's Thought World. A Comparison of Galatians and Philippians', in E. H. Lovering, Jr and J. L. Sumney (eds.), *Theology and Ethics in Paul and his Interpreters: Essays in Honor of Victor Paul Furnish* (Nashville: Abingdon Press, 1996) 114–31.

Walking between the Times: Paul's Moral Reasoning (Minneapolis: Fortress Press, 1991).

Sanday, W. and Headlam, A. C., *The Epistle to the Romans* (ICC; Edinburgh: T&T Clark, 1945[5]).

Sanders, E. P., 'Paul', in J. Barclay and J. Sweet (eds.), *Early Christian Thought in its Jewish Context* (Cambridge: Cambridge University Press, 1996) 112–29.

Paul and Palestinian Judaism (Philadelphia: Fortress Press, 1977).

Sandnes, K. O., *Paul – One of the Prophets?* (WUNT 2,43; Tübingen: Mohr/Siebeck, 1991).

Schatzmann, S., *A Pauline Theology of Charismata* (Peabody, MA: Hendrickson, 1987).

Schlatter, A., *Der Brief an die Römer* (Stuttgart: Calwer Verlag, 1928).

Erläuterungen zum Neuen Testament II (Calw: Verlag der Vereinsbuchhandlung, 1909).

Gottes Gerechtigkeit: Ein Kommentar zum Römerbrief (Stuttgart: Calwer Verlag, 1991[6]).

Paulus der Bote Jesu (Stuttgart: Calwer Verlag, 1985[5]).

Schlier, H., 'Die Erkenntnis nach den Briefen des Apostels Paulus', in *Besinnung auf das Neue Testament: Exegetische Aufsätze und Verträge* II (Freiburg: Herder, 1964) 319–39.

'Kerygma und Sophia. Zur neutestamentlichen Grundlegung des Dogmas', in *Die Zeit der Kirche* (Freiburg: Herder, 1956) 206–32.

Der Römerbrief (HThK 6; Freiburg: Herder, 1977).

'Über die Liebe. – 1 Kor. 13', in *Die Zeit der Kirche* (Freiburg: Herder, 1956) 186–93.

Schmithals, W., *Die Gnosis in Korinth* (Göttingen: Vandenhoeck & Ruprecht, 1969[3]).

'Die Korintherbriefe als Briefsammlung,' *ZNW* 64 (1973) 263–88.

Schnabel, E. J., 'How Paul Developed his Ethics', in B. Rosner (ed.), *Understanding Paul's Ethics: Twentieth-Century Approaches* (Grand Rapids, MI: Eerdmans, 1995) 267–97.

Law and Wisdom from Ben Sira to Paul (WUNT 2,16; Tübingen: Mohr/Siebeck, 1985).

216   *Bibliography*

'Wisdom', *DPL*, 967–72.

Schnackenburg, R., *Der Brief an die Epheser* (EKK 10; Neukirchen-Vluyn: Neukirchener Verlag, 1982).

The Moral Teaching of the New Testament (London: Burns & Oates, 1969⁵).

Die sittliche Botschaft des Neuen Testaments II. *Die urchristlichen Verkündiger* (HThK.S 2; Freiburg: Herder, 1988).

Schnelle, U., *Neutestamentliche Anthropologie* (Neukirchen-Vluyn: Neukirchener Verlag, 1991).

Paulus: Leben und Denken (Berlin: W. de Gruyter, 2003).

Schrage, W., *Der erste Brief an die Korinther (1 Kor 1,1–6,11)* (EKK 7/I; Neukirchen-Vluyn: Neukirchener Verlag, 1991).

Der erste Brief an die Korinther (1Kor 6,12–11,16) (EKK 7/II; Neukirchen-Vluyn: Neukirchener Verlag, 1995).

Der erste Brief an die Korinther (1Kor 11,17–14,40) (EKK 7/III; Neukirchen-Vluyn: Neukirchener Verlag, 1999).

The Ethics of the New Testament (trans. D. E. Green; Edinburgh: T&T Clark, 1988).

Ethik des Neuen Testaments (NTD 4; Göttingen: Vandenhoeck & Ruprecht, 1982).

Die konkreten Einzelgebote in der paulinischen Paränese: Ein Beitrag zur Neutestamentlichen Ethik (Gütersloh: Gerd Mohn, 1961).

'Zum Verhältnis von Ethik und Vernunft', in H. Merklein (ed.), *Neues Testament und Ethik* (Freiburg: Herder, 1989) 482–507.

Schrenk, G., 'θέλημα κτλ.', *TDNT* III, 52–62.

Schulz, S., *Neutestamentliche Ethik* (Zürich: Theologischer Verlag, 1987).

Schunack, G., 'δοκιμάζω', *EDNT* I, 341–43.

Schürmann, H., 'Die geistlichen Gnadengaben in den paulinischen Gemeinden', in *Ursprung und Gestalt* (Düsseldorf: Patmos,1970) 260–65.

'Die Gemeinde des neuen Bundes als der Quellort des sittlichen Erkennens nach Paulus', in T. Söding (ed.), *Studien zur neutestamentlichen Ethik* (Stuttgart: Katholisches Bibelwerk, 1990) 17–48.

Schweizer, E., 'Gegenwart des Geistes und eschatologische Hoffnung bei Zarathustra, spätjüdischen Gruppen, Gnostikern und den Zeugen des Neuen Testaments', in W. D. Davies and D. Daube (eds.), *The Background of the New Testament and its Eschatology* (Cambridge: Cambridge University Press, 1964) 482–508.

'Slaves of the Elements and Worshipers of Angels: Gal 4:3, 9 and Col 2:8, 18, 20', *JBL* 107 (1988) 455–68.

Scott, I. W., *Implicit Epistemology in the Letters of Paul: Story, Experience and the Spirit* (WUNT 2,205; Tübingen: Mohr/Siebeck, 2006).

Scroggs, R., 'The Heuristic Value of Psychoanalytic Model in the Interpretation of Paul', *Zygon* 13 (1978) 136–57.

'New Being: Renewed Mind: New Perception. Paul's View of the Source of Ethical Insight', in *The Text and the Times* (Minneapolis: Fortress Press, 1993) 167–83.

'Paul: ΣΟΦΟΣ and ΠΝΕΥΜΑΤΙΚΟΣ', *NTS* 14 (1967/68) 33–55.

'Salvation History: The Theological Structure of Paul's Thought (1 Thessalonians, Philippians, and Galaitans)', in J. M. Bassler (ed.), *Pauline*

Theology I. *Thessalonians, Philippians, Galatians, Philemon* (Minneapolis: Fortress Press, 1991) 212–26.

Sedley, D., 'Stoicism', in E. Craig (ed.), *Routledge Encyclopedia of Philosophy* IX (London: Routledge, 1998) 141–61.

Sellin, G., 'Das "Geheimnis" der Weisheit und das Rätsel der "Christuspartei" (zu 1Kor 1–4)', *ZNW* 73 (1982) 69–96.

Senft, C., *La première épître de Saint-Paul aux Corinthiens* (CNT VII; Geneva: Labor et Fides, 1979).

Sevenster, J. N., *Paul and Seneca* (NT.S 4; Leiden: Brill, 1961).

Sinclair, S. G., *Jesus Christ According to Paul: The Christologies of Paul's Undisputed Epistles and the Christology of Paul* (Berkeley: Bibal Press, 1988).

Smit, J. F. M., '"What is Apollos? What is Paul?" In Search for the Coherence of First Corinthians 1:10–4:21', *NT* 44 (2002) 231–251.

Söding, T., *Das Liebesgebot bei Paulus* (Münster: Aschendorff, 1995).

Sonntag, H., ΝΟΜΟΣ ΣΩΤΗΡ: *Zur politischen Theologie des Gesetzes bei Paulus und im antiken Kontext* (TANZ 34; Tübingen: Francke, 2000).

Spicq, C., *Agape in the New Testament* II (St. Louis: Herder, 1965).

Stacey, W. D., *The Pauline View of Man* (London: Macmillan, 1956).

Stalder, K., *Das Werk des Geistes in der Heiligung bei Paulus* (Zürich: EVZ-Verlag, 1962).

Standhartinger, A., *Studien zur Entstehungsgeschichte und Intention des Kolosserbriefs* (NT.S 94; Leiden: Brill, 1999).

Steinmetz, F.-J., 'Die Weisheit und das Kreuz', *Geist und Leben* 2 (1999) 112–26.

Stendahl, K., *Final Account: Paul's Letter to the Romans* (Minneapolis: Fortress Press, 1995).

Sterling, G. E., 'Platonizing Moses: Philo and Middle Platonism', in D. T. Runia (ed.), *The Studia Philonica Annual: Studies in Hellenistic Judaism* V (Atlanta: Scholars Press, 1993) 96–111.

'"Wisdom among the Perfect": Creation Traditions in Alexandrian Judaism and Corinthian Christianity', *NT* 37 (1995) 355–84.

Stoessel, H. E., 'Notes on Romans 12:1–2. The Renewal of the Mind and Internalizing the Truth', *Int.* 17 (1963) 161–75.

Stowers, S. K., 'Does Pauline Christianity Resemble a Hellenistic Philosophy?', in T. Engberg-Pedersen (ed.), *Paul beyond the Judaism/Hellenism Divide* (Louisville, KY: Westminster/John Knox Press, 2001) 81–102.

'Paul on the Use and Abuse of Reason', in D. L. Balch, E. F. Ferguson and W. A. Meeks (eds.), *Greeks, Romans, Christians* (Minneapolis: Fortress Press, 1990) 253–86.

Strecker, C., *Die liminale Theologie des Paulus: Zugänge zur paulinischen Theologie aus kulturanthropologischer Perspektive* (FRLANT 185; Göttingen: Vandenhoeck & Ruprecht, 1999).

Strecker, G., 'Ziele einer Neutestamentlichen Ethik', *NTS* 25 (1979) 1–15.

Strobel, A., *Der erste Brief an die Korinther* (Zürich: Theologischer Verlag, 1989).

Strom, M., *Reframing Paul: Conversations in Grace and Community* (Downers Grove, IL: InterVarsity Press, 2000).

Stuhlmacher, P., *Der Brief an die Römer* (NTD 6; Göttingen: Vandenhoeck & Ruprecht, 1998²).

'Glauben und Verstehen bei Paulus', *Evangelische Theologie* 26 (1966) 337–48.

Paul's Letter to the Romans (Edinburgh: T&T Clark, 1989).

'Zur hermeneutischen Bedeutung von 1Kor 2,6–16', in *Biblische Theologie und Evangelium* (WUNT 146; Tübingen: Mohr/Siebeck, 2002) 143–66.

Stuhlmacher, P. and Hagner, D. A., *Revisiting Paul's Doctrine of Justification: A Challenge to the New Perspective* (Downers Grove, IL: InterVarsity Press, 2001).

Sturm, R. E., 'An Exegetical Study of the Apostle Paul's Use of the Word Apoka-lypto/Apokalypsis: The Gospel as God's Apocalypse' (Unpubl. PhD dissertation, Union Theological Seminary, 1985).

Summers, S., '"Out of my Mind for God": A Social-Scientific Approach to Pauline Pneumatology', *JPT* 13 (1998) 77–106.

Theissen, G., *Psychological Aspects of Pauline Theology* (Philadelphia: Fortress Press, 1987).

Psychologische Aspekte paulinischer Theologie (FRLANT 131; Göttingen: Vandenhoeck & Ruprecht, 1983).

Die Religion der ersten Christen: Eine Theorie des Urchristentums (Gütersloh: Kaiser, 2000).

'Social Integration and Sacramental Activity: An Analysis of 1 Cor. 11:17–34', in *The Social Setting of Pauline Christianity* (SNTW; Edinburgh: T&T Clark, 1982) 145–69.

'Soziale Schichtung in der korinthischen Gemeinde. Ein Beitrag zur Soziologie des hellenistischen Urchristentums', in *Studien zur Soziologie des Urchristentums* (WUNT 19; Tübingen: Mohr/Siebeck, 1989³) 231–71.

Theobald, M., 'Glaube und Vernunft. Zur Argumentation des Paulus im Römerbrief', in *Studien zum Römerbrief* (WUNT 136; Tübingen: Mohr/Siebeck, 2001) 417–32.

Therrien, G., *Le discernement dans les écrits pauliniens* (Paris: Librairie Lecoffre, 1973).

Thielmann, F., *From Plight to Solution* (NT.S 61; Leiden: Brill, 1989).

Paul and the Law: A Contextual Approach (Downers Grove, IL: InterVarsity Press, 1994).

Thiselton, A. C., *The First Epistle to the Corinthians* (NIGTC; Grand Rapids, MI: Eerdmans, 2000).

Interpreting God and the Postmodern Self: On Meaning, Manipulation and Promise (Edinburgh: T&T Clark, 1995).

'Truth, ἀλήθεια', *NIDNTT* III, 874–902.

Thompson, M., *Clothed with Christ: The Example and Teaching of Jesus in Romans 12.1–15.13* (JSNT.S 59; Sheffield: Sheffield Academic Press, 1991).

Thomson, P. J., *Paul and the Jewish Law: Halakha in the Letters of the Apostle to the Gentiles* (Compendia Rerum Iudaicarum ad Novum Testamentum; Minneapolis: Fortress Press, 1990).

Thrall, M. E., *The Second Epistle to the Corinthians* (ICC; Edinburgh: T&T Clark, 1994).

Thurén, L., *Derhetorizing Paul: A Dynamic Perspective on Pauline Theology and the Law* (WUNT 124; Tübingen: Mohr/Siebeck, 2000).

Tobin, T. H., 'Was Philo a Middle Platonist? Some Suggestions', in D. T. Runia (ed.), *The Studia Philonica Annual: Studies in Hellenistic Judaism* V (Atlanta: Scholars Press, 1993) 147–50.

Tronier, H., 'The Correspondence between Philosophical Idealism and Apocalyp-
 ticism', in T. Engberg-Pedersen (ed.), *Paul beyond the Judaism/Hellenism
 Divide* (Louisville, KY: Westminster/John Knox Press, 2001) 165–96.
Turner, M., *The Holy Spirit and Spiritual Gifts* (Carlisle: Paternoster Press, 1996).
 *Power from on High: The Spirit in Israel's Restoration and Witness in Luke–
 Acts* (Journal of Pentecostal Theology. Supplement Series 9; Sheffield:
 Sheffield Academic Press, 1996).
 'Prophecy and Preaching in Luke–Acts', *NTS* 38 (1992) 66–88.
 'Spirit in Philo' (Unpubl. Paper, Aberdeen, 1991).
 'Spiritual Gifts then and now', *Vox Evangelica* 15 (1985) 7–64.
Ukpong, J. S., 'Pluralism and the Problem of the Discernment of Spirits', *Ecu-
 menical Review* 41 (1989) 416–25.
Van Spanje, T. E., *Inconsistency in Paul?: A Critique of the Work of Heikki
 Räisänen* (WUNT 2,110; Tübingen: Mohr/Siebeck, 1999).
Via, D. O., *The Revelation of God and/as Human Reception in the New Testament*
 (Harrisburg, PA: Trinity Press International, 1997).
Vollenweider, S., *Freiheit als neue Schöpfung: Eine Untersuchung zur Eleutheria
 bei Paulus und in seiner Umwelt* (Göttingen: Vandenhoeck & Ruprecht,
 1989).
 'Der Geist Gottes als Selbst der Glaubenden', *ZThK* 93 (1996) 163–92.
 'Viele Welten und ein Geist', in *Horizonte neutestamentlicher Christologie*
 (WUNT 144; Tübingen: Mohr/Siebeck, 2002) 193–214.
 'Weisheit am Kreuzweg. Zum theologischen Programm von 1Kor 1 und 2', in
 A. Dettwiler and J. Zumstein (eds.), *Kreuzestheologie im Neuen Testament*
 (WUNT 151; Tübingen: Mohr/Siebeck, 2002) 43–58.
Vos, J. S., *Die Kunst der Argumentation bei Paulus: Studien zur antiken Rhetorik*
 (WUNT 149; Tübingen: Mohr/Siebeck, 2002).
 'Het probleem van de onderscheiding der geesten bij Paulus', *Nederlands The-
 ologisch Tijdschrift* 52 (1998) 194–205.
Voss, F., *Das Wort vom Kreuz und die menschliche Vernunft: Eine Untersuchung
 zur Soteriologie des 1. Korintherbriefes* (FRLANT 199; Göttingen: Vanden-
 hoeck & Ruprecht, 2002).
Wallace, R. and Williams, W., *The Three Worlds of Paul of Tarsus* (London:
 Routledge, 1998).
Walzer, M., *Thick and Thin: Moral Argument at Home and Abroad* (Notre Dame:
 Notre Dame University Press, 1990).
Wanamaker, C. A., *The Epistles to the Thessalonians* (NIGTC; Grand Rapids,
 MI: Eerdmans, 1990).
Warnach, V., 'Ratio und Pneuma', in L. Scheffczyk, W. Dettloff and R. Heinzmann
 (eds.), *Wahrheit und Verkündigung* I (Munich: Schöningh, 1967) 429–48.
Weiß, J., *Der erste Korintherbrief* (KEK 5; Göttingen: Vandenhoeck & Ruprecht,
 1977[9]).
 Das Urchristentum (Göttingen: Vandenhoeck & Ruprecht, 1917).
Welborn, L. L., 'Character and Truth in 2 Cor 1.17', *ZNW* 86 (1995) 34–52.
Wendland, H. D., *Die Briefe an die Korinther* (NTD 7; Göttingen: Vandenhoeck
 & Ruprecht, 1964[10]).
Wengst, K., 'Das Zusammenkommen der Gemeinde und ihr "Gottesdienst" nach
 Paulus', *EvTh* 33 (1973) 547–59.

Westerholm, S., *Israel's Law and the Church's Faith* (Grand Rapids, MI: Eerdmans, 1988).

'Letter and Spirit: The Foundation of Pauline Ethics', *NTS* 30 (1984) 229–48.

Perspectives Old and New on Paul: The 'Lutheran' Paul and his Critics (Grand Rapids, MI: Eerdmans, 2004).

Westphal, M., 'Taking St. Paul Seriously: Sin as an Epistemological Category', in T. P. Flint (ed.), *Christian Philosophy* (Notre Dame: University of Notre Dame Press, 1990) 200–26.

Widmann, M., '1 Cor. 2.6–16: ein Einspruch gegen Paulus', *ZNW* 70 (1979) 44–53.

Wilckens, U., *Der Brief an die Römer (Röm 1–5)* (EKK 6/I; Neukirchen-Vluyn: Neukirchener Verlag, 1978).

Der Brief an die Römer (Röm 6–11) (EKK 6/II; Neukirchen-Vluyn: Neukirchener Verlag, 1980).

Der Brief an die Römer (Röm 12–16) (EKK 6/III; Neukirchen-Vluyn: Neukirchener Verlag, 1982).

Weisheit und Torheit: Eine exegetisch-religionsgeschichtliche Untersuchung zu 1 Kor 1 und 2 (Tübingen: Mohr/Siebeck 1959).

'Zu 1Kor 2,1–16', in C. Andresen and G. Klein (eds.), *Theologia Crucis – Signum Crucis: Festschrift für Erich Dinkler zum 70. Geburtstag* (Tübingen: Mohr/Siebeck, 1979) 501–37.

Williams III, H. H. D., *The Wisdom of the Wise: The Presence and Function of Scripture within 1 Cor. 1:18–3:23* (Leiden: Brill, 2001).

Williamson, R., *Jews in the Hellenistic World: Philo* (CCWJCW 1, ii; Cambridge: Cambridge University Press, 1989).

Willis, W., 'Bibliography: Pauline Ethics, 1964–1994', in E. H. Lovering, Jr and J. L. Sumney (eds.), *Theology and Ethics in Paul and his Interpreters: Essays in Honor of Victor Paul Furnish* (Nashville: Abingdon Press, 1996) 306–19.

'The "Mind of Christ" in 1 Corinthians 2,16', *Bib* 70 (1989) 110–22.

Wilson, R. M., 'How Gnostic were the Corinthians?', *NTS* 19 (1972–73) 65–73.

Winger, M., *By what Law? The Meaning of* Νόμος *in the Letters of Paul* (SBL.DS 128; Atlanta: Scholars Press 1990).

Wink, W., *Naming the Powers: The Language of Power in the New Testament* (The Powers 1; Philadelphia: Fortress Press, 1984).

Winston, D., 'The Sage as Mystic in the Wisdom of Solomon', in J. G. Gammie and L. G. Perdue (eds.), *The Sage in Israel and the Ancient Near East* (Winona Lake, IN: Eisenbrauns, 1990) 383–98.

Winter, B., *Philo and Paul among the Sophists* (MSSNTS 96; Cambridge: Cambridge University Press, 1997).

Winter, M., *Pneumatiker und Psychiker in Korinth* (Marburg: N. G. Elwert Verlag, 1975).

Wire, A. C., *The Corinthian Women Prophets* (Minneapolis: Fortress Press, 1990).

Wischmeyer, O., *Der höchste Weg: Das 13. Kapitel des 1. Korintherbriefes* (StNT 13; Gütersloh: Gütersloher Verlagshaus, 1981).

Witherington, III, B., *Conflict and Community in Corinth: A Socio-Rhetorical Commentary on 1 and 2 Corinthians* (Grand Rapids, MI: Eerdmans, 1995).

Paul's Narrative Thought World: The Tapestry of Tragedy and Triumph (Louisville, KY: Westminster/John Knox Press, 1994).

Wolff, C., *Der erste Brief des Paulus an die Korinther* (Berlin: Evangelische Verlagsanstalt, 1982²).

Wolfson, H. A., *Philo* II (Cambridge, MA: Harvard University Press, 1982⁵).

Wolter, M., *Der Brief an die Kolosser. Der Brief an Philemon* (ÖTK 12; Gütersloh: Gütersloher Verlagshaus, 1993).

'Die ethische Identität christlicher Gemeinden in neutestamentlicher Zeit', in W. Härle and R. Preul (eds.), *Woran orientiert sich Ethik?* (Marburg: Elwert Verlag, 2001) 61–89.

'Ethos und Identität in paulinischen Gemeinden', *NTS* 43 (1997) 430–44.

'Verborgene Weisheit und Heil für die Heiden. Zur Traditionsgeschichte und Intention des "Revelationsschemas"', *ZThK* 84 (1987) 297–319.

Wood, W. J., *Epistemology: Becoming Intellectually Virtuous* (Leicester: Apollos, 1998).

Wright, N. T., *The Climax of the Covenant* (Edinburgh: T&T Clark, 1991).

The Epistles of Paul to the Colossians and to Philemon (Leicester: InterVarsity Press, 1986).

Young, F. and Ford, D. F., *Meaning and Truth in 2 Corinthians* (Biblical Foundations in Theology; London: SPCK, 1987).

Yu, S. W., 'Paul's Pneumatic Epistemology. Its Significance in his Letters' (Unpubl. PhD dissertation, Duke University, 1998).

Zeller, D., *Der Brief an die Römer* (RNT; Regensburg: Friedrich Pustet, 1985).

'Die Menschwerdung des Sohnes Gottes und antike Religionsgeschichte', in idem (ed.), *Menschwerdung Gottes: Vergöttlichung von Menschen* (Göttingen: Vandenhoeck & Ruprecht, 1988) 141–76.

AUTHOR INDEX

PASSAGE INDEX

SUBJECT INDEX

spirits 64–9
  good and evil 47–51, 64–5
spiritual discernment 69, 74, 157–63, 176
  (*see also* discernment)
spiritual elitism 61–4, 168, 186
spirituality 16, 18, 46, 65, 68, 148–9, 170,
  188
status 137, 163, 167–8, 170, 177, 186,
  193
Stoic thought 121–38
subject of discernment 70–4
subjectivism 183
supernatural versus natural inspiration 61,
  146
symbiosis of mind and Spirit 171, 187,
  195 (*see also* mind, Spirit)

testing
  ethical matters 27–43
  prophecies 60–4
  spiritual phenomena 64–70
theme of judgement (*see* judgement)
theology
  as a comprehensive perception of
    reality 86–9
  contemporary 3–6, 194–7
  existential 81–6, 166–70, 178–85
  of Paul (*see* Paul)
  of Philo of Alexandria 107–9
Torah 30–5, 102–7
  touchstone of all knowledge 103–7

traditions, ethical 27–30
triumphalism 61–2, 69, 74, 93, 169
truth 16, 24 n. 17, 38, 56, 75–7, 88, 90, 94,
  97, 108–10, 121, 125, 27, 132, 135,
  177, 195
  existential dimension of 81–6
  foundationalist/coherentist 88
  and language 83
  and Paul's theology 75–100
  as propositional 83

understanding (*see also* mind, intellectual
    and reflective capacity)
  of reality 87, 149
  as a virtuous state of mind 122

valuation
  and disposition 128–35, 172–85
  and intentionality (*see* intentionality)
value system 116, 137, 163, 170, 193
visio dei 120
volition 152, 176
vox dei 160 (*see also* Spirit)

Weltanschauung 69, 87, 196
wisdom 27–44, 71, 85, 101–7, 112, 134,
  137, 147, 149 n. 44, 165, 166 n. 139,
  170
word of wisdom 47, 91
world switch 155 n. 71, 164, 171, 188,
  194